D1666989

THE CHALLENGES OF DIASPORA MIGRATION

The Challenges of
Diaspora Migration
Interdisciplinary Perspectives on Israel and Germany

Edited by

RAINER K. SILBEREISEN
University of Jena, Germany,

PETER F. TITZMANN
University of Zürich, Switzerland

YOSSI SHAVIT
Tel Aviv University, Israel

ASHGATE

Published by
Ashgate Publishing Limited
Wey Court East
Union Road
Farnham
Surrey, GU9 7PT
England

Ashgate Publishing Company
110 Cherry Street
Suite 3-1
Burlington, VT 05401-3818
USA

www.ashgate.com

British Library Cataloguing in Publication Data
A catalogue record for this book is available from the British Library

The Library of Congress has cataloged the printed edition as follows:
The challenges of diaspora migration : interdisciplinary perspectives on Israel and Germany / by Rainer K. Silbereisen, Peter F. Titzmann, and Yossi Shavit.
    pages cm. – (Studies in migration and diaspora)
  Includes bibliographical references and index.
  ISBN 978-1-4094-6424-2 (hardback) – ISBN 978-1-4094-6425-9 (ebook) –
  ISBN 978-1-4724-0783-2 (epub) 1. Israel–Emigration and immigration. 2.
Germany–Emigration and immigration. 3. Israel – Ethnic relations. 4. Germany –
Ethnic relations. 5. Jews, Soviet – Israel. 6. Jews, Soviet – Germany. 7. Immigrants
– Cultural assimilation – Israel. 8. Immigrants – Cultural assimilation – Germany.
9. Transnationalism. 10. Emigration and immigration – Research – Case studies. I.
Silbereisen, R. K. (Rainer K.), 1944- editor of compilation.

  JV8749.C43 2014
  304.8'43–dc23

2013041929

ISBN 9781409464242 (hbk)
ISBN 9781409464259 (ebk – PDF)
ISBN 9781472407832 (ebk – ePUB)

Printed in the United Kingdom by Henry Ling Limited,
at the Dorset Press, Dorchester, DT1 1HD

Contents

PART I: DIASPORA MIGRATION AND THE CONSORTIUM "MIGRATION AND SOCIETAL INTEGRATION"

PART II: FROM HERITAGE TO HOME COUNTRY: THE MIGRATION TRANSITION AND ADJUSTMENT

PART IV: RESEARCH ON DIASPORA MIGRATION AND ITS IMPLICATIONS FOR RESEARCH AND POLICY

List of Figures

List of Tables

List of Contributors

Irit Adler received her Ph.D. in Sociology from Tel-Aviv University in 2004. She is a researcher in B.I. and Lucille Cohen Institute for Public Opinion Research in Tel Aviv University, and coordinating the European Social Survey (ESS) and the Survey of Health Aging and Retirement in Europe (SHARE) projects. She currently teaches at Tel-Aviv University and the Tel-Aviv-Yaffo Academic College. Her main areas of interest are social stratification and housing inequality. Her recent publications in her main areas of interest include a chapter on inequality in home ownership in Israel, co-authored with Noah Lewin-Epstein and Moshe Semyonov, in *Home Ownership and Social Inequality in Comparative Perspective* (edited by Karin Kurz and Hans-Peter Blossfeld, 2004) and a paper on social inequality and place of residence, co-authored with Noah Lewin-Epstein and Yossi Shavit, in *Research in Stratification and Social Mobility* (2005).

Alexandru Agache is Research Associate in the Department of Developmental Psychology at the Ruhr-University Bochum. He is currently finishing his dissertation thesis on effects of family economic well-being on adolescents' future orientation at the University of Konstanz. Further research interests include child well-being indicators and fathers' involvement. He is the co-author of a German diagnostic manual on sleep disorders in children and adolescents, and he is a first or co-author on several papers currently under review.

Carmit Altman is on the faculty in the Counseling Education Program in the School of Education at Bar-Ilan University. Her Ph.D from Bar Ilan University examined linguistic and cognitive aspects of bilinguals among English-Hebrew, Russian-Hebrew and Georgian-Hebrew immigrants in Israel. Her post-doctoral work at CUNY's Graduate Center and Lehman College in New York dealt with narrative assessment among healthy immigrants with aphasia. Altman's current research focuses on psycholinguistic and sociolinguistic aspects of immigrants in early childhood and mature adults.

Sharon Armon-Lotem is Associate Professor in the Department of English and a member of the Gonda Multidisciplinary Brain Research Center at Bar Ilan University. Her main area of research is language acquisition in monolingual and bilingual children with and without Specific Language Impairment (SLI). She was the Chair of COST Action IS0804 "Language Impairment in Multilingual Societies" and the editor of *Issues in the Acquisition and Teaching of Hebrew* (with A. Feuer and B. Cooperman, 2009) and *Generative Approaches to Hebrew*

Linguistics (with G. Danon and S. Rothstein, 2008). Recent publications include "Language proficiency and executive control in bilingual children" in *Bilingualism: Language and Cognition* (with P. Iluz-Cohen 2013) and "Between L2 and SLI: Inflections and prepositions in the Hebrew of bilingual children with TLD and monolingual children with SLI" in the *Journal of Child Language* (2014).

Maya Benish-Weisman is a faculty member in the Department of Counseling and Human Development at the University of Haifa, Israel. Her research focuses on psychological aspects of immigration, ethnic identities, cultural aspects of peer relations, development in context, values and adolescence and behavior genetics. Her recent research has been published in the *Journal of Research on Adolescence*, *Child Development*, *International Journal of Intercultural Relations*, *European Journal of Social Psychology*, and the *Journal of Cross Cultural Psychology*.

Klaus Boehnke is a psychologist by training; he holds a chair in social science methodology at Jacobs University Bremen and is Vice Dean of the Bremen International Graduate School of Social Sciences (BIGSSS). His research spans most diverse topics of political socialization with publications in top journals of psychology and sociology, but also extending to education, political science, mass communication, health, and semiotics.

Zhanna Burstein-Feldman has a PhD from the English Linguistics department at Bar-Ilan University. Her PhD was on language and identity of Russian speaking Israeli parents and their adolescent children. Her research interests are in language and immigrant identity, L2 acquisition by young children, sociolinguistic issues in SLA, lexical retrieval processes in L1 attrition. She currently teaches at the EFL department and at the TASP program (a joint program of the English and Education departments) of Bar Ilan University.

Svetlana Chachashvili-Bolotin is a lecturer at the Ruppin Academic Center in Netanya, Israel. She holds a PhD in Sociology and Anthropology from Tel Aviv University. Her main areas of research include migration, social stratification, sociology of education and research methods. Since 2011, she has served as a Head of Research and Evaluation Department in the Education Division at the municipality of Ashdod, Israel.

Ella Daniel is a postdoctoral fellow at the Department of Psychology, University of Toronto, Mississauga. Her academic interests include values development, moral development, and cross cultural psychology. She focuses on ways in which the social environment influences moral development. She is the author of articles published in journals such as *Child Development*, the *Journal of Cross Cultural Psychology*, and the *Journal of Adolescence*.

Natalia Gagarina is a coordinator of a research division/area on multilingualism at the Center of General Linguistics in Berlin and an assistant professor at the Humboldt University. Her main areas of research are: language acquisition in monolingual and bilingual children, development of narratives, testing language proficiency and language support in bilingual children, and the education of the kindergarten teachers. Her publications include: *First Language Acquisition of Verb Categories in Russian* (2008), *Russian Language Proficiency Test for Multilingual Children* (with Annegret Klassert and Nathalie Topaj, 2010). She co-edited *Frequency Effects in Language Acquisition* (with Insa Guelzow, 2007), *The Acquisition of Verbs and their Grammar* (with Insa Guelzow, 2006) and is the author or co-author of articles in such journals as the *Slavic and East European Journal, Acta Linguistica Petropolitana, Bilingualism: Language and Cognition, Folia Linguistics* and *First Language.*

Felix Golcher is Statistical Advisor at Humboldt-Universität zu Berlin. His academic interests include statistical properties of language and text. He studied physics in Munich and Berlin and finished his PhD in Linguistics in 2013 at Humboldt-Universität zu Berlin.

Julia Jäkel is Research Associate in the Department of Developmental Psychology at the Ruhr-University, Bochum. Her research aims to contribute to the understanding of the long-term developmental mechanisms explaining resilience in individuals facing socio-cultural or biological adversity. She has published several papers in leading journals including: *Psychological Medicine, PLoS ONE, Developmental Medicine* and *Child Neurology.*

Frank Kalter is Professor of Sociology at the University of Mannheim and head of the sociological research department at the Mannheimer Zentrum für Europäische Sozialforschung (MZES). His major research interests include migration, integration of ethnic minorities, methods, and formal models. He is the author of *Chancen, Fouls und Abseitsfallen* (2003) and *Migration und Integration* (2008).

Annegret Klassert is a staff member at the Department Linguistik/ University of Potsdam and the Centre for Applied Patho- and Psycholinguistics (ZAPP) Potsdam. Her main areas of research are the lexical development in bilingual children, specific language impairment in bilingual children and the impact of external factors on bilingual language development. She is co-author of the book *Russian Language Proficiency Test for Multilingual Children* (with Natalia Gagarina and Nathalie Topaj, 2010).

Ariel Knafo is Associate Professor of Developmental Social Psychology in the Psychology Department at The Hebrew University of Jerusalem. His main research interests concern the development of individual differences in social behavior, particularly prosocial behavior and empathy, temperament, and personal values, focusing on the effects of heredity and parenting on children's development, and the impact of children on their parents. His work appeared in several journals, including: *Journal of Cross-Cultural Psychology*, *Development and Psychopathology*, *Child Development*, *Developmental Psychology*, *Family Science*, *Emotion*, and *Journal of Personality and Social Psychology*.

Irena Kogan is Professor of Comparative Sociology at the University of Mannheim. Her research interests include ethnicity and migration, structural assimilation of immigrants, social stratification and mobility and transition form school-to-work. She is the author of a number of articles in international journals dealing with immigrants' labour market integration and social stratification. Her recent book publications include a monograph, *Working through Barriers: Host Country Institutions and Immigrant Labour Market Performance in Europe* and two edited volumes, together with Michael Gebel and Clemens Noelke, *Europe Enlarged: A Handbook of Education, Labour and Welfare Regimes in Central and Eastern Europe* and *Making the Transition: Education and Labor Market Entry in Central and Eastern Europe*. Irena Kogan is currently co-directing a number of projects, including 'Children of Immigrants Longitudinal Survey in Four European Countries' funded by the Norface.

Katharina Kohl is a PhD student in Developmental Psychology at the Ruhr-University Bochum in Germany and part of the research team of the SIMCUR project (Social Integration of ImMigrant Children – Uncovering Factors Promoting Resilience). Her main research interests include immigrant children's academic adjustment and achievement, parental school involvement, and social relationships in class.

Chaya Koren received her PhD in 2008 from the University of Haifa and is Lecturer at the School of Social Work and Research Fellow at the Centre for the Study of Society (http://society.haifa.ac.il/) at the University of Haifa, Israel. Her main research method is qualitative with emphasis on qualitative methods of inquiry such as analysis of dyadic and family units, and the construction of typologies. Her areas of research are intergenerational relationships in the family, couplehood in old age, repartnering in old age, Gerontology, ageism, and forgiveness. She has published in peer reviewed journals such as *The Gerontologist*, *Qualitative Health Research*, *Journal of Social and Personal Relationships*, *International Psychogeri atrics*, *Sociological Focus*, *Qualitative Social Work*.

Cornelia Kristen is Professor of Sociology at Bamberg University, Germany. She is also in charge of the migration pillar of the National Education Panel Study (NEPS). Her major research interests lie in the fields of migration and integration, social inequality, and sociology of education. She has published many articles in refereed journals (for example, *European Sociological Review*,

International Journal of Comparative Sociology, *Kölner Zeitschrift für Soziologie und Sozialpsychologie, Zeitschrift für Soziologie*) and has been directing several projects on the processes of immigrants' and their children's integration.

Yoav Lavee is Professor of Family Studies and Director of the Center for Research and Study of the Family at the School of Social Work, Faculty of Social Welfare and Health Sciences, University of Haifa. He received his PhD degree in family studies from the University of Minnesota. His main fields of interests include stress processes in couples and families, assessment and correlates of marital quality, Israeli families – cross-cultural aspects, and family theory and methodology. Additional information can be obtained at http://sw2.haifa.ac.il/images/stories/cv/lavee_facultycv.pdf

Noah Lewin-Epstein is Professor of Sociology at Tel-Aviv University and past Dean of the Faculty of Social Science. He heads the International Graduate Program in Migration Studies and serves as director of the B.I Cohen Institute for Survey Research. His areas of interest include social inequality, migration and ethnic stratification, and comparative survey research. His research has been published in a variety of journal including *American Journal of Sociology*, *International Migration Review*, *European Sociological Review*, *Journal of Marriage and Family, and Research in Social Stratification and Mobility*. Noah Lewin-Epstein is past president of the Israeli Sociological Society and currently heads the secretariat of the International Social Survey Programme (ISSP).

Birgit Leyendecker is Professor of Developmental Psychology at the Ruhr University Bochum. Her main areas of research are cultural perspectives on child development and parenting, positive development of minority children, and resilience.

David Mehlhausen-Hassoen is Adjunct Lecturer in Social Work at the University of Haifa and the Tel-Hai College, Israel. His main areas of interest are: intrafamilial and spousal communication and conflict resolution, regulation mechanisms and emotional adjustment, and intergenerational family relations. He collaborates in research with The Center for Research and Study of the Family and The Center for Research and Study of Aging at the University of Haifa, and participated as Research Associate in several major research projects. He also is a clinical practitioner and supervisor of marriage and family therapy.

Gustavo S. Mesch is a Professor of Sociology at the University of Haifa, Israel. His main areas of research are: the information society, immigrant's social and political adjustment, youth and delinquency and the sociology of health and illness. He has co-authored *Wired Youth: Adolescence in the Information Age* (with Ilan Talmud, 2010).

Andrea Michel is a postdoctoral research associate at the Department of Child and Adolescent Psychiatry, Psychotherapy and Psychosomatics, University of Leipzig. Her main areas of research are: child and adolescent development, acculturation of immigrants, perceived discrimination and psychological adaptation. She is currently studying risk and protective factors in the association of childhood maltreatment and psychological outcomes in adolescence.

Anna Möllering is a social and clinical psychologist. Her research interests focus on intergroup attitudes and outgroup derogation, especially Terror Management Theory, as well as cultural values and psychoanalysis. She received her PhD at the Jacobs University Bremen and is currently completing her education as a psychoanalytic psychotherapist.

Bernhard Nauck is Professor of Sociology and Head of a Research Group on Family and Migration at Chemnitz University of Technology, Germany. His current research includes family, life span, intergenerational relationships, demography, social indicators, migration, interethnic relations, cross-cultural and international comparisons. Currently, he serves as a coordinator of pairfam – the German Family Panel – and as a co-P.I. of a study on 2000 genealogies of Turkish families in Europe and Turkey.

Tobias Roth is an assistant lecturer in the School of Social Sciences, University of Mannheim, Germany. He also works as a research assistant at the Mannheim Centre for European Social Research, University of Mannheim, Germany. His research interests include educational inequalities, educational decision-making and social capital. He is author of articles that have been published in journals such as *British Journal of Sociology of Education*, *Irish Educational Studies*, and *Kölner Zeitschrift für Soziologie und Sozialpsychologie*.

Abraham (Avi) Sagi-Schwartz is Professor of Psychology and Director of the Center for the Study of Child Development, University of Haifa, Israel. His main research interests are in the area of attachment and social-emotional development across the life span and across cultures, and development and adaptation under extreme life circumstances and experiences. His published work includes many contributions to edited volumes and articles in leading journals of psychology, psychiatry, pediatrics, social work, family, law, and human development. He is also Associate Editor of the *Early Childhood Research Quarterly*. Professor Sagi-Schwartz is the recipient of the 2007 Society for Research in Child Development Award for Distinguished International Contributions to Child Development.

Zerrin Salikutluk is a researcher at the Mannheim Centre for European Social Research (MZES) and lecturer for the professor of Sociology, Societal Comparison at the University of Mannheim. She is currently working on the project *Children* *of Immigrants Longitudinal Survey in Four European Countries* (CILS4EU). Her main research interests are social and ethnic stratification, educational aspirations and decisions.

David Schiefer is a psychologist and postdoctoral fellow at Jacobs University Bremen. His research interest and publications focus on ingroup identification and outgroup relations among both cultural majority and minority individuals, especially in the context of migration, and furthermore on individual and cultural values.

Yossi Shavit is the Weinberg Professor of Sociology of Inequality and Stratification at Tel Aviv University and President of the Israeli Sociological Society. He received his PhD from the University of Wisconsin-Madison (1983) and was previously on the faculty of the University of Haifa and the European University Institute (EUI). His main interests are in the areas of social inequality and the sociology of education. He has published several comparative studies on these issues and has studied them extensively in Israel. Shavit is a former Spencer and Alon Fellow and a member of the honorary Sociological Research Association. He has served as secretary of the Research Committee on Social Stratification and Mobility of the International Sociological Association (RC28) and has headed the SPS department at the EUI, the Sociology and Anthropology Department at TAU. He is currently Director of the Educational Policy Program at the Taub Center for Social Policy Studies in Israel.

Rainer K. Silbereisen (www.rainersilbereisen.de) is currently Research Professor of Human Development and Director of the Center for Applied Developmental Science (CADS) at the University of Jena, Germany, and member of the Board of Governors of the University of Haifa, Israel. He is Fellow of the American Psychological Association and the Association for Psychological Science, Member of the European Academy of Sciences (London), and Past-President of the International Union of Psychological Science IUPsyS). A psychologist by training, he has been involved in interdisciplinary research on the role of social change in human development, acculturation among immigrants, psychological development of entrepreneurship, and prevention of adolescent problem behavior, often in a cross-national format. Rainer K. Silbereisen was also the head of the research consortium on "Migration and Societal Integration", which represents the backbone of this book.

Olivia Spiegler is a PhD student in Developmental and Social Psychology at the Ruhr-University Bochum in Germany. She is also part of the SIMCUR project (Social Integration of Immigrant Children – Uncovering Factors Promoting Resilience). Her research interests focus on the development and change of social identities in the context of acculturation as well as on intergroup relations between immigrants and host nationals.

Anja Steinbach is Professor of Sociology at University of Duisburg-Essen, Germany. Her main areas of research are: intergenerational relations, stepfamilies, the division of household labour, demography, age and aging, migration, and interethnic relations. Recent publications as editor include *Intergenerational Relations Across the Life Course. Special Issue of Advances in Life Course Research* (2012) and articles in the journals *Comparative Populations Studies* and *Journal of Marriage and Family*.

Katharina Stoessel received her PhD at the University of Jena (Germany). She is currently a research associate at the distance teaching university FernUniversität in Hagen, Germany. Her research focuses on Diaspora immigrants, immigrants' cultural identification in the context of intergroup relations as well as on diversity inclusion in higher education.

Peter F. Titzmann is currently Associate Professor at the Jacobs Center for Productive Youth Development, University of Zürich, Switzerland. His general research interest is in the interplay between normative development and migration-related adaptation among adolescents with immigrant background. He investigated this interplay in various developmental outcomes, such as experiences of stress, delinquent behaviour, friendships, and autonomy development. His work was published in various book sections and journal articles, for example in the *Journal of Cross-Cultural Psychology*, *Child Development*, and *Developmental Psychology*.

Nathalie Topaj is a research associate at the Berlin Interdisciplinary Centre for Multilingualism (BIVEM) in the Centre of General Linguistics (ZAS) in Berlin. Her main research interests lie in bilingual or multilingual language acquisition (in particular involving German and Russian), narrative and pragmatic skills in bilingual children; the development of language support and test materials for language acquisition, and multilingual language education. She is co-author of the *Russian Language Proficiency Test for Multilingual Children* (with Natalia Gagarina and Annegret Klassert, 2010).

Takeyuki (Gaku) Tsuda is Professor of Anthropology in the School of Human Evolution and Social Change at Arizona State University. His primary academic interests include international migration, diasporas, ethnic minorities, ethnic and national identity, transnationalism and globalization, ethnic return migrants, and the Japanese diaspora in the Americas. He is the author of *Strangers in the Ethnic Homeland: Japanese Brazilian Return Migration in Transnational Perspective* (Columbia University Press, 2003) and also the editor of *Diasporic Homecomings: Ethnic Return Migration in Comparative Perspective* (Stanford University Press, 2009) and *Local Citizenship in Recent Countries of Immigration: Japan in Comparative Perspective* (Lexington Books, 2006).

Joel Walters works on the interface of psycholinguistic and sociolinguistic aspects of bilingualism in early childhood and in mature adults with and without language impairments. His book *Bilingualism: The Sociopragmatic-Psycholinguistic Interface* was published by Erlbaum/Routledge in 2005. Other papers have appeared in *Language Learning, Bilingualism: Language and Cognition, Journal of Multilingual and Multicultural Development.* His joint research (primarily with Sharon Armon-Lotem) has been funded by the Israel Science Foundation, GIF, and BMBF. He is currently Dean of the Faculty of Humanities at Bar-Ilan University.

Jessica A. Willard is a doctoral student at the Ruhr-Universität Bochum in Germany. She is part of the research team of the SIMCUR project (Social Integration of ImMigrant Children – Uncovering Factors Promoting Resilience). Her main research interests are bilingual language development and heritage language maintenance. She is currently studying the vocabulary development and language use of Turkish language speakers in Germany.

Steffen Zdun is Research Associate at the Institute for Interdisciplinary Research on Conflict and Violence at Bielefeld University, Germany. His main areas of research are: juvenile delinquency, desistance and crime prevention. He is author of articles that have been published in journals such as *Criminology and Criminal Justice, Sociological Focus, International Journal of Conflict and Violence, Journal of Scandinavian Studies in Criminology and Crime Prevention, New Directions for Youth Development* and *Journal of Social Work Practice.*

Acknowledgements

This book is the final product of the large research consortium "Migration and Societal Integration" and would not have been possible without the constant support and effort of many people, including those whose work appears here. As there are too many to name individually, we would like to say a general but heartfelt thanks to all the senior and junior scientists from inside and outside the consortium who invested substantial amounts of their time to conduct and present the innovative work that forms the basis of this book. We would, however, like to offer our particular thanks to the following: to the German Federal Ministry of Education and Research (BMBF), which provided the financial basis for the endeavor and without which the whole project would not have been possible; to Heinz Thunecke from the German Aerospace Center (DLR) who was very supportive of our work from the very first steps of the consortium to the presentation of final results; to Elke Schröder who coordinated and organized consortium meetings and enabled a lively exchange of results and ideas; to Verona Christmas-Best who was involved in the preparation of various manuscripts prior to publication; and last, but by no means least, to Annett Weise and Stefanie Gläser who provided invaluable support in the technical and fiscal administration of this large research endeavor.

The Editors

Series Editor's Preface

Over the past three decades there has been a burgeoning of research in migration. Starting with studies of the great movement westward from Eastern and Southern Europe at the end of the nineteenth century, and the migration of post-colonial economic migrants from the periphery to the core after the Second World War, research moved on to embrace refugees and forced migrants from the Middle East, Asia and Africa and, more recently, the impact of the emigration from the A8 and A2 countries. Allied to these studies was the introduction of new theories of migration which could accommodate the increasing diversity of movements and peoples. New nomenclatures were introduced; transnational, return migrant, circular migrant and global citizen became part of the migration specialist's lexicon. However, the protagonists in this volume fit into none of these categories, and are, as a number of the contributors acknowledge, an under researched group. They are diasporic migrants, people returning to their ancestral homelands from countries in which they, and their ancestors, had lived for many decades, sometimes for centuries.

The specific groups under the microscope are emigrants who had left the Former Soviet Union to settle in Germany and Israel. The break-up of the Soviet Union, and the creation of new nation states, resulted in an exodus by those who were concerned about their future economic opportunities and (their newly acquired) outsider identity. A major pull factor was the special entry provisions that Israel and Germany put in place for these diasporic incomers. It is the comparison of the psychosocial effects of the arrival and settlement on both diasporic immigrants and indigenes in those two countries that the chapters in this book consider. In keeping with the theme of this series, the contributors – the majority engaged in the joint research project 'Migration and Societal Integration' – are from a range of disciplines, including criminology, education, linguistics, psychology and sociology.

The process of settlement for any migrant is complex and requires adaption to a multiplicity of life activities. However, in many cases it is even harder for diasporic returnees, for they belong and yet don't belong. The young incomers, who are the main subjects of the book, were confronted with a cultural heritage with which they were unfamiliar and to which many found it difficult to adapt. Chapters in this volume highlight the variety of life course experiences facing the young cohorts on arrival in Germany and Israel. These include language acquisition, the continuation and cessation of violent behaviour – the latter commonly known as, 'knifing off'; approaches to, and development of, romantic relationships in the new environment and the transition from school to work and the associated expectations. With one or two exceptions the studies are taken beyond the binary comparative and not only contrast experiences of the diasporics in Germany and Israel, but put these within a broader framework, at times incorporating comparison with indigenes, at others, with those of Turkish immigrants in Germany and Israeli-Arabs in Israel. Through the researchers' recorded findings our knowledge of both the patterns of behaviour of the ethnic migrants and the conduct of young people generally, under various conditions, is enhanced.

The Challenges of Diaspora Migration provides a fascinating and overdue addition to our knowledge and understanding of the migrant experience, in this instance one infrequently explored. It is important to remember that the diasporic migrants featured in this study are not the only (possible) return ethnic wanderers. We can think of slaves from Africa transported between the 16th and 19th centuries, Japanese Brazilians who settled in Brazil at the beginning of the 20th century, the Welsh in Patagonia and Koreans in China and Japan. It may well be that their return experiences would differ from those in this volume, but a template upon which to base research into that migration and the opportunity to compare and contrast is now available thanks to this detailed and scholarly contribution to the complex world of migration study.

Anne J. Kershen
Queen Mary University of London
Winter 2013

PART I
Diaspora Migration and the Consortium "Migration and Societal Integration"

Chapter 1

Introduction: Migration and Societal Integration: Background and Design of a Large-Scale Research Endeavor

Rainer K. Silbereisen, Peter F. Titzmann, Yossi Shavit

Migration is not a new phenomenon – nevertheless with increased globalization, growing economic uncertainty, and political turmoil in many countries of the world, rising levels of migration have been seen in recent decades. This trend seems likely to continue. From 2010 onwards, the number of people of working age living in high-income countries will begin to decline, whereas the number of working-age people in low-income countries will very likely increase, as Hugo (2010) reported with reference to World Bank data. This disparity will be a major force for further migration from low-income to high-income countries. Other developments, such as affordable transportation facilities and modern communication technologies, mean that today's immigrants can keep in close and regular touch with their heritage society. Frequent visits to the heritage country, for example, are rather normative today so that immigration also needs to be seen from an increasingly dynamic perspective (Leyendecker, 2011; Portes, 2003).

New Migration Trends: Leaving and Returning

Macro-level economic changes and the comparably low costs of transportation mean that migration no longer follows the traditional paradigm of permanent migrant settlement and that temporary or circular migration is becoming more prevalent (Global Commission on International Migration, 2005). To demonstrate this point, and to show the complexity of migration systems, we can use Australia as an example, primarily because, in contrast to most other countries, Australia has a comprehensive system for recording data concerning immigration and emigration.

In Australia, one of the largest flows of migrants is between Asia and Australia. Here, migration is "best depicted as one in which circularity, reciprocity, and return are key elements" (Hugo, 2010, p. 2). At closer scrutiny, a number of different migration patterns can be distinguished – permanent movement (settlers), long-term movement (stay for 12 months or more), and short-term movement (usually stay for less than 12 months) as described by Hugo. Permanent movement, the classical case, occurs as flow in and flow out of the destination country; although immigration research tends to focus more on the incoming migration, the numbers from Australia show that the counter flow is about 50 percent for some heritage regions. In other words, for some areas about half as many migrants return to their heritage country as arrive in Australia. The same circularity, reciprocity, and return apply to long- and short-term movements. Returning migrants take home the skills, networks, resources, and experiences they made in the destination country, which can be seen as an asset for the country of origin. Return migration, therefore, can be seen as part of an interacting system between countries or regions, and whose size may have been underestimated due to a lack of reliable national data.

A particular case under the rubric of return migration is that of migrants returning from a Diaspora. The term Diaspora historically refers to the exile and dispersion of Jews from Roman Judaea that started around the 6th century BC, and resulting in people of Jewish descent living over many generations outside their ancestral homeland. Some left their ancestral homeland in pursuit of opportunity while others fled into the Diaspora to escape ethno-political persecution. Today, and in this book, the term Diaspora migration is used in a much broader sense so that it also includes the migratory return of ethnic groups to their ancestral homeland for economic and other opportunities, or due to non-migratory changes in country borders, for example as result of military conflicts and political decisions. In addition to Israel, many European countries, including Germany, serve as ethnic home countries with Diaspora spread across the world. These are groups of people who have lived away from their ancestral territories for many generations, and return to what they deem their traditional home, motivated by political, social, economic, or cultural reasons (Brenick and Silbereisen, 2012). Tsuda (2009) lists 24 countries from all around the globe that are confronted with the situation of returning migrants that share ethnic roots with the receiving society. Given, however, that data on immigration/emigration flows are limited, it is safe to assume that this is a conservative estimate. Such returning immigrants are typically well acculturated and established in the country of their birth but, in contrast to other immigrant groups, such as work migrants, ethnic return migrants (or Diaspora migrants) have often maintained their own ethnic or cultural communities and shared dreams of returning to their ethnic homeland (Weingrod and Levy, 2006).

Two principle driving forces behind the return to the ancestral territories can be distinguished (Berry, Kim, Minde, and Mok, 1987). Push factors emerge if and when life in the country of residence deteriorates in political, cultural, or economic terms. Pull factors originate in the country of destination such as the wish to gain from the groups' cultural, social, and human capital. In some instances, countries attempt to affect their demographic composition by offering Diaspora migrants economic and other incentives to immigrate, the prime example being Israel, which has managed to maintain a solid Jewish majority by attracting immigrants in large numbers from the Jewish Diasporas in Europe, the Arab world, and the former Soviet Union.

Until the complexity of migration streams became obvious, the possible positive impact of migration for the countries from which people are migrating, such as the promotion of trade and, more importantly, remittances sent to lower income countries, was widely overlooked. Indeed, the OECD has suggested that through such money transfers, "a three per cent expansion in international migration could add more to world incomes than a complete liberalization of all trade" (Katseli, Lucas, and Xenogiani, 2006, p. 48).

Nevertheless, there is still a lack of research focusing on the unique and understudied experiences and psychosocial outcomes of immigrants from Diaspora populations. Special issues of journals (Brenick and Silbereisen, 2012; Silbereisen, 2008) on a better understanding of return migration from the Diaspora in Europe represent an important step, but they have concentrated on psychological research only. In spite of the overall positive reception in the new country, the political promotion of immigration from the Diaspora, and independent of the actual or presumed cultural linkages, Diaspora immigrants seem to experience the typical strain associated with immigration found in other immigrant groups (see Titzmann and Stoessel, this volume). They have to align the interests of self, home country, and host country, which may be quite different from expectations nourished by cultural tradition. Of particular relevance for the acculturation to the new context is that their legal status as Diaspora migrants differs from the status of other immigrants, and that the acculturation expectations of the host society call for quick and comprehensive adaptation to the new circumstances. Indeed, the mismatch between the idealized hopes of Diaspora migrants and the high expectations for social integration by the new host country can result in a particularly difficult adaptation, often with high social costs.

Diaspora Migration to Germany and Israel

This book project evolved from the collaborative work of a group of researchers from various disciplines (psychology, sociology, education, criminology, linguistics) on migration from ethnic German and Jewish Diasporas originating in Eastern Europe and Central Asia (mostly countries of the former Soviet Union or the socialist block) to Germany and Israel. The drastic political and economic changes following the breakdown of the communist system opened up borders and allowed dreams to become true for many individuals in the Diaspora. That many individuals used this opportunity to return to their homelands is particularly evidenced by the major streams of migration from countries of the former Soviet Union to Germany and Israel in the early 1990s (see Figure 1.1). Earlier waves of Diaspora migrants entering Germany had been much less pronounced, although a few thousand ethnic Germans had immigrated to Germany shortly after World War II and both Israel and Germany received a noteworthy share of Diaspora migrants in the 1970s (Bundesverwaltungsamt, 2010). Israel, however, has received several very large immigration waves of

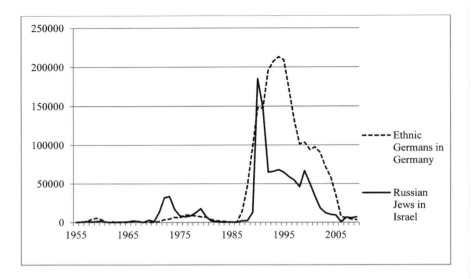

Figure 1.1   Number of immigrants to Israel and Germany 1955-2009

Diaspora Jews throughout its existence, as well as in the period preceding its establishment as a state (DellaPergola, 1998).

The more recent, post-Soviet, waves of immigration have caused a public debate and instigated substantial amounts of research in both Israel and Germany, largely because of the high numbers of immigrants, but also because of the crucial economic and social importance for the receiving societies that these groups adapt well to their new society. Research into the accommodation and integration of Diaspora migrants to Germany and Israel is also discussed in many other countries around the world because these groups are seen as prototypical cases of ethnic Diaspora migration.

As can be seen in Figure 1.1, in Israel, two waves of Diaspora immigration from the former Soviet Union can be clearly identified (Jewish Virtual Library, 2013; Mesch, 2003). The immigration wave of the 1970s is often referred to as the first immigration wave, and that of the 1990s as the second. The unprecedented return migration to Israel after World War II, and especially after the breakdown of the Soviet Union, was driven by push factors rooted in history, such as ethno-political discrimination, combined with bleak economic perspectives. At the same time, Israeli policy of providing a safe haven for those under pressure of discrimination and hardship represented a pull factor for people of Jewish descent and their families. The wish to increase the Jewish share of the population was certainly also relevant. The migrants themselves saw the chance to realize the romanticized dream of coming home to the ancestral land. All of the above was reinforced by media and personal contacts with those who had already left for Israel (Remennick, 2007).

With regard to the return migration of ethnic Germans and their families from their birth countries in Eastern Europe and Central Asia, although this had already begun in the years before the breakdown of the Soviet Union, it gained tempo and increased substantially in numbers after the political changes at the end of the 1980s (Dietz, 2006). In principle, these people shared roots with the German minorities that had migrated to Russia and other countries in the region as early as the reign of Catherine the Great in the 18th century. Mainly due to their skills as craftspeople, they were offered land and financial privileges and were allowed to keep their German culture and traditions. However, growing nationalism changed Russian attitudes toward these once welcomed ethnic Germans so that, especially after World War II, ethnic Germans were deported to Siberia or Kazakhstan, and were no longer allowed to maintain their German culture, or even to speak German in public, thus forcing them to adapt to Russian culture and Soviet society.

The pull and push factors among the German and Jewish people for immigration to their ancestral homelands, therefore, were alike. A further commonality between the two Diaspora groups, and with immigrants in general, is the link between economic uncertainties in their country of origin and the real or imagined affluence in their ancestral homeland. Although the idea of resettling in one's homeland gives direction to move to a particular country, the economic underpinnings are also very relevant (Silbereisen, 2008).

Diaspora immigrants in general tend to believe that once in the ancestral territories, acculturation will be easier than it is in reality, and people of the country of destination often share this expectation, although both views may have illusionary aspects. Although the two paradigmatic groups studied here had been born and raised abroad, they are assumed by governments and the public to be culturally similar to the native population in the receiving society (including its own heterogeneity), a view based simply on their historical common roots. In the case of ethnic German migrants ("Aussiedler," which literally means re-settlers; "Spätaussiedler" means late re-settlers and refers to those who arrived in Germany after January 1993) and the Jewish migrants to Israel, their integration is promoted by pre-migration preparations in the country of birth; by granting of German or Israeli citizenship; and by extensive support, including financial benefits once in the new country. This pro-active reception, especially the immediate granting of citizenship, is quite in contrast to other migrants to Germany and Israel; nor is it the norm for ethnic return migrants in other regions, such as Asia, where integration with full rights as citizens is not the rule (Tsuda, 2009).

Other factors may make assimilation into the new society difficult. For example, Diaspora groups typically are of mixed ethnic origin and it is not unusual for migrant families in Israel and Germany to have one partner of non-Jewish or non-German origin (Dietz, 2006), meaning that cultural affinity may differ within families. The children of migrating families may also find the move to the new country problematic; they were usually fully assimilated in the country of origin and often had to leave close friends behind. In addition, in spite of preferential treatment and extended support in the new country, all family members faced the risk of their prior achievements not being recognized in the new country, often leading to the downgrading of occupational qualifications in the local labor market.

This could also lead to a shift in the power balance between generations within families due to the more accelerated adaptation of the young (Titzmann, 2012).

The immigration of both Jewish and German Diaspora groups has a long history, and over time not only the social composition and number of the migrants changed but also, and in part as a response to these changes, the migration regimes in Israel and Germany were modified. For instance, until the end of the 1980s, ethnic German migrants were free to settle in Germany wherever they wanted, whereas later on they were required to settle according to target numbers for the various federal states of the country. Since the early 1990s, the command of German as requirement for immigration was reinforced, including the language competence of dependents who had never used or learned German in their birth country (Dietz, 2000). Moreover, within two years of the onset of immigration in the early 1990s, when only about half of the ethnic Germans in the former Soviet Union had migrated to Germany, the government introduced contingents. These and many other measures to manage the immigration of ethnic Germans changed the conditions for acculturation (Eisfeld, 2013).

Whereas in Germany migration policies enhanced regulation and constraint over time, in Israel the migration regime changed in the opposite direction. In the early decades of immigration, the state played a centralized role in immigration absorption: it built housing, created jobs, established absorption centers and actively directed immigrants to settle in the social periphery of the country. Since the late 1980s, this policy was replaced with a policy of "direct absorption" according to which immigrants from the FSU received a "basket" of cash and services and could choose among various strategies and modes of incorporation with state support. The basket included a lump sum of money, housing subsidies and numerous services including training and educational programs and subsidies (Doron and Kargar, 1993). Immigrants could choose where to live, whether to buy an apartment or rent one, and when and where to enter the labor market (Semyonov and Gorodzeisky, 2012). Nowadays, both Germany and Israel receive only small numbers of newly arriving Diaspora migrants from the former Soviet Union. Nevertheless, both countries still struggle with the integration of the substantial overall numbers of migrants, also because they want to avoid long-term segregation and the development of stable minorities (Al-Haj, 2004).

Despite all the good intentions of the governments involved to support the integration of Diaspora migrants, as Weingrod and Levy (2006) point out, there are many "paradoxes of homecoming," meaning that the Diaspora-homeland distinction is too simple in many cases. This would seem to be especially true for young immigrants, who may identify more easily with destinations other than Germany or Israel, or the country of birth. Young Ethiopian Jews, for example, tend to identify with the black Diaspora in other parts of the world due to experiences of discrimination. Moreover, the countries of birth have begun to see the potential of their former Diaspora citizens not only for developing relations with the new receiving countries (Germany and Israel), but also for their own future development. Thus, circular migration is promoted, so that – as noted when introducing the interactive system of international migration – "returning home" is not the end of the story.

The Research Consortium "Migration and Societal Integration"

The research consortium "Migration and Societal Integration," which started in 2006, with funding from the German Federal Ministry of Education and Research (BMBF), encompassed five interdisciplinary research groups. The consortium comprised researchers from eight German universities (Berlin, Bielefeld, Bremen, Chemnitz, Göttingen, Jena, Leipzig, and Mannheim) and four Israeli universities (Bar-Ilan, Haifa, Jerusalem, and Tel-Aviv). The aim was to identify specificities and commonalities in the migration experience of German and Jewish migrants, which concerned many aspects of a complex context-person interaction that could only be tackled from a multi-disciplinary view. Consequently senior researchers and young investigators in sociology, education, psychology, criminology, and linguistics were involved.

The research agenda was built around a few basic concepts. The first concept dealt with the issue of developmental transitions. We use the term transition for two kinds of changes relevant for migrants – one refers to more or less normative biographical transitions across the life span, such as the transition into formal educational institutions, and the other concerns the non-normative transition of migration from one country to another as the core element of migration experiences.

Normative biographical transitions, the first type of transitions studied, are periods in the life span when, due to normative changes in the ecology, such as entering into educational institutions or forming a family of one's own, the past alignment between individual and context becomes challenged (Bronfenbrenner, 2005). The life-course is characterized by a sequence of such biographical transitions that represent tasks to be resolved by individuals' goal-oriented actions. For the consortium, we chose the almost ubiquitous transitions in the educational sector on the one hand, and the less formal transitions to first romantic partnerships in adolescence and cohabitation in adulthood on the other. We deem the concentration on these transitions crucial, because they take place in the life span when major pathways to future success in life are formed. As one knows from research on the optimal timing of psychosocial interventions, this is also the window of opportunity for cost-effective improvements of later life chances (Heckman, 2006).

The other type of transition, the transition from one country to another, is a crucial life event and characterized by a substantial set of acculturative processes related to intergroup contact, identification, behavioral adaptation, and stress-related coping processes (Berry, Poortinga, Segall, and Dasen, 2002; Ward, 2001). Depending on the life stage, this transition and the ones mentioned in the previous paragraph can overlay each other and interact. A case in point is growing depressive mood – often taken as a sign of difficulties in adjusting to the transition to a new country, but also a common phenomenon for many individuals during the transitions related to puberty and adolescence. As Michel, Titzmann, and Silbereisen (2011) have shown, changes related to adolescence (normative development) and to migration (acculturation and adaptation to the new context) need to be carefully distinguished, because an age-normative increase in depressive symptoms can be counterbalanced by a decrease in depressive symptoms due to the sociocultural adaptation to the new context. The effect can be that longitudinal observations of adolescents do not reveal the typical increase in well-being one usually expects during early years in the new country.

The second basic concept that has guided the research of the consortium is acculturation, understood as the process and result of interaction between people of different ethnicities or cultures. As a general framework applicable to the whole consortium, we utilized a model by Berry (1997) with which to identify the important conditions and processes of acculturation. His heuristic approach became famous in the international migration literature, especially among psychologists, but it is not much different to the distinction of steps or strategies on acculturation used by other approaches more prominent in sociology (e.g., Esser, 1980).

Probably the best known contribution by Berry (1997) is his distinction of four "acculturation strategies," which were utilized in various projects of the consortium to identify different attitudes among immigrants. According to Berry's view, any migrant is faced with two basic questions. The first concerns how one values maintaining the cultural heritage and the second concerns how one values relations with the receiving cultural group. In our case the receiving groups refer to native Germans or veteran Israelis respectively. On the basis of these two dimensions, four strategies are distinguished. Integration (maintain heritage identity and build relations with host society), assimilation (only relations to host society are sought), separation from the mainstream (only relations to members of the heritage culture are sought), and marginalization (neither relations with members of the heritage culture nor with the receiving culture are sought). In many studies integration was shown superior to the other strategies in terms of positive psychosocial outcomes (Berry, 2005). The distinction between these categories received some criticism (for an overview see Van Oudenhoven, Ward, and Masgoret, 2006). Research often focused on the immigrants' strategies, despite the fact that Berry (2005) clearly stated that the success of immigrants' adaptation also depends on the four strategies of the larger society (parallel to the migrant strategies), namely, multiculturalism, melting pot, segregation, and exclusion. This was one reason for having native groups in nearly all studies of the consortium.

Findings suggest that there may be conflict between immigrants' and natives' acculturation strategies: Research for Israel showed that the hosts and the Russian-Jewish migrants preferred integration at first glance, but beyond this the host society preferred assimilation much more than the migrants. The tendency of the host society to expect assimilation of the Diaspora ethnic German immigrants was also shown for Germany (Zick, Wagner, van Dick, and Petzel, 2001). According to

Jasinskaya-Lahti et al. (2003) such discrepant acculturation orientations between host society and immigrants relate to higher psychological distress among the immigrants.

Besides the concept of transition and the theoretical approaches related to acculturation, the third major conceptual issue of the consortium was to compare the groups of Diaspora origin with other relevant groups within the two countries studied, as well as comparing results across the two countries. Such comparative studies of immigrant groups across countries are still quite scarce but can help in identifying similarities in adaptation and the generality of associations, on the one hand, and group-specific aspects of adaptation and limits of generality, on the other (Berry, Phinney, Sam, and Vedder, 2006; Slonim-Nevo, Mirsky, Rubinstein, and Nauck, 2009). Due to the limited knowledge of the specificities concerning the adaptation of Diaspora immigrants, such comparative research is needed, both comparisons with native groups and comparisons with other immigrant groups (e.g., work-migrants): established minorities can be highly informative with regard to the success and the perceived challenges among Diaspora migrant groups. For this reason, the studies presented in this book not only investigated the two Diaspora groups mentioned, but included natives in Germany and Israel (veterans), as well as minorities, namely Turks in Germany and Arabs in Israel. A special group of Russian Jewish immigrants to Germany was also included.

Conceptual Framework

The acculturation strategies and expectations just mentioned are an important element of the larger framework for studying acculturation (see Berry, 1997, for the full complexity of processes assumed). The major distinction in Berry's framework is between the group (macro) level and the individual (micro) level. This distinction may seem trivial, but it is important not only for understanding the acculturation experience of immigrants, but also for the collaboration of several disciplines in our research consortium, in that it reflects their major domains of scholarship.

The group level conditions are indirectly assessed by the comparison of Israel and Germany, and by the comparative investigation of different groups in each country. The financial situation in the two receiving countries in the mid-2000s reflects the economy before the world financial crisis. The government in Israel had been headed by Ariel Sharon since the beginning of 2003, followed by Ehud Olmert after 2006; both governments were conservative coalitions. In Germany, a coalition of the center-left and center-right parties had been in power since 2005, under the leadership of Chancellor Angela Merkel. Both Israel and Germany have an immigration policy based on similar ethnicity as criterion for acceptance (beyond other political issues). As far as the immigrant groups studied are concerned, there is also a commonality regarding the regions of origin in the former Soviet Union, which became a rather hostile context saturated with discrimination against both groups after the political changes of the late 1980s. One difference, however, that is noteworthy: whereas the ethnic Germans often used to live in rural areas, the Jewish Diaspora were more likely to live in larger cities (Slonim-Nevo et al., 2009). Concerning the conditions of the society of settlement, both countries are welfare states, although probably with better provisions in Germany than Israel. Both countries also have extensive support systems for Diaspora immigrants, in part beginning before actual migration. Over the years, and with increases in the number of ethnic German migrants, support in Germany became less generous; language tests before actual migration became obligatory; and the group comprised fewer ethnic Germans with a German background and more family and relatives of Russian origin (Dietz, 2006). One may also say that gradually, over time, these Diaspora immigrants form a different cohort due to other self-selection criteria (e.g., willingness to participate in language classes, chain-migration of extended family).

Attitudes toward immigrants and their integration in the population at large can be described as skeptical in both countries (Abali, 2009; Al-Haj, 2004) and are often reflected in experiences of group discrimination (Jasinskaja-Lahti et al., 2003; Titzmann, Silbereisen, and Mesch, 2011). The attitudes towards ethnic Germans among the native German population are rather "guarded." Often this aloofness is based on the reportedly higher delinquency rates (Heubrock, Voukava, and Petermann, 2008), although for the better part these simply reflect differences in social status and social participation (Raabe, Titzmann, and Silbereisen, 2008). To keep things in perspective, however, one should add that, according to a recent survey of the German Marshall Fund (GMF), public opinion to immigration overall is more positive in Germany than in other countries (The German Marshall Fund (GMF), 2011). A recent study in Israel on the attitudes of the veteran population towards the allocation of social rights to immigrants and Arabs reveals considerable discrimination against these groups (Raijman, 2009) but it is less severe vis-à-vis Jewish immigrants than Arabs or labor migrants.

Another group (macro-) level comparison in the research consortium refers to various groups within each country. These groups differ substantially with regard to their socio-economic and legal conditions. As the specific groups compared in each project are characterized in the single chapters, only a few facts are mentioned here. In Germany, many Turks are not German citizens, whereas all ethnic Germans are. In Israel, citizenship is not an issue, but legal rights and duties differ between the groups studied. For example, the State of Israel declares itself to be a Jewish state (Declaration of Independence, 1948). As such, it upholds the national aspirations, cultural values and interests of Jews while refusing to recognize, much less promote, the collective interests of its Arab citizens (e.g., Lustick, 1980). Although, most Arabs view Israel as a legitimate state and even as a Jewish state, many are alienated by the Jewish hegemony and feel unsafe in the state (Smooha, 2005). Many Arab citizens avoid taxation and very few serve in the military or national service.

Concerning the Turkish and Arab minorities included in the research, a major commonality is the rather traditional Islamic religious orientation, and in both cases their economic situation is less advantaged than that of the native/veteran population. None of the migrant groups studied appears substantially deviant in physical features from the local population, but the groups differ with regard to their tendencies to live in ethnic quarters or enclaves where the everyday spoken language and the language of commerce is more or less exclusively the ethnic language. Such segregation is less pronounced in Germany than in Israel, but even in Germany spatial segregation for some of the groups can be seen, especially in big cities, but no segregation in education can be found in Germany.

In sum, comparing the two countries with the specific groups in each country obviously does not allow an independent assessment of immigrant group and country as context of the acculturation. Nevertheless, at least the two Diaspora groups have much in common and the major differences between the two countries are that Israel could be deemed more experienced in dealing with immigration waves and that the level of segregation of ethnic groups is somewhat higher in Israel as compared to Germany. Such group-level conditions need to be taken into account, because the context and the group-level acculturation set the stage for the specific acculturation experience assumed to be the starting point of adaptation or maladaptation to a new cultural environment, as well as for the long(er)-term outcomes of this process (Berry, 1997). The specific experiences were the subject of a research project on the reasons for Diaspora immigrants to desist from or become involved in delinquency after the immigration process (Koren and Zdun, this volume, Zdun, this volume).

On the individual level, that is, the micro-level of inter-individual differences within specific ethnic groups, Berry's (1997) heuristic framework underscores the stress-coping process as a mechanism for acculturation-related adaptations, but other acculturation-related processes, such as social learning or inter-group processes (Ward, 2001) also exist and seem more relevant for specific research questions and outcomes (e.g., Gagarina et al., this volume; Walters, Armon-Lotem, Altman, Topaj, and Gagarina, this volume).

The advantage of Berry's model is, however, that it specifies a large number of moderating individual-level factors, which are themselves influenced by group level conditions. The first group of such factors concerned conditions that existed before immigration, including socio-demographics, pre-immigration acculturation, migration motivation, expectations concerning the resettlement, cultural specificity with regard to the country of destination, and stable personality features. Of particular interest for the research conducted in several projects of the consortium were the effects of socio-economic status, as indicated by educational level or financial affluence. More specifically, the consortium research enabled us to investigate a major issue concerning inequality in psychosocial outcomes between migrants (or different migrant or ethnic groups) and the local natives. Such ethnic inequalities are particularly notorious in relation to educational attainment, but the question of course is whether ethnic differences in psychosocial functioning are rooted in cultural differences or in socio-economic differentials (Heath, Rothon, and Kilpi, 2008). Because some migrants or minorities possess an educational and occupational skill level that is on average lower than the population average, such as the Turkish group in Germany, the socioeconomic background can partially explain inequalities between groups. In other words, rather than cultural sources proper, it may be the social class origin that explains the education and labor market disparity found (Kalter, Granato, and Kristen, 2007).

Concerning the inequalities mentioned, pertinent research demonstrated that social background covers about half of the gap in educational attainment, but that similar effects concerning the "ethnic penalty" in the labor market are much smaller (Heath et al., 2008). Obviously other factors play a role in explaining an ethnic or cultural gap. Such factors could be knowledge, discrimination, access to citizenship, and perhaps cultural orientation. Some chapters of this book deal with the question of whether socio-economic standing can explain away ethnic differences (e.g., Kristen, Chachashvili-Bolotin, Roth, and Adler, this volume; Lewin-Epstein, Salikutluk, Kogan, and Kalter, this volume; Silbereisen et al., this volume; Titzmann et al., this volume). The results across the different chapters suggest that whether or not various forms of social, economic, or cultural capital can or cannot explain away differences between the groups investigated depends on the outcome studied (educational vs. social cognitive).

Other moderating factors in Berry's (1997) model refer to the time during acculturation in the country of destination and the acculturation strategies mentioned earlier. These acculturation strategies were utilized in several projects for the investigation of adaptation in various domains of life, such as values, well-being and experiences involved in first romantic relations (Daniel, Benish-Weisman, Knafo, and Boehnke, this volume; Möllering, Schiefer, Knafo, and Boehnke, this volume; Nauck and Steinbach, this volume).

Methodological Framework

To address the research questions of all the projects, it was clear from the beginning that a variety of methods and scientific approaches would be needed to fulfil the aims of the research consortium. The methods and concepts therefore included ethnographic and linguistic approaches; concurrent, retrospective and prospective analyses; quantitative surveys; qualitative hypothesis-generating study formats; and panel studies.

As theoretical approaches on research concerning acculturation and the adaptation of immigrants revealed that comparative research is needed to identify similarities and group specificities in adaptation (Berry et al., 2006; Fuligni, 2001), the core methodological commonality across the projects has been the comparative nature of the studies. Nevertheless, comparative research is still quite rare, particularly comparative research involving Diaspora migrants and other immigrant groups, although there are some exceptions (e.g., Motti-Stefanidi and Asendorpf, 2012).

In conducting such research, different lines of methodology can be followed. A large number of immigrant groups differing in the combination of theoretically defined characteristics, such as the reasons for immigration or country of residence (Berry et al., 1987) could be investigated, or alternatively, a few groups that differ in some crucial aspect (e.g., Diaspora vs. non-Diaspora) and where results from one group can challenge the results in another (Kohn, 1987) can be studied.

The research consortium has chosen the approach by Kohn (1987), which has the advantage that the specific situation of the few groups investigated can be taken into account more thoroughly. The consortium investigated a variety of groups in two modern immigration countries: Israel (veteran Israelis, former Soviet Union Jews, and Israeli Arabs) and Germany (native Germans, Turks, former Soviet Union Jews, and ethnic Germans). The sampling of immigrant, minority, and native groups in two diverse receiving countries is a design that enables the exploration of specifics of the receiving context (mainly differences between countries can be expected), specifics of Diaspora migration (differences between Diaspora migrants and other immigrant/minority groups can be expected), and also normative universal processes, which may result from normative processes of dealing with age-related developmental tasks (e.g., the associations of predictors and outcomes do not differ across the groups studied).

The resulting data from this research are impressive. Altogether 17,000 individuals participated in the various projects so that the consortium is certainly among the largest endeavors conducted with regard to immigration research. Participants came from various regions within each country and, in most projects, were randomly selected from registry data. The research questions covered in the book focus on age groups ranging from kindergarten age to middle adulthood, and in some cases include multiple informant assessments. This suggests that the consortium produced an unusually large data set that will be available to other researchers through a well-documented archive, group number GN0081 (http://www.gesis.org/unser-angebot/recherchieren/datenbestandskatalog/). The specific aims and methods for all projects can be found on the consortium information portal (http://www.migration.uni-jena.de/).

Organization and Content of the Book

The research presented in the various parts of the book is guided by two common approaches. First, the effect of transitions on the psychosocial development of Diaspora immigrants is demonstrated. Such transitions can be the cultural transition from one country to another or transitions within the new society, such as the transition from school to work. Second, nearly all chapters present comparative research including data on Diaspora immigrants, ethnic minorities, and the majority population in their respective countries. This allows the way in which individuals of different background manage the transitions they encounter. Most of the chapters of this book resulted directly from the work of consortium research groups and have undergone several cycles of discussion and review. Earlier versions were presented at the concluding meeting of the consortium in

Berlin in 2010 and have since been revised, sometimes repeatedly, in response to input from colleagues and independent readers. Beyond these contributions, which form the core of the book, we invited outside experts to help in setting the stage for our approach as part of research in the broader field of Diaspora migration worldwide, and to provide suggestions concerning the relevance of the research for social policy above and beyond what had already been discussed by the consortium authors. The chapters are not research reports but have a broader scope, including carefully crafted expert views on pertinent research related to the particular topic. Our aim was to bring the chapters always "in tandem" – Israel and Germany (sometimes data from both countries are included in the same chapter).

Diaspora Migration and the Consortium "Migration and Societal Integration"

Part I of the book includes this introductory chapter and a chapter on Diaspora migration from a broader perspective. As readers will have realized, this introduction provides information on the process of coming home to a foreign land with special emphasis on immigration conditions in Israel and Germany. This chapter also describes the framework of the research consortium.

The second chapter in this part (Tsuda, this volume) deals systematically with the issue of Diaspora migration from a global view. According to Brubaker (2005) there is a tendency to refer to every population category that is geographically dispersed away from its territory of origin, as Diaspora. In Tsuda's view, however, the term should only refer to displaced people who have an imagined or real connection, of whatever degree and quality, with a prior home country, and who have seen the opportunity presented by the opening of borders, or found a way round closed borders to migrate to that country. Obviously, Germany and Israel are not the only examples of target countries for Diaspora migration. They are, however, rather special in that they have large population groups of shared ethnicity, particularly in the countries of the former Soviet Union and its allies in Europe and Asia. This is different to Finland and Greece with their much smaller Diasporas from the same region. Moreover, the initial displacement occurred in part a very long time ago, often repeatedly across new territories, and at a time when the present country of destination may not have existed in its current form. Diaspora migrants always share the experience that the original displacement did not occur during their own lifetime, which is in contrast to return migration, where people return to their birth-country, often in response to incentives to redress a brain drain or skills shortage. Tsuda avoided a Euro-centered view – there are many other Diaspora groups in the world. He gives examples such as the African Diaspora, one of the largest in modern times, the Asian Diaspora, and those involving Chinese and Indians who were also distributed in large numbers across the globe. Practically every national or ethnic conflict in our times produces new Diasporas.

From Heritage to Home Country: The Migration Transition and Adjustment

The focus of Part II is on the cultural transition from one country to another. The transition to a new country requires immigrants to acquire a new body of knowledge and a new set of behavioral skills with which to deal competently with the challenges of the new country. Learning the new language is probably the most important skill in this regard and extremely important for success in the new environment also among Diaspora migrants (Michel, Titzmann, and Silbereisen, 2012; Titzmann, Silbereisen, and Mesch, 2011). Although Diaspora migrants share some cultural or ethnic roots with the receiving society, most of them no longer speak the language of their ancestral homeland. This may be for a variety of reasons, such as the case of ethnic Germans living in the former Soviet Union who were forbidden to speak German in public. According to a Russian micro-census from 1994 (Dietz, 1999), German was used as the family language in only 13 percent of ethnic German families in Russia. This, together with interethnic marriages, reduced the German language proficiency of ethnic Germans substantially. Consequently, two chapters highlight language acquisition in Diaspora immigrant families as one of the most important sociocultural tasks following the transition to a new country (Walter et al., this volume, Gagarina et al., this volume).

Besides language acquisition, immigrants need to develop a value system of cultural belonging, which is part of their self-definition and fundamental to their aims in dealing with members of the host and heritage culture. Berry's (1997) acculturation strategies, as presented earlier in this introduction, guided the research of two of the chapters in this section. First, the chapter by Möllering et al. (this volume) explores the interaction of certain acculturation strategies and the context immigrants moved to as predictors for their well-being. The chapter by Daniel et al. (this volume) then focuses on the value system of immigrants and shows that, in Israel, the values endorsed by adolescents are related to acculturation strategies. Taken together, these two chapters remind us that the situation of Diaspora immigrants is rather complex concerning their cultural identity as far as the two culture reference systems are concerned.

The last two chapters of Part II view the transition from one country to another as a chance to break with the past. In this regard, immigration implies opportunities and risks for human development. For example, if an individual was on the path to delinquency in their country of origin, a radical change of people and context may lead to a total change of the developmental trajectory because the factors supporting delinquency are removed. An alternative scenario is, however, that someone well-adjusted in the home country can develop violent behavior under the new circumstances and challenges of the country of settlement. The two chapters (Koren and Zdun, this volume; Zdun, this volume) focus on discontinuities in adjustment and maladjustment. Koren and Zdun (this volume) address four groups that represent different statuses of violence before and after the immigration: those consistently showing violence; those who abstained from violence after immigration; those who started this behavior in the new country; and those who refrained from violence in both contexts. This chapter contains an in-depth examination of how experiences in different domains of everyday life, such as school, friends, or family, are linked to engagement in violent behavior in Germany and Israel. This chapter is compelling because it uncovers different motivations and characteristics of continuity and discontinuity in violent and non-violent behavior. In a similar vein, the chapter by Zdun (this volume) belongs to the very few studies on "knifing-off" in an immigration situation and addresses a currently unresolved question, namely, what exactly has to happen in order to refrain from past negative behavior (knifing-off) and then maintain the positive change.

Preparing for a Future: Transitions within the New Country and Related Opportunities

Part III takes the definition of transition further and moves the focus from transition between countries to look at how immigrants, minorities, and the majority population in Israel and Germany prepare for transitions within the new society. Such normative biographical transitions are crucial for the successful development of individuals (Bronfenbrenner, 2005), and ethnic or cultural differences in how such transitions are managed may be the background for the ethnic differences in the long-term adaptation of certain groups. In the modern Western world, it is the transition from school to work that often decides the future lives of individuals. For this reason, families try to see that their children and adolescents accomplish this transition successfully. In this section, two chapters present data on academic achievements of different immigrant groups. The focus of the Epstein et al. chapter (this volume) is on mobility aspirations, i.e., what occupational career plans are held in the different groups. The authors found that differences in aspirations existed, but were not substantial in magnitude. Furthermore, such aspiration differences could be explained by the social stratum individuals belonged to and by academic achievement. The results reported by Epstein et al. should be read in combination with results of the following chapter (Kristen et al., this volume). Kristen et al. investigated academic skills of immigrant and native students in Germany and Israel and uncovered differences between the two countries. The major difference was that the ethnic penalty in academic achievement is smaller in Germany despite the fact that the differences in educational background between native and immigrant parents are much larger in Germany compared to Israel. Furthermore, whereas this ethnic penalty was explained away in Germany by socio-economic differences, in Israel a difference remained even after controlling for such variables. These findings show that the country of residence needs to be taken into account for a thorough understanding of the academic adaptation of immigrant students.

Three more chapters in this section deal with biographical transitions within the new country. These chapters focus, however, on the informal transitions to first romantic relationship and to cohabiting as a couple. The major question in two chapters (Silbereisen et al., this volume; Titzmann et al., this volume) was whether these transitions affect the psychosocial functioning of individuals and whether they affect these outcomes differently for the Diaspora migrants, minority individuals, or members of the majority (in Germany: ethnic German Diaspora immigrants, Russian-Jewish immigrants, Turks, and natives; in Israel: Russian-Jewish Diaspora immigrants, Israeli-Arabs and veteran Israelis). Individuals were compared before and after the transition with regard to aspects of positive development (Lerner et al., 2005), namely, competence, confidence, connection, character, and caring (the Five Cs). In both countries, the transitions studied seemed to foster positive development, because those individuals after the transitions were better off in select psychosocial outcomes. In addition, results showed that transitions had similar effects across ethnic groups. The exception was the transition to a romantic relationship, which seemed to have a different effect among Israeli-Arab adolescents than among the other Israeli groups. Besides effects of transitions, ethnic differences in the Five Cs were found. In contrast to the results on academic achievement, however, these differences were never explained by economic, cultural or social capital, so that the effects seem cultural beyond being indicators of status differences.

A final chapter in Part III (Nauck and Steinbach, this volume) presents findings on the nature of the transition into early romantic relationships that usually occurs in adolescence. This transition is particularly affected by cultural norms and behaviors and the analyses showed clearly that immigrant groups differed with regard to selection criteria for potential romantic partners (e.g., status vs. appealing individual characteristics) and with regard to the experiences made in the first romantic relationships. Despite such differences, however, the groups were rather similar in partnership satisfaction, which suggests that different criteria for a fulfilling romantic relationship exist across the ethnic groups studied. Nauck and Steinbach combine German and Israeli data. However, they do not group ethnicities based on the country of settlement, they rather combine ethnic groups based on characteristics they deem important for selecting a romantic partner.

Research on Diaspora Migration and its Implications for Research and Policy

In Part IV, the final part of the book, contributors discuss opportunities for supporting and preparing individuals during the transition from one country to another and during transitions within the new country. First in this section, the chapter by Titzmann and Stoessel (this volume) moves away from the particular results of the consortium and addresses the question whether and how Diaspora migration differs from other types of immigration (e.g., among work-migrants). Taking the arguments from various theoretical viewpoints and empirical results together, Diaspora migration seems to have some similarities to other kinds of immigration, especially if the move to the homeland takes place after one's ancestors had been living in the Diaspora for many generations. The second half of the chapter is dedicated to the identification of challenges and directions for future research, which include comparative longitudinal research designs, person-oriented research, and the investigation of context-specific mechanisms through exploring interactions between the various factors involved.

The final two chapters emphasize conclusions that refer directly to issues of social policy. Leyendecker et al. (this volume) bring in the perspective from Germany and make a convincing plea for strengthening the role of first generation parents by encouraging them to teach their children their mother tongue and about their heritage culture, while at the same time facilitating their children's access to the language and culture of the host country. The advantages of bilingualism reviewed in this chapter reach from children's cognition and well-being to indicators for family relations and school success. The chapter by Mesch (this volume) complements this view with an Israeli perspective and identifies the various domains of life that represent challenges for the adaptation of Diaspora immigrants. A central issue is housing policy, as residential location can be a constraint or an opportunity in terms of access to education and labor market opportunities, and place of residence is known to shape the social, schooling and identity options open to immigrants. Other challenges discussed are related to social identity and to education. For all these challenges, Mesch offers opportunities and suggestions for how such issues can be resolved and about what needs to be considered when such policies are implemented. Both these chapters (Leyendecker et al., this volume; Mesch, this volume) complement each other and, although originating from a German or Israeli perspective, each chapter can give valuable recommendations for both receiving countries studied here.

Summary

The research covered in this book is unique in that it analyzes and compares systematically the acculturation processes and outcomes of Diaspora immigrants from the same territory in two destination countries. Moreover, the comparison includes groups of the majority population (native Germans or veteran Israelis) and other ethnic minorities, with a strong emphasis on life transitions and positive psychosocial outcomes. A central theme through most of the chapters is to look at the acculturation of Diaspora migrants and other immigrant groups through the lens of a transition (either the migration transition itself or normative transitions in the receiving country and how such transitions are managed by the different ethnic groups in the respective receiving country). The topics covered represent central topics of public debate and provide solid empirical evidence from one of the largest research endeavors in the study of Diaspora migration. The manifold methodological approaches and results presented by the various studies reported in the consortium chapters (Parts II and III) and their embedding in general views on Diaspora migration and their application to research and policy provide a broad picture of how Diaspora immigrants adapt to a new society. Further, the approach reveals the commonalities and differences between Diaspora migrants and other ethnic groups in the two countries studied, and illuminates potential consequences that may help in a better understanding of these groups and of the support they need for successful adaptation.

References

Abali, O. S. (2009). *German Public Opinion on Immigration and Integration*. Washington, DC: Migration Policy Institute.

Al-Haj, M. (2004). *Immigration and ethnic formation in a deeply divided society. The case of the 1990s immigrants from the former Soviet Union in Israel.* Leiden: Brill.

Berry, J. W. (1997). Immigration, acculturation, and adaptation. *Applied Psychology: An International Review, 46*(1), 5-34.

Berry, J. W. (2005). Acculturation: Living successfully in two cultures. *International Journal of Intercultural Relations, 29*(6), 697-712. doi: 10.1016/j.ijintrel.2005.07.013.

Berry, J. W., Kim, U., Minde, T., and Mok, D. (1987). Comparative Studies of Acculturative Stress. *International Migration Review, 21*(3), 491-511.

Berry, J. W., Phinney, J. S., Sam, D. L., and Vedder, P. (Eds.). (2006). *Immigrant youth in cultural transition: Acculturation, identity, and adaptation across national contexts*. Mahwah, NJ: Lawrence Erlbaum Associates.

Berry, J. W., Poortinga, Y. H., Segall, M. H., and Dasen, P. R. (2002). *Cross-cultural psychology: Research and applications* (2nd ed.). New York, NY: Cambridge University Press.

Brenick, A., and Silbereisen, R. K. (2012). Leaving (for) home: Understanding return migration from the diaspora. *European Psychologist, 17*(2), 85-92. doi: 10.1027/1016-9040/a000119.

Bronfenbrenner, U. (2005). A future perspective (1979). In U. Bronfenbrenner (Ed.), *Making human beings human: Bioecological perspectives on human development* (pp. 50-59). Thousand Oaks, CA: Sage Publications Ltd.

Brubaker, R. (2005). The 'diaspora' diaspora. *Ethnic and Racial Studies, 28*(1), 1-19. doi: 10.1080/0141987042000289997.

Bundesverwaltungsamt. (2010). Spätaussiedler und deren Angehörige [Ethnic Germans and their relatives]. Köln: Bundesverwaltungsamt.

DellaPergola, S. (1998). The global context of migration to Israel. In E. Leshem and J. T. Shuval (Eds.), *Immigration to Israel. Sociological perspectives* (pp. 51-92). New Brunswick, NJ: Transaction Publishers.

Dietz, B. (1999). Kinder aus Aussiedlerfamilien: Lebensituation und Sozialisation [Children in ethnic German families: Live situation and socialization]. In B. Dietz and R. Holzapfel (Eds.), *Kinder aus Familien mit Migrationshintergrund* (pp. 9-52). Munich: DJI Verlag.

Dietz, B. (2000). German and Jewish migration from the former Soviet Union to Germany: Background, trends and implications. *Journal of Ethnic and Migration Studies, 26*(4), 635-652.

Dietz, B. (2006). Aussiedler in Germany: From Smooth Adaptation to Tough Integration. In L. Lucassen, D. Feldman and J. Oltmer (Eds.), *Paths of Integration. Migrants in Western Europe (1880-2004)* (pp. 116-136). Amsterdam: Amsterdam University Press.

Doron, A., and Kargar, H. J. (1993). The Politics of Immigration Policy in Israel. *International Migration, 31*(4), 497-512. doi: 10.1111/j.1468-2435.1993.tb00681.x.

Eisfeld, A. (2013). (Spät-)Aussiedler in Deutschland [Ethnic Germans in Germany]. *Aus Politik und Zeitgeschichte, 63*(13-14), 51-57.

Esser, H. (1980). *Aspekte der Wanderungssoziologie* [Aspects of migration sociology]. Darmstadt: Luchterhand.

Fuligni, A. J. (2001). A comparative longitudinal approach to acculturation among children from immigrant families. *Harvard Educational Review, 71*, 566-578.

Global Commission on International Migration. (2005). *Migration in an Interconnected World: New Directions for Action.* Geneva: Global Commission on International Migration.

Heath, A. F., Rothon, C., and Kilpi, E. (2008). The Second Generation in Western Europe: Education, Unemployment, and Occupational Attainment. *Annual Review of Sociology, 34*(1), 211-235. doi: 10.1146/annurev.soc.34.040507.134728.

Heckman, J. J. (2006). Skill Formation and the Economics of Investing in Disadvantaged Children. *Science, 312*(5782), 1900-1902. doi: 10.1126/science.1128898.

Heubrock, D., Voukava, L., and Petermann, F. (2008). Sind Aussiedler aggressiver? [Are ethnic Germans more aggressive?]. *Zeitschrift für Psychiatrie, Psychologie und Psychotherapie, 56*(4), 293-299. doi: 10.1024/1661-4747.56.4.293.

Hugo, G. J. (2010). Circularity, Reciprocity, and Return: An Important Dimension of Contemporary Transnationalism. *ISSBD Bulletin, 58*(2), 2-6.

Jasinskaja-Lahti, I., Liebkind, K., Horenczyk, G., and Schmitz, P. (2003). The interactive nature of acculturation: Perceived discrimination, acculturation attitudes and stress among young ethnic repatriates in Finland, Israel and Germany. *International Journal of Intercultural Relations, 27*(1), 79-97.

Jewish Virtual Library (2013). Immigration to Israel: Total Immigration, by Country per Year (1948-2013). Retrieved May 16, 2013, from http://www.jewishvirtuallibrary.org/jsource/Immigration/immigration_by_country2.html.

Kalter, F., Granato, N., and Kristen, C. (2007). Disentangling recent trends of the second generation's structural assimilation in Germany. In S. Scherer, R. Pollack, G. Otte and M. Ganlg (Eds.), *From Origin to Destination: Trends and Mechanisms in Social Stratification Research* (pp. 214-245). Frankfurt: Campus.

Katseli, L. T., Lucas, R. E. B., and Xenogiani, T. (2006). *Effects of Migration on Sending Countries: What Do We Know?* Paris: OECD.

Kohn, M. L. (1987). Cross-national research as an analytic strategy: American Sociological Association, 1987 presidential address. *American Sociological Review, 52*(6), 713-731.

Lerner, R. M., Lerner, J. V., Almerigi, J. B., Theokas, C., Phelps, E., Gestsdottir, S., van Eye, A. (2005). Positive youth development, participation in community youth development programs, and community contributions of fifth-grade adolescents: Findings from the first wave of the 4-H study of positive youth development. *Journal of Early Adolescence, 25*, 17-71.

Leyendecker, B. (2011). Children from Immigrant Families – Adaptation, Development, and Resilience. Current Trends in the Study of Migration in Europe. *International Journal of Developmental Science, 5*(1), 3-9. doi: 10.3233/DEV-2011-002.

Lustick, I. (1980). *Arabs in the Jewish State: Israel's Control of a National Minority*. Austin, TX: University of Texas Press.

Mesch, G. S. (2003). Language Proficiency among New Immigrants: The Role of Human Capital and Societal Conditions: The Case of Immigrants from the FSU in Israel. *Sociological Perspectives, 46*(1), 41-58. doi: 10.1525/sop.2003.46.1.41.

Michel, A., Titzmann, P. F., and Silbereisen, R. K. (2011). Psychological adaptation of adolescent immigrants from the former Soviet Union in Germany: Acculturation versus age-related time trends. *Journal of Cross-Cultural Psychology, 43*(1), 59-76. doi: 10.1177/0022022111416662.

Michel, A., Titzmann, P. F., and Silbereisen, R. K. (2012). Language shift among adolescent ethnic German immigrants: Predictors of increasing use of German over time. *International Journal of Intercultural Relations, 36*(2), 248-259. doi: 10.1016/j.ijintrel.2011.10.002.

Motti-Stefanidi, F., and Asendorpf, J. B. (2012). Perceived discrimination of immigrant adolescents in Greece: How does group discrimination translate into personal discrimination? *European Psychologist, 17*(2), 93-104. doi: 10.1027/1016-9040/a000116

Portes, A. (2003). Conclusion: Theoretical Convergencies and Empirical Evidence in the Study of Immigrant Transnationalism. *International Migration Review, 37*(3), 874-892. doi: 10.2307/30037760

Raabe, T., Titzmann, P. F., and Silbereisen, R. K. (2008). Freizeitaktivitäten und Delinquenz bei jugendlichen Aussiedlern und Einheimischen [Leisure activities and delinquency among ethnic German adolescents from the former Soviet Union and native German adolescents]. *Psychologie in Erziehung und Unterricht, 55*(1), 39-50.

Raijman, R. (2009). Citizenship Status, Ethno-National Origin and Entitlement to Rights: Majority Attitudes towards Minorities and Immigrants in Israel. *Journal of Ethnic and Migration Studies, 36*(1), 87-106. doi: 10.1080/13691830903123245.

Remennick, L. (2007). *Russian Jews on Three Continents: Identity, Integration, and Conflict*. Brunswick, NJ: Transaction.

Semyonov, M., and Gorodzeisky, A. (2012). Israel: An Immigrant Society In J. Frideres and J. Biles (Eds.), *International Perspectives: Integration and Inclusion* (pp. 147-164). Montreal and Kingston: McGill-Queen's University Press.

Silbereisen, R. K. (2008). New research on acculturation among diaspora migrants. *International Journal of Psychology, 43*(1), 2-5. doi: 10.1080/00207590701804222.

Slonim-Nevo, V., Mirsky, J., Rubinstein, L., and Nauck, B. (2009). The impact of familial and environmental factors on the adjustment of immigrants: A longitudinal study. *Journal of Family Issues, 30*, 92-123.

Smooha, S. (2005). *Index of Arab-Jewish Relations in Israel 2004*. Haifa: University of Haifa.

The German Marshall Fund (GMF). (2011). Transatlantic Trends. Immigration. Retrieved May 20, 2013, from http://trends.gmfus.org/files/2011/12/TTI2011_Topline_final1.pdf

Titzmann, P. F. (2012). Growing up too soon? Parentification among immigrant and native adolescents in Germany. *Journal of Youth and Adolescence, 41*(7), 880-893. doi: 10.1007/s10964-011-9711-1

Titzmann, P. F., Silbereisen, R. K., and Mesch, G. (2011). Change in friendship homophily: A German Israeli comparison of adolescent immigrants. *Journal of Cross-Cultural Psychology, 43*(3), 410-428. doi: 10.1177/0022022111399648.

Tsuda, T. (Ed.). (2009). *Diasporic homecomings: Ethnic return migration in comparative perspective*. Palo Alto, CA: Stanford University Press.

Van Oudenhoven, J. P., Ward, C., and Masgoret, A.-M. (2006). Patterns of relations between immigrants and host societies. *International Journal of Intercultural Relations, 30*(6), 637-651. doi: 10.1016/j.ijintrel.2006.09.001.

Ward, C. (2001). The ABCs of acculturation. In D. Matsumoto (Ed.), *Handbook of culture and psychology* (pp. 411-445). New York: Oxford University Press.

Weingrod, A., and Levy, A. (2006). Social thought and commentary: Paradoxes of homecoming: The Jews and their Diasporas. *Anthropological Quarterly, 79*(4), 691-716.

Zick, A., Wagner, U., van Dick, R., and Petzel, T. (2001). Acculturation and prejudice in Germany: Majority and minority perspectives. *Journal of Social Issues, 57*(3), 541-557. doi: 10.1111/0022-4537.00228.

Chapter 2

Why Does the Diaspora Return Home?
The Causes of Ethnic Return Migration[1]

Takeyuki (Gaku) Tsuda

Introduction: The Return of the Diaspora

In recent decades, the total volume of ethnic return migration has increased significantly. In contrast to the return migration of first generation diasporic peoples who move back to their homeland (country of birth), *ethnic* return migration refers to later generation descendants of diasporic peoples who "return" to their countries of ancestral origin after living outside their ethnic homelands for generations.[1] Although a number of scholars have examined how diasporas have continued to evolve through further migratory scattering, relatively few have studied how certain diasporic peoples have also been returning to their ethnic homelands, a form of diasporic "in-gathering" or the "unmaking of diasporas" (Münz and Ohliger, 2003; Van Hear, 1998, pp. 47-48; see also Clifford, 1994, p. 304). In fact, certain diasporas are now characterized by a tension between centrifugal and centripetal migratory forces. The most prominent example of diasporic return are the millions of Jews in the diaspora who have migrated to Israel since World War II. The largest group of Jewish ethnic return migrants have been from the former Soviet Union, more than 770,000 of whom entered Israel between 1990 to 1999 (see Levy and Weingrod, 2005; Münz and Ohliger, 2003; Remennick, 2003). In Western Europe, four million ethnic German descendants from Eastern Europe return migrated to their ethnic homeland between 1950 and 1999 (see Münz and Ohliger, 2003). Other European countries, such as Spain, Italy, Greece, Poland, and Hungary have received much smaller populations of ethnic return migrants from Latin American and Eastern Europe (see Capo Zmegac et al., 2010; Cook-Martín and Viladrich, 2009; Fox, 2009; King and Christou, 2010; Skrentny et al., 2009). After the collapse of the Soviet Union, 2.8 million ethnic Russians living outside Russia in Eastern Europe, Central Asia, and the Caucasus returned to their ethnic homeland between 1990 to 1998 (see Pilkington, 1998). In East Asia, close to a million second and third generation Japanese and Korean descendants scattered across Latin America, Eastern Europe, and China have return migrated to Japan and Korea since the late

---

1 Although ethnic return migration is often referred to as "co-ethnic migration," "ethnic affinity migration," or "ethnic migration" in the literature, these terms will generally not be used in this chapter because of their greater ambiguity.

1980s (see Song, 2009; Tsuda, 2003). China and Taiwan have also been receiving ethnic Chinese descendants from various Southeast Asian countries. There has even been limited ethnic return migration to various Southeast Asian countries as well. Although most diasporic returnees are labor migrants from poorer countries, there is also a smaller but growing population of professionals and students from developed countries in North America and Europe who migrate to their countries of ancestral origin.

Not only is the total volume of ethnic return migration quite substantial, it is generally long term or permanent in nature. Diasporic returnees in the Middle East and Europe often migrate in order to settle permanently in their countries of ethnic origin. Although some ethnic return migrants (especially in East Asia) are sojourners who intend to remain only a few years in their ancestral homelands (as labor migrants and target earners), a number of them are prolonging their stays and settling, often with family members (see Tsuda, 1999). The exception here are professional and student migrants from the developed world, who generally remain in their ethnic homelands temporarily (e.g., see Jain, 2012).

The Economics of Ethnic Return Migration

Most diasporic descendants are not returning to their ethnic homelands simply to reconnect with their ancestral roots or explore their ethnic heritage. Instead, they are generally migrating from less developed countries to more economically prosperous ancestral homelands (often in the First World) in search of jobs, higher incomes, and a better standard of living. Although the desire to eventually return to the ancestral homeland is often invoked in definitions of diasporic peoples (Safran, 1991, pp. 83-84; Tölölyan, 1996, p. 14), most of their descendants, who are quite rooted in their countries of birth, would not do so without sufficient economic incentives. Ethnic return migrants are generally in search of better economic opportunities, not ethnic roots. In this sense, diasporic return from the developing world initially appears to be another form of international labor migration caused by widening economic disparities between rich and poor countries.

This is especially true with Russian Jews and ethnic Germans living in poorer Eastern European countries, ethnic Korean descendants in China and the former Soviet Union, as well as Latin Americans of European and Japanese descent, who started returning to their ethnic homelands when faced with economic crises in South America in the late 1980s. Even when economic disparities between sending and receiving countries are not large, the primary motive remains economic.[2] In these cases, ethnic return is to easily accessible neighboring countries with whom

---

2   This is the case for ethnic Hungarian descendants from Romania returning to Hungary or ethnic Russians from Soviet successor states returning to Russia, although economic causes for return migration are stronger for ethnic Hungarians than ethnic Russians (Brubaker, 1998, pp. 1059-1060).

diasporic descendants have maintained relatively strong linguistic and cultural ties, lowering the economic threshold for migration.[3]

Although ethnicity is generally not a "pull" factor that draws diasporic descendants to the ancestral homeland in search of ancestral heritage, it can be a "push" factor that forces them out of their country of birth. In the past, large ethnic return migration flows were instigated by ethnopolitical persecution caused by major geopolitical disruptions, such as the dissolution of empires, colonial regimes, and multi-ethnic states and not by direct economic pressure per se (see Brubaker, 1995, 1998; Capo Zmegac, 2005). For instance, the collapse of the Austro-Hungarian and Ottoman Empires led to the mass repatriation of ethnic Hungarians and ethnic Turks from Eastern Europe and the Middle East and the defeat of Germany after World War II caused the expulsion of 12 million ethnic Germans from Eastern Europe, most of whom resettled in West and East Germany. The end of European colonial empires caused large numbers of European descendants living in colonized territories to return to their ethnic homelands (especially in the case of Britain and France). In these cases, ethnic return migration was mainly caused by ethnic discrimination and persecution as diasporic peoples from the conquering homeland were left behind as their empires receded, becoming "enemy" ethnic minorities and former colonizers who lost their privileged sociopolitical status and were pressured, if not forced, to migrate back to their countries of ethnic origin.

In recent decades, ethnopolitical persecution has not caused any large-scale ethnic return migrations, which have become primarily economic in nature. For instance, although Jewish diasporic return to Israel began in the wake of the Holocaust after World War II, most Jews in the diaspora today migrate from less developed countries to Israel for economic reasons. Even diasporic returns caused by the dissolution of multi-ethnic states and empires have had a notable economic component in recent decades. The collapse of the Soviet Union was the most recent geopolitical event that enabled a number of ethnic minorities within its territories to return migrate to more economically developed ethnic homelands. Most notable of these are the diasporic return of Russian Jews to Israel and a second wave of ethnic German return migration from Eastern Europe after the Cold War (the two largest recent ethnic return migration flows). Perhaps the only example of large scale ethnic return migration caused by ethnopolitical persecution in recent decades was during the dissolution of the former Yugoslavia, which forced ethnic minorities such as the Croats and Albanians living outside their homeland territories to return migrate under threat of ethnic persecution and genocide.

Nonetheless, ethnic discrimination can play a role even in cases of economically-motivated return migration. For instance, continuing ethnic

---

3   This is also the case for Finland-Swedes who return to Sweden. Not only do they share strong cultural affinities with their neighboring ethnic homeland, because of free movement across borders, some see their move to Sweden as internal migration. As a result, many are moving without strong economic pressure (Hedberg and Kepsu, 2003; Hedberg, 2009).

insecurity and discrimination in Eastern Europe has sometimes worsened the socioeconomic situation of ethnic minorities in these countries, causing them to leave for their ancestral homelands. After the collapse of the Soviet Union, the millions of ethnic Russians and their descendants who were left outside their Russian homeland in Soviet successor states suddenly became ethnic minorities of diminished socioeconomic and political status subject to deteriorating ethnopolitical relations, discrimination, and an uncertain economic and ethnic future, causing Russia to allow their repatriation (Brubaker, 1995, pp. 208-209, 1998, pp. 1059-1061; Pilkington, 1998, pp. 123-138; Vishnevsky, 2003, pp. 162).[4] Likewise, the diasporic return of Russian Jews to Israel was caused by a combination of economic crisis, political instability, and increasing Russian nationalism, anti-Semitism, and discrimination (Remennick, 1998, pp. 247, 2007, pp. 36-37, pp. 42-43). The migration of ethnic Hungarian descendants from Romania to Hungary was a response to their comparatively dismal economic future in Romania, exacerbated by the perception of ethnic discrimination (Fox, 2003, p. 452). In these cases, diasporic return migration is still motivated by underlying economic causes, but ethnic discrimination and persecution serve as an additional impetus that helps "push" diasporic descendants out of their countries of birth.

Ethnicity seems to play a greater role for ethnic return migrants from the First World. Coming from rich countries, such individuals have much less economic incentive to migrate to their ethnic homelands (which are sometimes poorer countries) and therefore, their numbers are quite limited. Although many are seeking professional, educational, or business investment opportunities in their countries of ancestral origin, the desire to reconnect with their ethnic roots and explore their cultural heritage seems to be a stronger motive compared to ethnic return migrants from poorer, developing countries. This is especially the case with student ethnic return migrants, who usually have a desire to study their ancestral language and learn about the homeland culture.[5] Asian Americans in East Asia cite the desire to explore their ethnic ancestry as a reason for return migration (see Kim, 2009; Tsuda, 2009) as do Korean Japanese who return to South Korea (Kweon, n.d.).[6] Some later generation Asian Americans also feel they have become too assimilated in the United States and have lost their

---

4   In fact, ethnic Russian repatriates are classified as "forced migrants" by the Russian government despite the fact that they resemble economic migrants more than refugees. Another example of diasporic return that was partly motivated by worsening ethnic conditions are Estonian descendants in the former Soviet Union who migrated to Estonia (see Kulu, 1998).

5   Of course, there are also students who migrate to their ethnic homelands from developing countries. For instance, a number of Korean Chinese in South Korea seem to be students (see Choi, n.d.; Yang, n.d.).

6   Second generation Greek Americans have similar motivations for migration (Christou, 2006, pp. 1050-1051).

cultural heritage, thus motivating them to return to their homelands to recover their ethnic ancestry as a source of cultural authenticity. In the case of the Finland-Swedes who return to Sweden, cultural and linguistic affinity with their ethnic homeland as well as concerns about their weakening minority culture in Finland is a primary motive for return migration in addition to educational and professional opportunities (Hedberg and Kepsu, 2003; Hedberg, 2009). A limited number of individuals from the First World travel to their ancestral homelands as cultural heritage tourists in order to explore their ethnic roots, sometimes on organized tours sponsored by ethnic organizations and homeland governments that wish to recover ties to wealthy diasporic descendants abroad and promote their economic investment in the ethnic homeland (e.g., see Kibria, 2002b; Louie, 2001, 2002, 2003). The most notable examples of such organized ethnic tourism are to Israel, China, and South Korea.[7]

Transnational Ethnic Ties and Diasporic Return

Although diasporic returns have been caused more by economic pressures than by persisting ancestral ties across borders, such transnational ethnic affinities determine the direction of these migrant flows. In response to economic pressures, diasporic descendants have chosen to migrate to their ethnic homelands instead of to other advanced industrialized countries because of their nostalgic affiliation to their country of ethnic origin as well as the ethnically preferential immigration policies of homeland governments, which have enabled them to return migrate.

Imagining the Ethnic Homeland from Afar

Most ordinary labor migration flows are structured by pre-existing, social networks and institutional connections between sending and receiving countries, which provide transnational linkages enabling migrants to move across borders and relocate to foreign countries. In the case of ethnic return migration, however, most diasporic descendants have lost any substantial transnational social connections or cultural contacts with their countries of ethnic origin,[8] except in a few cases where the ethnic homeland is located in neighboring countries. Despite literature that suggests that transnational social connections with the ethnic homeland persist after the first immigrant generation (e.g., see Levitt and Waters, 2002; Smith, 2006), even most second generation diasporic descendants considered in this book do not have substantial contact with their parents' country of origin. Therefore, the transnational ethnic ties that channel diasporic return migrants to

---

7   Some white Americans of European descent have also returned to their ethnic homelands (as tourists or otherwise) in search of their ancestral roots.

8   There are, of course, cases where ethnic return migrants have maintained social connections to relatives in their homelands and use these social networks to migrate.

their ethnic homelands are based on an imagined, nostalgic ethnic affinity to an ancestral country which most have never visited. In this sense, their ethnic return migration is a type of "forged transnationality" (Schein, 1998)—the creation of new transnational connections instead of the continuation of pre-existing linkages.

Although most diasporic descendants have developed a nostalgic identification with their ethnic homelands (cf. Al-Ali and Koser, 2002), the strength of such sentimental ethnic attachments varies. For instance, Russian Jews do not have a strong transnational ethnic affiliation to Israel because of their cultural assimilation and suppression of nationalist sentiment among ethnic minorities in the former Soviet Union (see Remennick, 2003). Others, like the Argentines of Spanish and Italian descent, do not have a strong awareness of their ethnic heritage, but develop an appreciation for it while recovering their homeland nationality (Cook-Martín, n.d.).

Immigrant ethnic minorities sometimes develop strong transnational identifications with their countries of ethnic origin in response to the discriminatory exclusion and marginalization they experience in dominant society (e.g., see Espiritu, 2003, pp. 86-88; Levitt, 2001, pp. 19-20; Parrenas, 2001, pp. 55-59; Portes, 1999; cf. Kibria, 2002b), which makes them feel that they do not fully belong to their countries of birth. For instance, ethnic Hungarian descendants in Romania feel solidarity with the greater Hungarian nation partly in response to their adversarial relations with majority Romanians. Ethnic Germans in Eastern Europe seem to have had analogous experiences in the past when faced with discrimination. Some ethnic minorities (such as Asian Americans and Japanese descent *nikkeijin* in Latin America) are forever racialized as foreigners with essentialized cultural attachments to their native countries of origin because of their phenotypic differences from the mainstream populace, which can cause them to construct a romanticized view of their ethnic homeland as the country where they racially belong (Kim, 2009; Louie, 2002, p. 313-314; Tsuda, 2003, Chapter 2).[9]

However, ethnic minorities can also develop relatively strong homeland attachments because their ethnic ancestry and countries of origin are constructed and portrayed in a favorable manner. Indeed, most diasporic descendants imagine their ancestral homelands from afar in rather idealized, romantic, if not mythical ways (cf. Cohen, 1997, pp. 184-185). Many of these positive images come from their parents and grandparents, whose nostalgic romanticization of their homeland is a product of their prolonged separation from their countries of origin (see Grossutti, n.d.; Kim, 2009; Klekowski von Koppenfels, 2003, p. 316, 2009; Tsuda, 2003, Chapter 2; Viladrich, n.d.). Other images come from the globalized mass media and popular culture, which has become the primary means of imagining homelands from afar (Appadurai, 1996, p. 38, p. 49; Gupta and Ferguson,

---

9   This is sometimes reinforced by first generation immigrant parents who tell their assimilation-minded offspring that they cannot deny their ethnic heritage because of their distinctive racial appearance and bloodline (Kibria, 2002a, Chapter 3).

1992, p. 11). At times, such nostalgic longings for their country of ethnic origin can cause diasporic descendants to cling to archaic ancestral traditions that are no longer actively practiced in their ethnic homelands.

Positive identifications with ancestral homelands seem to be especially prominent among "positive minorities" who enjoy a relatively higher socioeconomic status than majority society and are ethnically respected, such as the Japanese Brazilians, Finland-Swedes, certain Asian Americans, and even the ethnic Hungarians in Romania (see Fox, 2003, p. 459; Hedberg, 2009; Hedberg and Kepsu, 2003, p. 72; Tsuda, 2003, Chapter 2). Some of these ethnic minorities can be positively stereotyped by mainstream society because of sociocultural qualities associated with their ethnic homelands, especially for those in developing countries whose ancestors came from more developed or First World countries. Of course, images of the ancestral homeland can vary over time depending on historical circumstances and ambivalent, conflicting perceptions often co-exist (see Louie, 2003; Tsuda, 2001).

Attachments to homelands are especially strong for diasporic peoples located in neighboring countries where ethnocultural links exist across national borders, as with the Hungarian Romanians and Finland-Swedes (Hedberg and Kepsu, forthcoming).[10] In addition, both of these groups are generally raised and educated in cohesive ethnic communities and have retained their ancestral languages to a certain extent. Unlike other diasporic descendants, such peoples never left their ethnic homelands to migrate to faraway countries and assimilate to foreign cultures. Instead, the ethnic homeland technically left them (in neighboring countries), when it lost territory and national borders shifted or were consolidated.[11]

Therefore, when diasporic descendants are faced with economic pressures to emigrate, many naturally have turned to their ethnic homelands instead of migrating to other advanced industrialized nations because of their sentimental ethnic attachments to their countries of ancestral origin. Not only did these countries seem more ethnically accessible, it was presumed that their co-ethnic status would facilitate their immigrant social integration.

In addition, such transnational ethnic affiliations have been substantiated by homeland governments, which have adopted immigration and nationality policies that reach out to their diasporic descendants abroad and allow them to return to their ethnic homelands. These governments have granted the right of ethnic return because of their own sense of ethnocultural affinity and historical connection to their diasporic peoples. In order to fully understand the factors which have enabled

---

10 In the case of Hungary, the government has actively reached out to its nearby diasporic communities and granted them various legal and social privileges in order to promote a greater Hungarian ethnic nation across borders (Fox, 2003, 2009; Joppke, 2005, pp. 247-250).

11 In other cases, such as the ethnic Germans in Eastern Europe and the Korean Chinese, diasporic descendants reside in nearby countries but actively emigrated abroad and were historically isolated from their homelands by Communist regimes.

diasporic return, therefore, we must analyze the rationales behind the ethnic return migration policies of homeland states.

Ethnic Return Migration Policy: Encouraging the Diaspora to Return "Home"

Although most liberal democratic states have abandoned the ethnically discriminatory, racist immigration policies of the past, which excluded certain immigrants by race or national origins, a number of them continue to have ethnic preference policies that privilege ethnically desirable immigrants (see Joppke, 2005), usually drawing from the country's pool of diasporic descendants abroad. The shift has therefore simply been from negative discrimination to positive discrimination in ethnic selectivity (cf. Joppke, 2005, p. 19). Governments have not only reached out across territorial borders to their first generation emigrants in order to ensure their continuing national loyalty and engagement in their home countries (Glick Schiller, 1997, pp. 160-161; Guarnizo, 1997, p. 305, p. 309; Smith, 2003), they have also attempted to incorporate second and third generation diasporic descendants into their "deterritorialized nation-states" by encouraging them to return to their ethnic homeland.

The ethnic preference policies of homeland governments are based on the essentialized assumption that ethnic descendants, despite being born and raised abroad, would be culturally similar to the host populace because of their shared bloodline. Diasporic descendants have been imagined as an integral part of a broader, deterritorialized cultural nation of "co-ethnics" living in other countries but united by common descent (cf. Joppke, 2005, p. 159), thus invoking a natural ethnic affinity between the nation-state and its diaspora. However, the specific reasons why homeland governments decided to welcome back their ethnic descendants from abroad vary according to geographical region.

Ethnic return migration policies in Europe (and Israel) are generally based on an ethnic protection or ethnic affinity rationale based on the historical connection of these countries to their diasporic peoples abroad (cf. Skrentny et al., 2009; see also Joppke, 2005, pp. 23-24). In Israel and Germany, these policies were initially implemented to protect their diasporic peoples from ethnic persecution. When the state of Israel was established after the Holocaust, all Jews were granted the right to return to their ancestral homeland partly to provide them a safe haven from future persecution as well as to build up and strengthen the Jewish state (Joppke and Rosenhek, 2009). Likewise, in Germany, ethnic German descendants expelled from Eastern Europe after World War II and those living in Communist countries during the Cold War were allowed to return as *Aussiedler* under the presumption of ethnic persecution.

In contrast, ethnic preferences in immigration policy and nationality law in other European countries (Spain, Italy, Greece, Hungary, Poland, and Russia) are based almost exclusively on an ethnic affinity rationale with diasporic descendants born abroad as part of a greater ethnic nation beyond state borders (Joppke, 2005, pp. 116-117, 245-246). Because of historical and racial ties to the diaspora, ethnic descendants are seen by their respective homeland governments as "our peoples" who therefore have a right to return to their ancestral homeland. Although some type of ethnic protection rationale can be invoked,[12] the underlying justification is based on a sense of state responsibility/obligation toward their diasporic descendants abroad (Cook-Martín, n.d.; Joppke, 2005, p. 246; Skrentny et al., 2009; de Tinguy, 2003, pp. 116-119).[13]

Unlike their European counterparts, East Asian as well as some Southeast Asian countries have invited back their diasporic descendants mainly for economic purposes (Skrentny et al., 2009; see also Joppke, 2005, pp. 158-159). Japan and South Korea have imported large numbers of ethnic return migrants in response to acute unskilled labor shortages caused by decades of economic prosperity coupled with low fertility rates. South Korea and China (and to some extent, Taiwan, the Philippines, Malaysia, Vietnam, Cambodia, and Laos)[14] have encouraged wealthy and highly-skilled ethnic descendants in the diaspora to return migrate in order to promote economic investment from abroad and to tap their professional skills. However, these countries generally decided to allow diasporic return because they assumed ethnic return migrants of shared descent and presumed cultural affinity would be easier to assimilate and socially integrate than other immigrants and would therefore not disrupt the country's ethnoracial balance.

Because of the different justifications that European and East Asian countries have used to welcome co-ethnic descendants from abroad, it is not surprising that the legal status they enjoy in their ethnic homelands is quite different. European countries (and Israel), which have accepted ethnic return migrants as peoples who deserve to be included in and protected by the nation-state, either grant them citizenship upon ethnic return (as in the case of Israel, Germany, Poland, and Greece to some extent) or allow them to recover their ethnic homeland nationality and become dual nationals, which gives them the right to return migrate (as in the case of Spain, Italy, Ireland, Poland, and Russia) (Cook-Martín and Viladrich, 2009; Grossutti, n.d., pp. 2-5; Iglicka, 1998, p. 1008; Joppke, 2005, pp. 245-247; Skrentny et al., 2009). Unlike most of the other countries, Spain and Italy do not have preferential ethnic immigration policies that specifically target co-ethnic descendants abroad and actively encourage them to return migrate.[15] Instead,

---

12   Joppke notes that the original purpose of the dual nationality law in Spain, which enables ethnic return migration, was to protect Spanish immigrants in Latin America, who were being forced to naturalize in their countries of residence in the late nineteenth and early twentieth centuries (2005, pp. 115-117). A protection rationale for ethnic preference immigration or dual nationality policies is also invoked by Greece (Skrentny et al., 2009).

13   Israel's policy also grants the right of ethnic return to all Jews as members of a deterritorialized diasporic community (regardless of whether they have been persecuted) and is therefore based on both an ethnic affinity and protection rationale.

14   See Cheng (2002, pp. 91-92) and Skrentny et al. (2009).

15   Spain does have preferential immigration policies toward Latin Americans and Filipinos based on linguistic and cultural affinities to peoples from its former colonies (Cornelius, 2004, p. 410; Joppke, 2005, pp. 114-129; Skrentny et al., 2009).

ethnic return migration is enabled through their *jus sanguinis* (descent-based) dual nationality laws, which their ethnic descendants (mainly in Argentina) have utilized to migrate to their ethnic homelands in response to economic crises at home.[16] The main exception to such policy trends in Europe is Hungary, which does not confer nationality to its co-ethnics abroad nor even has a stable guest worker program for them, forcing most ethnic return migrants to work illegally.[17] Hungary is also not interested in actively recruiting ethnic return migrants (Brubaker, 1998, p. 1055; Fox, 2009; Skrentny et al., 2009) because its economy is less prosperous and cannot support large numbers of immigrant workers and its ethnic descendants are mainly in surrounding countries, which creates certain policy constraints.[18] Likewise, although Russia remains committed in principle to accepting all ethnic Russians who return from Soviet successor states, it does not actively encourage repatriation because of the limited ability of its fragile economy to accommodate and integrate them (Brubaker, 1998, p. 1061; Pilkington, 1998).

In contrast to most European countries, ethnic return migrants in East Asia are generally given only preferential visas (and not citizenship) since they are being imported primarily as immigrant workers.[19] The Japanese government issues indefinitely renewable visas to ethnic return migrants, and China has even offered permanent residence to its highly-skilled diasporic returnees (Skrentny et al., 2009). In South Korea, ethnic Koreans from China and the former Soviet Union have been offered only a limited number of work visas (industrial trainee visas in the past and now, five-year visas under a new "Visit and Work Program"). Because most of its Third World diasporic descendants are located in neighboring and poorer China, the Korean government has been concerned about a flood of

---

16   The Spanish and Italian governments not only allow Spanish and Italian Argentines to retain dual nationality by descent, those (especially of the later generations) who have lost their ethnic homeland nationality are allowed to recover it. Many of them have done so in order to return migrate for the economic opportunities, especially during periods of Argentine economic crisis in recent decades.

17   Although Hungary granted restrictive three month guest worker visas to ethnic Hungarians in neighboring Romania as part of a 2001 "Status Law," many of its provisions have since been weakened or revoked. A referendum granting dual nationality to co-ethnics abroad was also defeated because of insufficient voter turnout. Skrentny et al. (2009) claim that there are other Eastern European countries that grant only preferential visas to co-ethnic returnees.

18   Hungary's ethnic descendants are in neighboring states because of the country's loss of territory after World War I. As a result, if Hungary actively encouraged them to "return" to Hungary, it would cause political tensions, raising fears of territorial "revisionism" among its neighbors. This is especially true in Romania, whose relations with Hungary have been especially tense because of the contested territory of Transylvania. Romania has in fact objected to Hungary's attempts to reach out to ethnic Hungarian descendants across its borders (Fox, 2003, p. 455; Joppke, 2005, pp. 249-250; Kovrig, 1994).

19   The exception seems to be Taiwan, which has recruited highly-skilled diasporic Chinese through European-style dual nationality laws (Cheng, 2003, pp. 91-92).

Korean Chinese labor migrants and has therefore not adopted a more open policy toward them. This has caused many of them to immigrate illegally, but with the tacit consent of the Korean government which has conveniently looked the other way (Lim, 2006, p. 241).

Such open ethnic immigration policies have been an important factor in facilitating diasporic return by enabling co-ethnic descendants abroad to secure access to their ancestral homelands by virtue of their ethnic heritage and descent (Van Hear, 1998, p. 48). Although these policies have not been a direct cause of ethnic return migration, they have certainly channeled these migration flows by determining their destination. Many diasporic descendants have chosen to return migrate to their ethnic homelands for economic reasons because of the much greater ease of entry compared to other countries of immigration (cf. Tsuda, 1999). If homeland governments had not openly admitted their diasporic descendants, most ethnic return migration flows would have remained quite small and many of the migrants would have headed to other advanced industrialized nations. In this sense, the transnational ethnic connections that enabled ethnic return migration were forged both "from below" by diasporic descendants, who imagined their ancestral ties to the ethnic homeland, and "from above" by the policies of these homeland governments, which have reached out to their ethnic descendants abroad and encouraged them to return "home" (see Guarnizo and Smith, 1998).[20]

Conclusion: Diasporic Return as a Migration System

Immigration specialists over the years have offered various theories for why people migrate, some based on simple economic explanations and others emphasizing transnational social networks, immigration policies, and even cultural/behavioral norms (see Castles and Miller, 2003, Chapter 2; Massey et al., 1998 for reviews). It is quite evident that any comprehensive understanding of population movements must adopt a dynamic and multi-causal "migration systems" approach that examines various transnational economic and sociopolitical connections between groups of sending and receiving countries, which serve as bridges and links that channel and direct migrants to specific countries (see Fawcett, 1989; Kritz and Zlotnik, 1992). Although ethnic return migration is initiated by economic forces that are similar to other forms of labor migration, it is also structured by transnational ethnic ties between sending and receiving countries. This includes both sentiments of nostalgic affinity among diasporic descendants with their ethnic homelands and homeland governments' ethnically preferential immigration

---

20   Although "transnationalism from above" usually refers to global processes (such as transnational capital, media, and supra-national organizations) that are above the nation-state, Guarnizo and Smith (1998, p. 29) warn us against equating it exclusively with global processes and note that transnationalism from above and below are relational and contextual terms.

and nationality policies, which are based on imaginings of a greater ethnic nation encompassing their diasporic descendants abroad.

Ultimately, ethnic return migration is a product of a complex dynamic between economics and ethnicity, with neither variable by itself sufficient to explain the causes of diasporic return. Global economic disparities and pressures explain why ethnic return migrants leave (emigration), but not where they go (immigration). Transnational ethnic ties between homelands and their ethnic descendants abroad explain where they go, but not why they leave. A full understanding of the migratory process, therefore, must simultaneously involve both economic pressures, which initiate migration, and transnational ethnic connections, which determine its destination.

The study of diasporic return migration therefore provides a new perspective to immigration studies by examining how migration can be structured by transborder ethnic ties between countries. Most other types of population movements (e.g., labor migrants, high-skilled and professional migration, etc.) are not ethnically motivated. In the case of refugees, ethnicity (in the form of political persecution) may be a cause of migration, but it simply "pushes" them out of the sending country and is not a transnational variable that "pulls" them to the receiving country as is the case with ethnic return migration. By illustrating how ethnic dynamics can influence the migration process, the study of diasporic return also highlights how migration can be the product of not only instrumental economic or political motives, but also expressive and affective ties of ethnoracial group belonging that are constructed (and even imagined) across national borders. Even in the absence of actual transnational social or institutional connections between sending and receiving countries, migration can still occur because of primordial and sentimental ethnic attachments that people have to distant ancestral lands.

References

Al-Ali, N., and Koser, K. (2002). Transnationalism, International Migration, and Home. In N. Al-Ali and K. Koser (Eds.), *New Approaches to Migration? Transnational Communities and the Transformation of Home* (pp. 1-14). London and New York: Routledge.

Appadurai, A. (1996). *Modernity at Large: Cultural Dimensions of Globalization.* Minneapolis: University of Minnesota Press.

Brubaker, R. (1995). Aftermaths of Empire and the Unmixing of Peoples: Historical and Comparative Perspectives. *Ethnic and Racial Studies, 18*(2), 189-218.

Brubaker, R. (1998). Migrations of Ethnic Unmixing in the 'New Europe.' *International Migration Review, 32*(4), 1047-1065.

Capo Zmegac, J. (2005). Ethnically Privileged Migrants in Their New Homeland. *Journal of Refugee Studies, 18*(2), 199-215.

Capo Zmegac, J., Vob, Ch., and Roth, K. (Eds.) (2010). *Co-Ethnic Migrations Compared: Central and Eastern European Contexts.* Berlin: Verlag Otto Sagner.

Castles, S., and Miller, M. J. (2003). *The Age of Migration: International Population Movements in the Modern World* (3rd ed.). New York: Guilford Press.

Cheng, L. (2002). Transnational Labor, Citizenship and the Taiwan State. In A. Rosett, L. Cheng and M. Y. K. Woo (Eds.), *East Asian Law: Universal Norms and Local Cultures* (pp. 85-105). New York: RoutledgeCurzon.

Choi, W. N.d. (2006). Ethnic Koreans from China: Korean Dreams, Adaptation, and New Identities. Paper presented at a conference on Korean ethnic return migration, University of Auckland, New Zealand, November 2006.

Christou, A. (2006). Deciphering Diaspora—Translating Transnationalism: Family Dynamics, Identity Constructions and the Legacy of 'Home' in Second-Generation Greek-American Return Migration. *Ethnic and Racial Studies, 29*(6), 1040-1056.

Cohen, R. (1997). *Global Diasporas: An Introduction.* Seattle: University of Washington Press.

Cook-Martín, D. N.d. The Long Way Home or Back Door to the EU? Argentines Claims of Ancestral Nationalities. Unpublished conference paper.

Cook-Martín, D., and Viladrich, A. (2009). Imagined Homecomings: The Problem with Similarity Among Ethnic Return Migrants in Spain. In T. Tsuda (Ed.), *Diasporic Homecomings: Ethnic Return Migration in Comparative Perspective* (pp. 133-158). Stanford: Stanford University Press.

Clifford, J. (1994). Diasporas. *Cultural Anthropology, 9*(3), 302-338.

Cornelius, W. A. (2004). Spain: The Uneasy Transition from Labor Exporter to Labor Importer. In T. Tsuda, P. Martin and J. Hollifield (Eds.), *Controlling Immigration: A Global Perspective* (2nd ed.) (pp. 387-429). Stanford: Stanford University Press.

Espiritu, Y. L. (2003). *Home Bound: Filipino American Lives Across Cultures, Communities, and Countries.* Berkeley: University of California Press.

Fawcett, J. T. (1989). Networks, Linkages, and Migration Systems. *International Migration Review, 23*(3), 672-680.

Fox, J. E. (2003). National Identities on the Move: Transylvanian Hungarian Labour Migrants in Hungary. *Journal of Ethnic and Migration Studies, 29*(3), 449-466.

Fox, J. (2009). From National Inclusion to Economic Exclusion: Transylvanian Hungarian Ethnic Return Migration to Hungary. In T. Tsuda (Ed.), *Diasporic Homecomings: Ethnic Return Migration in Comparative Perspective* (pp. 186-207). Stanford: Stanford University Press.

Glick Schiller, N. (1997). The Situation of Transnational Studies. *Identities: Global Studies in Culture and Power, 4*(2), 155-166.

Grossutti, J. N.d. From Argentina to Friuli (1989-1994): A Case of Return Migration? Unpublished manuscript.

Guarnizo, L. E. (1997). The Emergence of a Transnational Social Formation and the Mirage of Return Migration Among Dominican Transmigrants. *Identities: Global Studies in Culture and Power, 4*(2), 281-322.

Guarnizo, L. E., and Smith, M.P. (1998). The Locations of Transnationalism. In M.P. Smith and L. Guarnizo (Eds.), *Transnationalism from Below* (pp. 3-34). New Brunswick: Transaction Publishers.

Gupta, A., and Ferguson, J. (1992). Beyond 'Culture': Space, Identity, and the Politics of Difference. *Cultural Anthropology, 7*(1), 6-23.

Hedberg, C., and Kepsu, K. (2003). Migration as a Cultural Expression? The Case of the Finland-Swedish Minority's Migration to Sweden. *Geography Annals, 85B*(2), 67-84.

Hedberg, C. (2009). Ethnic "Return" Migration to Sweden: The Dividing Line of Language. In T. Tsuda (Ed.), *Diasporic Homecomings: Ethnic Return Migration in Comparative Perspective* (pp. 159-185). Stanford: Stanford University Press.

Hedberg, C., and Kepsu, K. Forthcoming. Identity in Motion: Finland–Swedish Migration to Sweden. *National Identities 10*(1).

Iglicka, K. (1998). Are They Fellow Countrymen or Not? The Migration of Ethnic Poles from Kazakhstan to Poland. *International Migration Review 32*(4), 0995-1014.

Jain, S. (2012). For Love and Money: Second-Generation Indian-Americans 'Return' to India. *Ethnic and Racial Studies* (published online).

Joppke, C. (2005). *Selecting by Origin: Ethnic Migration in the Liberal State.* Cambridge, MA: Harvard University Press.

Joppke, C., and Rosenhek, Z. (2009). Contesting Ethnic Immigration: Germany and Israel Compared. In T. Tsuda (Ed.), *Diasporic Homecomings: Ethnic Return Migration in Comparative Perspective* (pp. 73-102). Stanford: Stanford University Press.

Kibria, N. (2002a). *Becoming Asian American: Second-Generation Chinese and Korean American Identities.* Baltimore: Johns Hopkins University Press.

Kibria, N. (2002b). Of Blood, Belonging, and Homeland Trips: Transnationalism and Identity Among Second-Generation Chinese and Korean Americans. In P. Levitt and M. C. Waters (Eds.), *The Changing Face of Home: The Transnational Lives of the Second Generation* (pp. 295-311). New York: Russell Sage.

Kim, N. Y. (2009). Finding Our Way Home: Korean Americans, "Homeland" Trips, and Cultural Foreignness. In T. Tsuda (Ed.), *Diasporic Homecomings: Ethnic Return Migration in Comparative Perspective* (pp. 305-324). Stanford: Stanford University Press.

King, R., and Christou, A. (2010). Cultural Geographies of Counter-Diasporic Migration: Perspectives from the Study of Second-Generation 'Returnees' to Greece. *Population, Space and Place 16*(2), 103-119.

Klekowski von Koppenfels, A. (2003). Who Organizes? The Political Opportunity Structure of Co-Ethnic Migrant Mobilization. In R. Münz and R. Ohliger (Eds.),

Diasporas and Ethnic Migrants: Germany, Israel, and Post-Soviet Successor States in Comparative Perspective (pp. 103-132). London: Frank Cass.

Klekowski von Koppenfels, A. (2009). From Germans to Migrants: *Aussiedler* Migration to Germany. In T. Tsuda (Ed.), *Diasporic Homecomings: Ethnic Return Migration in Comparative Perspective* (pp. 227-259). Stanford: Stanford University Press.

Kovrig, B. (1994). Hungarian Minorities in East-Central Europe: To Create Harmony in an Ethnic Mosaic. *Bulletin of the Atlantic Council of the United States* 5(4). 3.

Kritz, M., and Zlotnik, H. (1992). Global Interactions: Migration Systems, Processes, and Policies. In M. M. Kritz, L. L. Lim, and H. Zlotnik (Eds.), *International Migration Systems: A Global Approach* (pp. 1-16). New York: Oxford University Press.

Kulu, H. (1998). Ethnic Return Migration: An Estonian Case. *International Migration* 36(3), 313-336.

Kweon, S. N.d. Returning Ethnic Koreans from Japan in Korea: Experiences and Identities. Paper presented at a conference on Korean ethnic return migration, University of Auckland, New Zealand, November 27-28, 2006.

Levitt, P. (2001). *The Transnational Villagers.* Berkeley: University of California Press.

Levitt, P., and Waters, M. C. (2002). *The Changing Face of Home: The Transnational Lives of the Second Generation* (pp. 295-311). New York: Russell Sage.

Levy, A., and Weingrod, A. (2005). *Homelands and Diasporas: Holy Lands and Other Places.* Stanford: Stanford University Press.

Lim, T. (2006). NGOs, Transnational Migrants, and the Promotion of Rights in South Korea. In T. Tsuda (Ed.), *Local Citizenship in Recent Countries of Immigration: Japan in Comparative Perspective* (pp. 235-269). Lanham, MD: Lexington Books.

Louie, A. (2001). Crafting Places through Mobility: Chinese American 'Roots-Searching' in China. *Identities* 8(3), 343-379.

Louie, A. (2002). Creating Histories for the Present: Second-Generation (Re) definitions of Chinese American Culture. In P. Levitt and M. C. Waters (Eds.), *The Changing Face of Home: The Transnational Lives of the Second Generation* (pp. 312-340). New York: Russell Sage.

Louie, A. (2003). When You Are Related to the 'Other': (Re)locating the Chinese Homeland in Asian American Politics through Cultural Tourism. *Positions: East Asia Cultures Critique* 11(3), 735-763.

Maeyama, T. (1996). *Esunishitei to Burajiru Nikkeijin* (Ethnicity and Brazilian Nikkeijin). Tokyo: Ochanomizu Shobo.

Margolis, M. L. (1994). *Little Brazil: An Ethnography of Brazilian Immigrants in New York City.* Princeton, NJ: Princeton University Press.

Massey, D. S., Arango, J., Hugo, G., Kouaouci, A., Pellegrino, A., and Taylor, J. E. (1998). *Worlds in Motion: Understanding International Migration at the End of the Millennium.* Oxford: Clarendon Press.

Moreira da Rocha, C. (1999). Identity and Tea Ceremony in Brazil. *Japanese Studies 19*(3), 287-295.

Münz, R., and Ohliger, R. (Eds.) (2003). *Diasporas and Ethnic Migrants: Germany, Israel, and Post-Soviet Successor States in Comparative Perspective*. London: Frank Cass.

Parreñas, R. S. (2001). *Servants of Globalization: Women, Migration and Domestic Work*. Stanford, CA: Stanford University Press.

Pilkington, H. (1998). *Migration, Displacement, and Identity in Post-Soviet Russia*. London: Routledge.

Portes, A. (1999). Conclusion: Toward a New World – The Origins and Effects of Transnational Activities. *Ethnic and Racial Studies 22*(2), 463-477.

Reichl, C. A. (1995). Stages in the Historical Process of Ethnicity: The Japanese in Brazil, 1908-1988. *Ethnohistory 42*(1), 31-62.

Remennick, L. I. (1998). Identity Quest Among Russian Jews of the 1990s: Before and After Emigration. In E. Krausz and G. Tulea (Eds.), *Jewish Survival: The Identity Problem at the Close of the Twentieth Century* (pp. 241-258). New Brunswick, NJ: Transaction Publishers.

Remennick, L. I. (2003). A Case Study in Transnationalism: Russian Jewish Immigrants in Israel of the 1990s. In R. Münz and R. Ohliger (Eds.), *Diasporas and Ethnic Migrants: Germany, Israel, and Post-Soviet Successor States in Comparative Perspective* (pp. 370-384). London: Frank Cass.

Remennick, L. I. (2007). *Russian Jews on Three Continents: Identity, Integration, and Conflict*. New Brunswick, NJ: Transaction Publishers.

Safran, W. (1991). Diasporas in Modern Societies: Myths of Homeland and Return. *Diaspora: A Journal of Transnational Studies 1*(1), 83-99.

Schein, L. (1998). Forged Transnationality and Oppositional Cosmopolitanism. In M. P. Smith and L. Guarnizo (Eds.), *Transnationalism from Below* (pp. 291-313). New Brunswick, NJ: Transaction Publishers.

Skrentny, J., Chan, S., Fox J. E., and Kim, D. (2009). Defining Nations in Asia and Europe: A Comparative Analysis of Ethnic Return Migration Policy. In T. Tsuda (Ed.), *Diasporic Homecomings: Ethnic Return Migration in Comparative Perspective* (pp. 44-72). Stanford: Stanford University Press.

Smith, R. C. (2003). Diasporic Memberships in Historical Perspective: Comparative Insights from the Mexican, Italian, and Polish Cases. *International Migration Review 37*(3), 724-759.

Smith, R. C. (2006). *Mexican New York: Transnational Lives of New Immigrants*. Berkeley: University of California Press.

Song, C. (2009). Brothers Only in Name: The Alienation and Identity Transformation of Korean Chinese Return Migrants in South Korea. In T. Tsuda (Ed.), *Diasporic Homecomings: Ethnic Return Migration in Comparative Perspective* (pp. 281-304). Stanford: Stanford University Press.

de Tinguy, A. (2003). Ethnic Migrations of the 1990s from and to the Successor States of the Former Soviet Union: 'Repatriation' or Privileged Migration? In R. Münz and R. Ohliger (Eds.), *Diasporas and Ethnic Migrants: Germany,*

Israel, and Post-Soviet Successor States in Comparative Perspective (pp. 112-127). London: Frank Cass.

Tölölyan, K. (1996). Rethinking *Diaspora*(s): Stateless Power in the Transnational Moment. *Diaspora: A Journal of Transnational Studies 5*(1), 3-36.

Tsuda, T. (1999). The Motivation to Migrate: The Ethnic and Sociocultural Constitution of the Japanese Brazilian Return Migration System. *Economic Development and Cultural Change 48*(1), 1-31.

Tsuda, T. (2001). When Identities Become Modern: Japanese Immigrants in Brazil and the Global Contextualization of Identity. *Ethnic and Racial Studies 24*(3), 412-432.

Tsuda, T. (2003). *Strangers in the Ethnic Homeland: Japanese Brazilian Return Migration in Transnational Perspective*. New York: Columbia University Press.

Tsuda, T. (2009). Global Inequities and Diasporic Return: Japanese American and Brazilian Encounters with the Ethnic Homeland. In T. Tsuda (Ed.), *Diasporic Homecomings: Ethnic Return Migration in Comparative Perspective* (pp. 227-259). Stanford: Stanford University Press.

Van Hear, N. (1998). *New Diasporas: The Mass Exodus, Dispersal and Regrouping of Migrant Communities*. Seattle: University of Washington Press.

Viladrich, A. N.d. Going back Home? Argentine Return Migrants in Transnational Perspective. Unpublished conference paper.

Vishnevsky, A. (2003). The Dissolution of the Soviet Union and Post-Soviet Ethnic Migration: The Return of Diasporas? In R. Münz and R. Ohliger (Eds.), *Diasporas and Ethnic Migrants: Germany, Israel, and Post-Soviet Successor States in Comparative Perspective* (pp. 155-172). London: Frank Cass.

Yang, Y.-K. N.d. The Return Migration of Korean Chinese (*Joseonjok*) from a Comparative Perspective. Paper presented at a conference on Korean ethnic return migration, University of Auckland, New Zealand, November 27-28, 2006.

Note

Material from this chapter is taken from "Why Does the Diaspora Return Home? The Causes of Ethnic Return Migration," in *Diasporic Homecomings: Ethnic Return Migration in Comparative Perspective*, Takeyuki Tsuda (Ed.). Stanford: Stanford University Press.

PART II
From Heritage to Home Country: The Migration Transition and Adjustment

Chapter 3

Language Proficiency and Social Identity in Russian-Hebrew and Russian-German Preschool Children

Joel Walters, Sharon Armon-Lotem, Carmit Altman, Nathalie Topaj, and Natalia Gagarina

Immigrant parents who are dominant in a minority language generally speak to their second generation children in their native language, while their children tend to respond in the language of the host society. This well-documented phenomenon usually leads to relatively rapid transition (language shift) over a single generation. It can also contribute to the development of multiple identities (e.g., Alba, 1999; Cameron, 2004; Portes and Schauffler, 1994; Weinreich and Saunderson, 2003), identities which are maintained or shift through early and later childhood and adolescence. This chapter explores the interface of language acquisition/ proficiency and immigrant identity in Russian-Hebrew and Russian-German preschool children. Beyond cross-language and cross-national comparisons of native speakers of Russian in two national contexts, we attempt to get at some of the complexities of identity in preschool children and their relationship to language proficiency.

Both language and identity are viewed here as complex and dynamic. The two constructs are modular in the sense that they function without reference to each other, but they also interact, with language reflecting different identities. Linguistic structure is traditionally divided into phonology, morphology, syntax, semantics, and lexicon, but investigation of language also includes more speaker-based phenomena such as proficiency, and attitudes. The identity construct includes personal as well as social identity, with a particular focus here on ethnolinguistic identity (Walters, 2005).

In the language domain, we focus on language proficiency as assessed by standardized tests for acceptance and placement of preschool children in educational programs which test expressive and receptive language abilities; for identity, we are concerned with ethnicity, ethnolinguistic identity, social preferences, and attitudes to speakers and languages, none of which are explicitly used as gatekeepers in schools, but all of which influence policy decisions in subtle and not so subtle ways.

As a construct, social identity has its origins in personality psychology (Erickson, 1968; Mead, 1964), in social psychology (Tajfel, 1982), and in sociology (Goffman, 1959). Uni-dimensional views of identity, based on classical variables such as social class, gender, ethnicity, nationality, territory, religion, family, and occupation have given way to more dynamic approaches, which allow for multiple, fluid identities.

A context-based, multiple identities approach is taken here to reflect what Bourdieu (1991) called *champs* (Fr.), i.e., macro-sociological contexts such as demography, kinship and culture. These contexts are embodied in the demographic patterns of the migrant preschool child's neighborhood and school population, in the presence of grandparents as caretakers, and in electronic media. Traditional sociological variables – socio-economic status (SES), class, occupation, nationality, gender, religion, and ethnicity – cut across these macro-categories. Weigert, Teitge and Teitge (1986) offer a five-way distinction among ego, individual, group, organization, and societal levels of identity. The multidimensional and flexible character of ethnic identity is prominent in this literature (Alba, 1990; Waters, 1990).

Identity is viewed as a bridge from the social context to the child's first language maintenance and second language acquisition and use. Parent's educational level, occupation, and SES are elements of economic identity. Nationality, ethnicity, and religion constitute political identity. Birth order, gender, and family relationships are relevant to one's family identity, while preschool, social activities, and media contact contribute to cultural identity. Processes such as migration, urbanization, secularization, and integration/alienation are also reflected in the migrant's composite identity, and its influence on the child's socialization patterns.

The present exploration of preschool social identity cannot examine a child's identities through choices of nationality, profession, family and social relations, and religious affiliation. We can, however, look at children's different identities, and at transitions linked to language development. We do so in two ways, one via responses to quasi-experimental questions and tasks and another through actual language behavior, in terms of proficiency in Russian vs. German/Hebrew and reported language use. We also look at parents' perceptions of children's language proficiency, use and attitudes. In this way we attempt to gain access to the child's identities and the effects of parents' social integration.

Language-identity relations have been widely investigated with tasks adapted from social psychology and sociolinguistics (Allard and Landry, 1994; Bourhis and Landry, 2008; Lambert, 1990; Sachdev, Arnold, and de Dios Yapita, 2006; Taylor, Meynard, and Rheault, 1977). Yet, preschool children are not represented in this literature, in part because of the notion that social identity develops later and in part because the methods of choice in this field, questionnaire and survey methods, are not appropriate for very young children.

Social identity is conceptualized here as a complex of (1) ethnic and ethnolinguistic identity, (2) social preferences, and (3) attitudes to speakers and languages. The ethnic/ethno-linguistic construct is centered on collective identity; social preferences focus on relational or interpersonal identity; and attitudes are an indirect way of getting at both collective and interpersonal identity (see Brewer and Chen, 2007; Roccas and Brewer, 2002 for the theoretical basis here).

Research Focus

The main question concerns the extent to which Language Proficiency is related to ethnolinguistic identity, social preferences for bilingual speakers of the target languages, and attitudes to speakers of different ethnic groups and their languages. The central hypothesis is that increased proficiency and language use together with interaction with speakers of the host language will be accompanied by a transition in social identity. That transition might take the form of assimilation from home language monolingualism to target language dominance. Alternatively, it may proceed from dominance in the home language to bilingualism. The former transition is expected to reflect a more unidimensional form of identity, while the latter would be evidence for multiple identities. Of primary interest is which components of identity are most related to language proficiency.

Method

Participants

Data from 65 Russian-German and 58 Russian-Hebrew bilingual children ages 4-7 and their parents were gathered. Children participated in a series of 30 to 45 minute sessions involving a standardized language test and three measures of social identity. Parents participated in sociolinguistic interviews which elicited data about their perceptions of their child's ethnolinguistic identity, social preferences and attitudes. In order to arrive at comparable samples, children with non-Russian-speaking parents, those at risk for language impairment, and those from non-middle class SES were excluded from the present analysis. The two samples were very similar for age, gender, birth order, and length of exposure to the target language in preschool (Table 3.1).

Table 3.1   Basic demographic information

	Germany (N=65)	Israel (N=58)
Age	M=65.78, range 47-86 mo	M=70.06, range 53-81mo
Gender	33 male, 32 female	26 male, 32 female
Birth order	35 firstborn, 30 later born	26 firstborn, 32 later born
L2 exposure	M=37mo, range 13-65mo	M=36mo, range 9-68mo

Linguistic Measures and Tasks

Standardized measures of language ability   in German and Hebrew, normed on native-born monolingual children, were administered. These instruments are the gold standard in educational settings for determining the expectations of the host societies for children of a particular age. Thus, use of these instruments was motivated by policies which use language tests as gatekeepers to certain school programs, and in the worst cases, to label children as 'language impaired.' The Hebrew Language Test (Goralnik, 1995) includes subtests for vocabulary, sentence repetition, comprehension, production, pronunciation, and storytelling. The German Screening SSV (Grimm, 2003) has two subtests: non-word repetition, and sentence repetition.

Ethnolinguistic self-labeling/Ratings of ethnolinguistic labels   Two sets of questions were developed. Children were asked: a) "Who are you?" and were given the following response options: Russian, Israeli, Jewish, new immigrant in Israel, and Russian, German, Jewish, immigrant, and Russian-German in Germany; b) to rate on a 10-point scale how much they agreed, liked, and wanted to be Russian, Israeli/German when they grew up. Parents were asked a parallel set of questions about their children in order to elicit perceptions of their children's identities.

Social preferences   were elicited from children via person perception narratives describing monolingual and bilingual 'friends' at a birthday party and on a desert island. Children were asked to rate how much they wanted to be with monolingual and bilingual children. Ratings were elicited for monolingual, dominant bilingual, and fully bilingual social partners in narratives like the following:

> A boy/girl invited you to come to his/her birthday party today. At the party there will be children who speak [a] Russian/ Hebrew/German only; b) very good Russian and very poor Hebrew/German; c) both languages very well; d) very good Hebrew/German and very poor Russian]. How much would you like to go to this party?

Findings

Children – Language, Identity and Preferences

Language proficiency   In terms of second language proficiency, approximately one third of the children in both national cohorts performed below the monolingual norm (more than 1 SD below the mean) on standardized tests of German and Hebrew (21/65 children in Germany and 22/58 children in Israel).

Ethnolinguistic identity labels and ratings   In response to the question "Who are you?", German immigrant children overwhelmingly preferred the Bicultural/ Russian-German label over unicultural Russian or German labels, regardless of language proficiency (65 percent and 80 percent of lower and higher proficiency children, respectively). In Israel, higher proficiency children preferred the Israeli label (65 percent), while lower proficiency children showed a slight advantage for the Bicultural label (41 percent). A distinctive feature of the German group is the presence of 'ethnic Germans' (*Aussiedler*) or migrants of German origin who grew up in Russia and immigrated to Germany under privileged resettlement programs. German immigrant children were generally unfamiliar with the *Aussiedler* label and thus did not offer this in the labeling task. In the rating task, they preferred the Russian-German category.

Table 3.2   Percentage of low and high proficiency children who preferred Russian, German/Israeli and bicultural labels

Research Setting	Germany		Israel	
Ethnic Label	Low Prof	High Prof	Low Prof	High Prof
Russian	.30	.11	.35	.26
German/Israeli	.05	.09	.24	.65
Bicultural	.65	.80	.41	.09

Table 3.2 shows clear transitions in identity, with major differences between the two proficiency groups. Low proficiency children in both groups show roughly the same percentage of children identifying themselves as Russian (30 percent and 35 percent). With the increase in proficiency, children in Germany strongly prefer Bicultural identity (80 percent); in Israel, they prefer Israeli identity (65 percent).

In the ethnolinguistic rating tasks, however, results showed stronger preference for German identity labels among higher proficiency children across all three rating tasks ("I am…; I like being…; When I grow up, I want to be…"). In the Israeli cohort, Israeli identity was preferred by the higher proficiency group but only for future identity ("When I grow up, I want to be Israeli").

These data show the importance of assessing language proficiency in the investigation of identity. They also show that the growth in language proficiency is accompanied by a transition in identity.

Children's social preferences   In the person perception tasks all children, regardless of language ability and regardless of situation (birthday party/desert island), preferred interaction with balanced bilinguals. Beyond this generalization, for the German cohort, children with lower L2 proficiency preferred to invite Russian-speaking monolinguals, while children with higher L2 proficiency preferred to invite German-speaking children to their birthday parties. For the Israeli group, both lower and higher language ability groups showed a slight (but non-significant) preference for Hebrew only and Hebrew dominant 'friends' in the desert island situation, but no clear preference for either language group in the birthday party situation.

Summary   The following parallels were documented for the two national cohorts. For language proficiency, a third of the children in each group did not reach age-matched monolingual norms on standardized measures. For ethnolinguistic identity, children in Germany tended to prefer bicultural identity and children in Israel preferred Israeli identity. And for social preferences, both groups preferred to interact with bilingual children.

Important differences were revealed here by looking at the relationship between identity and language proficiency. Low proficiency children in both groups preferred a Bicultural identity label, but high proficiency children in Germany manifested an even stronger Bicultural identity, while Israeli preschoolers strongly preferred Israeli identity. These transitions show that a shift in language proficiency is accompanied by a shift in identity. Bicultural identity attracted 80 percent of the high proficiency children in the German cohort, but only 9 percent of those in the Israeli cohort. This proficiency-identity relationship also finds support in the German cohort, where lower proficiency children preferred to socialize with L1/Russian-speaking monolinguals, while higher proficiency children preferred to interact with German-speaking children. For the Israeli cohort, no shift was evident, since both lower and higher ability groups preferred Hebrew only and Hebrew dominant 'friends' in the desert island situation.

In order to help clarify the findings here, we interviewed parents about their children's language proficiency, ethnolinguistic identity, social preferences, and attitudes.

Parent Perceptions of Children's Identity

Individual interviews conducted with parents of the children in the study lasted 90 minutes, and included a semi-structured spontaneous conversation/sociolinguistic interview, a sociolinguistic network task, and five sociolinguistic scales, completed together with the interviewer. The sociolinguistic interview addressed the following topics: information about the child's language acquisition history, family composition (siblings, grandparents), languages spoken and language policy at home, major transition periods (e.g. from home to preschool, from L1 to L2), friends and peers, and everyday activities.

Ethnic and ethnolinguistic identity   Parents responded to an ethnic labeling task ("Who is your child?"), and three ethnolinguistic rating tasks parallel to the tasks conducted with their children.

Ethnic labeling task: "Who is your child?"   Fifty percent of Israeli parents labeled their child Israeli/Israeli-oriented (e.g. 'a Russian/Russian-speaking Israeli', 'an Israeli of Russian origin'). Only 17 percent labeled their children Russian, and 9 percent called their child Bicultural. In contrast, more German parents labeled their children Russian (23 percent) or Bicultural (16 percent) than German (9 percent).

Many parents in both countries said that they did not discuss the identity issue with their children, as they did not consider it problematic. In addition, no parents reported their child to be ashamed of their Russian origin or to have experienced any discomfort in this regard. One child's mother even recalled how during a party in the girl's Hebrew-speaking preschool, her daughter together with other Russian-speaking children refused to sing a popular Russian song "Solnechnyj Krug" (The Sun Circle) in a Hebrew translation and insisted on singing it in Russian.

Many parents in both countries reported that their children viewed bilingualism as an advantage. In this vein, an Israeli mother recalled that her daughter introduced herself as follows: 'Hello, my name is Sh. I speak three languages: English, Russian, and Hebrew – you can choose whichever is better for you." Describing trips to Russia, parents from both groups reported encounters with monolingual Russian speaking peers, and the children's surprise that they did not understand German/Hebrew.

Other parents feel that their children have become more German/Israeli oriented. One mother recalled how a recently immigrated child came up to her son and spoke to him in Russian, to which her son (himself in his first year of Hebrew preschool) replied: "Don't speak Russian to me because I am an Israeli and I speak only Hebrew". Parents' sense of the transition to being Israeli/German is evident in Vi30's mother's remark that when on a visit to Russia, her daughter was identified as a foreigner not by having a distinct accent (since her Russian was accentless) but by being more "relaxed" and loud in public. This, her mother joked, was an indication of her daughter's shift to becoming Israeli.

Ethnolinguistic rating tasks Parents rated: 1. "My child is Russian/German /Israeli. How much do you agree?" 2. "How much does your child like being Russian/German/ Israeli?" 3. "How much do you want your child to grow up to be Russian/German/Israeli?"

For the first task ("My child is…"), a notable difference emerged in Israeli and German parents' ratings of their children's identity. More than half of the Israeli parents viewed their children as Israeli or Israeli-oriented (56 percent) or as Bicultural (31 percent). In contrast, German parents most often attributed Russian identity (31 percent) to their children. Recalling that two thirds of the families in Germany were ethnic Germans, it is not surprising that the Bicultural label 'Russian-German' was preferred (41 percent) over unicultural labels (Russian, German).

For the second task ("How much does your child like being Russian/German/ Israeli?", group differences again emerged. For the Israeli cohort, only 8 percent reported that their children "like being Russian/Russian-oriented." In contrast, 42 percent reported their children to "like being Israeli or Israeli-oriented," and 37 percent reported them to "like being Bicultural." In the German group, however, more parents reported their children to "like being Russian/Russian-oriented" (26 percent) than being German/German-oriented (11 percent).

For the third task ("How much do you want your child to grow up to be Russian/ German /Israeli?"), more than half of the Israeli parents want their children to grow up Israeli/Israeli-oriented (59 percent) rather than Russian (8 percent). Among German parents, preferences are split relatively equally between Bicultural (34 percent) and German/German-oriented identity (36 percent).

In order to get a clearer picture of the differences between the German and Israeli cohorts, parents' ratings were collapsed into Russian, Bicultural or German/Israeli identities and compared across the three ethnolinguistic rating tasks. In Israel, most immigrant parents see their children as Israeli or Bicultural rather than Russian. They feel their children 'like' being viewed as Israeli and Bicultural, with somewhat stronger preferences for Israeli identity. With regard to future identity, most parents think their children will prefer to be more bicultural than mono-cultural (either Israeli or Russian) when they grow up. In contrast, more immigrant parents in Germany perceive their children as Russian than Bicultural or German. Furthermore, although they feel that their children are not necessarily comfortable with being German, they believe that they would like to be seen as German (and Bicultural) rather than Russian in the future.

Overall, the findings for parents' ethnolinguistic labeling and ratings show stronger preference for Israeli/Bicultural identity in the Israeli cohort, and for Russian/Bicultural identity identity in the German cohort across all three rating tasks. Most parents in both countries, however, think that their children would like to be more integrated into the mainstream society, with greater preference for Israeli identity in Israel and for German and Bicultural identities, equally, in Germany.

Social preferences   Parents' perceptions of their child's social preferences were assessed via the child's relationships with peers, siblings and grandparents as well as by personal names. Data were elicited with a sociolinguistic network task in which parents were asked to name the child's social contacts and indicate the languages spoken with each person and the degree of his/her connection with that person. Analyses of sociolinguistic networks of German and Israeli children yielded different patterns for the two groups.

Peers   In Israel, it was found that, as Hebrew proficiency increases, almost all interaction among Russian-speaking bilingual children is done in Hebrew. However, this language pattern does not presuppose a switch in children's choice of friends. Many parents reported their children to opt for friends from Russian speaking immigrant families, and about the same number have friends from both Russian- and Hebrew-speaking families. Parents relate their children's choice of Russian friends to similarity in upbringing or mentality rather than to sociolinguistic factors (language maintenance), as evidenced by the fact that even Russian friends tend to interact in Hebrew. A similar pattern was observed for the German cohort. An additional factor responsible for children's choice of friends in Germany is the enclaved neighbourhood they live in.

Siblings   In Israel, having older siblings was found to contribute to the child's identity. Of the 25 children who spoke Hebrew with older siblings, 12 were classified by parents as Israeli, 11 as Bicultural and only 2 as Russian. In Germany, findings were similar (but not as clear cut due to the small amount of data available on this issue). Of the 12 children who had German-dominant older siblings, eight were classified as German/Russian-German, two as Bicultural and two as Russian. Thus, communication with older German-/Hebrew-dominant siblings leads to a consistent transition to L2 language dominance and a shift in identity.

Grandparents   In Israel, the involvement of Russian-speaking grandmothers (as primary care-takers and/or living with the nuclear family) was not found to be a major influence on Russian identity. Of the 46 children whose Russian-speaking grandmothers were actively involved in their upbringing, 15 were classified as Israeli and were highly proficient in Hebrew, 23 as Bicultural and only eight as Russian.

In Germany, the situation is markedly different. Only five Russian-speaking grandmothers were reported to be actively involved with their grandchildren. Since most mothers in the German group did not work outside the home, grandparents' assistance was not required.

Naming   Naming patterns also revealed differences in integrative identity among the two countries. While children in Germany were predominantly called by international names (e.g. Anna, Katherina/Katrin, Maria, Andreas, Paul, Alexander), the majority of children in the Israeli cohort were given Israeli names (Ofir, Eitan, Yael).

Summary   Similar patterns emerged for both national cohorts, with identity choices trumping language choices. Parents reported equal numbers of friendships with children from Russian immigrant homes and host-country homes, but the languages of interaction were overwhelmingly German and Hebrew. Older siblings dominant in German/Hebrew also contributed to identity transitions, and to labeling of children as German/Israeli or Bicultural rather than Russian. Due to different residential and child-rearing patterns, the role of grandparents was more meaningful in Israel than in Germany. In Israel grandmothers were primary caretakers in almost two thirds of the families, and the children in these families were identified more as Bicultural and Russian than in the Israeli group as a whole. By contrast, German immigrant children were by and large raised by non-working mothers, and grandparents did not play much of a role. Finally, naming patterns also influenced children's identity choices, with parents in Israel giving Israeli names and immigrant parents in Germany predominantly giving Russian names.

Language attitudes   Attitudes to languages were elicited a) by asking: "Which language does your child (like/not like) to speak most?", and b) by rating "How much does your child like to speak Russian and German/Hebrew?"

Language attitudes (direct questioning)   Almost identical patterns emerged in Germany and Israel for parents' responses to the question "Which language does your child like most?" Both groups overwhelmingly chose the target language (German/Hebrew) as the preferred language of their children (44 percent and 49 percent, respectively). The others were divided equally between preferences for Russian, and equal preference for both languages.

Language attitudes (rating task)   "How much does your child like Russian/ German/Hebrew?" Findings for the two groups were similar: parents in both Germany and Israel rated their children as liking both languages equally (47 percent and 48 percent respectively), or as liking German/Hebrew most (41 percent for German and 48 percent for Hebrew), with much less preference for Russian, especially among the Israeli children. Unlike the direct question task above, the rating task produced greater preference for 'both Russian and German/Hebrew' and less preference for Russian in both groups.

Language proficiency and language attitudes   Parents rated their child's language proficiency in both L1 and L2 ("How well does your child speak Russian/German/ Hebrew?"). These ratings were compared with their perceptions of the children's language preferences. Results for both groups, in particular for the German cohort, showed high correlations of parents' assessment of proficiency and preferences, suggesting that parent's perception of language attitudes may be influenced by or even derived from their estimation of their child's proficiency in that language. And yet, parents' perceptions of the child's proficiency were not always accurate. For example, two Israeli mothers who estimated their children's Russian proficiency as very low and claimed that they never heard them speak Russian, assumed their children had forgotten all their Russian. They were surprised to learn from the interviewer that their children scored high on Russian proficiency tests and were happy to hold a conversation and tell a story in Russian.

Comparison of Parents' and Children's Findings

Ethnolinguistic labels   For the children in the German cohort, Russian was the preferred label for both parents and children (31 percent and 36 percent, respectively). For the children in the Israeli cohort, the Israeli label was chosen most frequently by the parents (56 percent), while the Russian label was chosen more by their children (44 percent), followed by Israeli (34 percent) and Bicultural (22 percent). The strongest differences between parents' and children's choices of ethnolinguistic labels were found for Russian identity labels in the Israeli data (44 percent of children vs. 13 percent of parents), and for the Bicultural/Russian-German label in the German data (13 percent for children, 41 percent for parents).

On the whole, then, when choosing ethnolinguistic labels, Israeli parents viewed their children as more Israeli/Israeli-oriented and Bicultural than their children did. German parents, on the other hand, considered their children to be Russian more often than German or Bicultural, while their children showed relatively equal preference for each of the three identity labels.

Children's Russian identity can be seen in the following examples. One Israeli child enjoyed translating for her non-Russian speaking father. By doing so, she sensed her (linguistic) superiority; in her mother's words, she even "considers herself to be of a higher caste", making excuses for her father's lack of competence in front of their Russian speaking friends: "Our Daddy doesn't know Russian, just a little, so I will translate". Another child (Germany) bragged: "I'm a RUSSIAN hero, I'm a RUSSIAN soldier, when are we going back to Russia?"

Ethnolinguistic ratings   The three rating tasks ("I am Russian/German/Israeli; I like being Russian/German/Israeli; When I grow up, I want to be Russian/German/ Israeli") showed a somewhat different picture from the ethnolinguistic labeling task. In the German cohort, children expressed relatively equal preference for all identities. Parents, on the other hand, considered their children to be more Russian than German or Bicultural. In the Israeli cohort, parents viewed their children as more Israeli/Israeli-oriented and Bicultural than their children did.

Overall, then, most parents in both countries would like their children to be more integrated into the mainstream society, with more preference for Israeli identity in Israel and for Bicultural identity in Germany.

Social preferences and social interaction: peers, siblings, grandparents, names   Peer interaction among preschool immigrant children was found to be almost universally in the target languages, German and Hebrew. This held for interaction with other immigrant children and host society children alike. Thus, whether peer relationships were carried out on the preschool playground or in the homes, the language of interaction is a strong assimilating factor. Language shift was bolstered by older siblings who spoke the target language. The same identity shift toward the host culture was reflected in the Hebrew first names given to the children in Israel, which contrasted with a tendency to maintain Russian names in Germany. One of the only factors pushing toward Russian language maintenance was the presence of Russian-speaking grandparents in the home, either as caretakers or actually living with the nuclear family. But this was true only in Israel.

Language attitudes   Overall, there was a strong preference for two languages and the societal language over Russian. This was true for parents as well as children and for both national cohorts. One difference between parents' and children's attitudes concerned Russian, with children showing more positive attitudes to Russian than their parents thought they had (again true for both cohorts). Specifically, very few parents stated that their children prefer Russian (12 percent and 4 percent, for German and Israeli parents, respectively), while their children had a more positive attitude to Russian (41 percent and 31 percent, for German and Israeli children, respectively).

These attitude data, however, were not always an accurate reflection of children's language behavior, as illustrated by some of their comments during the parent interviews. Vi56 (Israel), assessed as Russian-dominant, was present at the interview with his mother and frequently intervened in the conversation in Russian. When asked directly, he blurted out, "ani sone russkyi" (Heb., I hate Russian). An Israeli child awaiting enrollment in a Hebrew-speaking kindergarten, stated in Hebrew, "nim'as li miharusit, ba li ivrit" (I'm fed up with Russian, I want Hebrew). A similar statement came from a child (in Germany) who was asked something in Russian during her parent's interview. The girl ran to the bathroom, put water in her mouth and came out pointing that she could not speak because her mouth was full (*nabrat' v rot vody* lit., 'put water mouth' 'to keep quiet'). A contrasting incident came from a child in Germany who spoke limited Russian, codeswitched a great deal, but was very interested in the Russian sessions, trying to learn from them and improve his oral proficiency.

Summary and Discussion

The present research cast a wide net, examining language proficiency, ethnolinguistic identity, social preferences, and attitudes in preschool immigrant children and their parents in two national cohorts. Substantively, the most important finding is that language shift is accompanied by shifts in identity, which differ in Germany and Israel. Methodologically, two features of the study are innovative: inclusion of a range of behavioural measures of language performance, and a comparison of child and parent data. All of these issues lead to a number of policy recommendations.

Language proficiency and ethnolinguistic identity   The children in this study began with the same home language (Russian) and were of comparable ages and length of exposure to the second language (German/Hebrew). A full third of the children in each cohort did not reach norm on standardized tests of the second language, despite a minimum of two years of exposure.

Yet, two thirds of the children performed within the monolingual norm; this implies that there are certain factors which may lead to more rapid achievement in L2 language acquisition. Both German and Hebrew are high on all three of Giles, Bourhis and Taylor's (1977) ethnolinguistic vitality measures (status, demography, and institutional support). Both languages are prestigious within their national entities. Demographically, German is spoken by more than 120 million people worldwide, Hebrew by 8 million, and despite large minority language populations, 20 percent in Germany (Haspelmath, 2011) and 50 percent in Israel (Spolsky and Shohamy, 1999), within their national borders, German and Hebrew enjoy demographic hegemony. Finally, institutional support for both languages is similar in both countries, ranging from dominance to near exclusivity in government, education, healthcare, banking and the media. Thus, linguistic vitality factors all lead strongly to language shift.

Our findings for ethnolinguistic identity show the importance of looking at language proficiency data. Taking low proficiency children as a starting point, we see that for both countries, relatively equal numbers of children prefer Russian (30-35 percent) or Bicultural (41-65 percent) ethnolinguistic labels. For high proficiency children, however, Bicultural identity was overwhelmingly preferred in Germany (80 percent) and Israeli identity was preferred in Israel (65 percent). Thus, language proficiency serves as an important measure of transition, changes in language showing parallels to shifts in identity.

Social interaction, identity, language use and language proficiency The proficiency-identity relationship also found expression in the person perception task, where lower proficiency children in Germany preferred to socialize with Russian-speakers and higher proficiency children preferred German speakers. In Israel both proficiency groups preferred to socialize with Hebrew speakers.

However, these differences are overridden by the fact that most children in both groups prefer to socialize with bilinguals (like themselves) and to interact in the societal language. Parents' interview data confirmed that the dominant language of interaction is German/Hebrew, but parents claimed that their children preferred Russian-speaking friends (who are bilingual).

This disjunct between language use and social preference shows that while language and identity may be mutually influential, the causal direction cannot be inferred from the present data (and may not be empirically testable). In any case, the two constructs have independent trajectories. More specifically, successful and even less than successful L2 acquisition (i.e. among low proficiency children) leads to German/Hebrew social interaction, but this language shift does not necessarily yield a parallel shift in ethnolinguistic identity, choice of friends, and attitudes, where Bicultural identity, and bilingual friends and attitudes were preferred.

Findings about *siblings, grandmothers and personal names* differ qualitatively from those just discussed. First, unlike language proficiency, ethnolinguistic identity, social preferences, and attitudes, they are 'external' to the child, part of his/her social context.

Siblings and grandmothers are both important features of the 'home' domain (Fishman, 1972). Grandmothers unequivocally represent L1 language and culture. Older siblings are the preschool child's bridge to the new culture; in addition to the societal language, they bring home socialization patterns, and cultural mores. A personal name, even though it originates in the home, is the child's calling card for 'presentation of self.' It reflects parental aspirations for the child's identity, on the one hand, and serves as a powerful identity marker in all social contacts with wider society. It instantly elicits attitudes and beliefs from children and adults in the host society. Names in Germany reflected both ties to the children's Russian origins and aspirations for social integration; those in Israel were indicative of identity shift, or at least aspirations for social integration. All of these features serve as the basis for contrasts between the home and the preschool, between L1 and L2, between the in-group and the out-group.

German-Israeli cohort differences   Across a variety of methods, differences emerged between the two national groups. Preschool children from Russian-speaking homes in Germany present with Bicultural identity, whereas children of comparable age and language proficiency in Israel show a clear shift to Israeli identity. Several explanations for this difference are offered. First, it is possible that the host societies differ in the welcome they extend to new immigrants, both in terms of government services and opportunities for social interaction with members of the host society. Another difference relates to the assimilationist or "melting pot" approach to immigration in Israel. Along with an emphasis of the Israeli preschool curriculum on national and Jewish holidays, this fosters an identity shift. The German curriculum stresses academic achievements with holidays and nationalism taking a secondary role. Furthermore, the mothers of preschool children in Israel work outside the home, since the host society does not pay them to stay at home. This facilitates cultural and linguistic integration in ways it does not in Germany. Thus, even though social preferences and social interaction with peers, siblings and grandparents show contrasting influences (peers and siblings favouring integration into the host culture and grandmothers inducing Russian identity), the overall trend is toward identity shift for both cohorts, but sharper for immigrant children in Israel than for those in Germany.

Ethnolinguistic identities and naming practices support these cohort differences. Two thirds of the parents were of ethnic German origin and enjoyed advantages of this status in Germany. International names, appropriate in Russian as well as German, are reflections of bicultural identity. For the Israeli cohort, the parents were Jews in Russia; they became Israelis in Israel, both situations reflecting mono-cultural identity. Israeli/Hebrew names are, thus, indicative of a sharper shift in identity.

Theoretically, the shift in identity as well as the differences between the two groups can be accounted for in terms of 'context' and its use in both sociolinguistics and child development.

Context is relevant as an explanation for shifts in identity as well as national cohort differences. It accounts for many of the parent-child differences reported in this study. In terms of identity, context includes national demographic, economic, political, cultural, and institutional influences/patterns, as well as, social interactional influences. Immigrant identity is derived from feelings of being part of a language/ cultural minority group and the size, residential pattern (enclaved or not), economic mobility, and cultural salience of that group contributes to the individual's identity.

These wider contextual factors are expressed in social interaction between immigrants and majority culture individuals, leading to social comparison and changes in identity. Social identity in adult immigrants is seen as an integral of societal and interpersonal factors. The shift from ethnic German identity in Russia to *Russland-Deutsche/Aussiedler* identity in Germany can be viewed as maintenance of Bicultural identity. The shift from Russian-Jewish identity to Israeli identity can be interpreted a shift from an ostracized small minority identity to a large and influential majority.

Among the factors which may account for these national group differences are:

a. Societal heterogeneity of the host country: Immigrants to Israel become one of many very different Israelis, the great majority of whom have immigrant backgrounds, making immigration part of Israeli identity, whereas group permeability may be difficult in a more demographically homogeneous Germany, where immigration is less a part of the national ethnic or discourse.

b. Motivations for migration: These were not examined here, but see Dittmar, Spolsky, and Walters et al. (1998) for a comparative study of Russian immigrants to Germany and Israel.

c. Integration into the work force: Two working parents are the norm in Israel, whereas many mothers in the German group stay at home. Moreover, the majority of the parents in Israel integrated into skilled and professional occupations, while in Germany the majority of parents were employed in skilled and semiskilled occupations.

d. Residential patterns: Even though enclaved options exist in Israel, the children in this study came from more integrated communities, while children in Germany came from families who tended to settle near other immigrants.

These sources of differences are relevant to the larger social context, and contribute to the formation of collective identity. None, however, is directly relevant to preschool children, whose socialization and language acquisition is more of a function of interpersonal relationships with parents, siblings, and peers. These relationships are the core of interactional sociolinguistics, defined initially by the question "Who speaks which language to whom, in what setting, and for what purpose?" (Fishman, 1965).

Interpretation of the data here on social preferences, and the varied contributions of grandparents, siblings, and naming practices was informed by Harris's (1995, 2009) "Group Socialization Theory," which argues cogently for peers, not parents, as the primary socialization agents and the crucial importance of context/situational effects, especially those acquired outside the home, as an explanation for differences among siblings and the development of the child's personality. While the contribution of parents and grandparents in the form of language input is indisputable, their influence on the child's identity is less robust. In terms of our cohort differences in child-rearing patterns are reflected in the children's identity. A more parent/family-centered pattern in Germany where a few of our mothers worked outside the home supports Russian identity, whereas a more peer-oriented child-rearing pattern in Israel may lead to more assimilatory identities.

Policy implications. The most important policy implication follows from the sheer complexity of the constructs addressed in this study. Language proficiency was investigated by standardized measures involving assessment of morphosyntax, vocabulary and narrative abilities using norms for monolingual children. These measures are used to assess language minority children in both countries, inter alia, as criteria for selection and enrolment in competitive schools. They are also used for diagnosis of communication disorders and placement in special education programs. In both countries bilingual children are potentially 'overdiagnosed' as language impaired, and subsequently overrepresented in special education programs, due to similarities between diagnostic indicators in monolinguals with impairment and patterns of errors in typically developing bilinguals. The findings that more than a third of the bilinguals do not reach monolingual norms even after two years of exposure calls into question the use of monolingual screening tools for this population. Interpretation of the results of such tools must take into consideration contextual factors as shown above.

Furthermore, understanding the relative and combined influence of context, identity, and language at such a young age facilitates decision making at the transition from preschool to school. This study of language and social identity in early childhood reveals the importance of the context in understanding transition and assimilation patterns even at this young age and for integrating this information into the decision making process. Increased awareness of the difference in child rearing patterns and the degree of integration in the work force may assist in identifying indicators of adjustment and maladjustment in social integration, and can help inform policymakers who make educational decisions regarding acceptance and placement of children in school programs.

References

Alba, R. D. (1990). *Ethnic identity: The transformation of white America.* New Haven, CT: Yale University Press.

Alba, R. (1999). Immigration and the American realities of assimilation and multiculturalism. *Sociological Forum, 14*(1), 3-25.

Allard, R., and Landry, R. (1994). Subjective ethnolinguistic vitality: A comparison of two measures. *International Journal of Sociology of Language, 108,* 117-144.

Bourdieu, P. (1991). *Language and symbolic power* (Raymond, M. and G. M. Adamson, Trans.). Cambridge, MA: Harvard University Press.

Bourhis, R. Y., and Landry, R. (2008). Group vitality, cultural autonomy and the wellness of language. In R. Y. Bourhis (Ed.), *The vitality of the English speaking communities of Quebec: From community decline to revival* (pp. 185-212). Montreal, Quebec: CEETUM, Université de Montréal.

Brewer, M. B., and Chen, Y. R. (2007). Where (who) are collectives in collectivism? Toward conceptual clarification of individualism and collectivism. *Psychological Review, 114*(1), 133-151.

Cameron, J. E. (2004). A three-factor model of social identity. *Self and Identity, 3,* 239-262.

Dittmar, N., Spolsky, B., and Walters, J. (1998). Convergence and divergence in second language acquisition and use: Towards an integrated model. In V. Regan (ed.), *Contemporary Approaches to Second Language Acquisition in Social Context*. Dublin: University College Press.

Fishman, J. A. (1965). Who speaks what language to whom and when? *La Linguistique, 2*, 67-88.

Fishman, J. (1972). Domains and the relationship between micro- and macro-sociolinguistics. In J. J. Gumperz and D. Hymes (eds.), *Directions in Sociolinguistics: The Ethnography of Communication* (pp. 435-453). Oxford, UK: Basil Blackwell.

Goffman, E. (1959). *The presentation of self in everyday life*. New York, NY: Doubleday, Anchor Books.

Goralnik, E. (1995). *Goralnik screening test for Hebrew*. Even Yehuda, Israel: Matan (in Hebrew).

Grimm, H. (2003). *SSV. Sprachscreening für das Vorschulalter. Kurzform des SETK 3-5. Manual*. Göttingen: Hogrefe.

Harris, J. R. (1995). Where is the child's environment? A group socialization theory of development. *Psychological Review, 102*, 458-489.

Harris, J. R. (2009). *The nurture assumption: Why children turn out the way they do*. New York: Free Press.

Kopeliovich, S. (2009). Reversing language shift in the immigrant family: A case study of a Russian-speaking community in Israel. Frankfurt: VDM Verlag Dr. Muller.

Kopeliovich, S. (2011). How long is 'the Russian street' in Israel? Prospects of maintaining the Russian language, *Israel Affairs, 17*(1), 108-124.

Lambert, W. E. (1990). Issues in foreign language and second language education. *Proceedings of the first research symposium on limited English proficient student issues*. Washington, DC: Office of Bilingual and Multicultural Education.

Mead, G.H. (1964). *On social psychology: Selected papers*. In A. Strauss (Ed.). Chicago, IL: University of Chicago Press.

Portes, A., and Schauffler, R. (1994). Language and the second generation: Bilingualism yesterday and today. *International Migration Review, 28*, 640-661.

Roccas, S., and Brewer, M. B. (2002). Social identity complexity. *Personality and Social Psychology Review, 6*, 88-106.

Sachdev, I., Arnold, D., and de Dios Yapita J. (2006). Indigenous identity and language: Some considerations from Bolivia and Canada. *BISAL, 1,* 107-128.

Strauss, A. L. (1959). *Mirrors and masks: The search for identity*. Glencoe, IL: Free Press.

Tajfel, H. (1982). *Social identity and intergroup relations*. Cambridge, England: Cambridge University Press.

Taylor, D. M., Meynard, R., and Rheault, E. (1977). Threat to ethnic identity and second-language learning. In H. Giles (Ed.), *Language, ethnicity and intergroup relations* (pp. 99-118). New York, NY: Academic Press.

Walters, J. (2005). *Bilingualism: The sociopragmatic-psycholinguistic interface.* Mahwah, NJ: Erlbaum/Taylor and Francis.

Waters, M. C. (1990). *Ethnic options: Choosing identity in America.* Berkeley, CA: University of California Press.

Weigert, A. J., Teitge, J. S., and Teitge, D. W. (1986). *Society and identity: Toward a sociological psychology.* Cambridge: Cambridge University Press.

Weinreich, P., and Saunderson, W. (2003). *Analysing identity:Cross-cultural, societal and clinical contexts.* London, England: Routledge/Taylor and Francis.

Ziv, Y. (2007). Social information processing in preschool children. In J.A. Zebrowski (ed.), *New Research on Social Perception* (pp. 47-74). Nova Science Publishers.

Chapter 4

Age, Input Quantity and their Effect on Linguistic Performance in the Home and Societal Language among Russian-German and Russian-Hebrew Preschool Children[1]

Natalia Gagarina, Sharon Armon-Lotem, Carmit Altman, Zhanna Burstein-Feldman, Annegret Klassert, Nathalie Topaj, Felix Golcher, and Joel Walters

This chapter investigates bilingual acquisition in language minority children from Russian-speaking backgrounds in Israel and Germany and the effects of selected background factors on bilingual knowledge of lexicon and morphosyntax. Background factors are divided into external factors (e.g., parent education and occupation, birth order and family size), those that the child brings to the language learning effort, and internal factors (age of onset and length of exposure to the second language), which reflect the child's language experience.

The aim of the chapter is to trace the effects of age, length of exposure and the amount of language use, i.e. input quantity, on the acquisition of both languages in a bilingual context. To that end, a comprehensive treatment of the linguistic performance in two languages and comparison of development/ attrition in the home /L1 and societal languages/L2 are provided.

Linguistic performance targeted in the two languages included lexical, morphological, and syntactic skills which were elicited via different experimental techniques. This variety of linguistic tasks and experimental techniques made it possible to test which skills were more sensitive/resilient to the background factors. Factors which are less influenced by bilingual language acquisition would then be those most useful for testing language impairment among bilinguals.

Research on the background factors influencing language acquisition processes among bilingual children has mainly involved English as either L1 or L2 (Hoff, 2006a, 2006b; Gleitman and Newport, 1995; Paradis, 2010) and the focus has been on the relationship between extralinguistic factors and language

1 The research reported on in this work has been supported by funding from the German Ministry for Education and Research (BMBF), grant numbers 01UG0711 and 01UW0702B.

development in English as the societal and target language. Pearson's (2007) focus on L1 is one exception. Pearson examined the role of five factors – input, language status, access to literacy, family language use, and community support – in learning a minority language. In extensive studies of Spanish-speaking children in Miami, she found that L1 input at home played an important role in children's maintenance of the minority language (cf. Klassert and Gagarina, 2010 for a similar result with Russian as a home language).

The extent to which L1 input at home leads to L1 maintenance is related to parents' socio-economic status (SES) (Lambert and Taylor, 1996). Lambert and Taylor found that mothers from low SES encouraged their children to learn L2/English in order to succeed educationally, while mothers from high SES encouraged L1 maintenance and saw additive bilingualism as a goal. On the other hand, Oller and Eilers (2002) found that children of professionals perform better in L2 than children from working class families, with hardly any difference in L1 maintenance. When there was a difference, however, children of working class mothers did better in L1. That is, high SES parents value L1 culture more than low SES parents, but seem to provide less support for L1 and more support for L2 at home, while lower SES parents encourage L2 acquisition as a key to academic success but do not support it at home. In contrast to the above studies, which focused on school age children and tested both written and oral skills, the present study investigates spoken language in children at the onset of bilingualism in preschool years.

Spoken language skills enable communication with parents, grandparents, siblings and peers, but may or may not help in the acquisition of reading and cognitively demanding tasks in the societal language, German or Hebrew. This issue is also related to the level of home language proficiency as well as literacy needed to succeed in second language acquisition.

Tucker (1999), in a World Bank study on the use of two languages in education, reports that it takes up to five years of exposure to reach a level of language proficiency adequate for academic performance, i.e. understanding basic tasks in kindergarten/elementary school. Our own findings (Abutbul-Oz, 2009; Walters et al., this volume) show that by the time children enter school (after 2-3 years of L2 exposure), a third of typically developing (TD) bilingual children still score below monolingual norms, and most of those who score within norms are still below the monolingual mean. Following Hakuta and Garcia (1989), social background factors influencing L2 acquisition and L1 maintenance should be considered in order to understand bilingual language development beyond purely linguistic dimensions (Hoff et.al., in press). De Houwer (1999), for example, explored a range of linguistic environments of four-year-old bilingual children and found the following environmental constituents to be crucial for language acquisition: mother, sibling and peer input and the impact of television.

Research Questions and Hypotheses

The following research questions and hypotheses address children's language proficiency and its interrelationship with chronological age, length of L2 exposure and input quantity.

Language Proficiency

Question: To what extent do Russian-German and Russian-Hebrew bilingual children perform at or below monolingual norms on standardized tests of the societal language (German/Hebrew)?

Hypothesis I. Bilingual children are predicted to perform below monolingual norms on standardized tests even after two years of exposure to the societal language.

Age, Length of L2 Exposure and Language Proficiency

Questions: How will the development/attrition of language proficiency in bilingual preschool children change as a function of chronological age? What effects would the length of exposure to L2 have on each of the child's languages? Which linguistic domains will be most affected?

Hypothesis II. As age increases, the gap between monolinguals and bilinguals in home language proficiency will widen and the gap in the societal language proficiency will narrow. Furthermore, the length of L2 exposure is expected to have a negative effect on the home language and a positive effect on the societal language. This hypothesis is grounded in studies showing progressively increasing dominance in the societal language of bilingual children (cf. Cobo-Lewis et al., 2002a, 2002b; Klassert, 2011). Lexicon is expected to be the domain which is most affected in both languages.

Input Quantity (Amount of Language Spoken inside the Home) and Language Proficiency

Questions: Will language proficiency in both languages correlate with input quantity in the home language and what kind of correlation will emerge? Which domains of language will be affected the most/least?

Hypothesis III. For the measures tested in this study, we predict a strong correlation between the amount of home language spoken with the children (at home and outside) and L1 proficiency, and a negative correlation with L2 development. Again, lexicon is expected to be the most affected domain in both languages.

Method

Participants

In Germany, all participants were from Berlin. Given the size of the city and the large number of Russian speakers, neighborhoods with high concentrations of Russian-speakers were identified first. Then, preschool/school registers provided by the local school administration were accessed from an electronic data base, and contacts were made through local associations offering courses and activities for Russian-speaking children. The aim of this procedure was to attain a broad geographic spread of Russian-German bilinguals with a range of socio-economic status of the parents.

In Israel, participants were recruited from the greater Tel-Aviv area, including the cities of Petach Tikva, Rishon LeZion and Netanya, all with large numbers of Russian-speaking residents. However, the recruiting procedure differed from that in Germany, since research approvals were required first from the Ministry of Education. Regional inspectors, who had direct access to school statistics, were contacted for advice regarding the choice of preschools and schools with Russian-speaking children.

The literature on bilingual language acquisition attests to a range of factors which influence the rate and process of language development. Age of onset in both languages, quality and quantity of input, migrant background and native languages are considered to be the most important (Hamers and Blanc, 2000; Rothweiler, 2007; Reich, 2008; Meisel, 2009).

Selection criteria were as follows:

• School: preschool and first grade elementary school children
• Ages: 4, 5 or 6 year olds
• Gender: half male, half female
• Language proficiency: Ability to communicate in both languages
• Parents' native language: Russian (first generation immigrants)
• Home language spoken with children: Russian
• Language input from birth: Russian
• German/Hebrew acquired in German/Hebrew dominant preschool (at least 60 percent monolingual German/Hebrew-speaking children)
• Initial exposure to German/Hebrew from ages 1-3 (early sequential bilinguals)
• Length of exposure to German/Hebrew: at least 1 year
• No severe health problems or diagnosed language and cognitive disorders

The following steps were taken to identify potential child participants:

– A short questionnaire and consent form filled out by parents clarified whether the child met the selection criteria and allowed parents to make a decision regarding participation in the project;

– Children's language performance was assessed during the first sessions (including spontaneous speech and language proficiency tests), clarifying whether the child was able to communicate in both languages. Children who showed very low performance in one of the target languages (Russian, Hebrew/German) to the extent that they could not understand and perform language and sociolinguistic tasks in one language were not included in the project. Similarly, several children who refused to talk in one of the target languages were excluded from further investigation.

– Other information obtained from parent interviews (e.g., language history which did not match the project criteria) as well as results from linguistic tasks (e.g., children at risk for language impairment) were taken into consideration.

Data were obtained through a series of spontaneous, semi-spontaneous and experimental data collection tasks in both L1 and L2 in 12-14 sessions (each session lasting 30-45 min. each) as well as via standardized language tests in L2 (Grimm, 2003 for German; Goralnik, 1995 for Hebrew). All interviewers were native speakers of Russian and German/Hebrew in order to ensure the child's best performance in the corresponding language session.

In Germany, of 225 consent forms distributed, 174 parental agreements were obtained. One third (N=61) did not meet the three main selection criteria (e.g., home language Russian, early onset of German, at least 60 percent German-speaking children in the preschool). Twenty-three children did not complete the study due to poor performance during the first session, change of residence, or refusal to cooperate. Ninety children were tested for the majority of the tasks.

In Israel, parental agreement was obtained for 120 children, following the distribution of 392 consent forms. Of those, 79 children met the selection criteria; the others were not included due to atypical development (language impairment, ADHD) or lack of sufficient knowledge of Russian.

The two groups were similar in terms of age, gender, birth order and number of siblings, age of L2 onset, and length of exposure to the societal language in preschool (see Table 4.1).

Linguistic Measures and Tasks[2]

Data from standardized tests as well as from lexical and morpho-syntactic tasks were analyzed for both groups. (An additional task involving elicitation of

---

2   Data from discourse and narrative tasks, non-word repetition and rapid automatic naming were not analyzed here.

Table 4.1   Basic background information

	Germany (N=90)	Israel (N=79)
Chronological age	M=65.49, range 47-86 mo	M=70.22, range 54-84 mo
Gender	44 male, 46 female	35 male, 44 female
Parents' education	M=13.10, range 10-18 yrs	M=13.95, range 9-21 yrs
Mothers' education	M=13.05, range 10-18 yrs	M=14.37, 9-21 yrs
Fathers' education	M=13.16, range 10-18 yrs	M=13.49, 10-20 yrs
Mother occupation	10 academic 28 skilled work 12 unskilled work 39 unemployed 1 no information	26 academic 30 skilled work 15 unskilled work 2 students 2 unemployed 4 no information
Father's occupation	20 academic 21 skilled work 34 unskilled work 5 unemployed 10 no information	19 academic 28 skilled work 18 unskilled work 1 unemployed 13 no information
Family status	73 married 7 separated in contact 8 no contact 2 no information	61 married 6 separated in contact 10 no contact 2 no information
Home language	87 Russian-dominant 1 Russian-speaking mother 1 Russian-speaking father 1 no information	67 Russian-dominant 7 one Hebrew-speaking parent 5 no information
Birth order	53 firstborn, 37 later born	40 firstborn, 39 later born
Number of siblings	M=1.82, range 1-5	M=1.87, range 1-4
Age of L2 onset	M=28.43 mo	M=45.34 mo
Age of entering L2 speaking daycare	12-46 mo	9-67 mo
L2 exposure	M=37.51 mo, range 9-65 mo	M=37.41 mo, range 9-75 mo

grammatical case was performed with the Russian-German group, since case is an important morphological category in those languages, but not in Hebrew). All tasks were designed to target structures which were both similar and contrastive for Russian and the societal language (German/Hebrew).

Standardized Tests

Standardized tests were administered in both German (Grimm, 2003) and Hebrew (Goralnik, 1995). The motivation here was policy-oriented, since those are the standards by which minority children are enrolled in or rejected from participation in mainstream educational frameworks. Moreover, while monolingual norms cannot be directly applied to assess bilingual children, they can be used for comparing the children within an age group. The German Screening SSV (Grimm, 2003) consists of two subtests, non-word repetition (NWR/PGN *Phonologisches Arbeitsgedächtnis für Nichtwörter*) and sentence repetition (SR/SG *Satzgedächtnis*). The Hebrew Language Test (Goralnik, 1995) contains subtests for vocabulary, sentence repetition, comprehension, expression, pronunciation and story-telling. The standardized scores on these tests were used as a developmental measure for comparing children who had attained lower and higher language proficiency.

Lexical Task: Verb-Noun Naming

A Noun-Verb naming task (Kauschke, 2007), originally created for German, was adapted to Russian (Klassert, 2011, Klassert et al., 2013) and Hebrew. The material for the German test was a picture-naming task involving pictures of objects and actions (see De Bleser and Kauschke, 2003; Kauschke, 2007). All items were common and typical members of their respective category. The stimulus items in German and Russian were all mono- or bisyllabic and monomorphemic. They were controlled for frequency and naming agreement of monolingual adults in both languages, and counterbalanced between both word categories in respect to these factors. The German item set consisted of 36 action pictures (targeting verbs) and 36 object pictures (targeting nouns). The Russian version contained 31 action and 31 object pictures. In Hebrew there were 35 verbs and 35 nouns; two items were removed for cultural reasons. Children were presented with pictures one at a time and asked to name each one. Responses were recorded as correct or incorrect. Self-corrections, phonetically or phonologically incorrect responses and inflected forms of the target items (regardless of morphological accuracy) were recorded as correct as long as the target word was unambiguously identifiable.

Morphosyntactic Tasks: Elicited Imitation and Sentence Completion

Elicited (sentence) imitation is an effective measure for targeting different syntactic structures (Armon-Lotem et al., 2006). Morphosyntactic and syntactic structures which were found to be particularly difficult for language minority children were examined. The task included three subtasks: sentence imitation targeting prepositions, verb inflections and complex syntax. Stimulus sentences varied in length from 4-10 words.

For prepositions, there were 48 items for both Russian and German, and 35 items for Russian and 30 for Hebrew. The sentences included prepositions in the target languages, which were either similar or different across languages, as well as stimuli with a preposition in one language but without a preposition in the other. Example (1) illustrates this latter contrast for German/Russian (where there is a preposition in German but not in Russian); example (2), in which there are two different prepositions for Hebrew *'im* 'with' and Russian *na* 'on', respectively, illustrates the former contrast:

1	Der	Junge	wartet	auf	seine Eltern	zu Hause.
	Ø	Malčik	ždjot	Ø	svoih roditelej	doma.

The boy is waiting for his parents at home.

2	Hamelex	hitxaten	'im	hanesixa	hayafa.
	Korol	ženilsja	na	krasivoj	princesse.

The king married the beautiful princess.

For verb inflections, there were 40 items in Russian, and 42 items in Hebrew. For complex syntax, there were 20 items each for Russian and Hebrew. An example of topicalization is given in (3):

3	Ètu	šapku		devočka	poterjala.
	This-ACC	hat-ACC		girl	lost.
	Et	ha-kova	ha-ze	ha-yelda	ibda.
	ACC	the hat	the-this	the girl	lost.

This hat, the girl lost.

Verb inflections and complex syntax tasks were not performed in German, since similar measures were elicited in the standardized test.

The sentence completion task was designed to target a wide variety of verb inflections. Children were asked to complete a sentence within a story context with the correct verb form. In Germany, Russian stimuli consisted of three stories, targeting 10 verbs with 70 items. The German stimuli contained three stories, 18 verbs and 38 items. In Israel, Russian stimuli involved 6 stories, 16 different verbs with various inflections and 133 items. The Hebrew stimuli (based on Dromi, et al., 1999) included three stories, 11 verbs, and 45 items. For the Russian-German bilingual children, the focus in German was on (third person) present and on past tense (participles), where the use of appropriate regular and irregular verb forms requires specific knowledge. For the Russian-Hebrew bilingual children, the focus was on the past tense in Hebrew, where person, number and gender are all marked, and differences in aspect (synthetic vs. analytic constructions) pose a problem for bilingual children and second language learners (Armon-Lotem, et al., 2006; Gagarina et al., 2007; Gagarina, 2011).

A task involving grammatical case elicited accusative and dative forms in both Russian and German. It consisted of six test questions eliciting accusative case forms, six eliciting dative forms and 2 fillers, yielding 12 test items in each language. Nouns were controlled for gender, animacy, inflectional/ declension class in both languages. Only those nouns for which case is marked unambiguously (on the determiner in German and on the noun in Russian) were included, for example:

4	Kogo	iščet	Ø	zebra?	(pingvina-ACC)
	Wen	sucht	das	Zebra	(den Pinguin-ACC)
	whom	looks-for	the	zebra	(the penguin-ACC)

Whom is the zebra looking for? (the penguin)

Sociolinguistic Measures

Sociolinguistic measures examined (1) ethnic and ethnolinguistic identity, (2) social preferences, (3) attitudes to speakers and languages and (4) language use. Language use data are reported here (for details of the other measures, see Walters et al., this volume). Information on language use was elicited via questions about the language used with different interlocutors (family members, peers) and in different situations (home, preschool, TV programs, etc.).

Results and Discussion

Language Performance

It was hypothesized that bilingual children would perform below monolingual norms on standardized tests even after two years of exposure to the societal language. The results for L2/German show that a significant number of children do perform below monolingual norms and increased exposure to L2 does not bring them up to norm. This finding is strongest for the sentence repetition task which requires more knowledge of syntactic structures than, for example, the non-word repetition task. Furthermore, in terms of deviation from the mean, 16 percent of the children were more than one standard deviation below the mean, regardless of increased exposure to L2. For L2/Hebrew, the results are similar: many children are more than one standard deviation below the monolingual mean for a combined score on all tasks, even for children with two years or more of exposure.

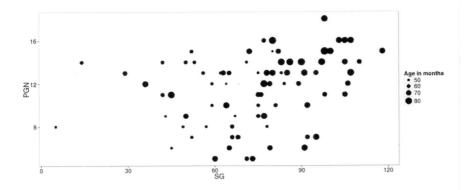

Figure 4.1   Non-word repetition, NWR (PGN Phonologisches Arbeitsgedächtnis für Nichtwörter) sentence repetition, SR (SG Satzgedächtnis) and age

Age, Length of L2 Exposure and Language Proficiency

While age was expected to have a positive influence on both languages of a bilingual child, length of exposure to L2 was predicted to have a negative effect for the home language, but a positive effect for the societal languages. This hypothesis is evaluated first for the standardized tests in the two societal languages, German and Hebrew, and then for the lexical abilities and morphosyntactic knowledge tested in each language, with tasks developed in the framework of the present project.

Standardized screening in German   SSV screening (Grimm, 2003) was used to test German language proficiency. Two subtests of the standardized screening were used: non-word repetition and sentence repetition. Both subtests showed an age dependency: $p < .05$ for non-word repetition, and $p < .0001$ for sentence repetition. The correlation of both scores is displayed in Figure 4.1 ($r = .30$, $p = .006$) with age in months indicated by the grey scale. Older children with higher scores are concentrated in the upper right quadrant. Thus, an increase in L2 exposure did not positively affect performance on standardized screening in German (see above for more details).

These analyses show that sentence repetition is more highly correlated with age than non-word repetition. This might indicate that phonological memory, which is engaged in non-word repetition, is less age-sensitive in preschool-children than phonological memory in sentence repetition, for which children need to have acquired more grammatical knowledge. Additionally, sentence repetition is more fine grained, simply due to the higher number of items, and could therefore contain more information. More speculatively, the sentence

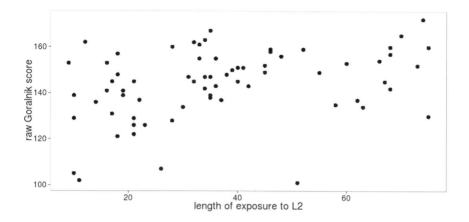

Figure 4.2   Raw Goralnik score and length of exposure to L2 in Russian-Hebrew speaking children

repetition task, especially the items involving complex syntactic structures, relies on more diverse knowledge, which may not be acquired until a later age. The phonological basis of non-word repetition may be more readily transferred from L1 knowledge, already in place at a young age in L1.

Standardized test in Hebrew   The raw scores of the Hebrew screening test are expected to increase as language develops. For monolingual children this development correlates with age (Goralnik, 1995). Yet, no such correlations were found for the bilingual children in the present study (p = .673). In contrast, length of L2 exposure yielded a significant correlation with the raw score, as can be seen in Figure 4.2.

A similar picture emerges when the subtests are evaluated for the influence of age and length of L2 exposure: children show significantly higher scores on vocabulary and expression with increasing age and length of exposure.

Since there is an inherently positive relationship between age and length of L2-exposure, these variables cannot be viewed as independent and, therefore, cannot be added simultaneously to the model. To avoid this problem, the age of the children was predicted from their length of L2-exposure and the residuals of this model were extracted and stored as another predictor variable, viz., *residualized* age. A high residualized age means that the child in question was relatively old for his length of L2-exposure. This yields two independent variables, L2-exposure on the one hand and the residualized age on the other. These two variables can be combined into a single model predicting the overall Goralnik score and performance on each of its subtasks. In this way, we can analyze the influence of these variables on the Goralnik scores separately.

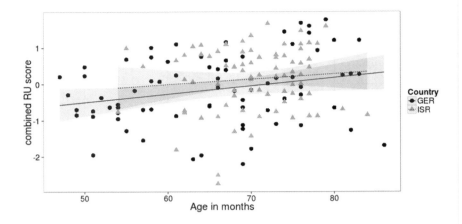

**Figure 4.3a   Combined score (the mean of the z-scaled values) for L1
Russian noun-verb naming over the age in months**

The results show that the residualized L2-exposure significantly correlates
with the overall Goralnik score ($p = .003$) and with the vocabulary ($p < .0001$)
and oral expression ($p = .009$) subtests. Thus, the residualized model containing
both variables is consistent with the univariate models reported above. The model
shows a negative influence of age (younger children perform better (e.g. picking
up new words more quickly) with the same length of L2-exposure, possibly a
reflection of their younger age of L2 onset. This interpretation is supported by
a number of acquisition studies on (bilingual) vocabulary development (Bloom,
2000; Paradis, 2008; Snedeker, et al., 2007; but see Goldberg, et al., 2008).

Thus, in the German data, sentence repetition is more highly correlated
with age than non-word repetition, and both subtests show low dependency
on length of exposure. For Hebrew, the significant correlation with the overall
Goralnik score was found for the residualized L2-exposure score.

Age effect on lexical and morpho-syntactic performance   While the standardized
screening/test evaluated the societal language, the tasks designed for the present
project were able to shed light on the home language as well. The correlations
between age and the L1/Russian lexical abilities on the combined Noun-Verb
naming tasks were significant in both cohorts (Figure 4.3a). The results show
further that Russian lexical performance in both countries is independent of
L2 exposure, indicating that while performance on verb-noun naming tasks
increases with age, increased length of L2 exposure does not lead to any
significant L1 attrition. This finding implies that L1 and L2 lexical abilities
operate on independent tracks, and improvement in one does not come at the

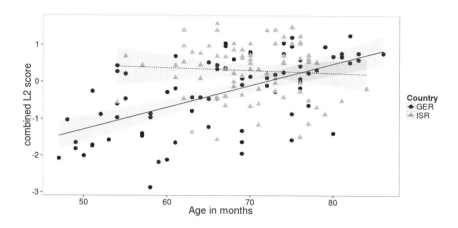

**Figure 4.3b   Combined score (the mean of the z-scaled values) for L2
German/Hebrew noun-verb naming over the age in months**

expense of the other. This implication will be discussed further in the context of
educational policy below.

For lexical performance in L2, age plays a strikingly different role in the two
cohorts (Fig. 4.3b): while German-speaking children show stronger development
for the older children, Hebrew-speaking children show a nearly flat slope across
the age spectrum, since as a group they show a relatively high command of the L2
lexicon from a younger age.

For morphosyntax, the tasks comparable in both cohorts and in all three
languages were sentence imitation/prepositions and sentence completion/verb
inflections. For L1/Russian, a slightly positive age dependency was found in both
cohorts (p < .001). For L2, however, the morphosyntactic developmental pattern
resembles the lexical pattern: for L2 German, age and morphosyntax are positively
correlated and for L2/Hebrew, there is no developmental change. However, these
differences were not significant. No other effects of age and length of L2 exposure
were found for L2 development in either country.

The results for the (additional) grammatical case tasks showed an effect of
age on the acquisition of case in Russian: Israeli children showed generally better
performance on Russian case than did German children. Performance on the
German case task correlated positively with both age and L2 exposure, though
these correlations were not very strong (p = .021). These different results both
for Hebrew and German and for the case tasks in Russian indicate a higher level
of language proficiency among the children in the Israeli cohort on all linguistic
performance tasks. Russian-German children reach the level of Russian-Hebrew
children by about 76 months.

Input Quantity and Language Performance

For input quantity, a strong positive correlation was predicted between the amount of L1/Russian used with children at home and outside and L1 development and a negative correlation was predicted between L1 language use and L2/German/ Hebrew development. That is, the more L1/Russian is used at home and outside, the more proficient the children will be in Russian and the less proficient they will be in L2/German/Hebrew. Findings are presented separately for each of the domains: at home and outside the home.

Language use at home and language performance   The amount of L1/Russian spoken at home was assessed by the reported language use of the parents (on a three point scale: *don't speak at all, speak a little, speak a lot*). A combined score was calculated for each household based on the amount of L1 and L2 spoken by the child's mother and father at home where the amount of L2 spoken was subtracted from the amounted of L1 spoken to yield a single score. Correlations were then calculated between this language input score and scores on the linguistic tasks (lexis, prepositions, verb inflections, complex syntax, grammatical case and non-word repetition).

For all tasks, apart from non-word repetition, a positive effect of L1/Russian spoken at home was found on linguistic performance in L1/Russian in both cohorts. The strongest correlation was registered for the grammatical case task ($p = .003$) and the correlation between the amount of Russian at home and case use, which was higher for the children in the Israeli group. For lexis, more Russian language use at home led to improved performance on the Noun-Verb task ($p < .0001$ for both, see Figure 4.4).

In addition, the three morpho-syntactic tasks performed in Russian showed a significant relationship with the amount of Russian spoken at home. The strongest relationship was found for the sentence completion task involving verb inflections ($p = .0009$) in both countries. All sentence repetition tasks showed the consistency of this relationship between L1/Russian language use and linguistic performance: for prepositions ($p = .024$ and $.003$ for Germany and Israel, respectively), for verb inflections ($p = .027$ for both Germany and Israel) and for complex syntax ($p = .007$ for both Germany and Israel).

The amount of L1/Russian spoken at home showed no negative effect on performance in German/Hebrew, and this finding was consistent for all tasks except lexical naming. For the lexical task, naming of nouns correlated negatively with L1/Russian language use ($p = .043$), but verb naming did not. The influence of L1/Russian home language use on lexical abilities is shown in Figure 4.5. The latter result supports the previous findings on the lower robustness of nouns in comparison with verbs in bilingual language acquisition (Klassert, et al., 2013).

In summary, there is a positive relationship between L1/Russian language use and all L1 tasks except NWR for both groups and no negative effect of L1/ Russian language use on L2 performance, again for both groups and for all tasks

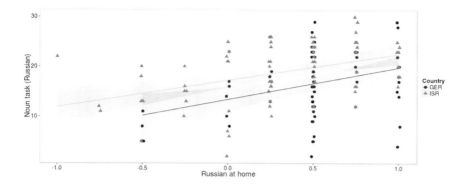

Figure 4.4   The effect of home language on noun task in Russian

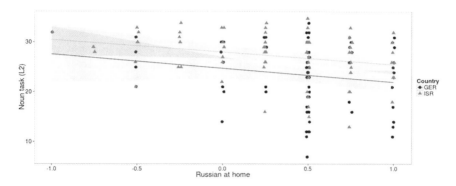

Figure 4.5   The effect of home language on noun task in German/Hebrew

(except lexical naming). To conclude, the amount of Russian spoken at home was shown to be the strongest predictor of competence in L1/Russian (like age) among the selected variables.

Conclusions

In this chapter, the effects of age, length of L2 exposure, and language input on the acquisition of both languages in bilingual Russian-German and Russian-Hebrew contexts were investigated for preschool children using a battery of similar phonological, lexical, and morpho-syntactic tasks. We aimed for a comprehensive overview of linguistic performance in the two languages in order to compare development in both the home and societal languages across the two cohorts.

Beginning with the effects of age and length of L2 exposure, the results of this paper show that in the German group, chronological age correlates with the development of language as measured by a standardized test of language proficiency, and this correlation is strongest for the sentence repetition task. Yet, despite this age related development, when comparing the results to monolingual norms, about one third of the children perform below those norms (Armon-Lotem, et al., 2011). Moreover, no correlation was found between age and the raw scores on the Hebrew standardized test. In terms of length of L2 exposure, both groups show positive correlations with linguistic performance, suggesting that both the amount of exposure and chronological age should be considered in setting norms for L2 proficiency. These results suggest that the use of standardized tests alone, without accompanying information about the amount of L2 input, might lead to misdiagnosis of bilingual children at risk for language impairment.

The variety of tasks used in the present study shows that different aspects of language develop at different rates in bilingual children, and shows different sensitivity to age and to length of L2 exposure. Evaluating these different linguistic facets in L1 suggests that the development of the home language is related to chronological age rather than length of L2 exposure, and crucially depends on the amount of L1 spoken at home. More precisely, negative correlations were not found between length of exposure to L2 and children's L1 performance. Notably, L1 performance could not be evaluated by monolingual norms; thus, we cannot conclude whether the children fall within such norms. These findings suggest that there is a strong need for tests specifically designed for bilingual children in both L1 and L2 (cf. Schulz and Tracy, 2011 *LiSe-DaZ* for L2 German; Gagarina, Klassert, and Topaj, 2010 for home language Russian).

The domain which showed highest sensitivity to both age and length of exposure is the lexicon. Yet, this was manifested differently for L1 and L2 across the two groups. On the L1 noun-verb naming task, both groups showed high sensitivity to age with no negative influence of the length of L2 exposure. The absence of negative correlations between length of L2 exposure and L1 lexicon might be explained by the fact that, generally, the lexicon is developing more rapidly during the earlier stages of language acquisition, thus length of exposure plays a less crucial role (cf. Bloom, 2000) losing its 'value' with age (as in the case of four- to six-year-old children in the present study). On the L2 noun-verb naming task, a correlation was found only for German, while no such correlation was found for Hebrew, where children seemed to perform rather well from the onset. The differences between the two languages in the societal language seems to be task-related, since the vocabulary subtest of the Hebrew standardized measure did yield a correlation with both age and length of exposure to L2.

With respect to the amount of L1 spoken at home, the results show a strong positive effect of the amount of Russian spoken at home on children's performance in that language, with no significant negative effects on German/ Hebrew performance, in most domains. That is, the use of L1 at home is a strong predictor of successful maintenance of this language; a high amount of Russian, spoken at home supports the development of the main language domains in Russian and does not impede the development of the societal language, German/ Hebrew, influencing it only to a minor extent in the domain of noun vocabulary. The latter result supports previous findings on lower robustness of nouns in bilingual language acquisition in comparison with verbs (Klassert, et al., 2013). Cummins's (1978, 1982) Interdependence Hypothesis suggests that one might even anticipate indirect positive effects of advanced development of the home language concurrent with acquisition of the societal language.

To conclude, the study showed that the development of lexicon in L1 is especially sensitive to input quantity in that language at home in both countries, whereas sentence imitation tasks in the morpho-syntax domains are more robust with regard to input in both the home and societal languages. Furthermore, the amount of L1 exposure alone cannot explain the development of linguistic performance in this study, since it interacts with chronological age and the length of L2 exposure.

Even today language clinicians and kindergarten teachers often discourage the parents of bilingual children from speaking in the home language to their children, and recommend using L2 in communication at home. In this respect, our findings have an important implication, suggesting that the use of the mother tongue (in our case Russian) by parents at home should be viewed favorably, since it has positive effects on L1 lexical and morpho-syntactic development and, at the same time, does not impede L2 development. Finally, we hope that further investigation of the effect of external and internal factors on language acquisition will provide a better understanding of bilingual development.

References

Abutbul-Oz, H. (2009). Person perception experiments on language preferences of Russian-Hebrew sequential bilinguals. Paper presented at ISB7, Utrecht.

Allard, R., and Landry, R. (1994). Subjective ethnolinguistic vitality: A comparison of two measures. *International Journal of the Sociology of Language, 108*, 117-144.

Armon-Lotem, S., Fine, J., Adam, G., Saiegh-Haddad, E., Blass, A., Harel, E., and Walters, J. (2006). *Verb inflections as an indicator of SLI in bilinguals: The role of task and cross-linguistic differences.* Tel Aviv: SCRIPT Conference on Literacy and Language.

Armon-Lotem, S., Gagarina, N., and Gupol, O. (2006). *Inflectional verb errors in the acquisition of Russian by bilingual and monolingual children.* Toronto: Language Acquisition and Bilingualism: Consequences for a Multilingual Society.

Armon-Lotem, S., Walters, J., and Gagarina, N. (2011). The impact of internal and external factors on linguistic performance in the home language and in L2 among Russian-Hebrew and Russian-German preschool children. *Linguistic Approaches to Bilingualism, 1*(3), 291-317.

Bloom, P. (2000). *How Children Learn the Meanings of Words*. Cambridge, MA: MIT Press.

Cobo-Lewis, A., Pearson, B. Z., Eilers, R. E., and Umbel, V. C. (2002a). Effects of bilingualism and bilingual education on oral and written English skills: A multifactor study of standardized test outcomes. In D. K. Oller and R. E. Eilers (Hrsg.), *Language and literacy in bilingual children* (pp. 43-63). Clevedon, UK: Multilingual Matters.

Cobo-Lewis, A., Pearson, B. Z., Eilers, R. E., and Umbel, V. C. (2002b). Effects of bilingualism and bilingual education on oral and written Spanish skills: A multifactor study of standardized test outcomes. In D. K. Oller and R. E. Eilers (Hrsg.), *Language and literacy in bilingual children* (pp. 98-117). Clevedon, UK: Multilingual Matters.

Cummins, J. (1978). Bilingualism and the development of metalinguistic awareness. *Journal of Cross-Cultural Psychology, 9,* 131-149.

Cummins, J. (1982). Die Schwellenniveau- und die Interdependenz-Hypothese: Erklärungen zum Erfolg zweisprachiger Erziehung. In: J. Swift (Hrsg.) *Bilinguale und multikulturelle Erziehung* (pp. 34-43). Würzburg: Königshausen + Neumann.

De Bleser, R., and Kauschke, C. (2003). Acquisition and loss of nouns and verbs: parallel or divergent patterns? *Journal of Neurolinguistics, 16* (2-3), 213-229.

De Houwer, A. (1999). Environmental factors in early bilingual development: The role of parental beliefs and attitudes. In E. Guus and L. Verhoeven (Eds.), *Bilingualism and Migration* (pp. 75-95). New York: Mouton de Gruyter.

Dromi, E., Leonard, L., Adam, G., and Zadunaisky-Ehrlich, S. (1999). Verb Agreement Morphology in Hebrew-Speaking Children with Specific Language Impairment. *Journal of Speech, Language and Hearing Research, 42,* 1414-1431.

Gagarina, N. (2011). Acquisition and loss of L1 in a Russian-German bilingual child: A case study. In S. N. Cejtlin (Ed.), *Monolingual and bilingual path to language* (pp. 137-163). Moscow: Jazyki slavjanskoj kul'tury.

Gagarina, N., Armon-Lotem, S., and Gupol, O. (2007). Developmental variation in the acquisition of L1 Russian verb inflection by monolinguals and bilinguals. In H. Caunt-Nulton, S. Kulatilake and I.-H. Woo (Eds.), *BUCLD 31 Proceedings Supplement* (pp. 1-11). Boston University.

Gagarina, N., Klassert, A., and Topaj, N. (2010). Russian language proficiency test for multilingual children. ZAS Papers in Linguistics 54, Berlin: ZAS.

Genesee, F., Paradis, J., and Crago, M. (2011). *Dual language development and disorders: A handbook on bilingualism and second language learning.* Baltimore, MD: Brookes.

Gleitman, L., and Newport, E. (1995). The invention of language by children: Environmental and biological influences on the acquisition of language. In

L. Gleitman and M. Liberman (Eds.), *Language: An Invitation to Cognitive Science*. Cambridge, MA: MIT Press.

Golberg, H., Paradis, J., and Crago, M. (2008). Lexical acquisition over time in minority L1 children learning English as a L2. *Applied Psycholinguistics, 29*(1), 41-65.

Goralnik, E. (1995). *Goralnik Diagnostic Test*. Even Yehuda: Matan.

Grimm, H. (2003). SSV. *Sprachscreening für das Vorschulalter*. Kurzform des SETK 3-5. Manual. Göttingen: Hogrefe.

Hakuta, K., and Garcia, E. E. (1989). Bilingualism and education. *American Psychologist, 44*, 374-379.

Hamers, J. F., and Blanc, M. H. A. (2000). *Bilinguality and Bilingualism*. Cambridge University Press.

Hoff, E. (2006a). How social contexts support and shape language development. *Developmental Review, 26*, 55-88.

Hoff, E. (2006b). Environmental supports for language acquisition. In D. K. Dickinson and S. B. Neuman (Eds.), *Handbook of Early Literacy Research, Vol. II* (pp. 163-172). New York: Guilford Publications.

Hoff, E., Core, C., Place, S., Rumiche, R., Señor, M., and Parra, M. (2012). Dual language exposure and early bilingual development. *Journal of Child Language, 39*, 1-27.

Kauschke, C. (2007). *Erwerb und Verarbeitung von Nomen und Verben*. Tübingen: Niemeyer.

Klassert, A. (2011). *Lexikalische Fähigkeiten bilingualer Kinder mit Migrationshintergrund. Eine Studie zum Benennen von Nomen und Verben im Russischen und Deutschen*. Universität Marburg, Dissertation.

Klassert, A., and Gagarina, N. (2010). Der Einfluss des elterlichen Inputs auf die Sprachentwicklung bilingualer Kinder: Evidenz aus russischsprachigen Migrantenfamilien in Berlin. *Diskurs Kindheits- und Jugendforschung, 4*, 413-425.

Klassert, A., Gagarina, N. and Kauschke, C. (2013). Object and action naming in Russian and Germanspeaking monolingual and bilingual children. *Bilingualism: Language and Cognition. FirstView* Article 1-16.

Lambert, W. E., and Taylor, D. M. (1996). Language in the lives of ethnic minorities: Cuban american families in Miami. *Applied Linguistics, 17(4)*, 477-500.

Meisel, J. M. (2009). Second Language Acquisition in Early Childhood. *Zeitschrift für Sprachwissenschaft, 28* (1), 5-34.

Oller, D. K., and Eilers, R. E. (2002). *Language and literacy in bilingual children*. Clevedon, UK: Multilingual Matters.

Paradis, J. (2008). *Are simultaneous and early sequential bilingual acquisition fundamentally different?* Paper presented at Models of Interaction in Bilinguals, University of Wales, Bangor, October 2008.

Paradis, J. (2010). Bilingual children's acquisition of English verb morphology: Effects of language dominance, structure difficulty, and task type. *Language Learning, 60,* 651-680.

Pearson, B. Z. (2007). Social factors in childhood bilingualism in the United States. *Applied Psycholinguistics, 28,* 399-410.

Reich, H. H. (2008). Die Sprachaneignung von Kindern in Situationen der Zwei- und Mehrsprachigkeit. In K. Ehlich, U. Bredel and H. H. Reich (Eds.), *Referenzrahmen zur altersspezifischen Sprachaneignung. Forschungsgrundlagen* (pp. 163-169). Berlin: Bundesministerium für Bildung und Forschung (BMBF).

Rothweiler, M. (2007). Bilingualer Spracherwerb und Zweitspracherwerb. In M. Steinberg (Ed.), *Schnittstellen der germanistischen Linguistik* (pp. 101-135). Stuttgart/Weimar: Metzler.

Snedeker, J., Geren, J., and Shafto, C. L. (2007). Starting over: International adoption as a natural experiment in language development. *Psychological Science, 18,* 79-87.

Schulz, P., and Tracy, R. (2011). Linguistische Sprachstandserhebung – Deutsch als Zweitsprache *LiSe-DaZ.* Göttingen: Hogrefe.

Tucker, G. R. (1999). *A global perspective on bilingualism and bilingual education.* Washington D.C.: ERIC Clearinghouse.

Chapter 5

Acculturation and Well-Being among Migrant and Minority Adolescents: A Cross-National and Cross-Ethnic Comparison

Anna Möllering, David Schiefer, Ariel Knafo, and Klaus Boehnke

Introduction

More than Just a Journey: Migration and Acculturation

Even though the history of migration is as old as humankind itself, the number of international migrants has never been higher than today (almost 191 million, according to the United Nations Division on International Migration 2006). The current high number of migrants in addition to the proverbial "shrinking" of the world as a consequence of faster communication and travel channels have led to more intercultural and interethnic contact than ever before in history. This is a challenge for both veterans and migrants.

The present chapter explores how this challenge affects the well-being of different migrant adolescent groups in two major immigration countries—Israel and Germany—in relation to the host societies' general attitude towards them and vice versa. To pursue this research question a basic theoretical framework is laid out regarding intercultural and interethnic contact.

How people deal with interethnic contact has, among others, been targeted by the concept of acculturation—a construct inseparably tied to the issue of migration. According to Arends-Tóth and Van de Vijver (2006a, p. 34), "… acculturation refers to changes that an individual experiences as a result of contact with one or more other cultures and of the participation in the ensuing process of change that one's cultural or ethnic group is undergoing". Acculturation is conceptualized as a process that takes place on several dimensions (Berry, Trimble, and Olmedo, 1986): the behavioral domain as well as the domain of attitudes and identity (e.g., Berry, Poortinga, Segall, and Dasen, 2002). In the following only the identity domain of acculturation will be addressed. According to Erikson (e.g., 1993) identity development is the most important developmental task during adolescence. Thus, since identity formation plays such a crucial role in adolescence and this study concentrates specifically on adolescents a focus on the identity aspect of acculturation seemed in place. In this regard, identity refers to the way individuals perceive themselves as members of the minority vis-à-vis the host society (Berry et al., 2002; Hutnik, 1991).

Classifying Acculturation Research

Studies on the concept of acculturation can be structured by categorizing them into three different types, namely studies dealing with *acculturation conditions*, *acculturation orientations,* and *acculturation outcomes* (Arends-Tóth and van de Vijver, 2006a).

    Acculturation conditions refer to variables on the group as well as the individual level. On the group level, characteristics of the society of settlement as well as the ethnic minority group are important. Openness of the society of settlement towards immigrants is crucial.

    Acculturation orientations can—according to Berry (e.g., Berry and Kim, 1988)—be classified into four different types resulting from answers to the following two questions: "Is my cultural identity of value and to be retained?" and "Are positive relations with the larger (dominant) society to be sought?" (Berry and Kim, 1988, p. 211). *Integration* describes an acculturation orientation in which aspects of the culture of origin are retained and an orientation towards the culture of the country of settlement also takes places. When individuals *assimilate,* they give up the culture of origin and instead are completely absorbed into the majority culture. *Separation* refers to an acculturation orientation in which the individual rejects the majority culture but maintains the culture of the society of origin. *Marginalization* can be described as the opposite of an integration orientation—individuals give up or lose their culture of origin and do not adapt to the majority society either.

    One of the most important issues regarding *acculturation outcomes* is an individual's subjective well-being, since it is closely related to many other acculturation outcome aspects (e.g., job performance, Wright and Cropanzano, 2004).

Acculturation in Two National Contexts: Israel and Germany

In the literature on acculturation orientations and their relation to well-being, little attention has been paid to the 'fit' between host societies acculturation expectations—an acculturation condition—and minority groups' actual acculturation orientations. However, obviously this 'fit' determines the relation between host society and ethnic minority which in turn impacts acculturation outcomes—like the well-being of an ethnic minority member—positively or negatively. The present chapter explores the relation between minority group members' acculturation orientations, state ideologies regarding migration as an indicator of host societies acculturation expectations and minority group members' well-being. This is done by taking into account two countries: Germany and Israel.

Similarities of the Societal Contexts of Israel and Germany

According to Bourhis et al. (1997), both countries share the same state ideology regarding migration: an ethnist ideology. Societies holding this view, typically expect immigrants to adopt the public values of the host country (such as the constitution of the state, or adherence to the civil and criminal code) and claim the right to intervene with private values (such as cultural, social and linguistic activities, or religious expression). Alternatively, ethnist ideology states refrain from pressuring immigrants into adopting the values of the host country altogether. This is the case if these societies do not have the intention of ever accepting immigrants as citizens anyway because they grant citizenship only on the basis of certain ethnic or religious qualities. Germany and Israel fall into that latter category (Bourhis et al., 1997), since they grant citizenship on the basis of the *jus sanguinis* (Germany) or religion (Israel)—though this religious affiliation is then actually also passed on via bloodline. With regard to ethnic minority groups that do fulfil the premises on which citizenship is granted, both countries expect an acculturation attitude oriented towards the host society (assimilation or integration).

Differences in the Societal Contexts of Israel and Germany

The State of Israel has always been an immigration country (e.g., Zerubavel, 1995). The idea of the early Zionists was to reunite the scattered Jewish communities to form a new nation (e.g., Liebman and Don-Yehiya, 1983; Metz, 1990). Therefore, the distinction between natives and immigrants is somewhat blurry. Even the citizens who were born in Israel have some kind of migration background, if only in previous generations (Rosenthal, 2005). However, there also is one ethnic group living in Israel that is neither Jewish nor does it have a migration background: the Arab population of Israel.

In contrast, the German society appears as a rather homogeneous one. It consists of a large German majority that has been living in this area for centuries. Only comparatively recently (within the last 40 years), a number of groups came to Germany as migrants. Another difference between the two countries is that Germany for a long time refused to see itself as an immigration country. Only when immigration numbers rose far beyond negligible percentages during the 1990's Germany did (to some degree) accept the fact that it is today one of the major immigration countries in the world.

Who Are They? Group Specific Characteristics and Acculturation

The current research compares four different ethnic minority groups. By doing so, cross-cultural differences between ethnic minority groups can be highlighted; we look at acculturation orientations of FSU immigrants to both Israel and Germany as well as Turkish migrants to Germany and non-migrant Arab citizens of Israel.

Former Soviet Union Immigrants to Israel

The vast majority of FSU immigrants who migrated to Israel were of Jewish heritage, reflecting immigration policies of the State of Israel. The most recent and most important immigration wave (around 920.000 people, Al-Haj, 2004) took place in the 1990s after the Soviet Union had loosened its strict regulations of outbound passage in 1989. Today around 15 percent of the Israeli population are of Russian heritage (Al-Haj, 2002).

Former Soviet Union Immigrants to Germany

FSU citizens who migrated to Germany typically were of German descent. Ancestors of these so-called *Aussiedler* had migrated from Germany to Russia during the 17th and 18th century (Schmitt-Rodermund, 1999). In line with a special article in the German constitution, they and their family were allowed to migrate to Germany and become German citizens upon arrival due to their German 'blood' ties. More than two million did so after the fall of the Iron Curtain. Today *Aussiedler* form Germany's largest minority group, although in strict legal terms they belong to the German majority.

Turkish Immigrants to Germany

A large number of immigrants from Turkey came to Germany as temporary guest workers in the 1960s (Böttiger, 2005). However, due to the originally poor economic situation in Turkey many guest workers and their families ended up staying in the host country. Today Turkish migrants form the second largest immigrant group in Germany.

Due to the *jus sanguinis*, naturalization is not easy for this migrant group: Only Turkish migrant children born in Germany after 1999 gain German citizenship automatically. Children born to Turkish migrants before 1999 have to decide between 18 and 23 whether they want to remain Turkish or change their citizenship to German (Alba, 2005).

Arab-Israeli Minority in Israel

In Israel, the second ethnic minority group in focus are Arab citizens. In the course of the establishment of the State of Israel and the preceding war, the majority of Arabs that had lived in the area that is now Israel fled or were forced to leave the territory of the new state (Ghanem, 2001; Stendel, 1996). Only 10 percent to 18 percent of all Palestinians stayed within the borders of the new state and have since then formed a minority in the new state of Israel (Ghanem, 2001; Rabinovitz,

2001; Stendel, 1996). The Arab communities can be seen as a parallel society (e.g., Sherer and Karnieli-Miller, 2004) that has established a distinct cultural and social life.

Hypotheses

Considering all unique features of the societal context and the characteristics of the respective minority groups the following hypotheses are formulated:

First it is expected that the four ethnic minority groups—FSU immigrants to Israel and Germany, Turkish migrants to Germany, and Israeli Arabs—follow different acculturation orientations, due to their unique characteristics and that of the social context of the host societies (Hypothesis 1). Adolescents in Israel and Germany with a migration background from the Former Soviet Union are being expected to show a strong identification with their Russian heritage, due to having settled in the Former Soviet Union for generations. At the same time they are assumed to attempt to integrate into the host society. The host countries support their attempt to feel as Israelis/Germans, due to the naturalization practice based on religious background and German ancestry, respectively. Hence, FSU immigrants to Israel and Germany will more likely report a bicultural acculturation orientation—integration.

Adolescents with a Turkish migration background and the Arab minority are expected to primarily hold a separation orientation. As has been described, it is rather difficult for both groups to feel part of and identify with the host society in light of the *jus sanguinis* policy of Germany and the self-definition of Israel as a Zionist-Jewish state. Moreover, both groups are culturally more distinct from the society of settlement compared to FSU immigrants, most of all in terms of religion. According to Ward, Bochner, and Furnham (2001) cultural differences between ethnic minority groups and host society can lead to conflicts. These conflicts also militate in favor of a separation orientation regarding these two minority groups.

Secondly it is hypothesized that individual acculturation orientations relate to well-being in line with assumptions laid out by Berry (e.g., Williams and Berry, 1991) (Hypothesis 2). An integration orientation is assumed to be related to the highest well-being, whereas marginalization is associated with the lowest well-being. Individuals holding a separation or assimilation orientation are hypothesized to score somewhere in between.

However, as mentioned earlier, Bourhis et al. (1997) argue that the 'fit' between host societies acculturation expectations and minority group members' actual acculturation orientations influences the relationship between the two groups. This 'fit' (and thus the relationship between groups) can differ depending on ethnic minority group characteristics and host societies' state ideology regarding migration and influences minority group members' well-being. Thus, the four acculturation orientations should be differentially related to well-being among different ethnic minority groups.

In the case of an ethnist state ideology integration and assimilation should relate more positively to well-being if the ethnic minority group 'fits' the criterion for granting citizenship because this would then be the acculturation orientation expected by the host society. On the other hand, separation is assumed to relate more positively to well-being if the minority group does *not* fulfill the criterion on which basis citizenship is granted because in this case separation would be the acculturation orientation expected by the host society.

Hence, with regard to the present ethnic minority groups we expect that integration and assimilation imply more benefitting potential for the individual's well-being among the FSU immigrants compared to the Turkish and Arab minority. Among the latter the relation between integration or assimilation and well-being could even be negative. Conversely, separation is hypothesized to relate more positively to well-being among Israeli Arabs and Turkish migrants compared to FSU immigrants. For FSU immigrants separation should relate less positively—or even negatively—to well-being in both Israel and Germany (Hypothesis 3).

Methods

Sample

All data were obtained using a paper–pencil questionnaire that participants filled in at school in the presence of a member of the research team.

Following the definition of the German Bureau of Statistics (*Statistisches Bundesamt*), participants were assigned as native Germans or Israelis, if both parents were born in the country. Alternatively, individuals were allocated to one of the four ethnic minority groups if at least one of the adolescent's parents was born in Russia (or another Former Soviet Union country) or Turkey. Since Arab Israelis cannot be distinguished from native Israelis by their country of origin, adolescents were categorized as belonging to this minority group if they attended an Arab school.[1]

All in all, the sample consisted of 1774 adolescents (811 male and 936 female, 27 did not report their gender) between 10 and 18. The allocation of participants to different ethnic groups resulted in the distribution pattern presented in Table 5.1 below.

Table 5.1   Distribution of participants according to ethnic group

Ethnic group	Turkish immigrants to Germany	FSU immigrants to Germany	FSU immigrants to Israel	Arab Israelis
	537	395	415	427

---

1   In Israel there exist different school systems for Jewish and Arab students.

Measures

Acculturation

As we have outlined, the most popular view on acculturation has been Berry's bi-dimensional model (e.g., Berry et al., 2002). To measure orientations towards both the culture of origin as well as the host culture, a common approach is to present participants identical items with reference to both cultures separately (e.g., Arends-Tóth and van de Vijver, 2006b; Tsai, Ying, and Lee, 2000).

Secondly, as reasoned above, it was decided to concentrate on identity formation when taking the acculturation perspective. Hence, we assessed acculturation using three items measuring identity centrality from a scale by Roccas, Sagiv, Schwartz, Halevy, and Eidelson (2006). The items measure the degree of subjective importance to be a member of both the cultural group of origin and the host-culture group. Thus, two short three-item scales assessed identification with the host society as well as with the ethnic minority group. The following three items were used (here presented in the form to measure identification with the German host society) "It is important to me that others view me as a German", "It is important to me to see myself as a German", "Being a German is an important part of who I am". The scales had a six-point response format, ranging from totally agree to totally disagree. Reliabilities of these scales among the four ethnic minority groups varied between $\alpha = .88$ and $\alpha = .94$.

Both identity scales formed the basis for calculating acculturation orientations. Arends-Tóth and van de Vijver (2006b) suggest a procedure that is based on the Euclidian distance concept. This procedure is grounded in the consideration, that an individual can be located on a two-dimensional matrix of orientation towards the culture of origin as well as towards the host culture (see Figure 5.1). In such a matrix, the extreme ends constitute the highest degree of a particular acculturation orientation (Figure 5.1). The distance of the individual's location to each extreme end (each corner of the matrix) can be calculated mathematically using the Euclidian distance formula. The Euclidian distance between two points x and y is the ordinary distance between these points as measured with a ruler. In a two dimensional plane the distance is given by the following formula (which is equivalent to the Pythagorean theorem): $\sqrt{(x_1 - y_1)^2 + (x_2 - y_2)^2}$. Resulting scores can be described as the proximity towards each of the acculturation types, based on their scores on both dimensions. Using this procedure, scores for four measures for each participant, one for each acculturation orientation, were calculated. For example, the respondent represented in Figure 5.1 has a positive orientation towards both the culture of origin and the host culture. Therefore, this person can be seen as closer to the prototypical integration orientation and more distant to the other orientations. Thus, after reversing the distance score, the respondent receives the highest score (indicating smallest distance) on the integration orientation. Scores on the four acculturation orientation scales can range from zero to 7.07.

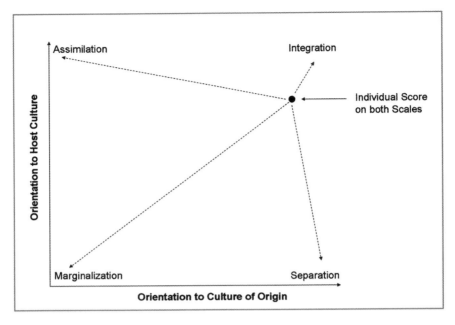

Figure 5.1   Measuring the acculturation orientations using the Euclidian distance procedure

Well-Being

In their large cross-cultural study on immigrant youth Sam, Vedder, Ward, and Horenczyk (2006) describe two aspects of an individual's well-being: Life satisfaction and self-esteem. Both are very widely used proxies for subjective well-being. Countless studies examining the impact of acculturation on a person's well-being used self-esteem (e.g., Dukes and Martinez, 1994; Giang and Wittig, 2006; Hutnik, 1991; Phinney, Chavira, and Williamson, 1992) or satisfaction with life as indicators (e.g., Ali, 2009; Lachance-Grzela and Bouchard, 2009; Libran, 2006; Vella-Brodrick, Park, and Peterson, 2009). The reason why self-esteem has been under scrutiny so often is that it constitutes an essential aspect of a person's self-concept (Rosenberg, 1979). It is highly vulnerable during adolescence, especially in the context of group membership (Umaña-Taylor, Diversi, and Fine, 2002). However, life satisfaction has also proven to be a valuable indicator of an individual's well-being. Sam et al. (2006) state that life satisfaction should be under scrutiny, since–like self-esteem–it is related to both the self-concept and the process of acculturation. Thus, in our study we decided to capture individual well-being by assessing both life satisfaction and self-esteem: The former with Diener's Life Satisfaction Scale (Diener, Emmons, Larsen, and Griffin, 1985) and the latter by using a short five-item version of Rosenberg's Self-Esteem Scale

(Rosenberg, 1965; only the positively worded items). Both scales can be considered classical measures regarding the respective concept and have been successfully used in a number of different cultural contexts (Farruggia, Chen, Greenberger, Dmitrieva, and Macek, 2004; Oishi, Diener, Lucas, and Suh, 1999; Pavot and Diener, 1993; Schmitt and Allik, 2005). Like the acculturation measure the self-esteem as well as the life satisfaction measure both had a six-point response format ranging from totally agree to totally disagree. Reliabilities of the self-esteem scale varied between $\alpha = .68$ and .91. The scale measuring life satisfaction showed a reliability of $\alpha = .65$ to .84.

Results

In the following sections, results will be presented according to the order of the hypotheses. Table 5.2 presents the means and standard deviations of all variables assessed.

Table 5.2   Means and standard deviations of variables included in the analyses

Variables	FSU Immigrants to Germany		Turkish Immigrants to Germany		FSU Immigrants to Israel		Arab Israelis	
	Mean[1]	SD	Mean[1]	SD	Mean[1]	SD	Mean[1]	SD
Ethnic Identification	4.66	1.47	5.35	1.12	4.63	1.63	5.33	1.26
Host Country Identification	3.12	1.59	2.69	1.65	4.35	1.63	3.64	1.89
Self-Esteem	5.54	1.00	5.79	0.91	5.96	1.05	6.19	1.00
Life Satisfaction	5.03	1.14	5.43	1.07	4.84	1.31	5.42	1.36

Note: [1]ANOVAs (post-hoc Scheffé tests) indicated significant mean score differences between all groups, except for the following: Ethnic Identification: FSU immigrants (Germany)—FSU immigrants (Israel); Turkish immigrants—Arab Israelis. Self-Esteem: Turkish immigrants—FSU immigrants (Israel). Life Satisfaction: Turkish immigrants—Arab Israelis; FSU immigrants (Germany)—FSU immigrants (Israel).

To examine the proposed hypotheses, correlational as well as structural equation analyses were performed. Hypothesis 1 expected different choices of acculturation orientations among the four samples. In Germany, individuals from both ethnic

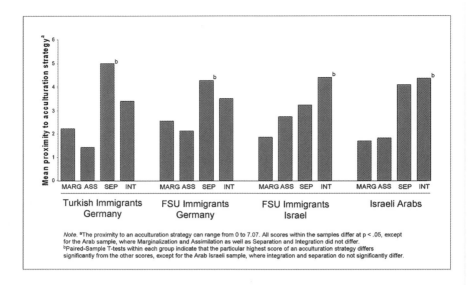

Figure 5.2   Mean scores of the orientation towards one of the acculturation orientations by sample

groups most often tended to separate, followed by the integration orientation. In Israel, immigrants from the FSU followed an integration orientation. Israeli Arabs, however, held the integration and the separation orientation similarly frequently (see Figure 5.2).

Hypothesis 2 predicted a stronger relationship between the acculturation orientations integration and marginalization and the indicators of well-being in contrast to both the relation between separation as well as assimilation and well-being. With regard to integration the relationship with the well-being indicators was assumed to be positive, for marginalization the relationship with well-being was expected to be negative. Results show that in line with the hypothesis integration was positively related to well-being (correlations with both well-being indicators ranged between $r = .15$, $p < .01$, and $r = .26$, $p < .01$); whereas resorting to a marginalization orientation was associated negatively with well-being (correlations ranged between $r = -.20$, $p < .01$, and $r = -.29$, $p < .01$). These findings pertain to members of all ethnic groups.

Furthermore and also as expected in the hypothesis, assimilation and separation were less coherently related to well-being. In Germany, separation and assimilation were not significantly related to either of the well-being indicators. In Israel assimilation was negatively related to self-esteem among the Arab adolescents, however only moderately in size (self esteem: $r = -.19$, $p < .01$). Separation, in turn, was marginally negatively related with life satisfaction ($r = -.14$, $p < .01$). Among the FSU immigrants to Israel separation was negatively related to self-esteem and life satisfaction, again the relation was only modest in the case of self-esteem (self-esteem: $r = -.11$, $p < .05$ life satisfaction: $r = -.24$, $p < .01$).

Hypothesis 3 postulated that the interrelation of acculturation orientations and the two well-being indicators is different depending on the societal and ethnic context. To test this assumption, structural equation models using AMOS 16 (Arbuckle, 2005) were conducted. Well-being was modeled as two related latent variables, each with five items as manifest variables, the above referenced self-esteem and life satisfaction items. Acculturation orientations were represented only by single observed indicators—the above described reversed Euclidian distance scores. Multi-group model tests were conducted for all four samples simultaneously. A model where the interrelations of an acculturation orientation and the well-being variables were allowed to vary freely between samples was compared to a model where these parameters were constrained to be equal across samples. If the constrained model showed a significantly worse model fit (significant increase in X^2), cross-sample differences were assumed. The multi-group model was estimated separately for each acculturation orientation indicator. Two model fit criteria were consulted to assess how well the specified models fit the data: standardized root mean square residual (SRMR) and root mean square error of approximation (RMSEA). The use of both indices has been recommended to detect possible model misspecifications with a sufficient sensitivity (Hu and Bentler, 1999; McCallum and Austin, 2000). A good model fit is indicated by SRMR $< .08$ and RMSEA $< .06$ (Hu and Bentler, 1999). The non-constrained models showed satisfying fit indices, when using the separation orientation as a predictor, $X^2 (164) = 960.37$, $p < .00$; SRMR $= .065$; RMSEA $= 0.05$; as well as assimilation, $X^2 (164) = 940.54$, $p < .00$; SRMR $= .06$; RMSEA $= 0.05$; marginalization, $X^2 (164) = 944.91$, $p < .00$; SRMR $= .065$; RMSEA $= 0.05$; and integration, $X^2 (164) = 954.9$, $p < .00$; SRMR $= .065$; RMSEA $= 0.05$.

The comparison of the samples as to the relation between acculturation orientations and well-being indicated cross-sample differences. Their extent, however, was only minor (see Figure 5.3). Assuming the relation between the separation orientation and life satisfaction to be invariant across samples led to a significantly less well-fitting, $\Delta X^2 = 9.35$, $\Delta_{df} = 3$, $p < .025$. Hence, the separation orientation seemed to relate differentially to life satisfaction. The estimates of the parameters of the structural equation model indicated that separation was related to life satisfaction only among the FSU immigrants in Israel, $\beta = -.22$, $p < .01$ but not among the other samples. In all other cases, cross-cultural differences only appeared by tendency but provided no significance in the multi-group comparisons. Thus, the FSU immigrants in Israel are obviously the only group that tends to suffer from holding the separation orientation.

Discussion

The aim of the present chapter was to obtain a more differentiated view of the interrelation of acculturation orientations and well-being by explicitly taking the

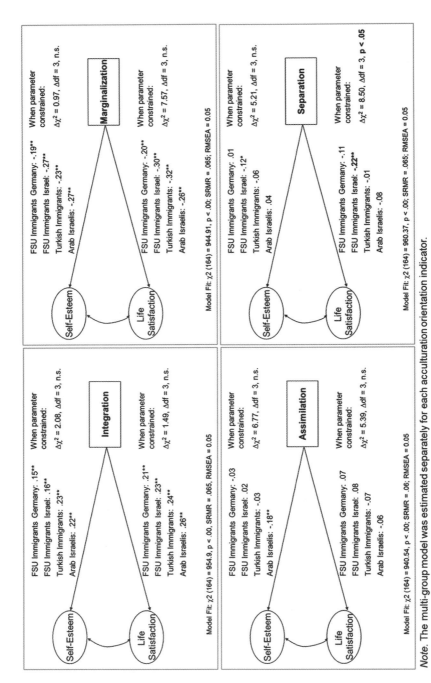

Note. The multi-group model was estimated separately for each acculturation orientation indicator.

Figure 5.3   Relationships between acculturation orientation and well-being: multigroup comparison models

societal as well as the ethnic minority group characteristics into account. It was assumed that both are important moderators when it comes to the relationship between acculturation orientations and well-being. Data indicate that assumptions are in part supported and, in addition, are interwoven. The study suggests that not all acculturation orientations are linked to well-being in the same way. Furthermore, results indicate that although there seems to be a stable relation of acculturation and well-being across countries, certain groups in certain contexts show unique relations. In the subsequent sections, each hypothesis will be discussed in detail.

With regard to Hypotheses 1 it can be stated that the four different ethnic minority groups do indeed differ in their preference for a particular acculturation orientation, however, not always as was expected. It was assumed that Turkish migrants to Germany would prefer to separate. This assumption could be confirmed. Furthermore, it was found that FSU immigrants to Israel most often showed the integration orientation. Again, this result confirmed our expectations.

However, contrary to expectations FSU immigrants to Germany most often reported the separation orientation, like their Turkish peers, instead of the expected integration orientation. At first glance this result seems astonishing: FSU immigrants to Germany are granted numerous advantages other ethnic minority groups immigrating to Germany are not granted: They, in their vast majority, automatically gain German citizenship when arriving in Germany due to their German ancestry. Also, in contrast to other immigrant groups, FSU immigrants to Germany often already possess rudimentary German language skills—the most important prerequisite to participate in the host society. Therefore, why do FSU migrant adolescents not identify with the German host society? One of the main reasons seems to be that the younger *Aussiedler* generations often feel attached to their Russian rather than their German heritage. This is due to the fact that after the oppression of the *Aussiedler* by Russians had ended (some time after the Second World War) a harmonization between Russians and *Aussiedler* took place. As a consequence, friendships and relationships between *Aussiedler* and Russians became more common. The children of "quasi-binational" (*Aussiedler*-Russian) marriages often strongly identify with their Russian heritage. Often Russian is the main language spoken at home and the norms and values in these families are coined by a strong Russian influence—which means that they are rather collectivistic as well as paternalistic. Strobl and Kühnel (2000), for example, found that when compared to German adolescents, *Aussiedler* had a more traditional understanding of gender roles. Also, in our sample, analyses not reported here showed that Russian immigrant adolescents emphasize tradition as well as conformity values significantly more strongly compared to their native German peers. Self-direction in turn was significantly more valued in the German sample.

These differences in values lead to differences between Russian immigrant and native German adolescents that are sometimes not easy to overcome: Hibert (2005), for example, notes that regarding peer contacts and friendships the contacts of *Aussiedler* are to a great extent focused on group interests and thus differ from the interests and peer contacts of German youth. Given the fact that *Aussiedler* often live in neighborhoods that are mostly inhabited by other *Aussiedler* families (Hibert, 2005), they often have a circle of friends consisting only of other *Aussiedler* (Dietz and Roll, 1998). This development is further amplified by discriminating attitudes *Aussiedler* adolescents sometimes have to face by their German peers. In 2006, the Shell Youth Study found that 30 per cent of the surveyed sample stated that they would not like to live next to an *Aussiedler* family (Schneekloth, 2006).

Thus, *Aussiedler* adolescents often find themselves in a country they do not identify with in a society where a considerable percentage of people hold discriminatory attitudes against them. Seen from this perspective it is not surprising that they mainly hold a separation orientation.

The other ethnic minority group that prefers a different acculturation orientation than expected is the group of the Israeli Arabs. It was hypothesized that these adolescents would mostly show a separation orientation. Arab Israelis, however, also state a rather strong sense of identification with Israel as a state, which results in an integrated acculturation orientation. It seems rather surprising that the Arab minority adolescents exhibit a strong Israeli identity given the fact that they have suffered decades of low socioeconomic status, as well as discrimination, and that—most importantly—they do not fit into the picture of Israel as a Zionist-Jewish state. This bicultural identification of the Arab Israeli adolescents can be interpreted in the way that Ghanem (2001) described: The Arab minority perceives itself as a firm part of the Israeli society and claims its rights as an equally recognized group within the state. They perceive themselves as Israelis, but as a distinct subgroup in the higher order group of Israelis—the *Arab* Israelis. This enables them to be attached to the country and at the same time remain unique and separate from its Zionist-Jewish self-definition. The Arab community in Israel has established a functional system of political and social institutions forwarding their aspiration for recognition as a minority group in Israel. According to Ghanem, these aspects make a national identification possible despite "...the ethnic character of the country" (Ghanem, 2001, p. 7).

The second hypothesis assumed that individual acculturation orientations relate to well-being in such a way that integration is associated with the highest and marginalization with the lowest well-being. Separation and assimilation were, in line with Berry (e.g., Berry et al., 2002), supposed to relate less strongly to well-being. These assumptions were confirmed: Integration was indeed positively associated with well-being among all ethnic minority groups. Also, a marginalization orientation was associated with lower well-being. Separation as well as assimilation were generally rather unrelated to well-being. Assuming a positive relationship between integration and well-being, a significantly negative relation between marginalization and well-being, and separation as well as assimilation to score in between, this was to be expected. These two acculturation orientations do not seem to offer as many resources for well-being as the integration orientation. This seems logical when considering that in contrast to integration, both separation and assimilation provide individuals with resources of only one cultural context. So the motto better safe than sorry seems to fit here literally.

Under Hypothesis 3 we expected that the relation of acculturation orientations and well-being would be different among the four minority groups. We assumed that for immigrants from the Former Soviet Union to both Israel and Germany, assimilation and integration have more potential for a positive well-being, compared to Turkish migrants in Germany and the Arab minority in Israel. This assumption rested on the fact that the state policies of the two countries much more easily enable FSU immigrants in both countries to feel attached to the host society. Separation in turn was hypothesized to have more positive effects for the Turkish immigrants to Germany and the Arab Israeli citizens, since this attitude is what the host society expects them to show. For FSU immigrants to Germany and Israel, separation was assumed to be less positively or even negatively related to well-being, since Israel and Germany put a certain pressure on these groups to participate in the host society. However, our data only partially support this hypothesis. Multi-group comparisons indicated that the interrelation of acculturation orientations and well-being was rather similar across all German groups. In Israel however, a difference was found: For Russian immigrants to Israel separation had a negative effect on life satisfaction. This finding is interesting, considering the fact that there still is an ongoing debate in the Israeli society whether FSU immigrants integrate or separate. Horenczyk and Ben-Shalom (2006) summarize studies that show both the Israeli identity as well as the Russian identity being related to well-being, whereas other studies found that it is only the Israeli identity. Possibly, the Israeli identity is more crucial for life satisfaction. To be attached only to the Russian heritage does not fit with the expectation of the majority society. Hence, if individuals of this group actually separate, then they are likely to face criticism.

Thus, results indicate that although it seems to a certain (if only small) extent relevant what a society expects from an individual and in what ways it defines citizenship, still the bicultural orientation is most essential for well-being. This finding seems to be universal across ethnic groups and contexts.

Strength and Limitations

One of the major strength of the present study lies in the large and varied sample. Besides comparing adolescents from various immigrant groups the study also explores the validity of the present hypotheses regarding a non-migrant ethnic minority group: Arab Israelis. Furthermore, two national contexts—Germany and Israel—are being taken into account, allowing to examine the influence the national context has on acculturation and well-being of ethnic minority group members. Regarding measures it is a strength of the present study to operationalize well-being with two measures: self-esteem and life satisfaction. By doing so a wider spectrum of the multi-faceted construct well-being was taken into account.

Regarding limitations of the present study it is important to mention that—as is the case in many studies—data are cross-sectional and for that reason results cannot directly indicate causal processes. Furthermore, our measure of acculturation focused on identification—an aspect of acculturation that is thought to play a central role for well-being in adolescence. Nevertheless, other aspects of acculturation, such as attitudes and behaviors, are not included and will be important to measure in this context in future research. Also, it cannot be ruled out that variables not assessed in the present study influenced individuals' acculturation orientations, their well-being, as well as the relation between the two in the chosen national contexts. From a methodological point of view, it needs to be mentioned that our measures of well-being included statements with a positive wording, meaning that a high agreement indicates high well-being. We chose to focus on positively-worded items because of the problems associated with negatively-worded items (e.g., overlap with depression measures, see for example Greenberger, Chen, Dmitrieva, and Farruggia, 2003).

When talking about acculturation orientations it has to be kept in mind that statements about preferred acculturation orientations of certain groups depend—at least to some extent—on the methodological approach with which they are measured. In the chapter by Daniel, Benish Weisman, Knafo, and Boehnke (in the present volume), which reports data from the same study, preference of acculturation orientations is assessed using a simpler median-split technique in the analyses of variance presented there. Here a Euclidian-distance measure was utilized, because the analytic strategy called for continuous interval-level variables. Slight differences in the assessment of acculturation preferences among the *Aussiedler* in Germany are owed to the differences in analytic strategies used in the two accounts.

A question that often remains in cross-cultural research is, "What is it that makes the difference?" From a methodological point of view, one needs to ask, "Can aspects such as culture or context be measured and therefore tested thoroughly?" (see e.g., Rohner, 1984). This leads to another rather open question: "What does ingroup identification and well-being mean in each of the groups under scrutiny?" Do the same levels of, for example, self-esteem and life satisfaction indicate the same level of psychological well-being in all groups? Although the used measures have been widely and successfully used cross-culturally the possibility remains that culture-specific normative differences to a certain extent affected participants' answers. Thus, in the four groups, stating a certain degree of ingroup identification, self-esteem or life satisfaction can to some extent be a social desirable and normative behavior. As a consequence the influence of interculturally different social norms regarding the measures used in the present research may have influenced the results to a certain extent.

Concluding Remarks

The research documented in this chapter has given new insights into the relationship between acculturation orientations and well-being by taking into account the ethnic minority group as well as the national context. Across all ethnic as well as societal contexts it was found that it is most beneficial for an immigrant adolescent's well-being to hold an integration acculturation orientation. Per se this result is not new.

However, contrary to the previous literature it was found in this study that not all acculturation orientations relate to well-being to the same extent. In Germany assimilation and separation were completely unrelated to this variable. In Israel correlations could be found but effect sizes were small. Thus results indicate (if only slightly) that certain acculturation orientations can relate differently to well-being, which is, in turn, to some extent dependent on the context. Consequently, it is argued here that it is of utmost importance in acculturation research to take into account the context, to not generalize results and theories overhastily.

References

Alba, R. (2005). Bright vs. blurred boundaries: Second generation assimilation and exclusion in France, Germany, and the United States. *Ethnic and Racial Studies, 28*(1), 20-49.

Al-Haj, M. (2002). Identity patterns among immigrants from the Former Soviet Union in Israel: Assimilation vs. ethnic formation. *International Migration, 40*, 49-70.

Al-Haj, M. (2004). *Immigration and ethnic formation in a deeply divided society: The case of the 1990s immigrants from the Former Soviet Union in Israel.* Leiden: Brill.

Ali, A. M. (2009). Acculturation and the subjective well-being of Somali immigrants in the United States: An explanatory mixed methods investigation. *Dissertation Abstracts International Section A: Humanities and Social Sciences, 69*(11-A), 4520.

Arbuckle, J. L. (2005). *Amos 6.0 user's guide.* Chicago: SPSS Inc.

Arends-Toth, J., and van de Vijver, F. J. R. (2006a). Issues in the conceptualization and assessment of acculturation. In M. H. Bornstein and L. R. Cote (Eds.), *Acculturation and parent-child relationships: Measurement and development* (pp. 33-62.). Mahwah, NJ: Lawrence Erlbaum Associates.

Arends-Tóth, J., and Van de Vijver, F. J. R. (2006b). Assessment of psychological acculturation. In D. L. Sam and J. W. Berry (Eds.), *The Cambridge Handbook of Acculturation Psychology* (pp.142-160). Cambridge: Cambridge University Press.

Berry, J. W. and Kim, U. (1988). Acculturation and mental health. In P.R. Dasen, J. W. Berry, and N. Sartorius (Eds.), *Health and Cross-Cultural Psychology: Toward Application* (pp. 207-236). London: Sage.

Berry, J. W., Poortinga, Y. H., Segall, M. H., and Dasen, P. R. (2002). *Cross-Cultural Psychology: Research and Applications* (2nd ed.). New York: Cambridge University Press.

Berry, J. W., Trimble, J. E., and Olmedo, E., L. (1986). Assessment of acculturation. In W. J. Lonner and J. W. Berry (Eds.), *Field methods in cross-cultural research* (pp. 291-324). Thousand Oaks, CA: Sage Publications.

Böttiger, H. (2005). *Migration in Deutschland* [Migration in Germany]. Göttingen: Sierke.

Bourhis, R. Y., Moise, L. C., Perreault, S., and Senecal, S. (1997). Towards an interactive acculturation model: A social psychological approach. *International Journal of Psychology, 32*(6), 369-386.

Daniel, E., Benish Weisman, M., Knafo, A., and Boehnke, K. (2014). Personal and culture-dependent values as part of minority adolescent identity. In R. K. Silbereisen, Y. Shavit, and P. Tietzmann (Eds.), *The Challenges of Diaspora Migration: Interdisciplinary Perspectives on Israel and Germany* (this volume). Farnham: Ashgate.

Diener, E., Emmons, R. A., Larsen, R. J., and Griffin, S. (1985). The Satisfaction With Life Scale. *Journal of Personality Assessment, 49,* 71-75.

Dietz, B., and Roll, B. (1998). *Jugendliche Aussiedler—Porträt einer Zuwanderergeneration* [Adolescent Aussiedler—portrait of a migrant generation]. Frankfurt am Main: Campus Verlag.

Dukes, R. L., and Martinez, R. (1994). The impact of ethgender on self-esteem among adolescents. *Adolescence, 29,* 105-115.

Erikson, E. H. (1993). *Identität und Lebenszyklus: Drei Aufsätze* [Identity and life cycle: Selected papers]. Frankfurt am Main: Suhrkamp.

Farruggia, S. P., Chen, C., Greenberger, E., Dmitrieva, J., and Macek, P. (2004). Adolescent self-esteem in cross-cultural perspective: Testing measurement equivalence and a mediation model. *Journal of Cross-Cultural Psychology, 35,* 719-733.

Ghanem, A. (2001). *The Palestinian-Arab minority in Israel 1948-2000: A political study*. Albany, New York: Suny Press.

Giang, M. T., and Wittig, M. A. (2006). Implications of adolescent's acculturation strategies for personal and collective self-esteem. *Cultural Diversity and Ethnic Minority Psychology, 12*(4), 725-739.

Greenberger, E., Chen, C., Dmitrieva, J., and Farruggia, S. P. (2003). Item-wording and the dimensionality of the Rosenberg Self-Esteem Scale: Do they matter? *Personality and Individual Differences, 35,* 1241-1254.

Hibert, O. (2005). Junge Aussiedler in der Bundesrepublik Deutschland: Wie Integration gelingen kann [Young Aussiedler in the Federal Republic of Germany: How integration can work]. In K. Feld, J. Freise, and A. Müller (Eds.), *Mehrkulturelle Identität im Jugendalter*. Münster: Lit. Verlag.

Hu, L., and Bentler, P. M. (1999). Cutoff criteria for fit indexes in covariance structure analysis: Conventional criteria versus new alternatives. *Structural Equation Modeling, 6*(1), 1-55.

Horenczyk, G., and Ben-Shalom, U. (2006). Acculturation in Israel. In D. L. Sam and J. W. Berry (Eds.), *Cambridge Handbook of Acculturation Psychology* (pp. 294-310). Cambridge: Cambridge University Press.

Hutnik, N. (1991). *Ethnic Minority Identity*. Oxford: Clarendon Press.

Lachance-Grzela, M., and Bouchard, G. (2009). The well-being of cohabiting and married couples during pregnancy: Does pregnancy planning matter? *Journal of Social and Personal Relationships 26*(2-3), 141-159.

Libran, E. C. (2006). Personality dimensions and subjective well-being. *The Spanish Journal of Psychology, 9*(1), 38-44.

Liebman, C., and Don-Yehiya, E. (1983). *Civil religion in Israel. Traditional Judaism and political culture in the Jewish state.* Berkeley: University of California Press.

McCallum, R. C., and Austin, J. T. (2000). Applications of structural equation modeling in psychological research. *Annual Review of Psychology, 51*, 201-226.

Metz, H.-C. (1990). *Israel: A country study.* Washington, DC: Federal Research Division, Library of Congress.

Oishi, S., Diener, E. F., Lucas, R. E., and Suh, E. M. (1999). Cross-cultural variations in predictors of life satisfaction: Perspectives from needs and values. *Personality and Social Psychology Bulletin, 25*, 980-990.

Pavot, W., and Diener, E. (1993). Review of the Satisfaction With Life Scale. *Psychological Assessment, 5,* 164-172.

Phinney, J. S., Chavira, V., and Williamson, L. (1992). Acculturation attitudes and self-esteem among high school and college students. *Youth and Society, 23*(2), 299-312.

Rabinowitz, D. (2001). The Palestinian citizens of Israel. The concept of trapped minority and the discourse of transnationalism in anthropology. *Ethnic and Racial Studies, 24*(1), 64-85.

Roccas, S., Sagiv, L., Schwartz, S., Halevy, N., and Eidelson, R. (2008). Toward a unifying model of identification with groups: Integrating theoretical perspectives. *Personality and Social Psychology Review, 12*(3), 280-306.

Rohner, R. P. (1984). Toward a conception of culture for cross-cultural psychology. *Journal of Cross-Cultural Psychology, 15,* 111-139.

Rosenberg, M. (1965). *Society and adolescent self image.* Princeton, NJ: Princeton University Press.

Rosenberg, M. (1979). *Conceiving the self.* New York: Basic Books.

Rosenthal, D. (2005). *The Israelis: Ordinary people in an extraordinary land.* New York: Free Press.

Sam, D. L., Vedder, P., Ward, C., and Horenczyk, G. (2006). Psychological and sociocultural adaptation of immigrant youth. In J. W. Berry, J. S. Phinney, D. L. Sam, and P. Vedder (Eds.), *Migrant youth in cultural transition: Acculturation, identity, and adaptation across national contexts* (pp. 117-142). Mahwah, NJ: Lawrence Erlbaum Associates.

Schmitt, D. P., and Allik, J. (2005). Simultaneous administration of the Rosenberg Self-Esteem Scale in 53 nations: Exploring the universal and culture-specific features of global self-esteem. *Journal of Personality and Social Psychology, 89,* 623-642.

Schmitt-Rodermund, E. (1999). Geschichte der Aussiedlung—Deutsche in der ehemaligen Sowjetunion [History of evacuation—Germans in the Former Soviet Union]. In R. K. Silbereisen, E.-D. Lantermann, and E. Rodermund (Eds.), *Aussiedler in Deutschland* (pp. 51-57). Leske + Budrich: Oppladen.

Schneekloth, U. (2006). Politik und Gesellschaft: Einstellungen, Engagement, Bewältigungsprobleme [Politics and society: attitudes, commitment, coping problems]. In K. Hurrelmann and M. Albert (Eds.), *15. Shell Jugendstudie, Jugend 2006* (pp. 104-144). Frankfurt am Main: Fischer.

Sherer, M., and Karnieli-Miller, O. (2004). Aggression and violence among Jewish and Arab youth in Israel. *International Journal of Intercultural Relations, 28,* 93-109.

Statistisches Bundesamt Deutschland. *Personen mit Migrationshintergrund, methodische Erläuterungen* [Persons with migration background, methodological explanations]. Available at: http://www.destatis.de/jetspeed/ portal/cms/Sites/destatis/Internet/DE/Content/Statistiken/Bevoelkerung/ MigrationIntegration/Migrationshintergrund/Aktuell,templateId=renderPrint. psml [accessed: 2 November 2009].

Stendel, O. (1996). *The Arabs in Israel.* Brighton: Sussex Academic.

Strobl, R., and Kühnel, W. (2000). *Dazugehörig und ausgegrenzt—Analysen zu Integrationschancen junger Aussiedler* [Appendant and excluded—analyses of the integration chances of young Aussiedler]. Weinheim, München: Juventa Verlag.

Tsai, J. L., Ying, Y.-W., and Lee. P. A. (2000). The meaning of "being Chinese" and "being American". Variations among Chinese American young adults. *Journal of Cross-Cultural Psychology, 31*(3), 302-332.

Umaña-Taylor, A. J., Diversi, M., and Fine, M. A. (2002). Ethnic identity and self-esteem among Latino adolescents: Making distinctions among the Latino populations. *Journal of Adolescent Research, 17,* 303-327.

United Nations (2006). *Inernational Migration Report 2006: A global assessment.* Available at www.un.org/esa/population/publications/2006_MigrationRep/ part_one.pdf [accessed June 20th, 2009].

Vella-Brodrick, D. A., Park, N., and Peterson, C. (2009). Three ways to be happy: Pleasure, engagement, and meaning—findings from Australian and U.S. samples. *Social Indicators Research, 90*(2), 165-179.

Ward, C., Bochner, S., and Furnham, A. (2001). *The psychology of culture shock.* Hove: Routledge.

Williams, C. L., and Berry, J. W. (1991). Primary prevention of acculturative stress among refugees. *American Psychologist 46*(6), 632-641.

Wright, T. A., and Cropanzano, R. (2004). The role of psychological well-being in job performance: A fresh look at an age-old quest. *Organizational Dynamics, 33*(4), 338-351.

Zerubavel, Y. (1995). *Recovered roots, collective memory and the making of Israeli national transition.* Chicago: University of Chicago Press.

Chapter 6

Personal and Culture-Dependent Values as Part of Minority Adolescent Identity

Ella Daniel, Maya Benish-Weisman, Klaus Boehnke, and Ariel Knafo

Immigrants and minority members often face two or more cultures, and choose their level of adaption to, or adoption of, each culture (Berry, 1997, 2001). A core component of any culture is its prioritization of values (Schwartz, 2008). Immigrants and minority members learn diverging value hierarchies from their multiple cultures, and as a result, may hold a complex value system (Daniel et al., 2012).

In this chapter, we propose that immigrants and minority members hold contextualized value systems relevant to the values of the country of residence and of the ethnic-group. We investigate the value priorities of countries (Israel and Germany) and of ethnic-groups (former Soviet Union immigrants, Arab citizens of Israel, Turkish immigrants). We examine the relations between these modal group values and the contextualized values of group members. Last, we examine the interaction between the contextualized values and acculturation strategies. The research adds to the existing literature in its focus on acculturation in value priorities across contexts, and in its large cross cultural sample.

Defining Values

Values are abstract trans-situational concepts or beliefs, describing desirable end states and varying in importance, that serve as guiding principles in people's lives (Rokeach, 1973; Schwartz, 1992). Schwartz (1992) identified ten universal values that can be distinguished by the motivational content they express (Table 6.1). The values hold dynamic relations of conflicts and compatibilities among them: action in pursuit of each value has psychological, practical, and social consequences that may hinder or promote the pursuit of other values (Schwartz, 1992). The relations among values create a circular structure, in which conflicting values are positioned on opposing sides, while compatible values are adjacent (e.g., Schwartz and Rubel, 2005). The ten value types are organized into two dimensions of higher-order values. The first dimension opposes openness-to-change values (emphasizing independent thought and action), with conservation values (emphasizing preservation of stability and traditional

Table 6.1   Definitions of Schwartz's ten universal values

Tradition: Respect, commitment and acceptance of the costumes and ideas that one's culture or religion imposes on the individual.

Benevolence: Caring for the welfare of the others who are closely related to me.

Universalism: understanding, appreciation, tolerance and protection of the welfare of all people and of nature.

Self-direction: The need for independent thought and action

Stimulation: The need for diversity, aspiration for change and excitement.

Hedonism: Pleasure and sensual satisfaction of the self.

Achievement: Acquiring personal success through demonstrating competence according to social standards

Power: requisite for social status and thus gaining control and dominance over other people.

Security: The need for protection of safety, harmony and stability of the social structure and of the self.

Conformity: limiting actions and urges that might violate social expectations and norms.

---

practices, and submissive self-restriction). The second dimension contrasts self-enhancement values (emphasizing the pursuit of one's own relative success and dominance over others), with self-transcendence values (emphasizing care for the welfare of others and accepting all as equals; Schwartz, 1992).

Applying Values to Different Cultural Contexts

Values are an important aspect of the identity, as they define who one is, and are experienced as reflecting the individual's true, authentic self (Gecas, 1982). For that reason, an action guided by one's values is experiences as a product of choice and free will, unbound by external coercion (Hitlin, 2003; Verplanken and Holland, 2002).

The identity has multiple components, each carrying a unique and context-dependent content (Donahue et al., 1993; Sheldon et al., 1997; Turner et al., 1994). The components include a personal identity, describing what is unique to individuals, and distinguishes them from all others; and social identities, describing the social groups the individuals belong to, and what distinguishes these social groups from out-groups (Turner et al., 1987; Turner et al., 1994). Each individual can have a number of social identities (Roccas and Brewer, 2002), like immigrants, who often hold an ethnic identity, as well as a country of residence identity (Hong et al., 2000; LaFromboise, Coleman and Gerton, 1993).

Like other identity aspects, values differ in importance between interpersonal identities, such as a family member, a student and a friend; and between social identities, such as a national group member or an ethnic-group member (Daniel et al., 2012; Seligman and Katz, 1994; Stelzl and Seligman, 2009). Similarly, we hypothesize that different values will be stressed in relation with different social identities.

H_1 Value priorities will differ between the country context and the ethnic-group context.

However, past studies did not investigate the basis of value differences across contexts. The current study attempts to uncover this basis by examining the cultural factors that are related to values across contexts.

Cultural Factors Associated with Value Importance

Values are acquired through formal and informal socialization. Families, schools, youth movements, and other social institutions aspire to instill values to youngsters (Boehnke, Hadjar and Baier, 2007; Chatman, 1991; Halstead, 1996; Knafo and Schwartz, 2001). Values are conveyed to society members directly, but also through laws, norms, organizational practices, and the media (Bardi, Calogero and Mullen, 2008; Bourdieu, 1972; Markus and Kitayama, 1994). These values become part of the individuals' value priorities.

Generally speaking, most majority members live in a relatively homogenous environment, surrounded by people culturally similar to themselves (Kelly and Evans, 1995). Adolescents typically share characteristics such as race, religion, and socioeconomic status with their family, and usually also with their friends from the neighborhood and school (Roccas and Brewer, 2002). Consequently, important socialization agents that influence the individual's values are embedded in a uniform environment (Bronfenbrener, 1986). For that reason, adolescents who are a part of a majority culture learn a relatively coherent set of values across contexts of their lives, when compared to minority members.

Immigrants and minority group members do not face such a consistent structure of the surrounding social world. The socialization agents they encounter are embedded in a multicultural environment, influenced by the ethnic, as well as the majority culture (Bronfenbrenner, 1986; Szapocznick and Kurtines, 1993). The family, in many cases, is heavily influenced by the ethnic culture. The school, on the other hand, often represents the majority culture. Therefore, minority adolescents are exposed to multiple value systems arising from the important agents in their lives, and their values in the context of the country and ethnic contexts can be influenced by these different values. We, thus, secondly hypothesize

H_2 *Values in different contexts will reflect the modal values of the respective life contexts.*

H_{2a} *Values in the context 'country' will reflect the modal values of the country of residence. The two migrant groups in Germany will have similar values in the context 'country', as will the two groups in Israel.*

H_{2b} *Values in the context 'ethnic-group' will reflect the modal values of the ethnic-group. The two groups of FSU immigrants will have similar values in the ethnic-group context; Turkish immigrants to Germany and Arab Israelis both come from Middle Eastern embedded cultures and may have similar values in the 'ethnic-group' context.*

Values and Acculturation

The identification with cultural values is an active process of choice, in which group members learn values and decide whether they wish to accept them. Among immigrants, this acceptance may be dependent upon their attitudes toward each of the cultures.

In the acculturation process, immigrants and minority group members form attitudes regarding two fundamental issues: to what extent should one adopt aspects of the majority culture, and to what extent should one maintain aspects of the culture of origin (Berry, 1997, 2001; Bourhis et al., 1997)? If the answers to the questions are dichotomized, four acculturation orientations may be discerned: Integration (valuing both dimensions), assimilation (valuing cultural adoption, but not cultural maintenance), separation (valuing cultural maintenance without cultural adoption), and marginalization (valuing neither dimension; Berry, 1997, 2001).

Preferences for cultural adoption and maintenance can vary across life domains or situations. One can, for example, seek economic assimilation at work but social integration among friends and acquaintances (Arends-Tóth and Van de Vijver, 2006). An important acculturation domain is group identification—minority group members can choose their level of identification with the (new) country of residence (cultural adoption) as well as with the ethnic-group of belonging (cultural maintenance).

We hypothesize that acculturation orientations, as assessed vis-à-vis group identification, can lead to different patterns of value contextualization. Variations in value importance between contexts will be reported by adolescents who identify with one culture only. In these cases, the adolescents will see the values of the cultures as highly contradicting, and therefore feel obligated to choose one group to identify with. Coherence between contexts will be reported by adolescents who identify with the two groups. These adolescents will see the values of the groups as complimentary, or succeed in creating integration among the values, and therefore can identify with the two groups without feeling torn between values.

H₃ Acculturation orientation in the identification domain will be related to the contextualization of values. A pattern of choosing one identification will be related to contextualized values, while a pattern of choosing two identifications will be related to similar value priorities across contexts.

The Cultural Groups Studied

We now turn to a description of the four cultural groups participating in this study. The four groups included former Soviet Union (FSU) immigrants to Israel, Arab citizens of Israel, FSU immigrants to Germany, and Turkish immigrants to Germany. These groups vary on several important aspects. They include three immigrant groups, and one minority group. They include commonalities and differences in country of residence (Israel versus Germany) and areas of origin (FSU versus the Middle East). This variation is crucial for answering the outlined research questions, and understanding how culture guides value importance.

The two groups immigrating from the FSU typically were repatriates who left the FSU following the fall of the Iron Curtain, starting 1989. In both Israel and Germany, they are not perceived as mere newcomers, but as immigrants who come back to the land of their ancestors. Israel and Germany actively supported repatriation in numerous ways: granting immediate citizenship, social security and material support (Jasinskaja-Lathi et al., 2003; Titzmann et al., 2011). In spite of the common ethnic origin with the majority group, the immigrants have turned out to be culturally different from the majority society, and experienced some difficulties in acculturation (Dietz, 2000; Horowitz, 2005; Jasinskaja-Lathi et al., 2003). Today, immigrants having migrated to Israel from the FSU since 1990 form 11.2 percent of the Israeli population (Israeli Central Statistical Bureau, 2006). FSU immigrants to Germany are 2.5 percent of the German population (Federal Bureau of Statistics, 2007).

Arab citizens of Israel are an ethnic and cultural minority who form 20.2 percent of the Israeli population (Israeli Statistical Bureau, 2009). They are divided between two main religions (Muslims: 80 percent, Christians: 20 percent). The Arab citizens of Israel live mostly in homogenous Arab villages or in segregated neighborhoods in mixed cities (Rabinowitz, 2001). Israel grants its Arab citizens equal civil rights. Nevertheless, Arab citizens often face discrimination in many spheres of life, such as resource allocation and land ownership. Most Palestinian citizens of Israel see themselves as part of the Palestinian nation, but also integrate in the Israeli society (Hareven, 2002).

Most immigrants from Turkey arrived in Germany as guest workers between the 1960s and the 1980s. Later, migrants entered Germany by way of family reunion, or as refugees and asylum seekers (Euwals et al., 2007). Today, citizens of Turkey form 3 percent of the German population (Federal Bureau of Statistics, 2007). Turkish immigrants are a low status group of immigrants in Germany, economically and in public opinions (Brüß, 2005; Vedder et al., 2007). In contrast to all other groups studied here, Turkish immigrants arrived in Germany on a temporary basis, and expected to eventually return home. As a consequence, they retained their ethnic identity for many years, and were encouraged to segregate (Vedder, Sam and Liebkind, 2007). Only relatively few Turkish immigrants hold German citizenship, even into third generation of residence in Germany, due to a strict policy of naturalization in Germany (Diehl and Blohm, 2003).

More details regarding the studied groups can be found in the Moellering et al. chapter in this volume.

The Current Study

In the current study, we will measure adolescents' personal values, and use their aggregate to understand which values are important to the national and ethnic-group studied. We will also measure values in the contexts 'country' and 'ethnic-group, and examine the differences between the contexts, and their relations to the modal values in the groups. Finally, the acculturation strategy of the adolescents will be measured to investigate possible relations to value importance in the contexts.

Method

Participants

Study participants were adolescents from the four ethnic-groups described above, in two age groups; early-adolescents (5th and 6th graders), and mid-adolescents (10th and 11th graders).

The immigrant adolescents immigrated themselves, or were born to a mother or a father who emigrated from the FSU or Turkey. Arab citizens of Israel and their parents were born in Israel. Descriptive information about the sample, including number of participants, mean age, sex distribution, immigration generation distribution and time since immigration is presented in Table 6.2. The questionnaires were collected between the months October 2007 and July 2009 in Israel, and October 2007 and July 2008 in Germany.

Procedure

We distributed questionnaires in school classes to all adolescents of the appropriate age groups. In Israel, we sampled schools randomly from the list of schools in

Table 6.2   Descriptive statistics of the sample

Country	Ethnicity	N	Age		Percent of first generation	First generation: time since immigration		Percent of males
			Mean	SD		Mean	SD	
Israel	FSU immigrants	498	14.74	2.1	61.6%	10.26	3.16	52.4%
	Arab Citizens	410	13.96	2.46	—	—	—	38.5%
Germany	FSU immigrants	400	13.63	2.51	57.9%	8.97	3.82	48%
	Turkish immigrants	538	12.86	2.51	9.8%	8.68	3.33	45.9%

two major urban centers, in towns populated by a large percentage of immigrants (Israeli statistical bureau, 2001), and in Arab villages and towns. In Germany, we approached all schools in the State of Bremen and in the close surroundings in the State of Lower Saxony. Of the schools approached, 35 percent of the schools agreed to participate.

Trained experimenters distributed the questionnaires to adolescents whose parents consented to participation. They explained the instructions of the questionnaires and answered questions. Questionnaires were anonymous, and participation was voluntary. The study was approved by the pertinent local ethical review boards in the two countries.

Measures

Personal values Personal values were assessed using the Portrait Values Questionnaire (PVQ 25; Schwartz et al., 2001), a measure suitable for use with adolescents (Knafo and Schwartz, 2003; Schwartz et al., 2001). Each portrait describes a person's goals, aspirations, or wishes, pointing implicitly at the importance of a single value. For example, the portrait "It is important to him to be rich. He wants to have a lot of money and expensive things," describes a person for whom power values are important.

Respondents indicated "How much like you is this person?" for each portrait. They checked one of six boxes labeled '*very much like me,*' '*like me,*' '*somewhat like me,*' '*a little like me,*' '*not like me,*' and '*not like me at all.*' Thus, respondents' own values were inferred from their self-reported similarity to people who are described in terms of particular values. The similarity judgments were transformed into a six-point numerical scale. Indexes for each value were computed by averaging all items measuring the value. In order to control for scale use, the scores were centered around each participant's mean, in a procedure recommended by Schwarz (1992).

Contextualized values   Contextualized values were measured by assessing the importance of values in different life contexts using the Values-in-Context Questionnaire (VICQ). The VICQ is an adaptation to life contexts of the Schwartz Value Survey (Schwartz, 1992). Each participant described the importance of his or her values in the context of the country of residence (Israeli or German), and in the context of the ethnic-group (Russian, Turkish, Arab).

In order to prevent fatigue effects during questionnaire filling, we chose to focus on four of the ten Schwartz (1992) value types. The values chosen represent four extremes of the two dimensions organizing Schwartz's structure of values. Each value was assessed using three items, chosen on the basis of their cross-cultural stability (Schwartz and Sagiv, 1995). The value items used for the value measurement were: Achievement (capable, ambitious, successful), self-direction (curious, creative, freedom), conformity (obedient, polite, self-discipline), and benevolence (honest, helpful, forgiving). Items were adapted to the country and ethnicity context. For example, the importance of the value of conformity was assessed in the country and the ethnic-group context, with the following items: "as an Israeli, it is important to me to be obedient", "as an Arab, it is important to me to be obedient".

The contexts were presented on different pages, and context and item order was balanced. The values were rated using a 6-point scale, ranging from '*very important to me*' to '*not at all important to me*'. Indexes for the values were computed by averaging all items measuring one value in the specific context. In order to control for scale use, the scores were centered around participants' mean answer in the context, across values. Adolescents were instructed to rate only the values relevant to groups they belonged to.

Acculturation orientations   Identification with country and ethnic-group was measured using the centrality-to-identity scale of the Identification Questionnaire (Roccas et al., 2008). The items were adapted to the contexts used in the current investigation. Exemplary items are: "Being a German is an important part of my identity", "It is important to me to view myself as Russian".

The centrality to the country and ethnic-group identity scores were split at the middle of the scale (3.5) and crossed, to create the four acculturation orientations. For example, integration orientation was defined by high centrality to identity of both the country and ethnic-group identity. Separation strategy was defined by high centrality to identity of the ethnic-group, but low centrality to identity of the country of residence.

Results

Personal Values

As a first step, we wanted to understand the cultural values of each ethnic-group. For that purpose, we compared the personal values of adolescents from the different groups. A Multivariate Analysis of Variance (MANOVA), in which we compared the 4 ethnic-groups as to the importance of the ten values, found a significant group effect for value importance, $F(30,5322) = 16.06, p <.01$. In nine of the ten values, there was a significant (p < .01) ethnic-group difference in the importance of values. Only in security values there was no difference between the ethnic-groups (Table 6.3).

The differences in personal value importance were guided by the membership in the origin culture, as well as the country culture. Conservation values (conformity and tradition) were more important to adolescents from Arab or Turkish ethnic-groups. Both groups originate from embedded cultures, which believe in the precedence of group interests over individual interests (Schwartz, 2008). In contrast, openness to change values (self-direction, stimulation, and to a lesser extent hedonism values) were more important to adolescents from FSU ethnic-group.

Self-transcendence values were more important to adolescents living in Germany, both from FSU and Turkish ethnic-groups. Achievement values were more important to both ethnic-groups in Israel, and especially to FSU immigrants to Israel. Power values were more important to FSU immigrants to Germany and Israel than to Arabs and Turkish immigrants. In general, it seems that ethnic culture was related to the level of openness to change versus conservation values. It was also related to the level of power values. The importance of self-transcendence and achievement values was related to the country of residence.

Description of Analyses

We compared value importance across contexts in separate two-factor (2 contexts X 4 values) repeated measures Analyses of Variance (ANOVA) for each cultural group. Next, we analyzed the frequencies of acculturation orientations in each group, to check which orientations were chosen by at least 10 percent of the adolescents (Table 6.4). Last, we conducted again the above mentioned repeated measures ANOVAs, this time for each group of adolescents choosing an acculturation orientation in the ethnic-group. The results of the analyses will be reported by ethnic-group, in order to describe each cultural context.

FSU Immigrants to Israel

The main effect of value importance using the VICQ resembled the cultural differences in personal values $F(3,1068) = 22.86, p < .01$. Achievement values were found most important and conformity values least important in the country

Table 6.3 Means and standard deviations of values

Values	FSU Israel		Arabs Israel		FSU Germany		Turkish Germany		F	p	partial η^2
	Mean	SD	Mean	SD	Mean	SD	Mean	SD			
Conformity	3.44a	0.85	3.93b	0.71	3.64c	0.73	3.82b	0.73	36.79	<0.01	0.06
Benevolence	4.22a	0.64	4.30ac	0.69	4.38bc	0.70	4.42b	0.68	8.57	<0.01	0.01
Universalism	4.06a	0.73	4.16ab	0.65	4.20b	0.74	4.26b	0.73	7.18	<0.01	0.01
Self-direction	4.36a	0.62	4.14b	0.66	4.27a	0.61	4.11b	0.63	15.71	<0.01	0.03
Stimulation	4.22a	0.94	4.05b	0.9	4.16ab	0.92	4.00b	0.92	5.54	<0.01	0.01
Hedonism	4.35a	0.93	4.13b	0.92	4.53c	0.85	4.39ac	0.79	14.54	<0.01	0.02
Achievement	4.51a	0.66	4.19b	0.67	3.94c	0.85	3.94c	0.81	60.62	<0.01	0.09
Power	3.34a	1.17	2.6b	1.39	3.18a	1.07	2.82b	1.24	31.78	<0.01	0.05
Security	4.01	0.98	4.09	0.95	4.03	0.92	4.12	0.99	1.34	<0.26	0.00
Tradition	3.24a	1.03	4.02b	0.91	3.44c	1.04	3.82d	0.91	60.23	<0.01	0.09

Note: Means having the same subscript are not significantly different at p<.01 in the Turkey honesty significant difference comparison.

Table 6.4   Frequency of acculturation strategies

		Integration		Assimilation		Separation		Marginalization	
Country	Ethnic-group	N	%	N	%	N	%	N	%
Israel	FSU Immigrants	219	62.39%	42	11.97%	77	21.94%	13	3.70%
	Arab Citizens	218	70.78%	16	5.19%	67	21.75%	7	2.27%
Germany	FSU Immigrants	105	44.68%	24	10.21%	90	38.30%	16	6.81%
	Turkish Immigrants	95	46.80%	4	1.97%	98	48.28%	6	2.96%

and ethnic contexts. No context main effect was found $F(1,356) = .98$, $p = .32$. There was also no interaction between value importance and context $F(3,1068) = 1.71$, $p = .16$ (Means and standard deviation overall and in every acculturation orientation are presented in Table 6.5).

FSU immigrants to Israel chose mainly an integration orientation to acculturation, Some FSU immigrants to Israel chose separation and assimilation orientations (Table 6.4). Among adolescents who chose a separation acculturation orientation we found a significant interaction between value content and context (Table 6.6, Figure 6.1a). These adolescents endorsed achievement values more in the ethnic context than in the country context, in contrast to the modal values of their group and hypothesis 2. They also supported benevolence values more in this context, in line with the modal values of their group. They supported self-direction values more in the country context than in the ethnic context, in contrast to the modal values of their group. No interaction effect was found among adolescents supporting integration or assimilation orientations.

Arab Citizens of Israel

The main effect of value importance using the VICQ resembled the cultural differences in personal values $F(3,945) = 22.74$, $p < .01$. Achievement values were found most important and conformity values least important in both contexts. No context main effect was found $F(1,315) = 1.10$, $p = .29$. However, a significant interaction was found between value importance and context $F(3,945) = 4.27$, $p < .01$. Arab citizens of Israel reported lower importance of self-direction values in the ethnic context than in the country context, and lower importance of benevolence values in the country context than in the ethnic context, thus demonstrating

Table 6.5 Means and standard deviations of values among FSU immigrants to Israel

Values		General		Integration		Separation		Assimilation	
		Country	Ethnic-group	Country	Ethnic-group	Country	Ethnic-group	Country	Ethnic-group
Achievement	Mean	4.14	4.19	4.15	4.17	4.16	4.29	4.11	4.10
	SD	0.52	0.42	0.48	0.39	0.60	0.45	0.59	0.47
Conformity	Mean	3.98	3.98	4.01	3.99	3.82	3.93	4.12	4.07
	SD	0.51	0.42	0.42	0.37	0.66	0.43	0.50	0.54
Benevolence	Mean	3.87	3.87	3.88	3.89	3.85	3.82	3.86	3.85
	SD	0.54	0.51	0.49	0.46	0.68	0.59	0.48	0.51
Self-direction	Mean	4.01	3.96	3.96	3.96	4.18	3.96	3.91	3.98
	SD	0.52	0.49	0.42	0.43	0.66	0.58	0.62	0.56

Table 6.6   ANOVA of context*value*identification with the ethnic-group

Strategy	Effect	FSU Israel			Arabs Israel			FSU Germany			Turkish Germany		
		F	p<	partial η2	F	p<	partial η2	F	p<	partial η2	F	p<	partial η2
Integration	Context	0.15	0.70	0.00	1.34	0.25	0.01	0.90	0.35	0.01	2.53	0.12	0.03
	Value	16.58	0.00	0.07	15.77	0.00	0.07	18.45	0.00	0.15	7.91	0.00	0.08
	Context*Value	0.20	0.89	0.00	1.96	0.12	0.01	9.03	0.00	0.08	28.92	0.00	0.24
Separation	Context	2.19	0.14	0.03	2.59	0.11	0.04	0.34	0.56	0.00	0.73	0.40	0.01
	Value	7.69	0.00	0.09	5.36	0.00	0.08	10.26	0.00	0.10	11.65	0.00	0.11
	Context*Value	3.51	0.02	0.04	3.29	0.02	0.05	4.87	0.00	0.05	17.65	0.00	0.15
Assimilation	Context	1.00	0.32	0.02				1.00	0.33	0.04			
	Value	2.10	0.10	0.05				6.65	0.00	0.22			
	Context*Value	0.31	0.82	0.01				8.94	0.00	0.28			

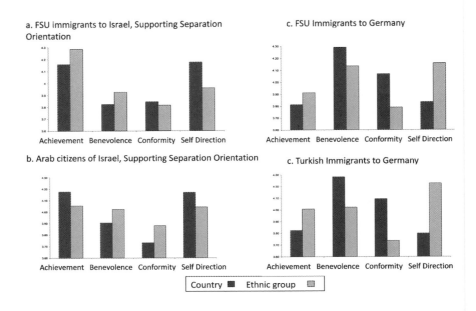

Figure 6.1   The importance of contextualized values across ethnic-groups

contextualized values that are similar to the modal values in the group (in line with hypothesis 2; means and standard deviation overall and in every acculturation orientation are presented in Table 6.7).

Arab citizens of Israel supported integration and separation acculturation orientations (Table 6.4). An interaction was found between value importance and context only among the adolescents endorsing a separation orientation, that was similar to the interaction reported for the overall cultural group (Table 6.6, Figure 6.1b). No such interaction was found among adolescents supporting an integration orientation.

FSU Immigrants to Germany

The main effect of value importance using the VICQ resembled the cultural differences in personal values $F(3,717) = 35.12$, $p < .01$. Benevolence values were found most important and achievement values least important. No context main effect was found $F(1,237) = 1.97$, $p = .16$. However, a significant interaction effect emerged between value importance and context $F(3,711) = 22.36$, $p < .01$, in line with hypothesis 2 (Figure 6.1c). FSU immigrants to Germany valued self-direction values more, and conformity values less, in the ethnic context than in the country context. They valued benevolence values more, and achievement values less, in the country context than in ethnic context (Means and standard deviations overall and in every acculturation orientation are presented in Table 6.8).

Table 6.7 Means and standard deviations of values among Arab citizens of Israel

Values		General		Integration		Separation	
		Country	Ethnic-group	Country	Ethnic-group	Country	Ethnic-group
Achievement	Mean	4.17	4.11	4.17	4.12	4.18	4.05
	SD	0.58	0.40	0.55	0.39	0.67	0.44
Conformity	Mean	3.91	4.00	3.94	4.01	3.91	4.02
	SD	0.59	0.45	0.59	0.43	0.56	0.45
Benevolence	Mean	3.82	3.87	3.84	3.86	3.73	3.88
	SD	0.55	0.40	0.53	0.38	0.62	0.45
Self-direction	Mean	4.09	4.02	4.05	4.00	4.17	4.04
	SD	0.57	0.45	0.56	0.42	0.53	0.49

Table 6.8   Means and standard deviations of values among FSU immigrants to Germany

Values		General		Integration		Separation		Assimilation	
		Country	Ethnic-group	Country	Ethnic-group	Country	Ethnic-group	Country	Ethnic-group
Achievement	Mean	3.81	3.91	3.83	3.95	3.83	3.92	3.73	3.83
	SD	0.57	0.46	0.53	0.38	0.56	0.46	0.61	0.62
Conformity	Mean	4.29	4.13	4.27	4.11	4.23	4.12	4.49	4.22
	SD	0.52	0.41	0.45	0.36	0.49	0.42	0.70	0.56
Benevolence	Mean	4.07	3.79	4.02	3.76	4.12	3.91	4.09	3.54
	SD	0.50	0.54	0.55	0.51	0.47	0.50	0.43	0.57
Self-direction	Mean	3.83	4.16	3.88	4.17	3.83	4.05	3.69	4.41
	SD	0.57	0.49	0.52	0.43	0.59	0.45	0.59	0.59

Table 6.9   Means and standard deviations of values among Turkish immigrants to Germany

Values		General		Integration		Separation	
		Country	Ethnic-group	Country	Ethnic-group	Country	Ethnic-group
Achievement	Mean	3.82	4.01	3.82	4.01	3.83	3.98
	SD	0.48	0.40	0.49	0.32	0.48	0.45
Conformity	Mean	4.28	4.02	4.25	4.07	4.29	4.02
	SD	0.54	0.43	0.56	0.36	0.52	0.42
Benevolence	Mean	4.09	3.74	4.18	3.72	4.03	3.70
	SD	0.45	0.57	0.46	0.44	0.43	0.67
Self-direction	Mean	3.80	4.23	3.75	4.21	3.84	4.27
	SD	0.58	0.40	0.59	0.38	0.54	0.42

FSU immigrants to Germany supported an integration, separation and assimilation acculturation orientations (Table 6.4). In contrast to hypothesis 3, a significant interaction (Table 6.6) between value importance and context was evident for adolescents of all acculturation orientations.

Turkish Immigrants to Germany

The main effect of value importance using the VICQ resembled the cultural differences in personal values $F(3,618) = 18.32, p < .01$). Benevolence values were found most important and achievement and conformity values least important. No context main effect was found, $F(1,206) = .09, p = .77$. However, a significant interaction was found between value importance and context, $F(3,618) = 40.86$, $p < .01$ (Figure 6.1d). In line with hypothesis 2, Turkish immigrants to Germany valued benevolence values more, and achievement values less, in the country than in the ethnic context. However, in contrast to hypothesis 2, they valued self-direction values more, and conformity values less, in the ethnic context than in the country context (means and standard deviations overall and in every acculturation orientation are presented in Table 6.9).

Turkish immigrants to Germany supported integration and separation acculturation orientations (Table 6.4). In contrast to hypothesis 3, a significant interaction (Table 6.6) between value importance and context was evident for adolescents supporting both acculturation orientations.

Discussion

Immigrants and minority members may negotiate conflicting cultural value systems in the process of acculturation. This study demonstrates the complexity of this process, by examining the similarities and differences in contextualized values between two countries and four ethnic-groups. We aggregated the values in each cultural group to gain an understanding of the modal values of the group. We then compared the values in the contexts of the ethnic-group and country of residence to these modal values. Thus, we could learn whether modal group values can be regarded as the source of values in a specific context.

Modal Group Values

The groups differed in their modal value priorities: conservation values were found characteristic of the Arab and Turkish groups, while openness to change values were found characteristic of immigrants from the FSU. These differences stand in line with known literature regarding cultural differences between Middle Eastern and FSU cultures, in which Middle Eastern cultures stress values of affiliation more than East European cultures (Schwartz, 2008). Power values were also important especially to immigrants from the FSU.

Values of self-transcendence were found most important to both German groups, while achievement values were found most important to both Israeli groups. Again, these differences stand in line with documented cultural differences, in which Western European groups value equality and social responsibility more than Israelis who value individual striving for success (Schwartz, 2008). This complex pattern of results shows that immigrants and minority groups adapt to certain cultural patterns of the majority society, while maintaining other patterns of their ethnic culture.

Values and Cultural Contexts

The main contribution of the current study is in studying values as part of a multi-faceted identity. In confirmation of the theory of contextualized values and Hypothesis 1, there was a significant interaction between the values and contexts in three of the cultural groups, indicating that immigrants and minority members value different values across contexts.

In general, values in the country aspect of identity were related to the modal values of the country of residence, while values in the ethnic-group aspect of identity were related to the modal values of the ethnic-group. Thus, the values prevalent in the culture may be internalized to create a context dependent value system.

As a striking exception, Turkish immigrants to Germany supported values that are not in line with the modal values in their group. In the ethnic-group context they supported self-direction and achievement values, while in the country context they supported conformity values. life as an immigrant pose a challenge of coping and succeeding in an unfamiliar environment, using a new language and behaving according to different norms. In order to succeed in such situation, one may need to use a different set of values. These values will be values of openness to change and self-enhancement. Turkish adolescents may consider their ethnic identity to be characterized not by the Turkish values, but by the values relevant to the immigrant role.

Acculturation Orientation and Values

The importance of addressing various nation-state contexts is exemplified by the finding that acculturation orientations were relevant to the context and value interactions among Israeli ethnic-groups only. For both FSU immigrants to Israel and Arab citizens of Israel, values differed by context only when adolescents endorsed a separation orientation. Adolescents who supported integration or assimilation orientations reported similar values across contexts. It may be that perceiving values as contradictory, the adolescents feel reluctant to identify with a new culture, and choose a separation orientation. In contrast, when perceiving values to be similar, adolescents feel free to identify with the majority culture, and adopt an integration or assimilation orientation.

In Germany, adolescents' acculturation orientation had no association with value importance across contexts. The difference between countries can result from the orientation of the majority society toward minorities. In Israel, the majority society supports assimilation orientation. Immigrants especially, and minority members to a lesser extent, are expected to identify with the Israeli nation and adopt its values and norms. In contrast, in Germany, a separation orientation is facilitated by the majority society (Jasinskaja-Lathi et al., 1993). In our results, a larger percentage of the German FSU immigrants chose the separation strategy than the Israeli FSU immigrants. In the Israeli reality, the choice of a separation orientation can carry a defiant meaning against the majority society. This meaning is absent in the German context. In Israel, such choice of strategy can stem from a strong sense of contradiction between the cultures. German adolescence who face a different environment, do not make similar choices.

Strengths and Limitations

The study utilized a large and varied sample. We have sampled schools randomly in Israel, and approached all schools in set parts of Germany. The large numbers of adolescents from each ethnic-group allowed us to draw conclusions with high confidence. The variety of cultural groups, including immigrants and minorities, from different cultural origins and destinations, makes the understanding of cultural effects possible.

Immigration research usually measures subjective perceptions of change in identifications, attitudes, behaviors, and values. Immigrants are requested to report their level of adaptation, as they perceive it. In contrast, in this study we studied actual adoption of contextualized values, by comparing values to the modal values of a group. Thus, the study added substantial information to the literature on value change following immigration.

The study employed questionnaires of values and identification. These self-report measures are vulnerable to multiple biases, including self-presentation and social desirability. Nonetheless, values are a subjective personal characteristic, and are not easily measured in any external way. Moreover, social desirability has been shown not to be a bias influencing the report of values, but a personality trait that is meaningfully related to value importance (Schwartz et al., 1997)

The current study concentrates on the acculturation orientations from an identification domain solely. Other domains of acculturation orientations, such us acculturation to cultural behaviors, may be related differently to value contextualization. In future studies, the scope of acculturation should be widened.

Moreover, in this study we focused on four values in the cultural contexts, out of Schwartz's (1992) ten values. The choice of the values was premediatated, surveying all value dimensions, and concentrating on values relevant to adolescent's lives. However, it would be very interesting to see how ethnic-group and country context interact in affecting the importance of other values, such as tradition and universalism. We plan to address this gap in future studies.

Policy Recommendations

In the current study, we found variations in adolescents' perceptions of their values across contexts, creating differentiated identities. It is crucial to understand whether these internal contradictions pose any threat to the adolescent's internal sense of integrity. If so, interventions can be implemented in order to assist the integration process. The country of residence, as well as the ethnic-group, created an environment that was associated with the contextualization of values. For example, only in Israel did identification with one's ethnic-group interact with the contextualized values. Further understanding of the exact elements that create differences among contextualized values may help professionals in supporting the identity formation of immigrant and minority adolescents.

Concluding Remarks

Living in complex cultural worlds, minorities and immigrants learn multiple values. The process of integrating these values into a coherent identity is challenging. Consequently, many adolescents believe in different values when thinking of different parts of their identities. It was shown that the modal values of the environment are integrated into the value system in the respective contexts and that individuals learn values from groups they belong to. From the sum of these experiences, a rich and complex identity is created.

References

Arends-Tóth, J., and Van de Vijver, F. J. R. (2006). Issues in the conceptualization and assessment of acculturation. In M. H. Bornstein and L. R. Cote (Eds.), *Acculturation and parent child relationships: Measurement and development* (pp. 33-62). Mahwah, NJ: Erlbaum.

Bardi, A., Calogero, R. M., and Mullen, B. (2008). A new archival approach to the study of values and value-behavior relations: Validation of the value lexicon. *Journal of Applied Psychology, 93,* 483-497.

Berry, J. W. (2001). A psychology of immigration. *Journal of Social Sciences, 57,* 615-631.

Berry, J. W. (1997). Immigration, acculturation, and adaptation. *Applied Psychology: An International Review, 46,* 5-34.

Boehnke, K., Hadjar, A., and Baier, D. (2007). Parent-child value similarity: The role of zeitgeist. *Journal of Marriage and Family, 69,* 778-792.

Bourdieu, P. (1972). *Outline of a theory of practice.* Cambridge: Cambridge University Press.

Bourhis, R. Y., Moïse, L. C., Perreault, S., and Senécal, S. (1997). Towards and interactive acculturation model: A social psychological approach. *International Journal of Psychology, 32,* 369-386.

Bronfenbrenner, U. (1986). Ecology of the family as a context for human development: Research perspectives. *Developmental Psychology, 22,* 723-742.

Brüß, J. (2005). Proud but isolated? Effects of in-group favouritism and acculturation preferences on inter-ethnic attitudes and contact between German, Turkish and resettler adolescents. *Journal of Ethnic and Migration Studies, 31,* 3-27.

Chatman, J. A. (1991). Matching people and organizations: Selection and socialization in public accounting firms. *Administrative Science Quarterly, 36,* 459-484.

Daniel, E., Schiefer, D., Möllering, A., Benish-Weisman, M., Boehnke, K., and Knafo, A. (2012). Value differentiation in adolescence: The role of age and cultural complexity. *Child Development, 83,* 322-336.

Diehl, C., and Blohm, M. (2003). Rights of Identity? Naturalization processes among "labor migrants" in Germany. *International Migration Review, 37,* 133-162.

Dietz, B. (2000). German and Jewish migration from the former Soviet Union to Germany: Background, trends and implications. *Journal of Ethnic and Migration Studies, 26,* 635-652.

Donahue, E. M., Robins, R. W., Roberts, B. W., and John, O. P. (1993). The divided self: Concurrent and longitudinal effects of psychological adjustment and social roles on self-concept differentiation. *Journal of Personality and Social Psychology, 64,* 834-846.

Euwals, R., Dagevos, J., Gijsberts, M., and Roodenburg, H. (2007). *Immigration, Integration and the Labour Market: Turkish Immigrants in Germany and the Netherlands.* [Online: IZA Discussion Paper No. 2677]. Available at SSRN: http://ssrn.com/abstract=978762

Federal Bureau of Statistics (2007). *Population with migration background.* [online: Results of the Microzensus 2005. Series 1, Volume 2]. from https://www-ec.destatis.de/csp/shop/sfg/bpm.html.cms.cBroker.cls?cmspath=struktur,vollanzeige.csp&ID=1020313 [accessed: 1 June 2009] (in German).

Gecas, V. (1982). The self-concept. *Annual Review of Sociology, 8,* 1-33.

Halstead, J. M. (1996). Values and values education in schools. In J. M. Halstead, and M. J. Taylor (Eds.), *Values in Education and Education in Values* (pp. 3-14). London: Falmer Press.

Hareven, A. (2002). Towards the year 2030: Can a civil society shared by Jews and Arabs evolve in Israel. *International Journal of Intercultural Relations, 26,* 152-168.

Hitlin, S. (2003). Values as the core of personal identity: Drawing links between two theories of self. *Social Psychology Quarterly, 66,* 118-137.

Hong, Y., Morris, M. W., Chiu, C., and Benet-Martinez, V. (2000). Multicultural minds: A dynamic constructivist approach to culture and cognition. *American Psychologist, 55,* 709-720.

Horowitz, T. (2005). The integration of immigrants from the former Soviet Union. *Israel Affairs, 11,* 117-136.

Israel Central Bureau of Statistics (2001). *Ranking of localities with over 5000 residents, according to the percentage of immigrants from the USSR (former) in to population of the locality.* [Online]. Available at http://www.cbs.gov.il/www/population/profil.pdf [accessed: 23 July 2009] (in Hebrew).

Israel Central Bureau of Statistics (2006). *Demographic profile 2006.* [Online]. Available at http://www.cbs.gov.il/www/publications/migration_ussr01/pdf/tab12.pdf [accessed: 9 July 2009].

Jasinskaja-Lathi, I., Liebkind, K., Horenczyk, G., and Schmitz, P. (2003). The interactive nature of acculturation: Perceived discrimination, acculturation attitudes and stress among young ethnic repatriates in Finland, Israel and Germany. *International Journal of Intercultural Relations, 27,* 79-97.

Kelley, J., and Evans, M. D. (1995). Class and class conflict in six western nations. *American Sociological Review, 60,* 157-178.

Knafo, A., and Schwartz, S. H. (2003). Parenting and adolescents' accuracy in perceiving parental values. *Child Development, 74,* 595-611.

LaFromboise, T., Coleman, H. L. K., and Gerton, J. (1993). Psychological impact of biculturalism: Evidence and theory. *Psychological Bulletin, 114,* 395-412.

Markus, H. R., and Kitayama, S. (1994). A collective fear of the collective: Implications for selves and theories of selves. *Personality and Social Psychology Bulletin, 20,* 568-579.

Rabinowitz, D. (2001). The Palestinian citizens of Israel, the concept of trapped minority and the discourse of transnationalism in anthropology. *Ethnic and Racial Studies, 24,* 64-85.

Roccas, S., and Brewer, M. B. (2002). Social identity complexity. *Personality and Social Psychology Review, 6,* 88-106.

Roccas, S., Sagiv, L., Schwartz, S. H., Halevy, N., and Eidelson, R. (2008). Toward a unifying model of identification with groups: Integrating theoretical perspectives. *Personality and Social Psychology Review, 12,* 280-306

Rokeach, M. (1973). *The nature of human values.* New York: Free Press.

Schwartz, S. H. (1992). Universals in the content and structure of values: Theoretical advances and empirical tests in 20 countries. *Advances in Experimental Social Psychology, 25,* 1-65.

Schwartz, S. H. (2008). *Cultural value orientations: Nature and implications of national differences.* Moscow: State University Higher School of Economics Press.

Schwartz, S. H., Lehmann, A., and Roccas, S. (1999). Multimethod probes of basic human values. In J. Adamopoulos and Y. Kashima (Eds.), *Social psychology and culture context: Essays in honor of Harry C. Triandis* (pp. 107-123). Newbury Park, CA: Sage.

Schwartz, S. H., Melech, G., Lehmann, A., Burgess, S., Harris, M., and Owens, V. (2001). Extending the cross-cultural validity of the theory of basic human values with a different method of measurement. *Journal of Cross-Cultural Psychology, 32,* 519-542.

Schwartz, S. H., and Rubel, T. (2005). Sex differences in value priorities: cross-cultural and multi-method studies. *Journal of Personality and Social Psychology, 89,* 1010-1028.

Schwartz, S. H., and Sagiv, L. (1995). Identifying culture-specifics in the content and structure of values. *Journal of Cross-Cultural Psychology, 26,* 92-116.

Schwartz, S. H., Verkasalo, M., Antonovsky, A., and Sagiv, L. (1997). Value priorities and social desirability: Much substance, some style. *British Journal of Social Psychology, 36,* 3-18.

Seligman, C., and Katz, A. N. (1996). The dynamics of value systems. In C. Seligman, J. M. Olson, and M. P. Zanna (Eds.), *The Psychology of Values: The Ontario Symposium, 8,* 53-75. Mahwah, NJ: Lawrence Erlbaum Associates.

Sheldon, K. M., Ryan, R. M., Rawsthorne, L. J., and Ilardi, B. (1997). Trait self and true self: Cross-role variation in the big-five personality traits and its relations with psychological authenticity and subjective well-being. *Journal of Personality and Social Psychology, 73,* 1380-1393.

Stelzl, M., and Seligman, C. (2009). Multiplicity across cultures: Multiple national identities and multiple value systems. *Organizational Studies, 30,* 959-973.

Szapocznik, J., and Kurtines., W. M. (1993). Family psychology and cultural diversity: Opportunities for theory, research and application. *American Psychologist, 48,* 400-407.

Titzmann, P., Silbereisen, R. K., Mesch, G. S., and Schmitt-Rodermund, E. (2011). Migration-specific hassles among adolescent immigrants from the former Soviet Union in Germany and Israel. *Journal of Cross-Cultural Psychology, 42*(5), 777-794.

Turner, J. C., Hogg, M. A., Oakes, P. J., Reicher, S. D., and Wetherell, M. S. (1987). *Rediscovering the Social Group: A Self-Categorization Theory,* Cambridge, MA: Basil Blackwell.

Turner, J. C., Oakes, P. J., Haslam, S, A., and McGarty, C. (1994). Self and collective: Cognition and social context. *Personality and Social Psychology Bulletin, 20,* 454-463.

Vedder, P., Sam, D. L., and Liebkind, K. (2007). The acculturation and adaptation of Turkish adolescents in north-western Europe. *Applied Developmental Science, 11,* 126-136.

Verplanken, B., and Holland, R. W. (2002). Motivated decision making: Effects of motivation and self-centrality of values on choices and behavior. *Journal of Personality and Social Psychology, 82,* 434-447.

Chapter 7

The Everyday Life Experience of Violent and Non-Violent Male Adolescent Immigrants from the FSU in Germany and Israel

Chaya Koren and Steffen Zdun

Introduction

Immigration from a communist society, such as the former Soviet Union (FSU), to a democratic society, such as Germany or Israel, is a stressful event, particularly during the transitional years of adolescence (Silbereisen, 2005). Eisner (1998) stressed the complex interrelationship between the social dynamics in the country of origin and the new living conditions in the receiving society, which might involve engaging in delinquency as a strategy for coping with life.

Various studies have examined the respective effects of immigrant delinquency and integration difficulties, but only few have addressed desistance of delinquent youth due to immigration (see Zdun, Chapter 8 in this volume). It appears worthwhile not only to differentiate between "desister" and "persister" types of youths among immigrants, but also to consider differences in their ways of "being-in-the-world". Thus, one of the aims of this chapter is to describe and compare these ways in the three life domains of school, friends and family, in the case of continuous/discontinuous violent/non-violent behaviour using qualitative methods. Although qualitative findings cannot generalise, they provide in-depth views of experiences as a basis for further investigation and intervention.

Background

This chapter is based on previous separate analyses of our German and Israeli data, which identified four groups of youth regarding continuity/discontinuity of behaviour: *novice* (Group A: non-violent in the FSU, violent in the receiving country),[1] *persister* (Group B: violent in both the FSU and the receiving country), *desister* (Group C: violent in the FSU, non-violent in the receiving country) and *never-violent* (Group D: non-violent in the FSU and in the receiving country) (Koren and Eisikovits, 2011; Zdun, 2012). A grounded theoretical model was

---

1   This group – as explained later – was found only in Israel.

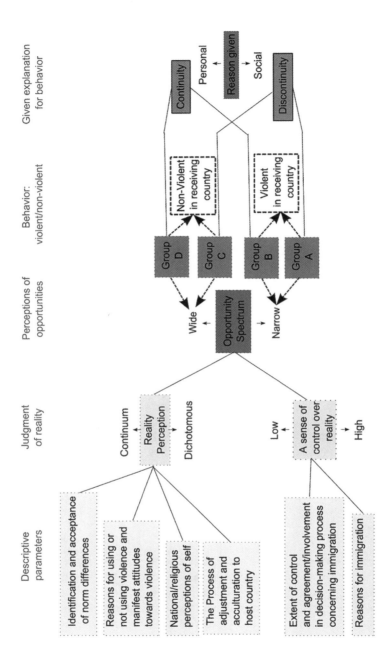

Figure 7.1   Grounded theoretical model of violent and non-violent male immigrant adolescents from the FSU

Note: Model appears in: Koren, C. and Eisikovits, Z. (2011). Continuity and discontinuity of violent and non-violent behavior: Towards a classification of male adolescent immigrants from the FSU in Israel. *Sociological Focus*, 44, 314-338.

developed accordingly to explain violent/non-violent behaviour after immigration (see: Koren and Eisikovits, 2011, p. 332).

The difference between the violent (novice and persister) and the non-violent (desister and never-violent) groups was in their judgment of reality and sense of control over reality. Youth who belonged to the violent groups held a dichotomous perception of reality and of themselves (as either Russian or Israeli/German) and had a low sense of control over reality (e.g., over the decision to emigrate). The non-violent groups perceived reality as a continuum (as being simultaneously Russian and Israeli, or a world citizen, rather than either German or Russian) and had a high sense of control over reality (e.g., over the decision to immigrate to Israel or taking responsibility for their reaction to their parents' decision to immigrate to Germany). These perceptions appeared to influence how they viewed their opportunities; the youth in the violent groups perceived them narrowly whereas the youth in the non-violent groups perceived a wide spectrum of opportunities. The latter, therefore, were able to choose non-violence, whereas the violent youths' construction of reality that was based on lack of opportunities led them to adhere to familiar behaviour patterns, including the use of violence.

The persister and never-violent groups, who were continuous in violence and non-violence, respectively, justified their behaviour by personal reasoning such as parental education and by personality traits. The novice and desister groups, who were discontinuous in their behaviour, based their reasons on social issues such as norm differences and their decision to conform to the norms of the receiving country. Persisters claimed to have been educated to hit back and experienced belonging to nowhere. In contrast, novices experienced parental disapproval of violence, felt more Russian because of their birth place, and Israeli only by residence rather than by a sense of belonging. Israelis and Germans gave different reasons for desisting from violence: Israelis mainly reported sensing control over the decision to immigrate for ideological reasons, such as Zionism. They identified norm differences between the home and receiving countries and behaved according to the Israeli mainstream. Germans, on the whole, were willing to use immigration as a means to improve their future prospects by using social support provided by the environment (e.g., family and friends), which helped their integration process. In both receiving countries, desisters perceived a wide range of opportunities.

Similar groups were documented in various criminology studies (e.g., Blumstein et al., 1988; Moffitt, 1993; Sampson and Laub, 1993). Previous research examined criminal careers and desistance processes, in particular, and considered the latter to be a fruitful interplay of social, structural and individual aspects. In contrast, onset and persistence were considered to reflect failure of this interplay. Non-violence has seldom been addressed, however, because of a lack of substantial information available on reasons for delinquency and changes in delinquent behaviour. Moreover, this type of research has largely neglected immigrants and behavioural changes in adolescence.

This notwithstanding, a large body of research has related delinquency among immigrants to risk factors (e.g., Decker and Weerman, 2005; Titzmann et al., 2008) and to various criminological theories. Empirical research and theoretical literature have demonstrated the meaning of trouble in school and of language acquisition difficulties, weak family bonds and delinquent peers, as well as other possible reasons for developing negative attitudes towards immigration and for becoming violent or maintaining violent behaviour. Decades ago, Sellin (1938) described the challenges facing immigrants, concluding that they preserved their culture, attitudes and behaviour especially when residentially segregated. However, this body of research aimed primarily to explain the delinquency phenomenon and rather neglected the contribution of immigration to desistance from violence.

The two specific immigrant groups addressed in our research (male adolescents from the FSU in Germany and in Israel) were chosen because of their comparable everyday pre-immigration experiences. In both the receiving countries, their difficulties with integration and delinquency are conspicuous. German (e.g., Haug et al., 2008; Zdun, 2007) and Israeli (e.g., Tartakovsky and Mirsky, 2001) research has repeatedly demonstrated the aforementioned risk factors as essential contributors to violent behaviour among these youth.

It is known also that negative and positive experiences in the three everyday life domains of school, friends and family might contribute to violence and non-violence respectively (e.g., Osgood et al., 1996; Sampson and Laub, 1993; Titzmann et al., 2008). Differences in teaching methods and lack of respect towards teachers in the receiving societies might motivate misbehaviour in school, which contributes to fights among pupils (Zdun, 2007). Leisure activities with friends might also cause trouble when interpreted as a disturbance by neighbours and passers-by (Kohl, 1998), and group conflicts could emerge between and within groups (Albrecht et al., 2007). Moreover, being in contact with delinquent peers and spending time in unstructured, unsupervised activities might contribute to violence whereas the opposite might encourage non-violence (Titzmann et al., 2008). Finally, weak family bonds and conflicts due to immigration could lead to more time spent with peers undergoing similar experiences whereas good family relationships are more likely to improve integration efforts and outcomes (Zdun, 2007). However, previous research has generally neglected to differentiate between continuous and discontinuous violent and non-violent behaviour.

Thus, an additional aim of this chapter is to address gaps in desistance and to focus on general research on delinquency among juvenile immigrants. The four groups were comparatively examined in both receiving societies to gain in-depth insights on differences and commonalities. Immigration was examined in the comparative context of violence and non-violence to gain further understanding of continuous and discontinuous delinquency.

Method

Qualitative measures can be used to investigate individual developments and interpretations. In-depth qualitative research is required, in particular, to examine

Table 7.1   Demographic characteristics and violence

	Israel	Germany
Age	Mean: 16,73 SD: 1,13	Mean: 16,70 SD: 1,36
Years in receiving country	Mean: 4,65 SD: 0,98	Mean: 4,55 SD: 1,87
Country of origin	Ukraine: 22 Kazakhstan: 6 Russia: 8 Moldova: 2 Kavkaz: 1 Belarus: 1	Kazakhstan: 18 Russia: 16 Ukraine: 3 Uzbekistan: 3
Religion of adolescents	Jewish: 14 Christian: 14 Christian/Jewish: 1 No religion: 11	Protestant/Baptist/ Mennonite: 18 Catholic: 5 Other: 6 No religion: 10
Parent's marital status	Married: 17 Divorced: 18 Mother widowed: 5	Married: 32 Divorced: 6 Mother widowed: 1 Living separately: 1
Financial situation of family	Very good: 0 Good: 13 Neither good nor bad: 11 Bad: 13 Very bad: 0 Do not know: 3	Very good: 2 Good: 14 Neither good nor bad: 23 Bad: 3 Very bad: 1

the logics and dynamics of continuity and discontinuity of violent and non-violent behaviour (Sampson and Laub, 1993). Through this approach, we were able to consider not only the circumstances but also their meanings and to arrive at in-depth descriptions and interpretations of experiences in both societies within several integration domains (school, friends and family).

Criteria for theoretical sampling were chosen as follows: Most of the participants had been involved in at least one violent incident as perpetrator; for comparative purposes, the others had not been involved in violent events since immigration. The Israeli and German samples each included 40 young male immigrants from the FSU. In the Israeli sample, the majority were from the Ukraine and in the German sample, the majority were from Kazakhstan. All Israeli participants and most German participants were pupils in the normative schooling systems and were not officially identified as delinquents. The age of the participants in Israel was between 15 and 19 years and in Germany between 14 and 20 years. The duration of residence in Israel was between three and six years and in Germany between two and nine years. The initial criterion for inclusion in

Table 7.2   Classification of violence use among adolescent immigrants from the FSU to Germany and Israel

	Violent in receiving country	Non-violent in receiving country
	Continuity of violent behaviour	Discontinuity of violent behaviour
Violent in FSU	Persisters Germany: 19 Israel: 11	Desisters Germany: 7 Israel: 8
	Discontinuity of non-violent behaviour	Continuity of non-violent behaviour
Non-violent in FSU	Novices Germany: 2 Israel: 16	Non-Violents Germany: 12 Israel: 5

the study was at least three years of residence in the receiving country to allow time for adjustment before engaging in violent behaviour. Four of the participants had resided in Germany for less than three years, but spoke the language and were already perpetrating violence, and were therefore included in the study.

Participants were asked to provide demographic information regarding socioeconomic status (SES). SES was approximately equal in all four groups in both countries. Participants were asked about their religious affiliation. The Israeli participants reported subjective religious affiliation, which was not necessarily consistent with official records. Although registered as having Jewish nationality, they might have identified with Christianity or claimed no affiliation to any religion. These subjective perceptions contributed to better understanding of the identity issues related to their immigration.

The cross-national comparison of the data showed manifold commonalities but also differences between and within the groups in both societies. Differences among the groups in both countries are presented in Table 7.2. The original research plan was to interview two groups in each country: 30 violent adolescents and a control group of 10 non-violent adolescents. However, during the interview process and the first stages of analysis, we identified four groups instead of two, producing the following unique distribution of participants: persisters and novices, who belonged to the violent group, and desisters and never-violent adolescents, who belonged to the non-violent group.

Most Israeli interviewees were recruited through clubs for normative youth, operated by municipal agencies throughout the country. About a quarter of the Israeli youth was recruited through schools, following permission from the Chief Scientist of the Ministry of Education. Semi-structured interviews were conducted in the homes of the adolescents. The German sample was recruited from different cities in Lower-Saxony and North Rhine-Westphalia and in Berlin. Interviewees were recruited with the assistance of teachers and social workers from schools and youth clubs in which the interviews were conducted.

The interview guide included the following opening request: "Tell me the story of your immigration". In addition, questions relating to immigration were asked, such as: "How was the decision made, by whom, when and why"? Questions were also asked about the use of languages, comparisons between the receiving country and country of origin regarding relationships with friends, teachers, parents, school and reasons and circumstances that triggered violent behaviour.

In both countries, interviews were conducted by the authors in Hebrew or German and lasted between one-and-a-half to two hours, were tape-recorded and transcribed verbatim. Interview transcriptions were 20 to 40 pages long. German data were coded using MAXQDA and Israeli data were coded using ATLAS.ti (two software programs used for qualitative data analysis). Codes were given in English for purposes of collaboration between the Israeli and German researchers. Open coding by individual cases was performed first. This enabled the development of content categories by units of meaning for each interview. Subsequently, cross-case analysis was performed by identifying themes that cut across interviews (Strauss and Corbin, 1990). Meetings were held periodically in both countries to compare codes and categories to arrive at agreed-upon themes. Quotes were chosen according to content richness, were translated from Hebrew or German into English and interpreted. Parallel quotes from both samples were identified to organise the themes for this chapter.

Findings

Data analysis revealed essential distinctions between all four groups in Israel, whereas the German data revealed no clear distinctions between novices and persisters, leaving just three groups. The only distinction found between novices and persisters in the German sample was the explanation for their behaviour, claiming to have been "too young" to fight before immigration. This implies that they would probably have engaged in violent behaviour if they had remained in the FSU. Apart from this, they expressed the same attitudes and explanations for violent behaviour as those who engaged in fights in both countries. Thus, novices were examined only in Israel. Each of the four groups was characterised by a unique theme illustrated through the everyday life domains of school, friends and family.

Novices were characterised by *convenience and frustration*. They considered their own convenience before anything else, and behaved in this way simply because they could. Persisters were characterised by *stubbornness and rigidity* in their attitude towards accepting the differences in the receiving country, when compared to the FSU. By doing things in their own way, they established an existence that served their purpose in a new environment and as such helped them to cope with the sense of insecurity. Desisters were characterised by *flexibility and positive outlook* on the reality in which they were living; as reflected in their quick adaptation to new circumstances and in perceiving the social environment as helpful with adjusting and integrating into the new society. They were positive about integration, and took responsibility for problems and difficulties and for changing these situations. The never-violent group was characterised by *personal resources that make the difference.* Most youths in this group seemed to have a positive attitude towards immigration, similar to the desisters. These juveniles had never been involved in violent behaviour, but we found variations among them relating to their adjustment. We interpreted their ability to adjust to immigration as being related far more to personal than to social resources.

School

Novices: convenience and frustration   The theme of convenience was relevant to discipline in school:

> I21(I): There, I did not disturb in class. Here, I disturb and get into fights... The teachers find it difficult to stand up to the children and take things to heart... There are more disturbances... They don't know how to discipline the pupils.

These youths perceived that the permissive environment would facilitate misbehaviour in the classroom. Thus, they engaged in violent and other types of behaviour that they would never have considered in the FSU, just because this was possible.

Persisters: stubbornness and rigidity   The persisters' "I did it my way" attitude was expressed in relation to school adjustment:

> I2(I): I didn't get along with them (the school regulations and teachers), but I got along with myself.

> I8(G): I don't like German schools and the way that I am treated there and in other institutions. People here don't like us. But I don't care about that. I don't want to live their life, I am not like them. If they would just understand what I want and what I'm like, they would treat me better and not always control me. But I will not behave in the way that they want.

These are examples of the "self-made man", who is able to succeed because he believes in his own abilities and is not defeated by the system. The youth in this group did not allow others to stand in the way of their achievements. They pushed the obstacles aside and practised self-reliance.

Desisters: flexibility and positive outlook   Desisters reported different attitudes and behaviour towards school, illustrated by flexibility in the classroom:

I32(I): We got to class and our teacher told us not to speak Russian. She said we must speak Hebrew with each other and I asked how we could speak Hebrew with someone who knows Russian better. It sounds ridiculous when a Russian speaks with a Russian in Hebrew. (The teacher said), that's how we'll learn Hebrew. OK, we speak Hebrew with Israelis who don't know Russian, but with Russians, we speak Russian. (The teacher said) we don't divide people, when there is someone in class who doesn't understand Russian, you must speak Hebrew. Somehow, the teacher is right.

I26(G): There are all the ethnic groups but no conflicts in school. We have no problems with each other. We are friends.

Q: Did you ever see a fight?

I26(G): No, never, not even in school. Here, strength is not important, what matters is intelligence…

Q: And how did you get used to the schools in Germany?

I26(G): Well, in the beginning, everything was different. But I learned from the others and made friends quickly, not just Russian friends…

Q: Which language do you use with your friends in school?

I26(G): We have to speak German. In the beginning, it was strange talking to my Russian friends in German, but it helped us learn faster.

The school regulations required all pupils to speak German or Hebrew, even among Russians, who found it easier to speak Russian among themselves. The youth in this group found this behaviour unnatural, but saw the logic behind the request. Their willingness to comply is one common indication of their flexibility.

Never-violent group: personal resources make the difference   Despite individual difficulties in the integration process, the dominance of personal resources as a factor of adjustment was experienced in school:

I38(I): I just got used to it (boarding school); I got used to it quite quickly. I really loved the place, the people, the staff. I never had difficulties with the people here, talking, getting to know each other, being with each other, living together, it wasn't hard for me.

I38(G): Well, the relationship with teachers is different in Germany. Sometimes, they even laugh with us. I like the school here very much because even if I have problems, teachers try to help. I had special language lessons and sometimes they sat with me after the classes and explained things that I didn't understand… This made it easy for me to adjust. I know that other immigrants complain a lot about the schools here, that everything is different. But I got used to the different methods and behaviours in school. I like the teachers and made friends easily.

The ability of the non-violent participants to take advantage of the formal support that they received from teachers, especially in Germany, appeared to be largely due to their good social skills and ability to integrate quickly.

Friends

Novices: convenience and frustration   The novices had "real friends" on whom they could rely to be violent for them:

> I21(I): If my friend is involved in a beating up, I'll always come and help him… Someone who won't abandon me when I'm in trouble; that's a real friend.

True friendship involved mutual loyalty, especially in times of need. It was a give and take situation; "I help my friend when he's in trouble and he helps me". They also had some close Israeli friends:

> I24(I): Most of my friends are Israeli; they actually helped me learn the language, understand the mentality, understand their style, how to dress, speech, behaviour. Those are my friends, who help the common new Russian immigrant, they are my friends. They help me become one of them… My advice is to get along with them, to get to know them. Learn their language, hang around with them, connect with them; that's all, just unite. It will be convenient, to become Israeli, learn the language, the dialect, the mode of speech, even a bit of the culture, to understand, absorb it, go along with it, go with the flow, to get along.

These participants made an effort to make friends with Israelis, who were able to help them adjust to the culture. They viewed friendship with Israelis as a means of integration into society; becoming friends out of convenience and for their own benefit. One of these benefits was language acquisition, for convenient adjustment to the new culture.

Persisters: stubbornness and rigidity   Persisters' attitudes towards friendship coincided with those of novices in some respects. However, rigidity was also illustrated when relating to friends:

> I2(I): Friends are those who, no matter what happens to me or in what situation I am in and I can help, then I'll do it, and I hope they'd do the same for me… My friend got stuck a while ago with his girlfriend and four Caucasians held a

knife to him... He called me and I came with a group of friends and we took care of things.

I12(G): Friends always fight for each other. I've helped them many times and they have helped me. It was like this in Russia and here, it is the same. People who don't help are no friends.

The youths expressed very deep commitment to their friends. They were willing to stand up for a friend in trouble and would use violence to help him. Such support and friendship appeared to go beyond the rules and laws of the country, and fighting was the source of many friendships.

I13(I): The day after we fought, I said I was sorry and he said he was sorry. We got to the classroom and he came over to me; I did this wrong and that wrong, and please forgive me. After that, we became best friends.

I14(G): I made some of my friends through fighting. This is normal and happens with many people I know. You fight with this guy and afterwards you realise that he's OK. After talking about what happened and who was wrong, there is no reason to become enemies. If I like someone and he thinks like me, then we should become friends.

The youth in this group had a unique way of starting friendships; they became very committed to each other after being involved in violent fights. Their stubbornness was expressed through the initial need to fight, which then developed into friendship following forgiveness.

Desisters: flexibility and positive outlook   In contrast, the desisters used friendship to express their optimistic attitude:

I33(I): In Kazakhstan, I had friends, but we were more separate. We weren't that close to each other and here, we came to a place where we both had problems, and I understand his kind of problems, and he understands mine, and that brought us together more. We are closer to each other.

I27(G): I have many different friends here... He (a friend) will respect me and my family. A friend isn't someone I just hang out with and drink beer... I like my German friends a lot because they helped me so much to integrate here, but I still have friends from Russia. They are also important because we came from the same place. We are also different in some way, but it is good to know people with whom you can talk about the past.

Leaving friends behind and having to create new friendships was one of the difficulties of immigration. Such situations can be interpreted in various ways.

The youth of this group were able to see the positive side, not only by acquiring new friends but also by relating to the quality of new friendships. They created close relationships of a unique nature that they had not experienced with their friends in the FSU, due to the shared experience of acculturation difficulties in the receiving society.

Never-violent group: personal resources make the difference   The following quotes illustrate the perception of the world as related mainly to personal resources of self and others:

> I19(I): I have many Israeli friends whom I can count on; also among the Russians there are good and bad people. It's true, they are just people, and another thing I can say is… I told some Israelis that in the Ukraine, I had Arab friends and they were my best friends ever. They said: "What, you were friends with Arabs?" I said: "You have to develop and grow up and get to know that not all Arabs are bad, some of them are OK." That's all.

> I11(G): In the beginning, I couldn't speak much German. And then... Well, I liked the people right away. That helped me and they were like me. So we made friends… It was never difficult for me to get acquainted with others. You just have to be open. I have friends from different countries and cultures. They think and behave differently, but we are just friends. We like each other and spend a lot of time together. I trust them and would always help them.

The participants emphasised personal resources also when relating to the type of friends they made. They considered individual characteristics to be more important than ethnic origin, which they might have disregarded completely, even when referring to youth from ethnic groups of potential enemy countries (in Israel).

Family

Novices: convenience and frustration   These youth acted according to their own convenience also within the family:

> Q: What do you do in situations of conflict? When your parents don't want something, but you do?

> I36(I): Look, it depends what the conflict is. What I want and what they want. For example, if it's going to the beach and there is something more interesting and I don't want to go, so I stay at home. If I feel like going out with my friends because I come home (from boarding school) only every two weeks, they understand. On the other hand, I should also understand that as I come home

only once in two weeks, maybe I should help take care of my little sister. I choose and make priorities, depending on what has to be done.

First and foremost, these youths chose to do what suited them; at times, they would consider taking part in family outings and responsibilities, but this was their choice and they would consider familial obligations at their own convenience. They were aware of this tendency and tried to balance between their own wishes and the needs of their family.

Their parents had a specific attitude towards violence for solving conflicts outside the family:

> I37(I): They (my parents) thought I was right. They come from the same (culture) that I do, but they think that violence should be the last resort when there is conflict. First, you have to solve the problem in a different way and only then use your physical body.

Their parents approved of the use of violence (only) as a last resort when all else had failed. If a conflict or misunderstanding could be solved without violence, then it should be. However, if physical force was the only choice, it was considered legitimate. Thus, it was preferable to solve conflicts through violence than not to solve them at all.

Persisters: stubbornness and rigidity   The theme of stubbornness and doing things in their own way was also reflected in relationships with and behaviour towards parents:

> I39(I): The court decided that my brother and I had to stay with my mother, because I wasn't yet 16 and didn't have the right to choose. I told my mother: "No, I'm staying with Dad". They separated because my mother found herself a boyfriend. She was unfaithful to him (my father), she spoke with him (her boyfriend) on the phone, and I fought with her because she wasn't paying attention to my brother... I love my mother but I didn't like the idea of moving out. I wanted to stay with my father, so at the last minute, after my mother had already packed everything, I told her I'm staying and she understood that it is her loss and she tried to convince me by bribing me... I went for one day and then came back to my father.

> I35(G): I didn't want to come here. I behaved very badly so that they would send me back home. I wanted them to kick me out of Germany.

> Q: So, you thought that your bad behaviour would bring you back?

> I35(G): Yes.

Q: Did you ever talk about that to your parents?

I35(G): Yes, but what should they do? They said: "We have no house in Uzbekistan anymore, we sold everything and now…" I still don't like the fact that they took me. Everything was better there.

Disregarding custodial decisions is an extreme example of stubbornly doing things in their own way. The incidents illustrated above occurred after immigration. The Israeli quote refers to parents who immigrated together and divorced after immigration. The youth believed that it was better to stay with his father than to move out with his mother. His decision was also based on moral issues, while being judgmental about his mother's behaviour. By doing so, he automatically sided with his father and did not hesitate to tell his mother that his choice to live with his father was her loss. His independent decision and his success in achieving his goal, in spite of the fact that his mother had custody, is indicative of stubbornness that paid off. The example from Germany shows the same type of stubbornness with which one youth opposed his parents' decision of immigration.

Adherance to norms that were already prevalent among youth in the FSU seemed to be accepted in the family when relating to parental approval for using violence:

I23(I): What scares me most about the police is what my parents will say. If I'm caught for theft, my father will kill me, but if I'm caught for fighting with someone, my parents will say something but not really severe. My father did similar things when he was young.

I4(G): If it's my fault, I get into trouble. But if I am not responsible, my parents say: "Okay. Whatever happens, happens". And if I were involved in a fight where someone was badly injured, then they wouldn't like that either.

As fighting and violence were accepted in the family to some extent, arrest for violence was taken lightly compared to offences such as theft. Family tradition appeared to be more important than the law. These parents accepted the violence as long as it did not harm the family's image or cause trouble with state institutions. No statement indicated any concern about the potential harm caused. Even mothers tolerated violence, especially when their sons were attacked. Violence in general was interpreted as an appropriate means of sanctioning disobedience and lack of respect. This might be interpreted as an intergenerational attitude of doing things their way, as opposed to in the legally accepted manner of the receiving country.

Desisters: flexibility and positive outlook   The flexibility of the desisters was also expressed through negotiation with parents:

I32(I): When I started smoking, my parents didn't know. Then all of a sudden, they found out and said they were against it, so I stopped smoking for three months and then started again, and decided I didn't care, and I told them. They said it was a shame and that it is my life, you can decide what you want. "We want you to stop smoking. If you don't stop, it's your decision". This happened about two weeks before we immigrated… When I started smoking again, when I came to Israel, I didn't have money and they (my parents) didn't give me money so that I wouldn't buy (cigarettes). I started smoking, and then I didn't. When I went to boarding school, they gave me money and I started smoking again and they agreed that they cannot stop me. If they would tell me to stop smoking, then I'd stop. But on the whole, they agree that I decide.

I36(G): Family life changed a lot here. My parents know that I have better friends and that I don't get into trouble any more. They give me a lot of liberties because they trust me. We talk a lot now about what we do. And now they listen to me much more. I guess it has also to do with me being older now, but my parents also changed somehow. We came here to live a better life, to have more opportunities. So, it is normal for them to allow me to get the best out of my life. They just want to know what I am doing, but they will not intervene and sometimes will even let me learn from my mistakes.

The youths described their parents as flexible, combining tolerance with their parental duty to express their opinion. Such parental attitudes seemed to nurture flexibility in their sons to listen to their point of view and to take responsibility for their actions. For instance, I32(I) stated that he would stop smoking if his parents would insist, but that this would be against his will. He was prepared to go against his will if his parents left him no choice. However, he emphasised that his parents gave him the freedom to decide, indicating their faith in his judgment. The interviewees in Germany also emphasised their parents' open-mindedness.

Never-violent group: personal resources make the difference   The personal ability to cope with family problems is illustrated as follows:

I5(I): I am simply very sensitive; it really touches me to the heart (referring to the father's situation, after their house burned down and he lost his job). Maybe some kind of change is around the corner, something that will change things. Maybe he'll get some kind of opportunity, something might happen. But the problem is that it doesn't always happen. Sometimes, you have to change yourself without an external factor.

I5(G): Since we have been in Germany, we (the family) help each other a lot. Even though it matters mainly what one does oneself and how hard one tries to integrate, it is necessary to support each other and remind each other that we will succeed if we don't give in.

The father described in the Israeli quote had experienced terrible misfortune since their immigration, and his personal resources were insufficient to overcome these tragedies. In the son's eyes, his father had reached the point at which he was waiting for an external solution. The son, on the other hand, believed in change that comes mainly from within. In this way, he explained his father's situation to himself and emphasised the difference between himself and his father, partially to reassure himself that he would not turn out the same way. The other interviewees of this group also mentioned the importance of mutual support to achieve personal goals.

Conclusions and Discussion

Each group was characterised by a unique theme that cut across each of the three everyday life domains in both countries. The comparison indicates that novices acted out of frustration and because of little or lack of social control they were able to "do things because they can" and were not intimidated not to act. Persisters seemed to be characterised by stubbornness and rigidity, and lacked social and institutional support. They reacted to this by perceiving themselves as self-made men, also if the results were negative, for instance, when they used violence. Desisters appeared to be characterised by flexibility and a positive outlook, which made it easier for them to seek actively and hence receive the required support for integration, and to act according to the social norms of the receiving countries. The never-violent group seemed to be characterised by personal traits that made a difference, and had less need to use this support. They counted more on individual competencies and motivation but perceived social and self-control as too strong at times, when they were not able to meet their own and others' expectations.

Overall, the findings suggest that issues regarding lack of discipline and adjustment in school were very relevant. Friends appeared to matter in terms of benefits and support in the case of problems and conflicts but also in regard to social integration. The relevance of family regarding social life was different for each of the four groups, who displayed varied reactions to and approval or disapproval of violent behaviour.

These findings were largely consistent with previous insights gained from criminology research. For example, our findings on persisters and desisters do not question previous research, but add some information about everyday interactions in the three life domains examined. However, the data also indicate that these juvenile immigrants are unique in certain aspects of desistance from and persistence of violence, which are more broadly examined by Zdun (Chapter 8 in this volume). For example, desistance might occur in early adolescence as a result of immigration and not only in early adulthood, for instance, due to marriage, parenthood, employment or military service (e.g., Maruna and Roy, 2007; Sampson and Laub, 1993). Such cases of early desistance appeared to be related to receiving sufficient and pro-social support and control from new friends, institutions and even the family. In contrast, young persisters as well as novices seemed to lack or reject support and therefore missed this opportunity to change their lives for the better. Finally, in regard to the never-violent participants, the findings partly coincide with Moffitt et al.'s (1996, p. 419) insights on "abstainers". The latter were defined as describing themselves as "overcontrolled, and also somewhat conventional, trusting, submissive, and socially inept. They described their personalities as sturdier and less reactive to stress than the other boys".

Moreover, the results are consistent with research on juvenile delinquency of immigrants (e.g., Titzmann et al., 2008; Zdun, 2007), indicating the fundamental relevance, for example, of adjustment in school, a non-delinquent environment, pro-social interactions and strong family bonds as well as substantial support for integration. The contribution of this chapter lies less in providing unique findings in this area of research but in encouraging more in-depth examination especially of non-delinquency, for example, by considering continuity and discontinuity in the course of immigration or other life events.

The aim of comparing German and Israeli data was not only to verify that our basic findings are unique to a specific country or group of immigrants, but also to identify "cultural" differences. It is interesting that the data showed no substantial differences in the general patterns noted in the three life domains. For example, despite differences in the school systems in the receiving societies, the youths' adjustment was similar in both countries. The main difference between the German and Israeli data was the emergence of the novices only in the Israeli sample. This appears to be an effect of sampling, however, because the original sample was recruited based on their violent or non-violent behaviour. With reference to findings of previous studies of this target group (Zdun, 2007), we assume that more specific sampling would also reach participants who started to use violence after immigration to Germany. However, further research would have to compare these participants with the novices in Israel, regarding similar attitudes and behaviour. Moreover, further studies are required to examine how far our findings can be verified in larger samples and with other populations of immigrants.

Our findings have various limitations. The qualitative sample cannot be used for generalisation. However, based on the *grounded theory* method, the findings can be representative of the phenomenon (Strauss and Corbin, 1990). Moreover, the sample was selective, as it excluded female youth and non-immigrants, and the sampled youth were relatively young at the time of immigration. It is also recommended to address a broader range of delinquency offences.

Keeping these limitations in mind, the findings indicate some pointers for prevention and intervention. First, such measures might acknowledge the specific characteristics that emerged from each of the four groups. Second, the meaning of familial support and especially the potential of the parents should be not underestimated, even though previous research often concentrated on the negative effects of weak family bonds (Zdun, 2007). Although our findings also demonstrate this problem, they indicate the potential of measures to strengthen family bonds and juveniles' respect for their parents, as well as to impart coping strategies to both generations to solve conflicts without using violence. In addition, our results emphasise the necessity of lasting adequate support to promote desistance, which has to consider a long-term process requiring a fruitful interplay of social, structural and individual aspects (Zdun, Chapter 8 in this volume). Finally, the family relationships and the strength of the parents of never-violent participants might also be addressed, to remove the impression that they can depend on self-reliance and should not expect familial support.

References

Albrecht, P.-G., Eckert, R., Roth, R., Thielen-Reffgen, C., and Wetzstein, T. (2007). *Wir und die anderen. Gruppenauseinandersetzungen Jugendlicher in Ost und West*. Wiesbaden: VS Verlag.

Blumstein, A., Cohen, J., and Farrington, D. (1988). Criminal Career Research: Its Value for Criminology. *Criminology*, *26*, 1-35.

Decker, S., and Weerman, F. (2005). *European Street Gangs and Troublesome Youth Groups*. Walnut Creek, CA: AltaMira Press.

Eisner, M. (1998). Konflikte und Integrationsprobleme. *Neue Kriminalpolitik, 10*, 11-13.

Haug, S., Baraulina, T., and Babka von Gostomski, C. (2008). *Kriminalität von Aussiedlern. Eine Bestandsaufnahme*. Nuremberg: Bundesamt für Migration und Flüchtlinge.

Kohl, E. (1998). *Projektbericht und Ergebnisse einer empirischen Untersuchung*. Duisburg: Diakonisches Werk.

Koren, C., and Eisikovits, Z. (2011). Continuity and discontinuity of violent and non-violent behavior: Towards a classification of male adolescent immigrants from the FSU in Israel. *Sociological Focus*, *44*, 314-338.

Moffitt, T. (1993). Adolescence-Limited and Life-Course-Persistent Antisocial Behavior: A Developmental Taxonomy. *Psychological Review*, *100*, 674-701.

Moffit, T., Caspi, A., Dickson, N., Silva, P. A., and Stanton, W. R. (1996). Childhood-onset versus adolescent-onset antisocial conduct problems in males: Natural history from ages 3 to 18 years. *Development and Psychopathology*, *8*, 399-424.

Osgood, D. W., Wilson, J. K., O'Malley, P. M., Bachman, J. G., and Johnston, L. D. (1996). Routine activities and individual deviant behavior. *American Sociological Review*, *61*, 635-655.

Silbereisen, R. K. (2005). Social change and human development: Experiences from German unification. *International Journal of Behavioral Development, 29*, 2-13.

Sampson, R. J., and Laub, J. H. (1993). *Crime in the Making: Pathways and Turning Points through Life*. Cambridge, MA: Harvard University Press.

Sellin, T. (1938). *Culture Conflict and Crime*. New York: Social Science Research Council.

Strauss, A., and Corbin, J. (1997). *Basics of qualitative research: Grounded theory procedures and techniques*. Thousand Oaks, CA: Sage.

Tartakovksy, E., and Mirsky J. (2001). Bullying Gangs among Immigrant Adolescents from the Former Soviet Union in Israel. *Journal of Interpersonal Violence, 16*, 247-265.

Titzmann, P., Raabe, T., and Silbereisen, R. K. (2008). Risk and protective factors for delinquency among male adolescent immigrants at different stages of the acculturation process. *International Journal of Psychology, 43*, 19-31.

Zdun, S. (2007). *Ablauf, Funktion und Prävention von Gewalt. Eine soziologische Analyse gewalttätiger Verhaltensweisen in Cliquen junger Russlanddeutscher.* Frankfurt: Peter Lang Verlag.

Zdun, S. (2012). Street Culture and Violence Among Young Migrants from the Former Soviet Union. *Sociological Focus, 45*, 143-158.

Chapter 8

Immigration as an Experience to Knife Off[1] from Delinquency: Desistance and Persistence among Male Adolescents from the FSU

Steffen Zdun

Introduction

This paper addresses the concept of *knifing off*, which conceptualizes the processes and individual actions that occur when an individual permanently withdraws from the specific social environments and opportunity structures that promoted their delinquency. It describes one of the very few explorations of knifing off among immigrants. The interview analysis is especially revealing in relation to the as yet unresolved question: What has to happen for a person to desist from past delinquency and maintain this change.

Criminologists largely agree that delinquency is tied to age and maturity (Agnew, 2001). Accordingly, desistance research focuses on behavioural changes in early adulthood (for example, relating to marriage, parenthood, employment, military service; see Maruna and Roy, 2007; Sampson and Laub, 2005). Other knifing-off options, such as the less fundamentally age-related experience of migration, tend to be neglected. Criminological research in general neglects migration as an explanation for decreasing delinquency, instead treating it as a risk factor for delinquency upon arrival. In fact, immigrant adolescents encounter and cope with inter-societal differences in norms and behaviour in various ways.

As elaborated in the previous chapter (Koren and Zdun, in this volume), continuity and discontinuity of delinquent behaviour both appear to be common responses to migration during adolescence. Although various changes in delinquency are discussed there, the empirical data was not used to examine knifing

---

1   Referring to the opportunities that help a person break away from 'contaminated' past situations (in particular risky or criminal activity). However, given that life changes are usually more temporary and dynamic in nature than implied by the amputation metaphor, the concept is more about promoting alternative behavioural opportunities than simply the elimination of structures promoting delinquency. An extensive description of the concept is provided by Maruna and Roy (2007).

off in relation to immigration. The following analysis is restricted to the German sample because the Israeli data lacks too many relevant aspects.[2] Comparisons are therefore based only on youth who desisted from or persisted in delinquency in the course of migration to Germany.

Desistance Research

More than two million ethnic German immigrants from the former Soviet Union have arrived in Germany since the early 1990s. They form an identifiable minority that even today is widely rejected by mainstream society on the basis of a small minority of delinquent adolescents who engage in *street offences* (such as shoplifting, assault and vandalism) and reject the receiving society and its norms.

Findings on their delinquency (Haug et al., 2008) coincide with the broad criminological consensus that a rather small group of 3 to 10 percent is responsible for a very significant proportion of juvenile crime in modern societies – between 40 to 60 percent – (for example, Blumstein et al., 1988). These *serious offenders* do not specialize in particular offences, although violence and petty offences predominate (Monahan et al., 2009). Furthermore, even though they often exhibit multiple risk factors (Sampson and Laub, 2003; Moffitt, 1993), it is impossible to predict who from this group will become a serious offender, nor to prognosticate processes of desistance.

Especially in the case of *episodic offenders*, juvenile delinquency is perceived as ubiquitous (Sampson and Laub, 2003), but criminologists disagree on when and under what conditions delinquency declines, how desistance arises and whether offenders can be categorized into groups that predict certain behaviour (Gottfredson and Hirschi, 1990; Moffitt, 1993; Sampson and Laub, 2005). Various theoretical explanations, which considerations of space preclude examining in greater detail here, address the issue from different perspectives and provide complementary insights.[3]

Sampson and Laub (1993) introduced the concept of *turning points*, integrating the significance of far-reaching life events. They identify social control as the main factor influencing changes in delinquency and turning points as events that explain changes in delinquency due to changes in social control. This differs only slightly from the concept of *knifing off*, which additionally requires an 'explicit removal of past options' (Maruna and Roy, 2007, p. 114) and related behavioural changes. Knifing off is not merely an environmental change, but includes the development of attitudes and practices.

Both concepts stress the significance of individual maturing processes conditioned by changes in social points of reference. Thus, on the basis of

---

2   Note that this research was originally designed to examine not desistance but the significance of norm conflicts among violent and non-violent youth.

3   A full description of these concepts is provided by Laub and Sampson (2001).

empirical findings that support an 'overwhelming power of age in predicting desistance from crime', Sampson and Laub (2005, p. 31) largely favour the self-control concept introduced by Gottfredson and Hirschi (1990). They especially reject basing predictions of change in delinquency on early childhood risk factors and recommend closer examination of the individual life-course. However, they cannot adequately explain why some youth change in the course of particular life events, while others remain delinquent.

Nevertheless, Sampson and Laub's approach goes further than most prior accounts, which were based mainly on quantitative longitudinal data, cohort statistics, or police and court sources. Teasing apart the interactions, perceptions and interpretations of individual development demands qualitative empirical data. This strand of research is gradually growing, grounded in the pioneering work of Bottoms and colleagues (2004) and Maruna (2001), who focus on *how* and *why* behaviour changes rather than *what* changes. This empirical shift is crucial because it allows more detailed consideration of *agency*. Agency is the 'confidence that they [individuals] have control over the activities in which they engage and the people with whom they associate' (Mulvey et al., 2004, p. 223). But little is known about agency's impact on desistance and persistence.

Current research on knifing off only partially integrates the processual nature of life events. Different *stages* need to be explored: a) preparation for an event, b) occurrence or execution and the initial period of familiarization with its consequences, and c) the habitualization of new attitudes, behaviour and social practice. If the latter is lacking, Maruna and Roy argue, 'knifing off alone, without the provision of new scripts for future identity development, may enhance pre-existing criminal tendencies rather than lead to desistance' (2007, p. 119). They go on to explain how such new scripts require a consistent change in attitudes and behaviour that covers various domains of life (and not just delinquency). The necessity of such a broad foundation is supported by my research with juvenile prisoners (Zdun, 2012b), which indicates that consistent non-delinquent behaviour tends to occur among those who develop new individual scripts.[4] Those stages in the knifing-off process deserve further consideration, but have not been examined systematically to date.

Criminological research on immigration largely fails to address these aspects adequately, but does offer some pointers. For example, stressful migration experiences and subsequent processes of social (dis)integration are identified as important triggers of (mal)adjustment. Decker and Weerman (2005) argue that the challenge of migration may favour the preservation of existing cultural and behavioural patterns rather than the adoption of new ones, especially where immigrants participate in delinquent youth groups. Baier et al. (2009), on the other

---

4   Inmates who maintain fatalistic life scripts tend to act inconsistently, for instance pretending to prison staff to have knifed off from delinquency, while still continuing secretly (Zdun, 2012b).

hand, argue that delinquency relates more to lack of social integration than to any particular ethnic origin or cultural practice.

It should be noted that such difficulties accumulate only among a minority within an ethnic group, whereas others find more successful means of adjustment (Albrecht, 2003). The experiences and perceptions of deprivation within such minorities appear to foster the maintenance, revitalization or intensification of delinquent behaviour internalized in the country of origin (Zdun, 2007). They display rejection of the migration experience and the receiving society, while gaining self-efficacy by claiming ethnic superiority. They also appear to be inadequately aware of opportunities in the receiving society, and quickly become frustrated by initial failures (Zdun, 2012a). Instead of encountering integration-supporting relationships they become isolated in delinquent groups; recognition for delinquency by disillusioned peers becomes their last resort (Decker and Weerman, 2005).

Even less is known about migration's impact on knifing off from delinquency through separation from former opportunities. Research often excludes pre-migration behaviour and thus fails to distinguish between desisters and non-delinquents, obviating opportunities to examine changes in delinquency at the individual level. Other research includes non-delinquent youth only for purposes of comparison, often going no further than describing differences in attitudes and experiences. My earlier research (Zdun, 2012a) does at least indicate that desistance from delinquency after immigration might result from fast adoption of the expectations and norms of the receiving society and hard work to profit from new opportunities. The desisters not only calmed down in a healthier social environment but actively sought support for integration. They gathered more positive experiences in everyday life than persisters, and interpreted negative events as exceptions.

Data and Methods

Qualitative data was analysed in this research. As Bottoms (2006) emphasizes, examining the logic and dynamics of changes in delinquency requires in-depth qualitative research. In addition, this kind of research rather allows for exploring the individual developments and interpretations involved (Flick, 1995).

The original sample comprised 40 young male immigrants from the FSU but included youth that were non-delinquent before immigration; they were excluded. Thus, the study considers 26 cases: 19 persisters (P) and 7 desisters (D). The original sampling was especially grounded in violent behaviour after immigration, with further information on delinquency in both societies collected during the interviews; i.e. the cases were not chosen according to delinquency before immigration.

Interviewees were 12-15 years old when they arrived in Germany and living there for 2-6 years. The young age at immigration might explain why there were just episodic offenders with sporadic violent and other delinquent behaviour but without criminal records before emigration. Due to the similarity in self-reported delinquency, level of violent encounters, living conditions before emigration, schooling, relationship with parents and involvement in delinquent youth groups, there were no clear-cut differences between later desisters and persisters before emigration. This suggests that migration might have altered their behaviour but this may also be based in methodological limitations or other reasons.

Interviews were conducted in several cities in three federal states of Germany. Interviewees were recruited with the assistance of teachers and social workers in schools and recreation centres for youth where the semi-structured interviews were done. The sampling was based in the above mentioned criteria and guided by those supporters that provided us with respective interviewees. Interviews lasting 90-120 minutes were tape-recorded and transcribed verbatim. Open coding was performed to identify units of meaning and content categories. Subsequently, cross-case analysis was performed to identify themes that cut across interviews (Strauss and Corbin, 1990).

Results

Preparation for Emigration

The data shows few pre-migration differences between respondents, so it would have been futile to seek predictions of later behaviour at that stage. The fights in which interviewees had been involved in the FSU usually entailed no more harm than bruises and black eyes. The honour of the individual or his family was a typical justification or motive for fighting. This occasionally even occurred among friends when they were drunk, but more often involved an impulsive response to provocation by rivals, competing for power and recognition.

> I24(D): I didn't like it when people insulted my parents. I hit them immediately.

> I6(P): You had to react to any kind of serious provocation to prove you're a man, especially when someone insults your family.

Both later desisters and persisters described such forms of showing off as a means of social positioning, but also related how they learned the rules of the street through the respect and sanctions of others.

> I13(D): I didn't grow up at home but in the streets. When I was twelve I often snitched on friends. I did so much shit, even to friends. They beat me up and told me how to behave. They explained how to live and survive. When you are twelve and he is eighteen and you insult him, you can't do that. At first they explained, but if I didn't get it, I was beaten up. When I did it again, I had to pay money. Then it didn't happen anymore.

I39(P): Over there, it was normal to fight sometimes. Every kid is involved, you can't stay out; even guys that don't fight here anymore. But it is not just there, I would say that it's normal to fight and do stupid things when you are young.

Most also came into contact with alcohol and tobacco through peers at a relatively young age. Even those who did not use drugs at this age came to regard it as a normal habit.

I40(D): I lived in a small town when I was ten. I met up with older guys, fifteen- and sixteen-year-olds. That's when the problems with drinking and smoking started.

I2(P): It was common to drink and smoke as a kid.

The relatively sparse data on personal agency basically indicates uncertainty about the decision to emigrate, but also hopes and plans. Respondents perceived the decision as having been made solely by their parents, and the anticipated emotional loss tended to increase their insecurity; some had completely rejected the whole idea of migration. However, most hoped it might improve their opportunities and were confident of coping with new and unknown social and living conditions.

I24(D): I didn't know what to expect from life here but I assumed that things would be different. Things are different, indeed, but I arrived willing to adjust my behaviour. I had no choice because my parents said that we had to go.

I25(P): I've got to tell you that it would have been alright to get not involved in fights anymore. I arrived with the idea that things would change, leaving the past behind. It would have been better to stay there, but now it's too late.

The data demonstrates that later persisters and desisters shared similar hopes, tended not to plan to remain delinquent and showed similar agency, in the sense of confidence that they could have control over the activities in which they engage and could desist from delinquency.

With respect to the social and structural situation, the parents were usually rather authoritarian and demanded respect from their offspring, especially obedience and politeness at home.

I14(D): Well, dad didn't hit me with a stick. If I behaved really badly and he had to complain twice, he used the belt... But it wasn't so severe.

I39(P): We had to do what our parents said; that wasn't questioned. If we did anything wrong they showed us that it was wrong in a way you don't forget.

Prior to emigration, responsibility for educational progress was largely attributed to the school, with most parents intervening only to apply sanctions if the child failed to meet their expectations. Because of this and the authoritarian nature of the school system, teachers were usually respected and truancy was uncommon. Even beyond school, parental control tended to be based on demanding respect and defending the family reputation rather than physical control. Respondents felt relatively free in their spare time, most of which they spent with peers. Older friends especially became role models of delinquency, which was usually treated by parents as a normal element of youth socialization as long as it did not go 'too far'.

> I35(D): For many parents it was normal that we fought. If someone got beaten up, the father might even say: 'Go back and beat him up too.'

> I29(P): Well, when a son comes to his father with a black eye and says: 'Oh, dad, someone hit me. I was beaten up,' he will reply: 'How many of them were there?' 'Three.' 'Did you at least hit back? You have to prove that you are stronger.'

So the social environment – state institutions at times as well – provided little support for rejection of delinquency.

Finally, all respondents reported perceiving pre-emigration living conditions as quite good and there was no relevant difference in parental education between desisters and persisters. With family income generally reported as having been around or slightly above average, subjective structural aspects did not serve as a predictor of individual post-immigration development.

The Move and Settling In: Desisters

One general reason why migration may contribute to knifing off is the abrupt loss of opportunity structures of delinquency. Specifically, the loss of old friends and lack of new ones in the initial period after arrival makes fights and other means of showing off at least temporarily more difficult. This period is tended to be used for observing new norms and practices and reflecting on earlier behaviour. Language difficulties may create misunderstandings, but also stimulate curiosity, explanation-seeking and making friends.

Desisters described this first period as rather confusing:

> I8(D): Many things were strange at first. I had no friends and had to make new ones to learn from them.

But how do we know that this development was not just a maturing process? And what contributed to knifing off completely? The change appears not to be an age- or maturity based form of desistance because the respondents arrived in Germany at the relatively young age of 12 to 15, while the aforementioned forms (parenthood, employment, etc.) tend to occur in young adulthood (Sampson and Laub, 2005). Secondly, knifing off seems to require a healthy interplay of agency with the social and structural situation. The empirical data indicates that the desisters avoided further delinquency largely due to positively perceived experiences and support, in the sense of an encouraging environment of non-delinquent friends and supportive institutional agents. Everyday experiences and reliable support strengthened agency, self-efficacy and the readiness to practise non-delinquent behaviour.

> I24(D): Well, I behaved better here right from the beginning because I wanted to do so and got a lot of help from my friends but also in school.[5]

The centrality of peer and institutional support is underlined by the prevalent inability of parents to provide much assistance in this period because they were themselves often more overwhelmed by the new situation than their offspring. Such help also contributed to rapid language acquisition, familiarization with new norms, non-delinquent behaviour and development of new goals and life scripts.

> I13(D): In the beginning it was difficult but then everything turned out well. I started believing in myself after half a year.

Once respondents felt assured in this behavioural shift, (singular) negative experiences of discrimination and failure no longer harmed their motivation to desist from delinquency, which instead increased due to positive experiences in other domains of life.

> I11(D): The majority is kind. There are people who say that Russians are bad, that they are all the same, that they drink and fight. This happened to me too, but I didn't mind about it. I also dislike this kind of immigrants. People who know me like me the way I am.

Such developments could even help compensate the emotional loss caused by migration.

The commitment of individual social workers and teachers who functioned as role models had a strong impact. Their contributions appear to have been especially crucial in helping or motivating respondents to actually realize new goals in life.

> I8(D): My friends were important but without the help of teachers and people from here [youth club] it would have been more difficult. In the beginning I was without any direction in life, they gave me one. I don't want to disappoint them.

Desistance often referred to a new future identity script grounded in conformity rather than delinquency. Residual problem behaviour remained, such as underage

---

5   Note that such friends were usually made only after weeks or months.

and/or excessive consumption of alcohol and tobacco, but this is also common among autochthonous adolescents and thus if anything an indicator of social integration.

Finally, note that despite the lack of tangible parental support, desisters usually at least received encouragement from the family.

> I35(D): I spend more time at home now. Things are better. Even if I have to help, it's a different atmosphere. They are happy about my change and I try to support them. Family means much more to me now and I like the new responsibilities.

This promoted the development of agency and the improved the relationship with parents. The adolescent's role and responsibilities in the family grew because they adjusted more quickly to the new circumstances than their parents, sometimes even helping them learn German. This also fed into the new script for living, strengthening values of family and social engagement.

The Move and Settling In: Persisters

Persisters were also separated from former opportunity structures of delinquency through immigration. Suddenly lacking friends and an environment in which they could attract attention and recognition, delinquency became the exception in the first months. They also observed differences in social norms and practices and compared them with their own socialization. Puzzling differences were also understood with the assistance of new friends.

> I4(D): I had to get used to the new situation. Many things were different and I had no friends. I didn't get in trouble at first because there were just no situations. But then I made friends who explained things.

Given the similarities to the situation for desisters, why did these respondents fail to knife off completely? Broadly speaking, experiences of initial failure, lack of social support and making the 'wrong' friends quickly led to loss of agency and new delinquency. Typical delinquent behaviours were illicit drug use and street offences to make money or relieve boredom. The selection, intensity and frequency of such acts was largely conditioned by group patterns and opportunity structures, in particular because many offences were committed together.

The negative development of persisters seems to relate mainly to lack of integrative support from peers, with whom persisters tended to be discontented. Firstly, these were the 'wrong' friends, perceived as less caring about others than the friends who had been left behind, as talking less about private problems, and as being alliances of convenience rather than true circles of friends.

> I25(P): If I have problems in the family, I won't discuss that with them [friends].
> It's your family and you mustn't tell them that kind of thing. You never know
> what they might do if they know too much about you.

Secondly, new friends provided support in fights, a space to express negative
experiences and recognition for delinquency, but offered little emotional support
(which the persisters in general lacked). In this group they were relatively
rarely exposed to socially acceptable behaviour, accumulated further negative
experiences with institutions and encouraged each other in defiant attitudes and
behaviour.

Parents were regularly described as too busy to cope with the new situation. In
contrast to the desisters, the atmosphere in the family often worsened and mutual
support declined. Specifically, deterioration of the financial and structural situation
was capable of eroding parental support and control.

> I32(P): My parents could no longer help me. My father was drinking and my
> mother just had a poorly paid job. I don't know why we came here. Everything
> is worse.

Displays of rejection of the parental decision to emigrate were common,
contributing to an impression of having been forced to go to Germany. Overall,
families tended to become dysfunctional and their authority was challenged,
fostering negative family dynamics. This increased the attractiveness of delinquent
peer groups that shared the same problems and became the main locus of social
interaction, although they had little to offer for the adolescent's development.
Persisters thus lost agency and options for positive development, defiantly sticking
to old internalized attitudes and behaviour and developing a rather fatalistic script
for the future.

> I4(P): I just had my friends. It was good to have them because they understood
> me. We spoke Russian and felt the same. Among them, I got used to behaving
> like we did at home. Why should we have changed for others?

Another element of this negative process was perceived lack of support from state
institutions. Frustration exacerbated by experiences of discrimination and initial
failure in various spheres of life (such as school, labour market) led to rejection of
the receiving society and its norms.

> I2(P): Once we were sitting at a playground. We weren't doing anything wrong.
> But the police came every day checking if we were up to anything. That was
> mean. Once they thought we had done something and we were handcuffed for
> hours. They searched us to see if we had drugs or weapons just because of what
> we did before.

Persisters quickly developed the impression that they were excluded from participation in mainstream cultural and societal goals. Poor language skills, difficulties with unfamiliar teaching methods, declining performance, and conflicts with teachers and other pupils were mutually reinforcing at school. Such experiences further minimized agency and self-efficacy and contributed to fatalism.

> I25(P): It was the same at school. Me and my friends were treated worse than others. And the way things are done in school here is strange anyway. It's difficult to learn. And teachers are so weak; I can't respect them.

Negative experiences in the public sphere sparked by defiant and delinquent behaviour further narrowed social interactions. The individual efforts of social workers were insufficient or perceived as irrelevant to personal matters, and youth clubs were mainly used for leisure activities with peers.

> I22(P): The youth workers like to discuss things and tell what we are doing wrong. But they live their naive lives. They don't understand our problems. Of course I want to have a nice house and a car some day. But I will not change for this.

Overall, persisters lacked positive role models after immigration, developed or maintained low failure tolerance and subsequently lost agency and the motivation to integrate, further narrowing their opportunities. They defined negative scripts for future identity grounded in maintenance – in some cases even expansion – of delinquency and lack of confidence in future opportunities.

Maintenance among Desisters

The stage following the initial relocation was a period of habitualization. Social bonds were strengthened and living conditions (in some cases) improved, stabilizing conformity, agency and self-efficacy. Previous delinquent behaviour became interpreted as a relic of former times in the FSU. Two forms of 'new identity' were identified in the empirical data; others may exist. Firstly, looking back, some respondents stated that they had never been really delinquent and just behaved that way for the sake of protection and peer recognition.

> I40(D): Well, at the age of twelve or sixteen all kids are a little bit crazy over there. They think: 'I'm cool. I can do anything.' Well, you want to show off. It has no meaning; you participate and help friends in need.

Immigration became a vehicle to leave this behind and seek non-delinquent friends.

Secondly, others settled down in a post-immigration environment with a low level of delinquency. Former delinquency was condemned, with migration interpreted as a means to overcome that and the new non-delinquent identity regarded as superior.

> I14(D): I came to live in a place without violence. It was strange in the beginning, but in a good way. It would be wrong to act any other way here. I would still help friends in trouble, but I never saw a fight. You can help them in better ways.

No further substantive differences appeared within either group, suggesting that the distinction might merely reflect different rationalizations of the knifing off process. The development of self-image did however promote self-efficacy grounded in a lasting positive interplay of the triad of agency and social and structural situation. Conformity became an unquestioned element of the new identity and was thus no longer perceived as noteworthy in everyday life. Situational motivation for desistance became less important and was replaced by new habits and a social environment that promoted conformity and would have been at least confused by a relapse, further minimizing opportunity structures for delinquency.

> I35(D): The fights in Russia seem so far away. I cannot really remember that life. I don't have any situations now where I even think about using violence. In the beginning, I had to get used to it, but now it all comes naturally.

These changes were also promoted by the family and institutions. Although further empirical scrutiny is required, the data indicates that positive developments for individual family members contributed to family relations in general. The significance of the adolescents in the family did not decline simply because the parents gradually coped better in the new situation and therefore required less assistance. This improved the family's well-being and allowed it to afford to live in relatively untroubled and non-disadvantaged areas, further minimizing opportunity structures for delinquency. More important, parents were able to pay more attention to their offspring, contributing to their goal-attainment.

> I8(D): Things in the family got better when we arrived. Nowadays, it is even better. We respect each other and my parents have much more trust and confidence in me. They don't control my activities but they do support my achievements.

However, it must be noted that the data does not necessarily indicate a clear-cut distinction between well-off desisters and poor persisters several years after immigration. Instead, differences related to both the atmosphere in the family and its perception of possible future progress.

Finally, the relevance of institutions as role models and supporters of desistance decreased over time. Instead, they became agents promoting habitualization, assisting the process of integration and contributing to the individual realization of new life scripts. Interestingly, desisters also actively sought help from a range of institutions.

> I14(D): There were some people who helped me a lot. They explained how to do things. It was important that I had them. But of course I also seek help from others, now that I am used to this.

This is noteworthy because such efforts require adjustment, trust and integration into society.

Maintenance and Developments among Persisters

Developments among persisters were far more heterogeneous and disorganized. Those who arrived relatively young, in particular, often became more violent in fights and committed new types of offences. This appears to relate less to migration than to developmental processes in adolescence that may trigger delinquency. Learning processes also mattered, with delinquent behaviour adopted from peers. On the other hand, in Germany older adolescents usually became less delinquent at about age 18. They usually believed that they had become too old or finally realized that delinquency might negatively affect their future opportunities.

> I6(P): When you're young it is normal to fight. I'm more mature now.

In general, maintenance of delinquent behaviour among persisters appeared to be largely age- and maturity-based. Interestingly, even the active persisters in the sample anticipated that they might become less delinquent as adults, due to the normative expectations acquired in the FSU. Note that the reduction in delinquent behaviour at the age of about 18 must therefore not be misinterpreted as an indicator of social integration but is instead another means of maintaining internalized attitudes from the society of origin. This is also indicated by plans mentioned by some interviewees to educate their own children in 'traditional' ways. And even if fighting as a source of recognition, shoplifting and the use of illicit drugs declined and were interpreted as immature, violence itself was often still accepted as a means of resolving conflicts – just the number of incidents decreased.

> I22(P): I don't reject violence absolutely. I would still fight if it was necessary. This is normal and my sons should do the same. My life just changed; I rarely get into trouble any more.

This reduction in brawling was mainly based on a conscious decision and seemed to be largely tolerated by peers from the FSU milieu. This can thus be interpreted as a maturity-based form of desistance, one grounded not necessarily in removal of the social environment but in a deliberate removal of prior behaviour; to that extent it is also agency-based.

In other cases the change seemed largely to involve a reduction in opportunity structures for delinquency due to spending less time with male friends and more with a girlfriend or at work.

> I29(P): I also changed for my girlfriend. I quit fighting and hung out less with friends. One time they called me: 'There's a fight.' I just replied: 'It's good that I'm not there.' The police came, now they have to do some community service. I am glad I was with my girl and not in the police car.

Thus the initial post-migration loss of agency to desist from delinquency caused by negative experiences and quick maladjustment might partly be compensated by age- and maturity-based forms of desistance in early adulthood, as outlined above. While these do not necessarily require integration in the receiving society, individual agency and motivation to reduce delinquency still appear crucial. Although persisters often still felt unwelcome in society and rejected various norms and institutions, they became used to reacting less aggressively and more instrumentally (see Zdun, 2012b).

> I22(P): I really don't like the behaviour of people in public institutions. They treat me worse and reject me. So I don't care about their rules. I know what they expect and I act that way when it helps me. I learnt that resistance is not always useful.

The data indicates that even such a development might contribute to calming down. Moreover, it was helpful when persisters finally defined realistic life goals and devoted more time and energy to pursuing them. By increasing their efforts they may gather positive experiences and gain self-efficacy.

> I16(P): I didn't do well at school but finally decided that I have to change some things and get vocational training. I tried hard and was on my own. There wasn't much help. But I did it and I'm doing vocational training now.

However, these successes should not be overestimated, because most persisters still lacked language abilities, schooling, goal-attainment, positive role models and/or effective support. This makes them more susceptible to recidivism. Quite a few repeatedly failed to achieve their goals and relapsed into delinquency; some even used illicit drugs to compensate for these experiences.

> I39(P): I tried different things but they didn't really interest me. Everything is getting worse all the time. I don't know what people expect from us. I did an internship, went to work every day. You do the same things as the others but don't get any money for the job. So I quit. You get frustrated and angry. Maybe this is why I still act like this [laughs].

Furthermore, they often kept their friends, with whom they shared experiences of failure and dealt with them in similar ways, indicating that in some respects the forms of delinquency are refined in early adulthood rather than abandoning delinquent behaviour completely.

The low chances of positive development even seem to be reinforced by negative attitudes toward state institutions, which interviewees largely contacted only as applicants for social welfare; other forms of support were refused (thus avoiding institutional control).

> I6(P): The people at the job centre and other offices treat me badly. They assume that I don't want to work, and I have lost my motivation due to this. They pretend that they want to help but I don't trust them.

Social institutions such as youth clubs were rarely perceived as relevant supporters and at most used for leisure activities, seldom for personal development. This was partly because of an individual lack of interest in certain measures, but also a lack of a supportive infrastructure that additionally contributed to habitualizing rejection of the receiving society, reducing opportunities to integrate and maintaining rather fatalistic views of life.

Conclusions

The data suggests migration can serve as a form of knifing off based not only on a changed environment but also on a consistent development of attitudes and behaviour in different domains of life. While the comparison shows that desisters and persisters may not differ in terms of delinquency, agency, and social and structural situation before migration, they develop in quite different ways upon arrival. Immigrants tend to knife off when their agency and motivation are acknowledged and when they receive adequate assistance and social control from new friends and institutions, minimizing opportunity structures for delinquency and compensating for lack of family support and control. Prior delinquency quickly becomes irrelevant and may later even be (re)interpreted as immature, while – according to Maruna and Roy (2007) – new scripts for identity based on conformity and social engagement are developed.

On the other hand, persistence appears to be fostered by repeated experiences of initial failure in the crucial period of transition from one society to another that quickly generate fatalistic views of life and are especially reinforced by friendships with peers who share similar problems and provide opportunity structures for delinquency. The data suggests further counterproductive effects where dysfunctional families become increasingly unable to supply emotional support and create another source of everyday conflicts, fostering the loss of agency and self-efficacy. Finally, a lack of positive relationships with institutional agents reinforces a negative image of society, which is rejected along with its norms. Under these conditions young immigrants are more likely to resume delinquent behaviour as an easily available source of recognition.

Nevertheless, delinquency may be aged- and maturity-based among immigrant persisters, allowing – according to Sampson and Laub (2005) – for processes of desistance in early adulthood. In other words, while frustration and delinquency might increase initially when the social and structural situation develops poorly and agency and self-efficacy are subsequently lost, early persistence after immigration might still be overcome. But the data does not permit identification of which specific forms of social support and control promote desistance and persistence. However, unless further research proves otherwise, exposure to and perception of forms of support and control seem to be crucial, while particular the sources and content appear to be secondary.

Later desistance or reductions in delinquency – after a number of years of residency – appear to be rooted in individual development rather than experiences of migration and social integration. But as we know from desistance research (Mulvey et al., 2004), such processes include relapses into delinquent behaviour and unstable agency, demonstrating inadequate individual competence in coping with failure. These findings support Maruna and Roy's observation (2007) that knifing off is insufficient as long as new scripts for future identity are lacking (see Zdun, 2012b). It should be added that a stable and positive interplay of the triad of individual agency and social and structural situation also appears to be necessary.

Overall, while it seems misguided to assume that certain post-immigration experiences or pathways might be predicted beforehand or in the early stages of immigration, the aforementioned patterns do serve to explain which kinds of experiences and support contribute to knifing off or persistence and the development of new life scripts.

These findings are, however, subject to various limitations. Due to its qualitative nature the sample is non-representative. Our approach did not aim for representativeness of the population but – following *grounded theory* – representativeness of the empirically generated theoretical concepts (Strauss and Corbin, 1990). The sample is selective: female adolescents and non-immigrant controls were excluded and the interviewees were relatively young at the moment of immigration. Different sampling methods would bear potential to generate broader insights. It would also appear worthwhile to address a broader range of delinquent behaviour. Although the study was not restricted to violent offences, information about other forms of delinquency was not systematically collected.

The data is retrospective. Bottoms (2006) argues that such data bears a risk of bias. Cognitive developments, fading memory of prior events and changing interpretations of experiences during the life-course are the main problems of retrospective research.

Another shortcoming is that the interviews provide insufficient data for in-depth analysis of the first stage of emigration, the process of preparation. Specifically, information is lacking on delinquent behaviour, as the interviewees were asked about offences prior to migration in general, but not specifically about this period.

They also supply little information on individual agency in changing or maintaining behaviour after migration. Finally, the actual importance of social support for desistance from friends and institutions deserves further investigation, along with the significance of individual competency and personality for integration.

Despite these shortcomings, the results are valuable because they confirm previous findings on knifing off and desistance, and contribute insights into the previously neglected meaning of immigration. The findings suggest that immigration is a powerful event that can contribute not only to temporary knifing off but under certain conditions also to permanent desistance from delinquency. But it should be noted that such life events are not causal factors for desistance or persistence; they merely provide new chances and opportunities. How opportunities are used and how an individual develops depends largely on individual personality as well as the structural situation and support from the social environment and institutions. The findings demonstrate the relevance of the interplay of these aspects in reinforcing the dynamics of developmental processes.

References

Agnew, R. (2001). An Overview of General Strain Theory. In: R. Paternoster (Ed.), *Essays in Criminological Theories* (pp. 161-174). Los Angeles: Roxbury.

Albrecht, G. (2003). Sociological Approaches to Individual Violence and Their Empirical Evaluation. In: W. Heitmeyer and J. Hagan (Eds.), *International Handbook on Violence Research* (pp. 611-656). Dordrecht: Kluwer Academic.

Baier, D., Pfeiffer, C., Simonson, J., and Rabold, S. (2009). *Jugendliche in Deutschland als Opfer und Täter von Gewalt: Erster Forschungsbericht zum gemeinsamen Forschungsprojekt des Bundesministeriums des Innern und des KFN.* Hannover: KFN.

Blumstein, A., Cohen, J., and Farrington, D. (1988). Criminal Career Research: Its Value for Criminology. *Criminology, 26*, 1-35.

Bottoms, A. (2006). Desistance, Social Bonds, and Human Agency: A Theoretical Exploration. In: P.-O. Wikström and R. Sampson (Eds.), *The Explanation of Crime* (pp. 243-290). Cambridge: Cambridge University Press.

Bottoms, A., Shapland, J., Costello, A., Holmes, D., and Muir, G. (2004). Toward Desistance: Theoretical Underpinnings for an Empirical Study. *The Howard Journal, 43*, 368-389.

Burnett, R. and Maruna, S. (2004). So "Prison Works", Does It? The Criminal Career of 130 Men Released from Prison under Home Secretary, Michael Howard. *The Howard Journal, 43*, 390-404.

Decker, S., and Weerman, F. (2005). *European Street Gangs and Troublesome Youth Groups.* Lanham: Rowman and Littlefield.

Flick, U. (1995). *Qualitative Forschung: Theorie, Methoden, Anwendung in Psychologie und Sozialwissenschaften.* Reinbek: Rowohlt.

Gottfredson, M., and Hirschi, T. (1990). *A General Theory of Crime*. Stanford: Stanford University Press.

Haug, S., Baraulina, T., and Babka von Gostomski, C. (2008). *Kriminalität von Aussiedlern. Eine Bestandsaufnahme*. Nuremberg: Bundesamt für Migration und Flüchtlinge.

Laub, J., and Sampson, R. (2001). Understanding Desistance from Crime. *Crime and Justice, 28*, 1-69.

Laub, J., and Sampson, R. (2003). *Shared Beginnings, Divergent Lives: Delinquent Boys to Age 70*. Cambridge, MA: Harvard University Press.

Maruna, S. (2001). *Making Good: How Ex-Convicts Reform and Rebuild their Lives*. Washington, DC: American Psychological Association.

Maruna, S., and Roy, K. (2007). Amputation or Reconstruction? Notes on the Concept of "Knifing Off" and Desistance from Crime. *Journal of Contemporary Criminal Justice, 23*, 104-124.

Moffitt, T. (1993). Adolescence-Limited and Life-Course-Persistent Antisocial Behavior: A Developmental Taxonomy. *Psychological Review, 100*, 674-701.

Monahan, K., Steinberg, L., Cauffman, E., and Mulvey, E. (2009). Trajectories of Antisocial Behavior and Psychosocial Maturity from Adolescence to Young Adulthood. *Developmental Psychology, 45*, 1654-1668.

Mulvey, E., Steinberg, L., Fagan, J., Cauffman, E., Piquero, A., Chassin, L., Knight, G., Brame, R., Schubert, C., Hecker, T., and Losoya, S. (2004). Theory and Research on Desistance from Antisocial Activity Among Serious Adolescent Offenders. *Youth Violence and Juvenile Justice, 2*, 213-236.

Sampson, R., and Laub, J. (1993). *Crime in the Making: Pathways and Turning Points Through Life*. Cambridge, MA: Harvard University Press.

Sampson, R., and Laub, J. (2003). Life-Course Desisters? Trajectories of Crime Among Delinquent Boys Followed to Age 70, *Criminology, 41*, 555-592.

Sampson, R., and Laub, J. (2005). A Life-Course View of the Development of Crime. *The Annals of the American Academy of Political and Social Science, 602*, 12-45.

Strauss, A., and Corbin, J. (1990). *Basics of Qualitative Research: Grounded Theory Procedures and Techniques*. California: Sage.

Strobl, R., and Kühnel, W. (2000). *Dazugehörig und ausgegrenzt: Analysen zu Integrationschancen junger Aussiedler*. Weinheim: Juventa.

Zdun, S. (2007). *Ablauf, Funktion und Prävention von Gewalt: Eine soziologische Analyse der Verhaltensweisen in den Cliquen junger Russlanddeutscher*. Frankfurt: Peter Lang.

Zdun, S. (2012a). The Normative Struggle of Young Street Culture Migrants from the Former Soviet Union. *Sociological Focus, 45*, 143-158.

Zdun, S. (2012b). The meaning of agency in processes of desisting from delinquent behaviour in prison: An exploratory study among juvenile inmates in Germany. *Journal of Social Work Practice, 26*, 459-472.

PART III
Preparing for a Future: Transitions within the New Country and Related Opportunities

Chapter 9

Mobility Aspirations of Immigrant and Native Youth in Germany and Israel

Noah Lewin-Epstein, Zerrin Salikutluk, Irena Kogan and Frank Kalter

Introduction

Many young men and women appear to follow a rather straightforward path to socioeconomic success while others falter and fall far behind. In order for society to address these differences in educational and occupational attainments it is first necessary to understand their underlying mechanisms. One of the more important factors associated with differences in socioeconomic success of young adults is the educational and occupational aspirations they espouse. Status attainment research has repeatedly demonstrated that such aspirations and expectations are among the most important predictors of eventual socioeconomic attainment (e.g., Feliciano and Rumbaut, 2005; Goyette and Xie, 1999; Perlmann and Waldinger, 1997; Waldinger and Perlmann, 1998).

Educational and occupational aspirations and their realization take on particular importance when it comes to immigrant youth. To a large extent aspirations represent an important stage in the process of incorporation and the extent to which immigrant youth are able to realize their aspirations can serve as a useful indicator of the barriers they face. Whereas research dealing with educational aspirations in the context of migration has been expanding (Kao and Tienda, 1995; Kao and Tienda, 1998; Heath and Brinbaum, 2007; Jonsson and Rudolphi, 2011), the formation of occupational and mobility aspirations among young immigrants and the extent to which they differ from those of native-born are still understudied, leaving a gap between the strategic importance of aspirations for the successful integration of the second generation of immigrants and current knowledge about its conditions (Portes, 1996; Rong and Brown, 2001; Zhou, 1997). Furthermore, while the literature on intergenerational social mobility is vast (for a recent review see Breen and Jonsson, 2005), subjective social mobility, which refers to one's perceived movement up or down the social ladder as compared to the previous generation, has received rather little attention.

The current chapter aims to contribute to our understanding of the integration of second generation immigrants by studying their occupational and mobility aspiration in comparison to those of their native-born peers. We focus in particular on the role of educational achievements, family resources and parental expectations. The population under study consists of immigrants from the FSU in Israel and Germany. Although they originated from different areas of the FSU and have somewhat different socio-demographic characteristics they share three important similarities: they are returning Diasporas who benefit from full citizenship rights; they possess relatively little financial means; and by comparison to most immigrant groups they are skilled and more highly educated.

Occupational and Mobility Aspirations of Immigrant Youth – Theoretical Considerations

Differentiated Occupational Aspirations

Aspirations are goals an individual strives for. These goals can be set in regard to educational degrees, occupational careers or other life domains. In view of the importance attributed to the transition into employment in market economies, occupational aspirations have been the subject of both theoretical conceptualization and empirical investigation for over half a century. Occupational aspirations can be expressed either in absolute terms based on a particular occupation or, more broadly, an occupational category to which one aspires, or they may be measured in relative terms (higher/lower, better/worse) using parental occupations as a reference. In the latter case one speaks of subjective mobility aspirations, that is whether youths expect to achieve higher socioeconomic status (as measured by one's occupation) as compared to their parents.[1]

The development of occupational aspirations and choices has been conceptualized by some researchers (e.g., Holland, 1997; Gottfredson, 1981) as primarily a function of individuals' aptitudes and personality traits, whereas others have emphasized the fact that individuals' choices are embedded within a social context. This context consists of both the immediate family environment and the more elusive social and cultural structure (e.g., Sewell and Hauser, 1975; Vondracek, Lerner, and Schulenberg, 1986; Yates, Harris, Sabates, and Staff, 2011). The latter position, which we adopt here, views individuals' aptitudes as important determinants of aspirations in as much as they receive recognition from the social environment in the form of educational achievements, parental expectations and those of peers.

When considering the aspirations of teenagers, the impact of family, or more specifically parents, cannot be overstated (Sewell and Hauser, 1975; Schoon and Parsons, 2002). The structural position of the family within the stratification system represents both material and cultural resources that affect offspring aspirations. Beliefs and expectations of parents are instilled in children by means

---

1   With regard to mobility aspirations, research has identified actual occupational mobility as the strongest predictor of one's subjective evaluation of mobility; and that one's educational gains relative to parents, irrespective of the actual occupational outcome, increase the sense of subjective mobility (Kelley and Kelley, 2009).

of the socialization process, and the extent of material resources at the family's disposal impact on the opportunities or constraints their offspring face. To address these relationships more systematically we posit a contextual model (Schoon and Parsons, 2002) according to which teenage occupational aspirations are affected by their educational attainment as well as the family's position in the stratification system. This structural position encompasses material, cultural, and social resources all of which are likely to affect offspring's aspirations directly or indirectly (through educational attainment). In the following paragraphs we elaborate briefly on each of these components.

Educational achievements constitute an important factor in the formation of both educational and occupational aspirations. The achievements that youths display as they grow up serve as means for self-assessing their capabilities and skills and forming a view of what they might expect in the future. For instance, students who reported having good scholastic achievement were more likely to pursue a professional occupation status while students who reported lower achievements, pursued semi-professions (Patton and Creed, 2007). Furthermore, children's achievements in school are likely to influence the expectations parents have for their children (Goldenberg, Gallimore, Reese, and Garnier, 2001), which in turn affect children's own expectations.

Family background shapes the aspirations of offspring in multiple ways. Not surprisingly, studies have typically found that economic resources positively influence aspirations. The more abundant resources available to youths from higher socioeconomic backgrounds contribute to their educational achievements and also provide a safety net against failure. Such youth are then able to aspire higher and take greater risks. Indeed, empirical findings support this proposition and reveal a positive relationship between material assets of the family and occupational aspirations as well as occupational achievements (Schoon and Parsons, 2002; Yates, Harris, Sabates, and Staff, 2011).

Family background differentiation is also expressed through distinct cultural capital. A rough indicator of such distinction is the educational level of the parents. Researchers have shown that highly educated parents attribute higher value to education. Consequently they place higher demands on their children, which in turn affect their educational achievements and, indirectly, their aspirations.

The third relevant resource is social capital, both within and between families. In line with Coleman's assertion regarding the importance of family social capital for offspring aspirations and attainment (Coleman, 1988), we expect that both within-family norms and the status of parental networks will have a positive impact on offspring aspirations. Within-family social capital refers primarily to education- and occupation-related interactions between parents and their children, including transmission of respective norms within the family.

The between-family social capital is created from the interactions with people at school, in the neighborhood, community, etc. Social capital embedded in these networks provides substantial information on occupational opportunities and their requirements and future assistance in attaining these expectations.

Although the direction in which family social capital will affect aspirations is very much dependent on the dominant values and beliefs espoused by the family members (Hao and Bonstead-Bruns, 1998) studies have generally found a positive relationship between family social capital and offspring's occupational aspirations (e.g., Marjoribanks, 2002).

Migration Status and Occupational Aspirations

The above factors have been shown to affect youth occupational aspirations in general (in various societal contexts). Yet their implications are likely to vary by population group. Correll (2004) has convincingly argued that cultural beliefs regarding the structural position of various groups constrain the development of career aspirations. Her study focused specifically on gender but the argument can be extended to groups defined by immigration status in as much as these are fairly well-defined collectives. In light of the disadvantages typically associated with migration, immigrant families are likely to posses fewer or less transferable resources than average native families.

In fact, several conceptual models have been developed with the specific aim of linking immigrant status to the formation of aspirations. One such model is the "positive selection" model. It emphasizes the fact that many immigrants are highly motivated and enjoy an edge over native-born due to certain qualities and values that they posses. It is assumed that these traits are transmitted to their offspring. Immigrant parents instill in their children dispositions and skills that are then revealed in higher aspirations and achievements of second generation immigrant youth compared to the native-born (Krahn and Taylor, 2005). The second generation has the advantage of being socialized in the dominant culture and language and hence, is in a position to better realize the wished educational success (Kao and Tienda, 1995).

The "positive selection" model has been substantiated by research showing that most immigrant youth hold very high ambitions and hopes for their future (Feliciano and Rumbaut, 2005). The underlying circumstances that result in high aspirations among immigrants, at times higher than those of natives, have important consequences for the future of immigrant youth. To the extent that the high occupational aspirations are driven by accurate self-assessment of their skills and opportunities, and supported by high motivation they will lead to high achievements and upward social mobility. Yet, there is also the possibility that high aspirations are not aligned with abilities, educational achievements and opportunities. In this case there is greater risk of "fractured transitions"; that is of not finding employment and remaining on the margins of the labor market. This is especially true for those who grow up in disadvantaged socioeconomic backgrounds (Yates, Harris, Sabates, and Staff, 2011).

Not every immigrant group aspires for high educational degrees and occupational success in a host society. Contrary to the first theoretical stream, lower aspirations can be explained by the so called "second generation revolt" (Perlmann and Waldinger,

1997) or the "second generation decline" (Gans, 1992). It suggests that immigrant youth denounce the normative mobility aspirations. This phenomenon is typically brought about by a combination of exogenous factors such as discrimination, together with endogenous factors relating to their family background. According to this view, perceived hurdles and fewer opportunities for social success dampen aspirations and influence educational and occupational choices, resulting in lower achievement (Fouad and Byars-Winston, 2005; Rong and Brown, 2001). This was shown to be the case especially where race and color are involved, and social barriers are particularly high (Fouad and Byars-Winston, 2005)

The two theoretical frameworks outlined above lead to different expectations regarding occupational aspirations of immigrants' children in comparison to natives. In view of the fact that in both Germany and Israel the immigrant groups under study are viewed as returning Diaspora we expect them to align themselves with the mainstream. We therefore lean toward the positive selection hypothesis rather than the second generation revolt hypothesis. In accordance with this we expect immigrant youth to display higher mobility aspirations compared to those of the native-born youth. We should note in this respect that first generation immigrants of working age typically experience occupational downgrading in the migration process. High aspirations of their offspring may thus also reflect the hope of recovering the "lost" status.

While we generally expect to find high mobility aspirations among immigrant youth from the FSU, differences may exist between the German and Israeli cases. To the extent that family characteristics of the immigrant populations in the two countries differ, this may have an effect on their offspring's aspirations. Additionally, structural constraints and different mobility regimes in Germany and Israel may impact on the extent to which the aspirations of immigrant youths resemble those of native-born youths in the two societies. In view of the importance of the context of immigration, the next section will outline some relevant features of the two countries.

The Immigrant Populations in Israel and Germany: The Setting

The most recent Jewish wave of immigration from the former USSR (FSU) to Israel, so-called the Great Russian "Aliyah",[2] began in 1988. About 830,000 immigrants from the FSU arrived in Israel by the end of the 1990s, of which 40 per cent were children and youngsters under the age of 30. During the same period Germany experienced immigration of ethnic German immigrants (called also "Aussiedler" or "Spätaussiedler"). Between 1988 and 1998 almost 2.5 million ethnic Germans entered Germany; in 1990 alone, almost 400,000 "Aussiedler" entered Germany (OECD 2007). Since 1993 immigration of ethnic Germans has

---

2   The term which literally means ascent is the term used for the gathering of Jewish Diaspora in the land of Israel.

been limited to those coming from the successor states of the former Soviet Union under certain quotas.

The vast majority of FSU immigrants to Israel arrived under the Israeli Law of Return while most FSU immigrants to Germany entered Germany with the status of "Spätaussiedler", i.e. claiming German ancestry and receiving German citizenship upon arriving. According to official German administrative data, the majority of ethnic Germans that immigrated between 1993 and 2007 from the FSU came from Kazakhstan (50.6 per cent), and Russian Federation (39.8 per cent).[3] As for Israel, of all immigrants from the FSU that arrived between 1990 and 1995, 79 per cent previously resided in the European part of the FSU and 21 per cent arrived from its Asian republics. Most of FSU Jewish immigrants left their homeland because of a socioeconomic crisis and growing anti-Semitism. Socio-economic difficulties and lack of prospects in the FSU were the main reasons for emigration of ethnic Germans as well. Many chose Israel or Germany due to the lower barriers to entry due to their returning Diaspora status.

The majority of FSU ethnic Germans possess some type of vocational education, either at the secondary level (19.1 per cent) or at post-secondary and lower tertiary level (29.8 per cent) (Konietzka and Kreyenfeld, 2001; Kogan, 2004). About 20 per cent of FSU "Aussiedler" had university education, which is quite similar to the proportion of native-born Germans with the university education (Kogan, 2011). The education that ethnic Germans obtained abroad prior to migration was recognized by employers far more frequently than the education of other immigrants, but when it comes to the access to highly qualified positions ethnic Germans appear to encounter considerable difficulties (Greif, Gediga, and Janikowski, 1999; Janikowski, 1999; Westphal, 1999; Kogan, 2011, 2012). It should to be noted, however, that even back in the former Soviet Union only 38.4 per cent of 'Aussiedler' worked in high-status positions compared, for example, to over 75 per cent among Jewish immigrants arriving from the same source country to Germany in the similar time-period (Liebau, 2011).

The two main characteristics of the FSU immigrants to Israel are a very high rate of tertiary education, including academic education and a very low proportion of immigrants with economic means (Sikron and Leshem, 1998). The percentage of persons with 13 years of education or more was 58 per cent among immigrants from the European republics and 43 per cent among those who immigrated from the Asian republics. In terms of economic integration, most of the immigrants that were employed in the USSR joined the Israeli labor market some time after arrival. Despite their academic background, most of them were employed as a semi-professionals, non-professionals and service employees several years after their migration.

Whereas most FSU immigrants to Israel are Jewish, from the European parts of the FSU, have an urban background, are highly educated, not religious and

---

3   The next two sending countries are Kyrgyzstan with only 3.8 per cent of all immigrants and Ukraine with just 2.7 per cent of all FSU ethnic Germans.

with low fertility (Horowitz and Leshem, 1998; Sikron, 1998), FSU immigrants to Germany originate largely from agricultural communities in the former Asian republics of the FSU (Dietz, 2000; Slonim-Nevo, Mirsky, Nauck, and Horowitz, 2007) and possess mainly blue-collar job qualifications. A comparison between FSU immigrants in Germany and Israel reveals that ethnic German immigrants brought with them somewhat lower qualifications and experience in occupations of lower socio-economic status compared to the Jewish counterparts who arrived in Israel with higher educational credentials. The latter also held occupations representing the higher end of occupational distribution. Due to the lower educational and occupational endowments of ethnic Germans' we expect that their children would express, on average, more modest occupational aspirations than the native-born population, whereas the opposite should be true for Israel.

Aside from differences in the composition of the migrant population, structural differences between Germany and Israel are likely to play a role as well. Israel has been shown to be one of the more open societies to social mobility (high fluidity) among economically advanced countries (Breen and Jonsson, 2005; Goldthorpe, Yaish, and Kraus, 1997; Yaish, 2002). Germany, on the other hand, has been shown to be one of the least open societies (Breen and Jonsson, 2005); that is a country with fewer opportunities for mobility. In view of this, we might expect Israeli youth to have greater mobility aspirations than German youth. In each of the societies, immigrant youth are likely to have higher mobility aspirations than native-born youth due to the fact their immigrant parents generally experience occupational downgrading in the migration process. Taking these two factors together suggests that the difference in mobility aspirations between immigrants and native will be larger in Germany than in Israel.

Research Methodology

For the analyses we use data from the project "Young Immigrants in the German and Israeli Educational Systems". The study focuses on the second and third transitions in the educational systems, which take place after the ninth and eleventh grades in Israel and after the ninth and tenth grades in Germany. According to the project design in Germany, students attending ninth grade of lower secondary school (Hauptschule) or comprehensive school, and tenth grade of intermediate secondary school (Realschule) or comprehensive school were interviewed.[4] In Israel the sample was drawn based on the student file provided by the Ministry

---

4   The major focus of the project in Germany was to analyse transitions from education to vocational training. Students attending the highest track in the German educational system (Gymnasium) were hence excluded from the data collection. This was mainly due to the fact that the ninth and tenth graders at the Gymnasium make their transition to vocational training or higher education at later stages (Grade 12 or 13) and thus are not in a comparable situation to their peers from lower educational tracks.

of Education, whereby students in ninth and eleventh grades from Hebrew (non-religious) public schools in cities with more than 10,000 residents were included in the sampling frame.

In Germany, the data were gathered in three federal states with fairly comparable structure of their educational systems – Hamburg, Hesse and North Rhine-Westphalia. Around half of sample was randomly selected from the population register from eighteen cities in these federal states. Another half of the sample encompasses students surveyed in 74 schools in the three federal states. On account of missing values and non-participation of mothers our final sample is comprised of 461 immigrant youth and 520 natives in Israel and 357 immigrant youth and 454 natives in Germany.

The present study examines the occupational and mobility aspirations of youth during their school years. Students were asked in what occupation they want to work when they grow up. We use the International Socio-Economic Index of occupations (ISEI) to indicate the status, or social standing, of the occupation reported by respondents (Ganzeboom, De Graaf, and Treiman, 1992). We then employ the socioeconomic standing of the occupations respondents as a measure of their occupational aspirations. Mobility aspirations of respondents pertain to expectations for subjective intergenerational mobility and are measured as the extent of agreement with the following statement: "It is important for me to work in an occupation that is better than the occupations of my parents'"; the values ranging from 1 – strongly disagree to 5 – strongly agree.

The independent variables included in our analyses are those that have been theorized to influence youth aspirations. The central variable of interest is migration status. We constructed a dichotomous variable that receives the value of "0" for natives (that is offspring of parents who were born in Israel/Germany) and a value of "1" for FSU immigrants. School achievement is used to predict respondents' occupational aspirations. It is measured as the standardized (z-scores) average of three grades reported by the respondent for Mathematics, English, and the native language (Hebrew/German).

Family characteristics are included as additional predictors. They include weighted family income per capita, measured based on monthly household income.[5] Parents' education is coded "1" if at least one parent has a university degree and "0" if neither parent completed university education. The position of the household in the occupational hierarchy is measured as the ISEI score of the parent with the higher score. Mother's educational aspirations for her offspring are coded "1" if the mother expects academic education and "0" otherwise. The variable "Perceived parental occupational expectations" is based on children's responses to the statement, "My parents would not be satisfied if I find employment in an

---

5   Income was reported by the mother in New Israeli Shekel in Israel and Euro in Germany. It was divided by the number of persons in the household, whereby the head of the household received a weight of '1'; and each further person in the household received the weight of '0.5'.

occupation that has lower status than theirs." The scale ranges from "1" strongly disagree to "5" strongly agree. It shows the extent to which parents communicate their expectations to their children and therefore reflects the inner-family social capital. The between-family social capital is captured by the number of persons with high status occupations that mothers know (ranging from 0 to 4), computed on the basis of the information provided in the position generator (Van der Gaag, Snijders, and Flap, 2008; Lin, Fu, and Hsung, 2001).[6]

In our analyses we take account of the students' grade level using a dichotomous variable to distinguish ninth- and eleventh-graders in Israel. In Germany we distinguish ninth-graders in "Hauptschule" (low educational track), ninth graders in comprehensive schools, tenth graders in "Realschule" (middle educational track) and finally tenth graders in comprehensive schools. All multivariate analyses also control for respondents' gender. The list of variables and their definitions are provided in Table 9.A.1 in the Appendix.

Descriptive Overview

In the first step of our analysis we provide some descriptive evidence on occupational and mobility aspirations among FSU immigrant youth in Germany and Israel compared to their native-born peers in both countries. The upper panel of Table 9.1 provides detailed information on youths' subjective intergenerational mobility aspirations. It is evaluated based on the extent to which respondents agreed or disagreed that for them it is important to work in an occupation better than that of their parents. In both the Israeli and German samples we find that more immigrants than natives choose the "agree" and "strongly agree" response categories. This is also reflected in their significantly higher mean scores. A review of the mean scores leads to three conclusions: first youth mobility aspirations are generally higher in Israel than in Germany; second, in both societies immigrant youth report higher aspirations than natives; and three, the gap between immigrants and natives is larger in Germany than in Israel.

Since the overall lower occupational aspirations in Germany might be an artifact of the sample selection (i.e., exclusion of the higher educational track students),[7] the results for Germany are shown for the entire sample and separately for those in comprehensive schools. Students of the German comprehensive schools are quite

---

6   The position generator is presented to respondents as a list of twelve occupations with varying prestige scores. Respondents are asked about whether they personally know someone pursuing each of the listed occupations.

7   The overall German sample is negatively selected as students at the higher school track (Gymnasium) are excluded from the data per project's design. Due to structural constraints related to the stratification feature of the German education system, students enrolled in lower school tracks are more likely to have lower occupational aspirations.

Table 9.1   Descriptive information on immigrant and native youth in Israel and Germany

		Israel			Germany (all)			Germany (comprehensive schools only)		
		Immigrant Youth	Native Youth	Sig.	Immigrant Youth	Native Youth	Sig.	Immigrant Youth	Native Youth	Sig.
Important to work in an occupation better than that of my parents	% Strongly disagree	5.42	13.65	***	9.52	18.72		9.60	20.55	
	Disagree	6.94	12.88		16.25	31.28		14.65	30.43	
	Neither disagree nor agree	15.62	19.62		27.45	32.16		27.78	32.02	
	Agree	33.41	25.38		28.57	14.32		25.76	12.25	
	Strongly agree	38.61	28.46		18.21	3.52		22.22	4.74	
	Mean	3.93	3.42	*	3.30	2.53	***	3.36	2.51	***
	S.D.	1.14	1.38		1.21	1.06		1.25	1.09	
Aspired occupational status (ISEI)	Mean	56.51	59.33		48.53	49.56		49.21	50.47	
	S.D.	24.42	20.24		14.85	15.89		15.45	16.89	
	(N)	(358)	(402)		(315)	(367)		(173)	(197)	

				sig			sig			sig
Perception of parental expectation	Mean	3.73	2.70	***	3.06	2.14	***	3.19	2.08	***
	S.D.	1.31	1.51		1.33	1.04		1.33	1.08	
Average school grades (z-standardized)	Mean	-0.01	0.04	***	-0.18	0.11	***	-0.17	0.27	***
	S.D.	1.00	1.01		1.04	1.00		1.05	0.95	
Parents' education: University degree	%	66.81	44.42	***	13.73	22.47	***	12.12	26.88	***
Parents' occupation (ISEI)	Mean	40.03	46.32	***	33.85	48.51	***	33.36	49.57	***
	S.D.	19.13	15.62		11.61	14.05		11.21	14.23	
Income per capita	Mean	3.64	4.13	***	0.71	1.05	***	0.71	1.09	***
	S.D.	1.67	1.67		0.24	0.38		0.24	0.39	
Network members with high prestige	Mean	0.54	2.53	***	1.04	2.19	***	0.96	2.15	***
	S.D.	0.78	1.15		1.04	1.36		1.38	1.03	
Aspiration of mother (university)	%	74.19	77.31		59.66	59.66		54.55	67.59	*
N		461	520		357	454		198	253	

Note: * p<0.10, ** p<0.05, *** p<0.01 (two-group mean-comparison test; Wilcoxon rank-sum test for importance to work in a better occupation and the perception of parental expectations).

comparable to the Israeli students. The fact that the results are similar in both cases strengthens our confidence in the validity of the results.

A second way of gauging the status aspirations of immigrant and native youth in German and Israel is based on the status of the occupations they aspire to. As some respondents found it difficult to specify the occupation of their choice the results are based on a sub-sample of students.[8] The findings here are less conclusive than with regard to mobility aspirations. In general occupational aspirations of Israeli youth are considerably higher than in Germany. Again this may reflect the fact that students attending Gymnasium were not included in the sample. As to the native – immigrant comparison, we find that on average natives in Israel aspire to slightly higher prestige occupations than immigrant youth (59.3 vs. 56.5, respectively). In Germany there appear to be no statistically significant differences, although, natives have a slightly higher score in both samples.

The conclusion arising from these findings is that immigrant youth realize that they must aspire to a longer distance upward intergenerational mobility just to keep on par with native youth in terms of their desired occupational status. This conclusion is supported by the observation that immigrant students in both Germany and Israel have a stronger perception than native students that their parents would not be satisfied if they ended up working in an occupation with lower status than their own.

Before turning to more rigorous analyses of the occupational and mobility aspirations using multivariate modeling we examine key social and demographic characteristics of the population groups under study. Average school grades of natives and immigrants are quite similar, with natives showing a slightly higher performance, especially in Germany. A substantially higher portion of German parents had higher education, compared to the parents of immigrant youth. The proportion of parents with higher education is generally larger in Israel than in Germany,[9] but interestingly immigrant parents are more likely than natives' parents to have higher education. This is a reflection of the unique immigration from the FSU that arrived in Israel during the last decade of the twentieth century.

As might be expected, family income and occupational status of native families are considerably higher than the corresponding figures for immigrants in both Israel and Germany. The socioeconomic differences are also manifested in the social networks of immigrant and native mothers. In both societies natives have access to higher-status network resources than immigrants and the difference is somewhat larger in Israel. Finally, mothers of native youth have

---

8   Approximately 20 percent of the respondents did not specify an occupation. Non-response on this item was slightly higher in Israel than in Germany and was lowest among immigrant youth in Germany. Therefore, the sample for the analysis of occupational aspirations consists of 358 immigrant and 402 natives in Israel and 315 immigrant and 367 natives in Germany.

9   Again this is at least partially a reflection of the study design in Germany which excludes students enrolled in Gymnasium.

higher educational aspirations for their offspring than do immigrant mothers. The difference is especially pronounced in the sample of the German comprehensive school students.

Occupational Aspirations

Although univariate descriptive statistics provide some insights into the similarities and differences between immigrant and native youth, more elaborate models are necessary in order to determine the sources of these differences. We therefore, turn now to multivariate estimation using OLS regression models, starting with occupational aspirations as the dependent variable (see Table 9.2). In line with the theoretical propositions outlined at the outset our primary objective is to evaluate whether aspirations are affected by immigrant status. Hence, the base model aims to estimate the gross difference between immigrant and native youth (taking into account compositional differences). It includes, in addition to immigrant status, gender, and school cohort. Indicators for students' school grades, as well as family attributes, are introduced in the second model in order to examine the contribution of achievements and structural position to the formation of aspirations. The additional factors include family economic, cultural and social resources; maternal aspirations with regard to adolescents' educational attainment; and youths' perceptions of parental expectations.

The first two columns in Table 9.2 present results for Germany and the two columns on the right hand side of the table pertain to Israel. From Model 1 it is evident that immigrant youth have lower occupational aspirations than native youth, but the difference is statistically significant only in Israel. Likewise there are no gender differences in Germany, whereas in Israel boys have lower aspirations on average than girls. School grade level and track make a difference in Germany (occupational aspirations are higher in upper levels and tracks) but no difference was found in Israel between students in the ninth and eleventh grades.

Adding school achievements and family characteristics improves the models' goodness of fit, especially in Germany. A miniscule R^2 in the initial model increases to 21 per cent in Germany and reaches 14 per cent explained variance in Israel. Upon controlling for these characteristics the effect of migration status remains non-significant in Germany and is reduced to statistical insignificance in Israel. We may conclude, then, that immigrant and native youth populations in both countries do not seem to differ much with respect to occupational aspirations. The differences noted at the outset are largely related to the unequal position of the adolescent populations in the stratification system. Once these differences are accounted for (by means of multivariate modeling) aspirations appear quite similar.

Turning to additional findings, the results presented in Table 9.2 show that higher grades in major school subjects increase students' occupational aspirations in both countries, but the estimate is statistically significant only in Germany. Maternal educational aspirations for their offspring influence students' own occupational

Table 9.2   Occupational aspirations of immigrants and native students in Israel and Germany (results of the OLS regression)

	Germany		Israel	
	Model 1	Model 2	Model 1	Model 2
FSU origin (vs. native-born)	-1.041	0.094	-2.997*	-0.123
Composition				
Male (vs. female)	0.056	0.464	-14.607***	-13.548***
School cohort in Germany (Ref: 9th grade lower secondary)				
9th grade comprehensive	7.829***	5.752***		
10th grade intermediate secondary	11.438***	7.764***		
10th grade comprehensive	11.155***	7.180***		
School cohort in Israel Ref: 9th grade)				
11 grade			-1.369	-1.447
Student's achievements				
Z-Standardized grades		2.413***		1.236
Family attributes				
Parental education: University (vs. not university)		3.321**		-0.723
Parental occupational status (ISEI)		0.012		-0.047
Income per capita (in 1000 Euros/NIS)		1.788		0.145
Network members with high prestige		0.671		0.609
Maternal aspiration (university vs. below)		8.302***		5.163**
Perception of parental expectation		1.243***		-1.393**
Intercept	41.140***	31.158***	67.548***	67.073***
R2	0.068	0.212	0.111	0.136
N	682	682	760	760

Note: * $p<0.10$, ** $p<0.05$, *** $p<0.01$

Source: 'Young Immigrants in the German and Israeli Educational System' study, authors' own calculations.

aspirations in both countries. In Germany parental education (when at least one of the parents has a university degree) also has a positive effect on the formation of youth's aspirations. Other parental attributes, such as income, occupational status and parental social capital do not have a direct effect on aspirations in neither Germany nor in Israel. Finally in Germany, students' perceptions of parental expectations concerning their occupational future seem to independently play a significant positive role in the formation of adolescents' own occupational goals. In Israel there seems to be the opposite effect, a finding for which we have no immediate explanation.

Subjective Mobility Aspirations

We follow the same analytic strategy as above when examining subjective intergenerational mobility aspirations (Table 9.3). We start out with a basic model that captures compositional differences and then add school grades and family resources. From Model 1 it is evident that after accounting for gender and school level FSU immigrants have significantly higher subjective mobility aspiration than natives in both Germany and Israel (b=0.77 and b=0.51, respectively). Gender has no effect on mobility aspirations but school level seems to make a difference in Germany. The negative effects observed among students from the tenth grade compared to the ninth-graders might be indicative of a ceiling effect or that as students mature they moderate their expectations. Indicators of family status are mostly negatively associated with mobility aspirations (model 2). That is, the higher the parental education, occupational status and family income the weaker the mobility aspirations of offspring. The coefficient estimates are statistically significant in the Israeli sample, but only the coefficient for parental education is significant in Germany. This pattern may represent a ceiling effect and is not surprising when we recall that mobility aspirations are relative to parents' current occupational position; so the higher the current position of the parents the less certain respondents are that they will work in a better occupation.

Family social capital has no effect on mobility aspirations in Israel when other family characteristics are controlled, but in Germany there is a statistically significant negative relationship. This is counter to our expectations and may derive from the fact that this variable captures some aspects of family socioeconomic standing that were not fully captured by our measures of parental education and occupation. Maternal aspirations have no direct effect on adolescents' mobility aspirations in Germany and Israel, but nevertheless have a positive effect. If youths perceive a stronger parental wish that they should not work in an occupation lower than the one of their parents, youths themselves aspire to longer distance mobility.

As a general finding, expanding the initial models with indicators of the socioeconomic background and school grades considerably improves the model fit in both Germany and Israel. Furthermore, we found that the effect for immigrant status diminishes in Israel and Germany once family attributes are taken into account, but still remains significant.

Table 9.3   Subjective mobility aspirations of immigrant and native students in Israel and Germany (results of the OLS regression)

	Germany		Israel	
	Model 1	Model 2	Model 1	Model 2
FSU origin (vs. native-born)	0.770***	0.248***	0.509***	0.225**
Composition				
Male (vs. female)	0.099	0.059	0.094	0.053
School cohort in Germany (Ref: 9th grade lower secondary				
9th grade comprehensive	-0.168	-0.083		
10th grade intermediate secondary	-0.426***	-0.220*		
10th grade comprehensive	-0.319**	-0.184		
School cohort in Israel (Ref: 9th grade)				
11 grade			-0.068	-0.079
Student's achievements				
Z-Standardized grades		-0.025		-0.027
Family attributes				
Parental education: University (vs. not university)		-0.213**		-0.262***
Parental occupational status (ISEI)		-0.003		-0.011***
Income per capita (in 1000 Euros/NIS)		-0.038		-0.056**
Network members with high prestige		-0.062**		0.013
Maternal aspiration (university vs. below)		0.052		0.128
Perception of parental expectation		0.400***		0.272***
Constant	2.723***	2.118***	3.406***	3.492***
R2	0.121	0.292	0.040	0.210
N	811	811	981	981

Note: * $p<0.10$, ** $p<0.05$, *** $p<0.01$

Source: 'Young Immigrants in the German and Israeli Educational System' study, authors' own calculations.

Discussion and Conclusions

The study reported in this chapter utilized a contextual model according to which teenage occupational aspirations are affected by their educational attainment as well as their family's position in the stratification system. This structural position encompasses material, cultural, and social resources. The structural disadvantages of immigrant populations in host societies are well documented. Consequently a simple model of occupational aspirations should predict lower aspirations among immigrant youth. Yet, the theoretical literature on immigrant incorporation is more ambiguous with regard to the second generation. The positive selection model (Feliciano and Rumbaut, 2005) suggests that persons who decide to immigrate and risk starting over in a new society are more likely than others to possess certain positive traits (whether motivation, determination, or perseverance) which they instill in their offspring as well. These traits help the offspring overcome social and cultural barriers and reach higher than their structural position would suggest. An alternative theoretical model, the "second generation decline" (Gans, 1992), suggests that immigrant youth may denounce the normative mobility aspirations as appear to be unattainable, and they opt for alternative modes of expressing themselves.

The empirical section of our chapter set out to study immigrant youth from one source country (the former Soviet Union) in two destinations that differ in the rigidity of their social structures and mobility regimes. In line with expectations it was found that in both countries immigrants were located in lower structural positions on average. Yet their occupational aspirations, measured in occupational status scores, were just slightly lower than the aspirations of native youth. Consistent with these findings, immigrant youth held stronger mobility aspirations than similar age natives. In this regard the results of our study do not provide support for the "second generation decline" proposition; rather, they are in line with positive selection thesis. We remind the reader that our study focused solely on immigrants from the former Soviet Union who possessed important assets, including a well-respected culture and historic affinity to the receiving societies. We may surmise, then, that under such conditions the likelihood of the second generation decline is unlikely.

The multivariate analyses we conducted with respect to occupational and mobility aspirations led to an important conclusion; namely, that whatever aspiration differences exist between immigrant and native youth, they are largely the result of immigrants' structural position in society and their achievements in school. Once these factors are statistically controlled the effect of immigrant status is reduced. A further finding is the greater fit of the models to the data in Germany than in Israel. That is, the variation in youth occupational aspirations in Germany is more clearly related to school performance and family's position in the stratification system. This is what one would expect from a more structured and rigid system.

While the results of the study are generally favorable with respect to the social integration of immigrant youth as exemplified by their aspirations we should emphasize the fact that the conclusions are derived from the central tendencies we found in the data. It is clearly possible that some immigrant youth renounce the aspirations typical of the majority, but our findings suggest that this is no more likely among immigrant youth than among natives.

References

Breen, R., and Jonsson, J. O. (2005). Inequality of opportunity in comparative perspective: recent research on educational attainment and social mobility. *Annual Review of Sociology, 31*, 223-243.

Coleman, J. S. (1988). Social capital in the creation of human capital. *American Journal of Sociology, 94*, 95-120.

Correll, S. J. (2004). Constraints into preferences: gender, status, and emerging career aspirations. *American Sociological Review, 69*(1), 93-113.

Dietz, B. (2000). German and Jewish Migration from the Former Soviet Union to Germany: Background, Trends and Implications. *Journal of Ethnic and Migration Studies, 26*, 635-652.

Feliciano, C., and Rumbaut, R. G. (2005). Gendered paths: Educational and occupational expectations and outcomes among adult children of immigrant. *Ethnic and Racial Studies, 28*, 1087-1118.

Fouad, N. A., and Byars-Winston, A. M. (2005). Cultural context of career choice: Meta-analysis of race/ethnicity differences. *Career Development Quarterly, 53*, 223-233.

Gans, H. J. (1992). Second generation decline: Scenarios for the economic and ethnic futures of the post-1965 American immigrants. *Ethnic and Racial Studies, 15*, 173-192.

Ganzeboom, H. B. G., De Graaf, P. M., and Treiman, D. J. (1992). A standard international socio-economic index of occupational status. *Social Science Research, 21*, 1-56.

Goldenberg, C., Gallimore, R., Reese, L., and Garnier, H. (2001). Cause or effect? A longitudinal study of immigrant Latino parents' aspirations and expectations, and their children's school performance. *American Educational Research Journal, 38*(3), 547-582.

Goldthorpe, J. H., Yaish, M., and Kraus, V. (1997). Class mobility in Israeli society: A comparative perspective. *Research in Stratification and Social Mobility, 15*, 3-28.

Gottfredson, L. S. (1981). Circumscription and compromise: A developmental theory of occupational aspirations. *Journal of Counseling Psychology, 28*, 545-579.

Goyette, K. A., and Xie, Y. (1999). Educational expectations of Asian American youths: Determinants and ethnic differences. *Sociology of Education, 72*(1), 22-36.

Greif, S., Gediga, G., and Janikowski, A. (1999). Erwerbslosigkeit und beruflicher Abstieg von Aussiedlerinnen und Aussiedlern. In K. J. Bade and J. Oltmer (Eds.), *Aussiedler. Deutsche Einwanderer aus Osteuropa* (pp. 81-107). Osnabrück: Universitätsverlag Rasch.

Hao, L., and Bonstead-Bruns, M. (1998). Parent-child differences in educational expectations and the academic achievements of immigrants and native students. *Sociology of Education, 75*, 175-198.

Heath, A., and Brinbaum, Y. (2007). Explaining ethnic inequalities in educational attainment. *Ethnicities, 7*(3), 291-305.

Holland, J. L. (1997). *Making vocational choices: A Theory of Vocational Personalities and Work Environments* (3rd ed.). Odessa, Florida: Psychological Assessment Resources.

Horowitz, T., and Leshem, E. (1998). The immigrants from the FSU in the Israeli cultural sphere. In M. Sikron and E. Leshem (Eds.), *The Profile of the Aliya: The Absorption Process of the Immigrants of the Former USSR, 1990-1995.* (pp. 291-333). Jerusalem: Magnes and the Hebrew University (In Hebrew).

Janikowski, A. (1999). Berufliche Integration der Aussiedler und Aussiedlerinnen, in Aussiedler in Deutschland. In R. K. Silbereisen, E.-D. Lantermann and E. Schmitt-Rodermund (Eds.), *Akkulturation von Persönlichkeit und Verhalten* (pp. 113-142). Opladen: Leske+Budrich.

Jonsson, J. O., and Rudolphi, F. (2011). Weak performance – strong determination. *European Sociological Review, 27*(4), 487-508.

Kao, G., and Tienda, M. (1995). Optimism and achievement: The educational performance of immigrant youth. *Social Science Quarterly, 76*(1), 1-19.

Kao, G., and Tienda, M. (1998). Educational Aspirations of Minority Youth. *American Journal of Education, 106*(3), 349-384.

Kelley, S. M. C., and Kelley, C. G. E. (2009). Subjective social mobility: data from 30 nations. In M. Haller, R. Jowell and T. Smith (Eds.), *Charting the Globe: The International Social Survey Programme 1984-2009* (Chapter 6). London: Routledge.

Krahn, H., and Taylor, A. (2005). Resilient teenagers: Explaining the high educational aspirations of visible-minority youth in Canada. *Journal of International Migration and Integration, 6*(3-4), 405-434.

Kogan, I. (2004). Last Hired, First Fired? The Unemployment Dynamics of Male Immigrants in Germany. *European Sociological Review, 20*(5), 445-461.

Kogan, I. (2011). New immigrants – Old Disadvantage Patterns? Labour Market Integration of Recent Immigrants into Germany. *International Migration, 49*(1), 91-117.

Kogan, I. (2012). Potenziale nutzen! Determinanten und Konsequenzen der Anerkennung von Bildungsabschlüssen bei Zuwanderern aus der ehemaligen

Sowjetunion in Deutschland. *Kölner Zeitschrift für Soziologie und Sozialpsychologie, 64*(1), 67-89.

Konietzka, D., and Kreyenfeld, M. (2001). Die Verwertbarkeit ausländischer Ausbildungsabschlüsse. Das Beispiel der Aussiedler auf dem deutschen Arbeitsmarkt. *Zeitschrift für Soziologie, 30*(4), 267-282.

Liebau, E. (2011). *Arbeitsmarktintegration von hochqualifizierten Zuwanderern – Erklärung des spezifischen Integrationsmusters in den deutschen Arbeitsmarkt von Aussiedlern und jüdischen Kontingentflüchtlingen aus der ehemaligen Sowjetunion.* Inaugural dissertation, Universität Mannheim.

Lin, N., Fu, Y.-C., and Hsung, R.-M. (2001). The position generator: Measurement techniques for investigations of social capital. In N. Lin, K. Cook and R. S. Burt (Eds.), *Social Capital: Theory and Research* (pp. 57-81). New York: Aldine de Gruyter.

Marjoribanks, K. (2002). *Family and School Capital: Toward a Context Theory of Students' School Outcomes.* Norwell, MA: Kluwer Academic Publishers.

OECD. (2007). *Jobs for Immigrants. Labour market Integration in Australia, Denmark, Germany and Sweden.* Paris: OECD.

Patton, W., and Creed, P. (2007). The relationship between career variables and occupational aspirations and expectations for Australian high school adolescents. *Journal of Career Development, 34*(2), 127-148.

Perlmann, J., and Waldinger, R. (1997). Second generation decline? Children of immigrants, past and present – A reconsideration. *International Migration Review, 31*(4), 893-922.

Portes, A. (1996). Introduction: Immigration and its aftermath. In A. Portes (Ed.), *The New Second Generation* (pp. 1-7). New York: Russell Sage Foundation.

Rong, X. L., and Brown, F. (2001). The effects of immigrant generation and ethnicity on educational attainment among young African and Caribbean blacks in the United States. *Harvard Educational Review, 71*(3), 536-565.

Schoon, I., and Parsons, S. (2002). Teenage aspirations for future careers and occupational outcomes. *Journal of Vocational Behavior, 60*(2), 262-288.

Sewell, W. H., and Hauser, R. M. (1975). *Education, Occupation, and Earnings: Achievement in the Early Career.* New York: Academic Press.

Sikron, M., and Leshem, E. (1998). *The Profile of the Aliya: The Absorption Process of the Immigrants of the Former USSR, 1990-1995.* Jerusalem: Magnes and the Hebrew University (In Hebrew).

Sikron, M. (1998). The human capital of immigrants and their absorption in the labor market. In M. Sikron and E. Leshem (Eds.), *The Profile of the Aliya: The Absorption Process of the Immigrants of the Former USSR, 1990-1995* (pp. 127-181). Jerusalem: Magnes and the Hebrew University (In Hebrew).

Van der Gaag, M., Snijders, T. A. B., and Flap, H. (2008). Position generator measures and their relationship to other social capital measures. In N. Lin and B. H. Erickson (Eds.), *Social Capital: An International Research Program* (pp. 27-48). Oxford: Oxford University Press.

Slonim-Nevo, V., Mirsky, J., Nauck, B., and Horowitz, T. (2007). Social participation and psychological distress among immigrants from the former Soviet Union: A comparative study in Israel and Germany. *International Social Work, 50*, 473-488.

Vondracek, F. W., Lerner, R. M., and Schulenberg, J. E. (1986). *Career development: A life-span developmental approach.* Hillsdale, NJ: Erlbaum.

Waldinger, R., and Perlmann, J. (1998). Second generations: Past, present, future. *Journal of Ethnic and Migration Studies, 24*(1), 5-24.

Westphal, M. (1999). Familiäre und berufliche Orientierung von Aussiedlerinnen. In K. Bade, and J. Oltmer (Eds.), *Aussiedler: Deutsche Einwanderer aus Osteuropa.* Osnabrück: Universitätsverlag Rasch.

Yaish, M. (2002). The consequences of immigration for social mobility: the experience of Israel, *European Sociological Review, 18*(4), 449-471.

Yates, S., Harris, A., Sabates, R., and Staff, J. (2011). Early occupational aspirations and fractures transitions: a study of entry into "NEET" status in the UK. *Journal of Social Policy, 40*(3), 513-534.

Zhou, M. (1997). Segmented assimilation: Issues, controversies, and recent research on the new second generation. *International Migration Review, 31*(4), 975-1008.

Appendix: Table 9.A.1   Variables and definitions

Name	Description	Values
ISEI status of the aspired occupation	ISEI based on the 4-digit ISCI-88 in Germany and on the 3 digit CBS in Israel	
Subjective intergenerational mobility aspirations	Agreement on the item "It is important for me to work in an occupation that is better than the occupations of my parents"	Values range from 1 – strongly disagree to 5 – strongly agree
FSU-origin	A dummy variable	Coded 1 for FSU immigrants and 0 for natives
Gender	A dummy variable	Coded 1 for boys and 0 for girls
Grade in Israel	A dummy variable	Coded 0 for 9th and 1 for 11th
Grade and school type in Germany	A set of dummy variables	9th graders at Hauptschule, 9th graders at comprehensive schools, 10th graders at Realschule and finally 10th graders at comprehensive schools
Average school grades (Z-standardized)	Average school grades in Hebrew/German, Mathematics and English, as reported by the respondent	
Family income per capital	Based on mothers' reports of the family monthly income divided by the number of household members. The first person was weighted with 1 and every additional person with 0.5.	Values range from 2,000 NIS to 25,000 NIS in Israel and 500 Euros to 4,500 Euros in Germany

Parental occupation	Occupation of the parent with the higher occupational prestige measured by ISEI	Range from 16 to 88
Parental education	A dummy variable	Coded 1 for university degree and 0 for no university degree
Mother's educational aspirations	Mothers are asked what do they think will be the highest level of education that their child will attain in Israel how sure they are that her child will reach a university degree in Germany	Coded 1 for academic education and 0 otherwise in Israel and range from 1 – impossible to 5 – very sure in Germany, recoded as 1 if the mother is (very) sure that her child will attain university degree and 0 otherwise
Perception of parental expectations	Students should indicate, how much they agree with the statement "My parents would not be satisfied if I have to work in a lower occupation than theirs"	Values range from 1 – strongly disagree to 5 – strongly agree
Number of persons with high ISEI in mother's network	Based on the position generator which embraces 12 occupations stratified by their occupational status (ISEI). Mothers indicated whether they know someone working in occupations belonging to 4 most prestigious ones: engineer, lawyer, secondary school teacher and computer scientist	Values range from 0 to 4

Chapter 10

Achievement Differences between Immigrant and Native Fourth Graders in Germany and Israel[1]

Cornelia Kristen, Yossi Shavit, Svetlana Chachashvili-Bolotin, Tobias Roth, and Irit Adler

In this chapter, we study the educational achievements of native-born children and of immigrant children from the Former Soviet Union (FSU) in Israel and Germany. Based on a unique comparative data set, we investigate how immigrant and native-born children in the two countries compare with respect to cognitive and language competencies as well as school grades, and attempt to account for these differences. Our interest is in the socio-economic and cultural factors that affect achievements of immigrants and natives and in differences between the two countries in this regard. The major questions of this chapter are:

- Are there differences in competencies and achievements between FSU immigrants and natives in Germany and Israel?
- How do the two countries compare with respect to these differences?
- To what extent are these differences attributed to differences between the groups in socio-economical background and in cultural capital?

The comparison of children from immigrant families who came from the FSU to natives, in Israel and Germany offers a rare opportunity to analyze the integration processes of a rather similar group of immigrants in different national settings. The comparative design not only allows us to take into account processes that contribute to inequalities in education more generally and that therefore should apply to immigrants in Israel and Germany in a similar manner, but also to consider the conditions of absorption that are associated with the specific institutional context. To highlight certain characteristics of this institutional make-up we start with a description of recent migration flows from the FSU to Israel and Germany as well as the associated policies and then consider differences between the countries in relevant educational institutions. This is followed by a

1 This study was generously supported by grant no. 01GWS070 and 01GWS071 from the German Federal Ministry of Education and Research to the universities of Leipzig and Mannheim. Liliya Leopold provided invaluable research assistance.

presentation of the empirical evidence on the immigrants' scholastic achievements in two countries. After a summary of theoretical accounts of the effects of the socio-economic and cultural background of immigrant and native children on their achievements we describe the data, variables, methods, and the results. Finally, the last section compares the results for the two countries, and formulates conclusions and questions for further research.

Recent Immigration from the FSU to Israel and Germany

Immigration from the FSU to Israel

The recent mass immigration to Israel from the FSU began in September 1989. By the late 1990s approximately 830,000 people immigrated, increasing Israel's population by over 10 percent in a decade. The vast majority of FSU immigrants to Israel arrive under the Israeli Law of Return, namely, they are recognized by the State as Jews or persons of Jewish extraction, and as such are offered Israeli citizenship upon arrival. In addition to its impressive scope, the immigration from the FSU had two additional important characteristics: very few of the immigrants came with economic means and a very high percentage of adult immigrants held an academic degree (Sicron, 1998).

Furthermore, in contrast to the immigration of the 1970s, when Israel's immigration policy followed the "melting pot" model, which aimed to absorb and assimilate the immigrants within the dominant society, in the 1990s the state adopted a "cultural pluralism" model which recognizes cultural differences between immigrant groups and encourages their preservation (Horowitz, 1998; Leshem and Sicron, 1998).

In the earlier period immigrants were first directed to "absorption centers" where they were housed, fed, and taught Hebrew and, when needed, vocational skills. In the second period, by contrast, a policy of "direct absorption" was implemented whereby immigrants were dispatched with a modest stipend to fend for themselves in the various markets (the real estate market, the labor market, and the social services) where they could implement their integration into Israeli society according to their individual or group preferences and priorities (Lissitsa, 2006). However, since apartments are more expensive in the large urban centers, many immigrants sought affordable housing in either peripheral communities or in the poorer neighborhoods surrounding the urban centers (Horowitz, 1998). This geographic distribution also affected the distribution of immigrant students among schools in the country: while in some peripheral communities immigrants comprise over 20 percent of the student population (Zionit and Ben-Arye, 1995), where the educational level was much lower than in the center of the country, in the middle class neighborhoods of the main cities only 10 percent or less of the student population are immigrants. Additionally, during the first five months of migration adult immigrants receive the right to study at "ulpan" (Hebrew language courses) free of tuition. The "ulpan" is designed to teach adult Israeli immigrants the basic language skills (conversation, writing, and comprehension). However, according to studies presented to the Knesset's Immigration and Absorption Committee in January 2008, 60 percent of Israeli immigrants over the age of 30 who graduated from "ulpan" instructional courses were unable to read, write or speak Hebrew fluently (Fridman, 2008).

Immigration from the FSU to Germany

Two major groups of immigrants from the FSU moved to Germany since 1989: ethnic Germans ("Spätaussiedler") and Jewish refugees ("Kontingentflüchtlinge"). In its attempt to rebuild the Jewish community which had been annihilated during the Holocaust, Germany has encouraged Jews from the FSU to immigrate. Between 1993 and 2007 around 200,700 Jewish immigrants from the FSU came to Germany (Bundesministerium des Innern, 2008). Given its small size this group's educational performance has not been studied and also in our study it was not possible to identify them in sufficient numbers in the relevant age group. Our focus therefore is on Spätaussiedler from the FSU.

Spätaussiedler are descendants of the German emigrants who moved from Germany to several regions of the Former Soviet Union since the eighteenth century. Tsarina Catherine II invited foreigners from Europe to settle in Russia and promised them many advantages. Since the end of the nineteenth century, however, the German descendants lost all their privileges and during the First and the Second World Wars they were deported into the German settlements on the Volga, in Siberia, and in Kazakhstan (Schumann, 2003). In the 1990s, the German government encouraged FSU citizens of German ancestry to immigrate back to Germany.

Between 1990 and 2007 Germany absorbed about 2.1 million Spätaussiedler, that is about 2.7 percent of the German population (Bundesministerium des Innern, 2008). Thus, whereas in Israel FSU immigrants constitute a sizable group in the population, in Germany, Spätaussiedler are a small minority. In addition, Spätaussiedler are less educated than FSU immigrants in Israel, but both groups arrived in their countries of destination without substantial economic means. Like Jewish immigrants in Israel, Spätaussiedler can claim citizenship of the host country upon arrival. Compared to other migrant groups, the immediate access to German citizenship puts Spätaussiedler in a favorable position and signals that their stay is meant to be permanent. This could affect their future plans accordingly. For example, it could increase the motivation to learn the new language and to invest in the education of their offspring within the new context (Nauck, Diefenbach, and Petri, 1998).

In addition to the privileged legal status, until 2005 Spätaussiedler were not required to pay tuition fees for the language courses. While attending these six month courses the students receive full financial support and accommodation (Söhn, 2008). This policy aimed in particular at the integration of this group and up until 2005 distinguished them from for example labor migrants or political refugees who did not receive similar language support. Since 2005 they, as most other immigrant groups, can attend additionally an integration course which provides instruction on life in Germany, the society's norms and values.

Both their legal status and the specific measures the state takes to support Spätaussiedler has set them apart from other immigrant groups within the German context. Especially with regard to language learning, a key competence for school success, this might translate into more favorable conditions for the descendants of FSU immigrants compared to other immigrant groups. They may nevertheless face similar problems in terms of coping and adapting.

The Israeli and German School System

The Israeli School System

At present, education in Israel is free and compulsory up to age 16 (tenth grade for most on-track students), but over 90 percent of the Israeli-born students continue to twelfth grade: a year of pre-school is followed by six years of primary school, three years of lower secondary school and three years of upper secondary education. The upper secondary level is differentiated into academic and vocational (technological) track. Both tracks now prepare students for the matriculation examinations which are required for admission to university and post-secondary colleges.

The education system in Israel consists of five main types of schools: Jewish state schools, Jewish state-religious schools, Arab state schools, Arab Christian schools, and Jewish independent schools, most of which belong to the Jewish ultra-orthodox communities. Virtually all FSU immigrants are enrolled in non-religious Jewish state schools. Therefore, we restricted our sample to students attending non-religious schools. The mean achievements of students attending non-religious state schools are similar to the mean achievement in religious state schools (Feniger, 2009) but much higher than the mean in Arab state schools (e.g., Shavit and Blank, 2012). Thus, the exclusion of religious school students from the sample is unlikely to substantially bias our results while the exclusion of Arab schools biases it upwards. And yet, given that FSU immigrants do not usually attend Arab schools it would be misleading to compare their achievements to those of Arab students.

The German School System

In Germany compulsory education begins at age six with primary school, which takes four years in most federal states and is followed by the first educational transition into three different tracks of secondary education (Anweiler, 1996; Cortina, Baumert, Leschinsky, Mayer, and Trommer, 2003): Hauptschule (general elementary education, grades 5-9) leads to a minimum qualification, Realschule (general intermediate education, grades 5-10) leads to a medium-level qualification. Both degrees have traditionally constituted the preparation for an apprenticeship, even if typically for different realms of apprenticeship. The Gymnasium (general education for university entrance, grades 5-12/13) leads traditionally to university or applied university studies.

The professional education system is dominated by vocational training in the dual system, i.e. a combination of general education (conveyed by vocational schools) and vocational training in firms. Training within the dual system lasts between two and three years, depending on one's general educational preparation and the kind of apprenticeship chosen. General and vocational training are separate streams in the German education system.

Compared to Israel, Germany's school system is highly stratified (Allmendinger, 1989). Students are sorted early into different educational tracks which lead to distinct qualifications with the differences between these qualifications being well recognized in the labor market (Müller and Shavit, 1998). Upon the completion of upper secondary education, however, the German system of higher education is relatively less stratified (Allmendinger, 1989). In other words, educational inequality in Germany is largely determined by whether individuals enter and complete one of the more demanding forms of secondary schooling. Accordingly, with the focus of our study being on the achievements of fourth graders in the comprehensive elementary school system we direct our attention to a crucial stage in immigrant children's school careers.

Differences between Immigrants and Natives in Educational Achievement and Grades

As a starting point for addressing the question of how to account for differences in educational achievements between immigrants and natives we consider the main factors that have been shown to affect educational achievement in advanced societies. Previous research shows that the most important resources affecting the educational achievements of students are parental education (e.g., Sewell and Hauser, 1975) and economic circumstances (Duncan, Yeung, Brooks-Gunn, and Smith, 1998).

Educated parents are better able to assist their children with their school and to interfere on their behalf with teachers (Lareau, 2000). In addition, parents' education enhances the educational aspirations, and motivation of children (e.g., Gabay-Egozi, Shavit, and Yaish, 2009; Hauser, Tsai, and Sewell, 1983).

Children raised by educated parents are also endowed with higher levels of cultural capital which is conducive to success in school. Bourdieu and Passeron (1977) have argued that school curricula reflect the codes and values of the dominant culture in society and defined cultural capital as familiarity with these codes and values. The dominant culture is the culture of the privileged social strata. Children raised in these strata internalize the values of the dominant culture effortlessly and enjoy an advantage in the educational process. In this way, the intergenerational transmission of cultural codes facilitates the reproduction of educational and social inequality between generations. Recently, scholars like De Graaf and Kraaykamp (2000) found that the main component of cultural capital that affects educational achievement is not the students' familiarity with highbrow culture or participation in it but rather their exposure to books and reading at home. Children who were raised in affluent homes and whose parents are educated are more likely to benefit from the availability of books in the home and to do well in school.

Children's educational attainment is also affected by their family's income both because high-income families can afford the direct and opportunity costs of education and because economic circumstances affect children's cognitive development. The effects of family income on cognitive development and educational attainment are larger in the early ages (0-5) than in adolescence. Moreover, family income in childhood has a stronger effect on educational attainment at the secondary level than does contemporaneous family income (Duncan et al., 1998). This suggests that the effect of family income on educational attainment is mediated by developmental processes rather than simply the ability to afford the costs of schooling. As Duncan and associates point out, preschool ability sets the stage for subsequent educational achievements, and children raised in poverty are less likely to develop the cognitive skills necessary for educational success.

This brief review of the literature on the educational attainment process, in combination with the differences between FSU immigrants and natives in Israel and Germany, leads us to expect the following: In Israel, where FSU immigrants are educated but poor, the disparities in educational achievements between native and immigrant students are due primarily to differences between the two groups in economic background. In Germany, where FSU immigrants are both less educated and poorer on average than the native population, both the education and economical resources of the parents account for differences between native and FSU immigrant students in achievement.

Previous Studies on FSU Immigrants and Achievement in Germany and Israel

Since the beginning of mass immigration from FSU, several studies have investigated the educational achievements of immigrants in Israel (Fogel, 2007; Horowitz, 1998; Levin, Shohamy, and Spolsky, 2003; Sever, 2002). Most of these studies focus on achievements at the secondary school level such as on drop-out rates (see for example Sever, 2002), matriculation rates, and track placement (Chachashvili-Bolotin, 2007). These studies find that in addition to parental education and the economic circumstances of the family which affect educational achievements in most populations, tenure in Israel is an important determinant of achievement among FSU students (Fogel, 2007). Furthermore, the results indicate that although FSU immigrant parents are well educated by comparison to the local population, drop-out rates among their children have been higher than those of native Israeli students (Fogel, 2007). Studies have also found that immigrant adolescents are more likely than native Israeli students to attend vocational rather than academic secondary education (Chachashvili-Bolotin, 2007; Fogel, 2007). This has been attributed to two main reasons: first, many immigrant students come from poor families and they seek an education that would prepare them for immediate entry into well-paying jobs in the labor market rather than to further education. Second, immigrants tend to prefer vocational training which does not require a mastery of high-level Hebrew in which they suffer a handicap (Chachashvili-Bolotin, 2007).

Levin and her colleagues (2003) study the educational achievement of immigrant children in primary education. In addition to studying the determinants of middle- and high-school achievement in math and Hebrew, they studied achievements in fifth grade. Their main result is that the mean advantage of Israeli-born students relative to immigrants is largely due to differences between them in the mean economic circumstances.

Leopold and Shavit (2012) studied the effects of cultural capital on the scholastic achievement of Israeli natives and of immigrants from the Former Soviet Union. They show that the effects of cultural capital on actual learning do not vary between immigrant and native students but that the two groups differ markedly in the effects of cultural capital on teachers' evaluations: Teachers' evaluations of native students are affected by their cultural capital, whereas this relationship is weak among immigrants.

In Germany, children from immigrant families frequently encounter difficulties in school. At the first transition at the end of primary education they not only more often enter the lowest secondary track than their German peers (e.g., Konsortium Bildungsberichterstattung, 2006), but they also perform worse in terms of test scores (e.g., Müller and Stanat, 2006; Walter, 2008). These differences appear already early on in kindergarten (Becker and Biedinger, 2006) and continue on throughout primary school (Kristen, 2008; Schwippert, Hornberg, and Goy, 2008). Empirical studies reveal a typical pattern with children of Turkish origin facing the most pronounced disadvantages while other groups such as Greek immigrants seem to reach better results (Alba, Handl, and Müller, 1994; Kristen and Granato, 2007; Müller and Stanat, 2006; Nauck et al., 1998; Walter, 2008). Pupils from the FSU are intermediate. Furthermore, once parental education and occupation, economic resources and language use are taken into account disparities in test results completely disappear between descendants of FSU immigrants and native German students (Müller and Stanat, 2006; Walter, 2008).

Analysis

We analysed survey data from the "Immigrant children and youths in the German and Israeli educational systems" study on fourth grade students and their mothers in Germany and Israel. The data were collected under the auspices of the German-

Israeli Research Consortium "Migration and Societal Integration". We made an effort to apply measures that are as similar as possible given two countries with institutional and cultural contexts that are far from identical. It is clear, however, that our measures, especially those on competencies in different realms, may not measure the same in both educational contexts with the same validity. Keeping this limitation in mind, we discuss similarities and differences in the immigrant native gap across countries.

Data

The Israeli sample was drawn randomly from a list of all fourth grade students attending Hebrew (rather than Arabic) non-religious public schools in towns and cities with a population of 10,000 or more. The sampling frame included information on students' name, names of parents, address, immigration status, and date of birth. The sample was stratified by immigration status and consisted of two strata: students whose mothers immigrated from the FSU since 1989 (hereafter, immigrant students), and native students of Israeli born mothers. Other students (e.g., immigrants from other countries) were not included in the sample. Our final Israeli sample of fourth grade students included 271 native students and their mothers and 310 immigrant students and their mothers.

The German data were collected in the federal states Hamburg, Hesse, and North Rhine-Westphalia. More than two-third of the interviews were conducted in North-Rhine-Westphalia. We applied two sampling strategies. The first one was based on a stratified random sample of official data from local registration offices in 18 cities. Registry data usually includes information about name, address, country of birth, and citizenship. If the country of birth was missing, a so-called onomastic process was applied. According to this method names are assigned to languages to identify the origin of a person. In the second sampling strategy we contacted students via schools. Using official school statistics of the three federal states, schools with a high share of migrants were selected and contacted. Fourth grade students with parents born in the former Soviet Union and native fourth graders were interviewed. Their mothers were contacted via telephone. Our final German sample of fourth grade students included 202 native students and their mothers and 160 students from Spätaussiedler families (hereafter, immigrant students) and their mothers.

Variables

The questionnaires included, among other questions, two standardized tests: a test of reading comprehension in Hebrew/German consisting of 12 items in Israel and 21 items in Germany and a non-verbal cognitive test of analogies consisting of 25 items. The reading proficiency test for Germany was based on a subtest from the Hamburger school achievement test (Behörde für Schule, Jugend und Berufsbildung Hamburg, 2000). The non-verbal test was based on the German KFT-test (Heller and Perleth, 2000) and was identical for both countries. The sums of correct answers to each of these two tests are our first dependent variables. In addition, we study differences in school grades in Hebrew or German respectively as well as grades in math. For Germany, we reversed the values so that, as in the Israeli case, a higher value indicates a better grade. The dependent variables were standardized with a mean of zero and a standard deviation of one.

Children's socio-economic background is measured by the following variables: Parental education is a dummy variable indicating whether at least one parent has a university degree or not. Household income is measured as income per capita divided by 1000. It is a sum of earnings, income from self-employment, pensions, governmental transfers, rent, and any other income. Using the Central Bureau of Statistics' formula (CBS 2013), income was adjusted for the number of standard adults in the household. The formula adjusts income for the economies of scale that are enjoyed by large households. To consider missing income values, we include a separate dummy indicating whether this information has been available.

Cultural capital is measured by two indicators. One typical indicator which is commonly used in large-scale student assessments is the number of books in the home. Respondents could choose between six categories (1=0-10 books, 2=11-25 books, 3=26-100, 4=101-200, 5=201-500, and 6=500+). In the regressions it is treated as a metric variable. The other indicator is mother's cultural activities. This variable sums the number of activities that the mother attends frequently (ballet/ dance performances, classic concerts, rock/pop concerts, movies, the theatre, museums/art exhibitions). For each activity mothers were asked to indicate the frequency of their attendance. The response categories were: several times a week, several times a month, twice in six months, once a year or less, and never. Each activity that was attended frequently (from several times a week to twice in six months) was recoded into a dummy variable. The activity index sums these dummies and ranges from zero (no activities) to six (all activities).

We estimated linear regression models for each dependent variable and report unstandardized regression coefficients. In Germany, we estimated robust standard errors to take into account the clustering of students within schools, whereas in Israel clustering was negligible. In all models, we include controls for gender, and whether the child was interviewed at home or in school. The latter variable is only relevant for Germany since in Israel all students were interviewed at home. We also control for student's age at the time of the interview (measured in months).

Descriptive Results

Table 10.1 presents means and standard deviations of the variables by immigration status. When comparing Israeli immigrants and natives to their German counterparts we find the following: in Germany a larger proportion of native parents have attended higher education, than immigrants (47 percent vs. 24 percent respectively). In Israel, by contrast, native and immigrant parents exhibit similar proportions of

Table 10.1   Descriptive statistics for native and immigrant students in Israel and Germany (standard deviation in parentheses)

Variables	Israel		Germany	
	FSU	Natives	FSU	Natives
	1	2	3	4
Boys	0.51 (0.50)	0.49 (0.50)	0.48** (0.50)	0.56 (0.50)
Parental university education	0.45 (0.50)	0.50 (0.50)	0.24** (0.40)	0.47 (0.50)
Income per capita (in € for Germany and in ₪ for Israel)	2.77** (1.30)	3.39 (1.43)	0.59** (0.25)	0.98 (0.39)
Number of books at home	3.05** (1.20)	3.49 (1.16)	3.24** (1.07)	4.46 (1.23)
Mother's cultural activities	1.20** (1.47)	1.73 (1.43)	1.23** (1.35)	2.03 (1.52)
Reading comprehension test [z-scores]	6.71** (2.47) [z=-0.19]	7.66 (2.12) [z=0.19]	12.66** (4.82) [z=-0.28]	15.00 (4.56) [z=0.21]
Non-verbal cognitive test [z-scores]	14.11** (7.08) [z=-0.13]	16.02 (6.89) [z=0.13]	16.53 (7.02) [z=-0.10]	17.71 (6.55) [z=0.08]
Grade Math [z-scores]	87.46 (9.94) [z=-0.06]	88.78 (10.90) [z=0.07]	2.66 (0.82) [z=-0.03]	2.70 (0.87) [z=0.02]
Grade German/Hebrew [z-scores]	85.67** (10.20) [z=-0.12]	88.11 (10.51) [z=0.12]	2.50 (0.84) [z=-0.09]	2.63 (0.87) [z=0.06]
Age in months	117.25** (5.20)	115.76 (4.66)	120.86 (6.81)	119.86 (6.25)
Interview conducted at home	–	–	0.60** (0.48)	0.81 (0.40)
N	271	310	160	202

Note: The asterisks (**) indicate significant ($p < 0.01$) differences between natives and immigrants within each country.

higher education (45 percent and 50 percent). Evidently, the FSU immigrants to Israel are better educated than those who immigrated to Germany. In both countries, mean income is significantly higher among natives than among immigrants but the differences are larger in Germany (over a standard deviation) than in Israel (under half a standard deviation). Natives also have more books at home on average, and are more involved in cultural activities, compared to immigrants in the two countries. Here too the differences are much larger in Germany.

Whereas the native-immigrant differences in socio-economic and cultural background are much larger in Germany than in Israel, surprisingly the opposite is

Table 10.2   OLS regression reading comprehension test (in z-scores)

	Israel			Germany		
	Model 1	Model 2	Model 3	Model 1	Model 2	Model 3
FSU	-0.35**	-0.27**	-0.23**	-0.35**	-0.04	0.05
	(0.08)	(0.08)	(0.08)	(0.10)	(0.11)	(0.11)
Boy	-0.05	-0.02	0.00	-0.09	-0.05	-0.06
	(0.08)	(0.08)	(0.08)	(0.09)	(0.08)	(0.08)
Age	-0.02*	-0.01	-0.01	-0.02**	-0.02*	-0.01+
	(0.01)	(0.01)	(0.01)	(0.01)	(0.01)	(0.01)
Parental education		0.32**	0.19*		0.26*	0.24*
		(0.08)	(0.09)		(0.11)	(0.12)
Income		0.13**	0.10**		0.64**	0.65**
		(0.03)	(0.03)		(0.14)	(0.15)
Income (missing)		0.04	-0.03		-0.01	-0.01
		(0.18)	(0.17)		(0.35)	(0.35)
Books at home			0.13**			0.10*
			(0.04)			(0.04)
Cultural activities			0.05+			-0.06
			(0.03)			(0.05)
Interview at home				0.46**	0.34**	0.34**
				(0.13)	(0.13)	(0.12)
Constant	0.47**	-0.22	-0.59**	0.27	-0.50*	-0.84**
	(0.12)	(0.16)	(0.19)	(0.19)	(0.22)	(0.25)
R2	0.045	0.121	0.147	0.095	0.179	0.192
N	581			362		

Note: + $p<0.1$, * $p<0.05$, ** $p<0.01$

true for three of the four indicators of educational achievements and competencies. In Israel the achievements of native students are higher than those of immigrants, except for math in which the two groups obtain similar mean grades. In Germany, the achievements of immigrant students are only lower than those of natives in reading comprehension.

Multivariate Analysis

We now turn to the multivariate analysis of the differences between FSU immigrants and native students in competencies and achievements. For each

Table 10.3   OLS regression non-verbal test (in z-scores)

	Israel			Germany		
	Model 1	Model 2	Model 3	Model 1	Model 2	Model 3
FSU	-0.26**	-0.19*	-0.16*	0.01	0.16	0.20
	(0.08)	(0.08)	(0.08)	(0.10)	(0.12)	(0.13)
Boy	-0.18*	-0.14+	-0.13+	-0.02	-0.01	-0.02
	(0.08)	(0.08)	(0.08)	(0.11)	(0.11)	(0.11)
Age	-0.01	-0.00	-0.00	-0.02**	-0.02*	-0.02*
	(0.01)	(0.01)	(0.01)	(0.01)	(0.01)	(0.01)
Parental education		0.44**	0.36**		0.25*	0.24*
		(0.08)	(0.09)		(0.11)	(0.12)
Income		0.09**	0.06+		0.26	0.28
		(0.03)	(0.03)		(0.17)	(0.17)
Income (missing)		0.23	0.18		-0.28	-0.28
		(0.17)	(0.18)		(0.28)	(0.28)
Books at home			0.08*			0.05
			(0.04)			(0.04)
Cultural activities			0.05+			-0.04
			(0.03)			(0.04)
Interview at home				0.32**	0.22*	0.21+
				(0.12)	(0.11)	(0.11)
Constant	0.37**	-0.26	-0.51**	0.24+	-0.09	-0.27
	(0.12)	(0.16)	(0.19)	(0.14)	(0.22)	(0.28)
R2	0.031	0.117	0.132	0.031	0.065	0.070
N	581			362		

Note: + $p<0.1$, *$p<0.05$, ** $p<0.01$

dependent variable and for each country, we estimate a series of OLS regressions. The first regression estimates the gross difference between immigrants and natives, and subsequent models control for the socio-economic and cultural characteristics of families/mothers and inspect how these controls change the net difference between the two groups in the dependent variables.

In Table 10.2 we present the estimates of a linear regression analysis for scores in reading comprehension (in z-scores). The results for the two countries are remarkably similar. As one would expect, in both countries native students obtain significantly higher scores than immigrant students. The unadjusted native-immigrant gap is 0.35 of a standard deviation in both countries. In both countries

Table 10.4   OLS regression Hebrew/German grade test (in z-scores)

	Israel			Germany		
	Model 1	Model 2	Model 3	Model 1	Model 2	Model 3
FSU	-0.22**	-0.15+	-0.11	-0.12	0.18	0.25*
	(0.08)	(0.08)	(0.08)	(0.10)	(0.11)	(0.12)
Boy	-0.24**	-0.21**	-0.19*	-0.16	-0.13	-0.15
	(0.08)	(0.08)	(0.08)	(0.10)	(0.09)	(0.09)
Age	-0.01+	-0.01	-0.01	-0.02**	-0.02*	-0.02*
	(0.01)	(0.01)	(0.01)	(0.01)	(0.01)	(0.01)
Parental education		0.48**	0.39**		0.47**	0.35**
		(0.08)	(0.09)		(0.12)	(0.12)
Income		0.11**	0.08*		0.43**	0.32*
		(0.03)	(0.03)		(0.15)	(0.16)
Income (missing)		0.01	-0.03		0.10	0.08
		(0.17)	(0.17)		(0.19)	(0.19)
Books at home			0.07*			0.10+
			(0.04)			(0.05)
Cultural activities			0.06*			0.04
			(0.03)			(0.04)
Interview at home				-0.01	-0.14	-0.15
				(0.09)	(0.09)	(0.10)
Constant	0.45**	-0.26	-0.49**	0.61**	-0.06	-0.41
	(0.12)	(0.16)	(0.18)	(0.13)	(0.19)	(0.26)
R2	0.038	0.146	0.163	0.036	0.125	0.141
N	581			362		

Note: + p<0.1, *p<0.05, ** p<0.01

parental education and family income have positive effects (Model 2), and the effects of parental education are very similar in magnitude as are the effects of income when considering the exchange rate between the Euro and the Shekel (approximately 5). The effects of books at home are also quite similar (Model 3).

However, whereas in Germany the immigrants' disadvantage is fully accounted for by the socio-economic differences between natives and immigrants, this is not true for Israel. In Israel, controlling only for parental education does not explain any of the immigrants' disadvantage (not shown here). This is probably due to the fact that by contrast to Germany, in Israel there are no differences in parental education between native and immigrant students. Adding family income to the

Table 10.5   OLS regression math grade (in z-scores)

	Israel			Germany		
	Model 1	Model 2	Model 3	Model 1	Model 2	Model 3
FSU	-0.12	-0.05	-0.01	-0.07	0.14	0.23+
	(0.08)	(0.08)	(0.08)	(0.10)	(0.12)	(0.12)
Boy	0.03	0.05	0.07	0.10	0.12	0.10
	(0.08)	(0.08)	(0.08)	(0.10)	(0.09)	(0.10)
Age	-0.01	-0.01	-0.00	-0.03**	-0.02*	-0.02*
	(0.01)	(0.01)	(0.01)	(0.01)	(0.01)	(0.01)
Parental education		0.46**	0.37**		0.37**	0.24*
		(0.08)	(0.09)		(0.11)	(0.11)
Income		0.13**	0.09**		0.29+	0.18
		(0.03)	(0.03)		(0.16)	(0.17)
Income (missing)		-0.13	-0.17		0.01	-0.01
		(0.17)	(0.17)		(0.16)	(0.16)
Books at home			0.06+			0.11**
			(0.04)			(0.04)
Cultural activities			0.07*			0.04
			(0.03)			(0.04)
Interview at home				0.03	-0.07	-0.09
				(0.10)	(0.10)	(0.10)
Constant	0.25*	-0.50**	-0.71**	0.47**	0.01	-0.40
	(0.12)	(0.16)	(0.19)	(0.16)	(0.24)	(0.29)
R2	0.009	0.120	0.137	0.035	0.088	0.109
N	581			362		

Note: + $p<0.1$, *$p<0.05$, ** $p<0.01$

equation (Model 2) explains some of the net gap between immigrants and natives in both countries but in Israel a significant immigrant handicap remains. Cultural capital, as measured by number of books and mothers' cultural activities, does not contribute to our understanding of the gap between natives and immigrants in reading comprehension (Model 3).

Table 10.3 presents the regressions for the non-verbal cognitive test for both countries. The results are very different in the two countries. First, whereas in Israel, immigrant children perform worse than natives, in Germany the two groups perform on par. Second, in Israel parental education, income and cultural capital affect test scores while in Germany only parental education does and its effect is smaller than in Israel. Finally, the model explains much less variance in Germany than in Israel. Having seen these results, it occurred to us that the dependent variable was measured less reliably in Germany than in Israel but the Alpha Cronbach coefficient is about equal in the two countries (0.95 and 0.92 in Germany and Israel respectively).

Table 10.4 displays the regression results for grades in language (Hebrew/German). In Israel, but not in Germany, there is a significant gap in favor of native students. It is striking that in Germany, where we did find significant differences in reading comprehension, we do not find a significant difference between immigrant and native students in language grades. This is a remarkable result since disparities between immigrants and natives are usually most pronounced in the language realm.

With this exception however, the results for the two countries are quite similar: the effects of parental education are positive, significant and of similar magnitudes in the two countries, as are the effects of books. In both countries the effects of family income are positive and significant as well.

Controlling for socio-economic background and cultural capital explains much of the initial discrepancies between immigrant and native students in Israel while in Germany, net of these variables immigrant students seem to obtain higher grades in language than natives.

There are no significant differences between immigrant and native students in math grades in either country (Table 10.5, Model 1). In both countries parental education, family income, and cultural capital measured by the number of books at home have positive effects on math grades. Mothers' cultural activities have a significant positive impact in Israel only. As seen in the previous table, in Germany once we control for parental education, family income, and cultural capital (Model 3), immigrant children obtain higher marks in math.

Conclusions

The results of this paper are both clear and mysterious but in either case they leave us optimistic. Studies on the educational, occupational, and economic attainments of immigrants sometimes speak of an immigration penalty that immigrants pay in the host society (e.g., Heath and Cheung, 2007). The penalty is defined as the net disadvantages that immigrants suffer relative to natives, while controlling for differences between the groups in socio-economic characteristics. Small penalties indicate that immigrants have been integrated in the host society. Our results reveal gross differences between immigrant and native children in both competencies and achievements in fourth grade but including socio-economic and cultural characteristics of the families explain most of the gaps. Therefore, by and large, gross differences are not primarily due to immigrant penalties. This good news gives cause for optimism regarding both the future course of integration of FSU immigrants in Germany and Israel. The achievements of FSU immigrant students suggest that their future achievements and attainment will probably be as high as those of natives of equal socio-economic background.

Our results are especially optimistic for Germany and a bit less optimistic for Israel. As expected, we find that much of the scholastic disadvantage of immigrant children in Israel are due to their economic disadvantage. And yet, even when controlling for income as well as for parental education and cultural capital, a significant immigrant penalty remains with respect to test scores. In Germany by contrast, the immigrant penalty is smaller to begin with and is fully explained by socio-economic differences between immigrant and native children and their families. In fact, when adjusted for socio-economic and cultural background, immigrant students in Germany seem to obtain higher grades than their native counterparts.

Important differences between the two countries reflect in the educational distribution of immigrant parents. FSU Jews who came to Israel are better educated than FSU Spätaussiedler who came to Germany. This translates into a differential impact of education in accounting for the immigrant-native gap across countries. In Germany, the pattern for immigrant students resembles that of other immigrant groups, in particular the descendants of classic labor migrants, who typically come from families with lower educational levels, whereas in Israel immigrant students of FSU origin constitute a special case in the sense that they stem from highly educated, but poor families.

Another result that differs between the two contexts concerns the discrepant result in reading comprehension and school grades in language. The findings show that in Israel the native-immigrant gap persists even after considering economic resources. As noted, research on immigrants' education has shown that if such differences remain, they often pertain to the language realm.

The surprising result of our study concerns the discrepancy between countries in the magnitude of the native-immigrant gaps among parents and children. On the one hand we found that there are larger differences in Germany between immigrants and natives in parental education, income, and cultural capital than in Israel. For example, in Germany, the gap between immigrant and native parents in education is over a standard deviation whereas in Israel parental education in the two groups is virtually identical. And yet, among children the native-immigrant gaps in non-verbal competencies and in language grades are smaller in Germany than in Israel whereas in reading comprehension the gap is similar in the two countries (about 40 percent of a standard deviation). In math grades there are no native-immigrant gaps in either country. These results seem to indicate that conditions in Germany might be different to reduce the immigrant penalty so drastically in a generation. Could it be the financial support that Spätaussiedler have received or the acculturation and language courses that they receive? Is it the greater motivation of Spätaussiedler to integrate in the host society that explains this success? Or are the differences at least partly related to a limited cross-cultural comparability of our competence measures? Unfortunately, we cannot adjudicate between these explanations. As always, more research is called for.

References

Alba, R., Handl, J., and Müller, W. (1994). Ethnische Ungleichheiten im deutschen Bildungssystem. *Kölner Zeitschrift für Soziologie und Sozialpsychologie, 46*(2), 209-237.

Allmendinger, J. (1989). Educational systems and labor market outcomes. *European Sociological Review, 5*(3), 231-250.

Anweiler, O. (1996). Deutschland. In O. Anweiler (Ed.), *Bildungssysteme in Europa. Entwicklung und Struktur des Bildungswesens in zehn Ländern* (pp. 31-56). Weinheim: Beltz.

Becker, B., and Biedinger, N. (2006). Ethnische Bildungsungleichheit zu Schulbeginn. *Kölner Zeitschrift für Soziologie und Sozialpsychologie, 58*(4), 660-684.

Bourdieu, P., and Passeron, J.-C. (1977). *Reproduction in education, society and culture*. London: Sage Publications.

Bundesministerium des Innern (2008). *Migrationsbericht 2007*. Nuremberg: Bonifatius.

Central Bureau of Statistics (2013). Adjusted Private Disposable Income. http://www1.cbs.gov.il/reader/Milon/Milon_ByTerm_E. html?MyID=157&OnlyFinal=1. Retrieved 4 February, 2013.

Chachashvili-Bolotin, S. (2007). *The effects of the immigration on educational attainments of immigrants and native Israelis*. Thesis submitted to the Senate of Tel Aviv University in partial fulfillment of the requirements for the degree of Doctor of Philosophy.

Cortina, K. S., Baumert, J., Leschinsky, A., Mayer, K. U., and Trommer, L. (2003). *Das Bildungswesen in der Bundesrepublik Deutschland. Strukturen und Entwicklungen im Überblick*. Reinbek: Rowohlt.

De Graaf, N. D., de Graaf, P. M., and Kraaykamp, G. (2000). Parental cultural capital and educational attainment in the Netherlands: A refinement of the cultural capital perspective. *Sociology of Education, 73*(2), 92-111.

Duncan, G. J., Yeung, W. J., Brooks-Gunn, J., and Smith, J. R. (1998). How much does childhood poverty affect the life chances of children? *American Sociological Review, 63*(3), 406-423.

Feniger, Y. (2009). *Educational opportunities in Israeli state religious education: Learning climate, student achievement and educational inequality*. Thesis submitted to the Senate of Tel Aviv University in partial fulfillment of the requirements for the degree of Doctor of Philosophy.

Fogel, N. (2007). *Immigrants from the former USSR: Differences in educational achievements by geographic origin – 2003/04*. Working paper 33, Central Bureau of Statistics – The Chief Scientist Department, Jerusalem.

Fridman, L. S. (2008). *Undoing the ulpan* [Online: Haaretz newspaper]. Retrieved from http://www.haaretz.com/print-edition/opinion/undoing-the-ulpan-1.238456 [accessed: 05 September 2012].

Gabay-Egozi, L., Shavit, Y., and Yaish, M. (2009). Curricular choice: A test of a rational choice model of education. *European Sociological Review*, *26*(4), 447-463.

Hauser, R. M., Tsai, S.-L., and Sewell, W. H. (1983). A model of stratification with response error in social and psychological variables. *Sociology of Education*, *56*(1), 20-46.

Heath, A. F., and Cheung, S. Y. (2007). The comparative study of ethnic minority disadvantage. In A. Heath and S. Y. Cheung (Eds.), *Unequal chances: Ethnic minorities in western labour markets. Proceedings of the British Academy* (pp. 1-44). Oxford: Oxford University Press.

Heller, K. A., and Perleth, C. (2000). *KFT 4–12+R – Kognitiver Fähigkeitstest für 4. bis 12. Klassen, Revision (KFT 4-12+R)*. Göttingen: Beltz.

Horowitz, T. (1998). Immigrant children and adolescents in the educational system. In E. Leshem and M. Sicron (Eds.), *Profile of an immigration wave: The absorption process of immigrants from the Former Soviet Union, 1990-1995* (pp. 368-405). Jerusalem: The Magnes Press, The Hebrew University.

Konsortium Bildungsberichterstattung (2006). *Bildung in Deutschland: Ein indikatorengestützter Bericht mit einer Analyse zu Bildung und Migration*. Bielefeld: Bertelsmann Verlag.

Kristen, C., and Granato, N. (2007). The educational attainment of the second generation in Germany: Social origins and ethnic inequality. *Ethnicities*, *7*(3), 343-366.

Kristen, C. (2008). Schulische Leistungen von Kindern aus türkischen Familien am Ende der Grundschulzeit: Befunde aus der IGLU-Studie. *Kölner Zeitschrift für Soziologie und Sozialpsychologie, Sonderheft 48*, 230-251.

Lareau, A. (2000). *Home advantage: Social class and parental intervention in elementary education*. Second Edition. Lanham: Rowman and Littlefield.

Leopold, L., and Shavit, Y. (2011). Cultural capital does not travel well: Immigrants, natives and achievement in Israeli schools. *European Sociological Review*, doi:10.1093/esr/jcr086.

Leshem, E., and Sicron, M. (1998). *Profile of an immigration wave: The absorption process of immigrants from the Former Soviet Union, 1990-1995*. Jerusalem: Magnes Press and the Sapir Forum for Economic Policy (in Hebrew).

Levin, T., Shohamy, E., and Spolsky, D. (2003). *Academic achievements of immigrant students: Findings and recommendations for decision makers*. Ministry of Education. Department of the Chief Scientist (in Hebrew).

Lissitsa, S. (2006). *Integration of immigrants from the CIS in Israel: The emergence of a transnational diaspora*. Thesis submitted to the Senate of Tel Aviv University in partial fulfillment of the requirements for the degree of Doctor of Philosophy.

Müller, W., and Shavit, Y. (1998). *From school to work: a comparative study of educational qualifications and occupational destinations*. Oxford: Clarendon Press.

Müller, A., and Stanat, P. (2006). Schulischer Erfolg von Schülerinnen und Schülern mit Migrationshintergrund: Analysen zur Situation von Zuwanderern aus der ehemaligen Sowjetunion und aus der Türkei. In J. Baumert, P. Stanat and R. Watermann (Eds.), *Herkunftsbedingte Disparitäten im Bildungswesen. Vertiefende Analysen im Rahmen von PISA 2000* (pp. 221-255). Wiesbaden: VS Verlag für Sozialwissenschaften.

Nauck, B., Diefenbach, H., and Petri, K. (1998). Intergenerationale Transmission von kulturellem Kapital unter Migrationsbedingungen: Zum Bildungserfolg von Kindern und Jugendlichen aus Migrantenfamilien in Deutschland. *Zeitschrift für Pädagogik, 44*(5)*, 701-722.

Schumann, R. (2003). *Fremde Heimat – Deutsche aus Russland – von der Ansiedlung bis zur Rückwanderung.* Berlin: Verlag am Park.

Schwippert, K., Hornberg, S., and Goy, M. (2008). Lesekompetenz von Kindern mit Migrationshintergrund im nationalen Vergleich. In W. Bos, S. Hornberg, K.-H. Arnold, G. Faust, L. Fried, E.-M. Lankes, K. Schwippert and R. Valtin (Eds.), *IGLU-E 2006. Die Länder der Bundesrepublik Deutschland im nationalen und internationalen Vergleich* (pp. 112-125). Münster: Waxmann.

Sever, R. (2002). *High-school drop-outs in the context of the immigrant integration process.* Jerusalem: Taub Center for Social Policy Studies in Israel (in Hebrew).

Sewell, W. H., and Hauser, R. M. (1975). *Education, occupation, and earnings. Achievement in the early career.* New York: Academic Press Inc.

Shavit, Y., and Blank, C. (with I. Fast) (2012). Discipline and achievement in Israeli schools. In R. Arum and M. Velez (Eds.), *Improving learning environments in schools: Lessons from abroad.* Stanford University Press.

Sicron, M. (1998). The immigrants' human capital and their integration in the labor force. In E. Leshem and M. Sicron (Eds.), *Profile of an immigration wave: The absorption process of immigrants from the Former Soviet Union, 1990-1995* (pp. 127-182). Jerusalem: The Magnes Press,The Hebrew University.

Söhn, J. (2008). Bildungsunterschiede zwischen Migrantengruppen in Deutschland: Schulabschlüsse von Spätaussiedlern und anderen Migranten der ersten Generation im Vergleich. *Berliner Journal für Soziologie, 18*(3), 401-431.

Walter, O. (2008). Herkunftsassoziierte Disparitäten im Lesen, in der Mathematik und in den Naturwissenschaften: Ein Vergleich zwischen PISA 2000, PISA 2003 und PISA 2006. *Zeitschrift für Erziehungswissenschaft, Sonderheft 10,* 149-168.

Zionit, Y., and Ben-Arye, A. (1995). Immigrant children in Israel. Jerusalem: The Council for Children and the Center for Research and Policy Development.

Chapter 11

Transitions to Romantic Involvement and Living Together: A Comparison of Psychosocial Outcomes between Natives and Immigrants in Germany

Rainer K. Silbereisen, Peter F. Titzmann, Andrea Michel,
Avi Sagi-Schwartz, Yoav Lavee, and David Mehlhausen-Hassoen

The research addressed in this chapter is rooted in the psychological and sociological notion that biographical transitions provide new opportunities for the transaction between contexts and individuals and as such instigate new adaptation and longer-term development of psychosocial functions (e.g., Walsemann, Gee, and Geronimus, 2009). Among such transitions are more formal transitions from kindergarten to school, or from school to work, but also more informal transitions such as first romantic relationships, marriage, and parenthood. Although our project also had investigated transitions to kindergarten and school (Silbereisen, Titzmann, Michel, Sagi-Schwartz, and Lavee, 2012; Stoessel, Titzmann, and Silbereisen, 2011), this chapter concentrates on transitions to romantic involvement in adolescence and living together in adulthood.[1] Our question was whether the presumed potential of transitions for the instigation of psychosocial development pays off alike across natives, immigrants, and minorities, or whether there are dissimilarities which open or reduce differences in psychosocial development between the groups. Because about one-fifth of the German population share a so-called migration background, this question is of great public interest.

The data reported here are the German portion of a German-Israeli research project. The results for the Israeli part can be seen in the following chapter (Titzmann et al., this volume). In Germany, three different groups of

1 This project "Regulation of Developmental Transitions in Second Generation Immigrants in Germany and Israel" was funded by the German Federal Ministry of Education and Research (BMBF; reference number 01GWS068) as part of the research consortium on "Migration and Societal Integration" (Director: Rainer K. Silbereisen). All responsibility concerning the content of this publication is with the authors. We thank our other colleagues and collaborators from the Chemnitz-Haifa-Jena team: Susanne Clauß, Falk Gruner, Mohini Lokhande, Bernhard Nauck, Anja Steinbach, and Katharina Stößel. We want to express our gratitude to all study participants for their collaboration.

immigrants were studied. Among them are people of often distant German ethnicity (*Aussiedler*) who gain citizenship, typically resettling from successor countries of the former Soviet Union where they lived as a Diaspora, and groups of Russian Jewish refugees, also from the former Soviet Union that enjoy privileged residence permits in Germany (Dietz, 2000). Further, we included a group of Turkish immigrants who are residents but in most cases without German citizenship. All of these groups were compared with native Germans. Beyond legal differences, there is also notable variation in terms of acculturation and biographical success among these migrant groups, despite often extended periods of German residency (Nauck, 2001; Woellert, Kröhnert, Sippel, and Klingholz, 2009).

Hypotheses

The basic theoretical notion behind our study was that biographical transitions challenge established ways of adjustment and thereby offer opportunities to gain new experiences that ultimately support developmental progression among the individuals involved (Ryff and Heidrich, 1997). The transition to romantic involvement in adolescence is certainly a major developmental task for young people (Zimmer-Gembeck, 1999). It is a dyadic relationship in contrast to relationships with peer groups, and it is characterized by the expression of mutual affection and the initial union of sexuality and passion (Connolly and McIsaak, 2009). Concerning psychosocial development, the experience of sharing activities and exchanging views with an intimate partner puts into perspective the role of peers, helps to develop a new sense of responsibility, and also represents a push to think and judge more long-term (Brown, 1999). The appropriate timing and level of sexual contact among young people is a core element of cultural belief systems, and concerning native Germans it is well known that adolescents are involved rather earlier in romantic relationships as compared to other ethnic groups. The questions of timing and romantic activities are particularly relevant for Turkish adolescents where tradition imposes strict limits on any intimate relationship (Boos-Nünning and Karakaşoğlu, 2007). Families of repatriate Germans are also known to have more traditional role expectations than native Germans (Schmitt-Rodermund and Silbereisen, 2009). In comparing the groups of natives and immigrants, the question is whether similar effects of the transition on psychosocial outcomes will be found in spite of possibly different average levels of romantic involvement across groups, and whether possible gaps in psychosocial adaptation between groups diminish or increase.

Concerning the transition to living together in a shared household in early adulthood, differences between the ethnic groups are also to be expected. As in other Western countries, in Germany marriage is no longer the only acceptable living arrangement among adults who entertain a committed sexual relationship (Smock, 2000). Many people in individualistically-oriented societies begin such a relationship with cohabitation, whereas in collectivist societies a shared household comes only subsequent to marriage (Diener, Gohm, Suh, and Oishi, 2000). According to country-wide census data for Germany (Statistisches Bundesamt [Federal Statistical Office], 2008), among the younger cohorts (18-25 years) about 85 percent of native Germans who live together with their partner are not married; among immigrants this figure is less than half (40 percent). Living together with a partner implies many new challenges and offers opportunities for psychosocial development. For example, the closer encounter increases the likelihood of conflicts (Chen et al., 2006), particularly concerning the alignment of daily duties (Batalova and Cohen, 2002), and can also help the partners to learn resolution strategies. Cohabitation also involves changes in the social networks, and can carry expectations concerning an increase in the commitment to the partnership (Grau, Mikula, and Engel, 2001). The ethnic groups studied differ in the degree of egalitarian orientation towards partnership, with a rather gender-stereotyped profile among Turks (Diehl, König, and Ruckdeschel, 2009; Sakallı, 2001), as well as probably among the German repatriates (Remennick, 2005). Our question here was again whether the experience of living together as a couple is related to psychosocial outcomes, and if so, whether this association varies between the groups.

Psychosocial Outcomes

We used the so called Five Cs – that is, Competence, Confidence, Connection, Character, and Caring (Lerner et al., 2005) as a framework to define outcomes of psychosocial functioning. Using this framework allowed defining outcomes that are comparable across the transitions on the one hand and transition-specific on the other. Achievements in these five general domains are deemed to be the prerequisite for individuals to realize their developmental potentials concerning the self, family, community, and civil society.

Experiences related to transitions certainly do not represent the only predictors of the psychosocial outcomes of interest. Against this backdrop the conceptual model guiding our research assumed that the psychosocial outcomes were also related to two additional conditions above and beyond the experiences inherent in the transitions themselves, namely, family resources and regulation strategies in dealing with transition-typical challenges. Family resources were differentiated as economic, social, and cultural capital (Bourdieu, 1986). Regulation strategies were classified as engagement or disengagement when dealing with stressful situations (Heckhausen and Schulz, 1993). Engagement indicates that individuals actively try to change a challenging situation, whereas disengagement means that individuals avoid dealing with such issues. As we were interested in commonalities and differences in the role of this set of predictors across native and immigrant groups, main and moderating effects of group membership were added. In addition, these variables allowed us to compare the effect of transitions with the effect of the other correlates of the psychosocial outcomes. Ethnicity effects might, for example, be explained away by differences in resources, such as the economic or educational standing of the participants or their family (see for example Epstein et al. or Kristen et al., this volume).

Design and Assessments of the Study

Sample

The sample was organized by a matrix comprising transitions studied, target persons assessed, and ethnic groups compared. Concerning romantic involvement, the adolescents reported about the outcome variables and whether or not they had already made the transition to romantic involvement, whereas mothers reported on background variables, such as economic, cultural and social capital. On the transition to living together, all information was gathered from the young adults themselves. As the design comprised cross-sectional comparisons of groups differing in transition status we aimed at "age brackets" for sampling enough respondents before and after the transition: 15 to 18 years for romantic involvement, and 20 to 30 years for living together. These are ages where we had reason to assume that the size of the groups formed before and after the transition would be about equal.

Utilizing random selection from data supplied by the registry offices in two large cities in different federal states in the West of Germany, and with the help of many especially trained interviewers, we achieved a total sample of 1219 participants in Germany. This number includes the Russian Jewish immigrants for whom we had to rely on snowball sampling supported by people known in their community. Data collection took place from autumn 2007 to spring 2008. The particular cities chosen for data collection were selected because of their large populations of immigrants from all the groups studied. A breakdown of the samples is given in Table 11.1.

Measures

Data were gathered by standardized interviews conducted by specially trained bilingual interviewers fluent in German and the language of the respective immigrant group. Economic capital was indexed by self-assessment of the financial situation on a scale from 1 (it's never near enough) to 5 (the family is able to afford everything) regarding their family's affluence. Cultural capital was determined by the respondents' highest educational level achieved, and social capital addressed respondents' so-called weak ties (Granovetter, 1973). To assess weak ties, a list of occupations ordered by increasing prestige was provided (from unskilled laborer to physician), and participants were asked to check whether they knew people of these occupations (meant to be outside their family or close

Table 11.1   Sample sizes by ethnic group and transition

	Adolescence			Early Adulthood	
	Adolescent Before[a]	Adolescent After[a]	Mothers	Before[b]	After[b]
Native Germans	33 (24%)	102 (76%)	135 (100%)	75 (62%)	46 (38%)
Ethnic German repatriates	20 (24%)	62 (76%)	82 (100%)	53 (75%)	18 (25%)
Russian Jewish immigrants	26 (36%)	47 (64%)	73 (100%)	98 (78%)	27 (22%)
Turkish immigrants	36 (30%)	85 (70%)	121 (100%)	66 (82%)	14 (18%)
Total	115 (28%)	296 (72%)	411 (100%)	292 (74%)	105 (26%)
		822		397	
			1219		

Note: Percentages in brackets refer to the share of respondents in an ethnic group who have not yet made ("Before") vs. already made the transition ("After"); [a] before/ after first romantic involvement; [b] currently living together with partner no = before, yes = after. Only for the adolescent transitions both mother and adolescent participated.

acquaintances) well enough to ask them informally for advice. The score of social capital was calculated as the mean of the prestige (International Socio-Economic Index of Occupational Status; Ganzeboom, De Graaf, and Treiman, 1992) of all occupations in which the respondent knew someone, a procedure suggested by van der Gaag, Snijders and Flap (2008). The range of scores is between 0 (not knowing any person of the professions presented) and 56 (knowing persons of all professions presented).

Following Heckhausen and Schulz's (1993) model of developmental regulation, regulation strategies were conceived as involving an individual's engagement or disengagement in dealing with transition-typical challenges. Participants read two vignettes formulated with the help of experts that characterized problematic situations requiring a reaction. The vignettes for the transition to first romantic involvement, for example, referred to the desire of adolescents to develop more autonomy from parents. Respondents were asked to choose the level of their endorsement for three statements concerning regulation strategies. A list entailing the vignettes and the response scale used can be found here (http://www.migration. uni-jena.de/project1/The_Assessment_of_Regulation_Strategies.pdf).   In   the example, engagement referred either to own attempts at changing the situation described, or to encouraging oneself to try harder, or to seeking help from others in order to be successful. These behaviors are typically shown when the obstacles to success seem controllable. Disengagement, in contrast, is often revealed when perceived controllability is low. Here we asked whether participants opted for this strategy in order to avoid self-blame or whether they simply stopped thinking about the situation described in the vignette.

The selection of psychosocial outcomes was guided by the principle of the Five Cs – Competence, Confidence, Connection, Character, and Caring (Lerner et al., 2005). Competence in dealing with the transition to romantic involvement was assessed as competent behavior in relation to dating using three items taken from Levenson and Gottman (1978). These items addressed how often the adolescent felt able to maintain a romantic relationship based on mutual understanding, and whether an adolescent was able to sense how a potential romantic partner feels about him/her. Competence for the young adult group was indexed together with Confidence by general self-efficacy (Jerusalem and Schwarzer, 1992). An example item is "I am confident that I could deal efficiently with unexpected events." Assessment of all other Cs was accomplished in the same way for both age groups. Connection referred to partnership preferences that could be traditional (based on parental agreement and the match of religion or ethnicity) or economic (status, finances, and education were prominent). This measure, which was based on Hetsroni (2000), required respondents to rate the importance of these characteristics on a scale between 1 (not important) and 6 (very important). Character was assessed via a scale of delinquent beliefs (Finckenauer, 1995). Participants responded by indicating whether they agreed to four items such as "Taking things from stores doesn't hurt anyone." Caring was measured by the sum of civic engagement activities for the benefit of others. The measure was inspired by the 2006 Shell-Youth-Study (Hurrelmann and Albert, 2006) and presented items like "I have been actively involved with supporting good relations between people of different cultures" or "I have been actively involved with animal welfare or environmental protection."

In addition we assessed background characteristics related to migration status, information concerning the nature of the transitions studied, and the experiences they likely convey. Concerning adolescence, we used questions concerning involvement in sexual activities according to Smith and Udry (1985). For young adults we gained some more information on the nature and background of the relationship (i.e., whether they are married or intend to marry).

Following recommendations by Bollen (1989), concerning all variables comprising several items, confirmatory factor analyses ensured that factor loadings applied equally well across ethnic groups, gender and age groups. Thus, any differences between groups in the associations cannot be due to a lack of measurement equivalence. The alpha-consistency of all scales was higher than .60, despite the fact that some of the scales consisted of three items only.

Transitions

Regarding romantic involvement, the transition was defined as made when adolescents reported that they have had a girlfriend or boyfriend at some stage.

If they indicated that they had not yet had a romantic partner, adolescents were classified as pre-transition. There were almost no differences in the share of adolescents who had made the transition to romantic involvement (the Russian Jewish group had a somewhat lower share, though). Concerning adulthood, we ascertained whether or not the young adults currently live together with their partner in a shared apartment, independent of their marital status, which is referred to as cohabitation in the following. About one-third of the native German adults reported cohabiting, whereas only about one-fifth of Turks reported living together with their partner (see Table 11.1). Given the identical age brackets chosen for the groups, the differences in the share of transitions accomplished probably reflect cultural differences.

As we cannot investigate causal effects of transitions on psychosocial outcomes with our cross-sectional design, we wanted at least ensure that individuals before the transition did not differ significantly from individuals after the transition. We performed a number of analyses of variance (ANOVAs) to test for such differences. Variables under scrutiny were socio-demographic aspects (age of target, age of mother, gender, religiosity, number of children in the family, employment status, partnership of mothers), family resources (economic, cultural and social capital as well as educational aspirations), and several acculturation-related variables for the immigrant groups (length of residence, use of German, citizenship, identification with host culture). The results revealed only few significant differences between individuals before and after the transition. Most of these were related to age, but this variation was not large and was statistically controlled in all analyses.

Results on Differences between the Groups in Resources and Psychosocial Outcomes

In the following we report results of ANOVAs with post hoc tests comparing groups of immigrants and natives in mean levels of the variables which we later used as predictors for the psychosocial outcomes. Concerning cultural capital, across the transitions to romantic relations and living together as a couple, the Jewish group and the native Germans had the highest educational level, followed by the German repatriates, with the Turkish group coming last by some distance. Economic capital, however, did not show much difference across all groups. Finally, there was almost a cleavage in the results for social capital. Native Germans were closely followed by the Jewish group, with the repatriates and especially the Turks reporting very low levels of ties to people outside the family who, by their occupations, signify the accessibility to networks of knowledge and social influence. Although these differences were less pronounced among the young adults, the general picture also applied here.

Concerning regulation strategies vis-à-vis transition-typical challenges, the first result to be mentioned is that the endorsement of engagement in solving a problem was higher than that of disengagement. This is plausible given the principle of

Table 11.2   Means (standard deviation) of psychosocial outcomes of ethnic groups and respondents for transition to romantic involvement and living together as a couple

	Native Germans	Russian (Repatriates)	Russian (Jewish)	Turkish Immigrants	F values (df)
Adolescents: Transition to Romantic Involvement					
Dating competence	3.9 [a] (1.0)	4.0 [a] (1.0)	3.8 [a, b] (1.1)	3.5 [b] (1.3)	4.48 (3,404)
Self-efficacy	4.1 [b] (0.7)	4.3 [a, b] (0.9)	4.1 [b] (0.8)	4.4 [a] (0.9)	4.20 (3,405)
Self-esteem	4.9 (0.7)	4.8 (0.9)	4.8 (0.9)	4.8 (0.9)	0.76 (3,405)
Traditional partner preferences	2.4 [d] (1.1)	3.3 [b] (1.1)	2.8 [c] (1.1)	4.3 [a] (1.5)	57.84 (3,404)
Economic partner preferences	3.2 [c] (1.1)	4.0 [a, b] (1.1)	3.7 [b] (1.1)	4.2 [a] (1.3)	20.26 (3,403)
Delinquent beliefs	0.8 [b] (1.0)	1.1 [a, b] (1.2)	0.8 [b] (0.9)	1.3 [a] (1.2)	5.95 (3,405)
Civic engagement	4.0 (2.2)	3.6 (2.5)	3.6 (2.2)	3.5 (2.4)	1.15 (3,405)
Young Adults: Living Together as Couple					
Self-efficacy	4.1 [b] (0.8)	4.4 [a] (0.9)	4.3 [a] (0.8)	4.5 [a] (1.0)	3.91 (3,390)
Traditional partner preferences	2.2 [d] (1.2)	2.7 [c] (1.4)	3.2 [b] (1.3)	4.2 [a] (1.5)	37.26 (3,390)
Economic partner preferences	3.1 [b] (1.0)	3.6 [a] (1.2)	3.7 [a] (1.2)	3.9 [a] (1.2)	8.66 (3,390)
Delinquent beliefs	0.6 [c] (0.9)	0.8 [a, b, c] (0.9)	1.1 [a] (1.0)	0.9 [a, b] (1.0)	5.33 (3,390)
Civic engagement	3.1 [a] (2.3)	2.0 [b] (2.1)	3.0 [a] (2.2)	2.8 [a] (2.3)	3.82 (3,390)

Notes: Means with different superscripts within a row are significantly different at $p < .05$ with post hoc LSD-test (least significant difference) as part of an ANOVA. All results are controlled for age and gender.

controllability of the challenges expressed in the vignettes. If such situations can be controlled, then engagement is generally the better strategy in terms of well-being (Heckhausen and Schulz, 1993). As far as differences between the groups are concerned, irrespective of engagement or disengagement, the Turkish group endorsed the regulation strategies more highly than all other groups. Although the origins of this difference cannot be determined from the current data, a possibility is that the higher endorsement overall among the Turks points to a higher level of challenges during the transition. An alternative explanation may be that the challenges are experienced as more distressing, which is known to result in both more engagement and more disengagement compared to other situations (O'Farrell, Murray, and Hotz, 2000).

In Table 11.2, the means for the psychosocial outcomes studied are shown for all ethnic groups and transitions. For the sake of brevity we will confine ourselves to some substantial ethnic differences. First of all, Turkish adolescents scored lower in dating competence than the other three groups, which probably reflects the more traditional orientation of Turkish families, which do not necessarily allow dating among their offspring (Duyan and Duyan, 2005). The most substantial difference we found, however, regarded partner preferences. In both age groups, economic aspects were more highly endorsed among the three immigrant groups than in the native German group, and for traditional partner preferences, i.e. the tendency to prefer same-ethnic partners, Turks scored substantially higher than all other groups. Turkish individuals cannot easily envisage a relationship with a partner from a different ethnic background.

The Role of Transitions

Our main research question concerned the association between developmental transitions and psychosocial outcomes. This was addressed by a set of regression analyses that included all social groups studied, natives and immigrants, conducted separately per outcome in hierarchical sequence, in which a set of interaction terms between groups and transition, and between groups and regulation was introduced as a last step. Results of this last step tell us whether the role of transition and regulation for the outcome in question differs by ethnic group, that is, natives versus the three immigrant groups. The interactions addressed our most interesting question, because they can reveal a discrepancy in psychosocial outcomes between ethnic groups assessed before and after the transition. As the hierarchical regression revealed that effects of earlier steps were not explained away by variables entered later, only the results of the final step are shown in Table 11.3a (adolescent outcomes) and Table 11.3b (young adult outcomes).

Taking partnership preferences (an example of Connection in the language of the Five Cs) as a case in point, transitions played a role in the sense that traditional partnership preferences were lower among adolescents after the transition, whereas no effect was found for economic partnership preferences. Partnership preferences

Table 11.3a   Regression results for the transition to romantic involvement (standardized coefficients)

	Dating competence	Self-esteem	Self-efficacy	Traditional partner preferences	Economic partner preferences	Delinquent beliefs	Civic engagement
Age of the child	-.022	.116 *	-.005	.031	-.029	-.058	-.025
Sex (1 = male. 2=female)	-.112 *	-.178 **	-.213 ***	.204 ***	.242 ***	-.157 **	.088 +
Repatriate (Dummy = 1)	.048	.016	.129 *	.316 ***	.261 ***	.081	-.089
Russian Jewish (Dummy = 1)	-.024	-.018	.020	.151 **	.195 **	-.044	-.116 +
Turkish (Dummy = 1)	-.100	-.038	.209 **	.533 ***	.266 ***	.240 ***	.010
Social capital	.000	.074	.045	.093 *	-.015	-.007	-.024
Economic capital	.002	.029	.001	.056	-.025	-.047	.021
Cultural capital	.065	-.001	.012	-.173 **	-.141 *	.077	.216 **
Transition (0=no vs. 1=yes)	.415 ***	-.022	-.014	-.210 ***	-.085 +	.030	.114 *
Engagement target	.236 ***	.190 ***	.196 ***	.035	.119 *	.001	.049

Disengagement target	.033	-.026	-.020	.011	.106 *	.000	-.048
Repatriate x transition	-.069	.104+	.075	.060	-.007	-.044	-.031
Jewish x transition	-.019	-.022	-.014	.034	.025	-.004	-.050
Turkish x transition	-.002	-.041	-.036	.039	-.008	.040	-.021
Repatriate x Engagement	-.050	.016	.073	.038	.067	.025	-.007
Jewish x Engagement	-.088 +	-.003	.078	.032	.046	-.020	.001
Turkish x Engagement	-.082	-.066	.037	.000	.053	.053	.111 +
Repatriate x Disengagement	-.009	-.022	-.022	-.007	-.073	-.018	-.052
Jewish x Disengagement	.018	-.057	.033	-.022	-.024	.016	-.040
Turkish x Disengagement	-.140 *	.019	.125 *	.057	-.038	-.005	-.077
R2	.31	.10	.14	.40	.24	.09	.07

Note: $^+$ p < .10; * p < .05; ** p < .01; *** p < .001

Table 11.3b Regression results for the transition to living together as a couple (standardized coefficients)

	Self-efficacy	Traditional Partner preferences	Economic Partner preferences	Delinquent Beliefs	Civic Engagement
Age	.018	.038	.022	.020	.065
Sex (1 = male. 2=female)	-.155 **	.190 ***	.332 ***	-.053	.083
Repatriate (Dummy = 1)	.194 **	.114 *	.172 **	.036	-.135 *
Russian Jewish (Dummy = 1)	.189 **	.293 ***	.255 ***	.214 **	.029
Turkish (Dummy = 1)	.243 ***	.532 ***	.275 ***	.131 *	-.071
Social capital	.128 *	.070	.009	-.095 +	.202 ***
Economic capital	.118 *	.010	.104 *	-.049	.070
Cultural capital	.051	.013	.126 *	-.096	-.099 +
Transition (0=no vs. 1=yes)	.142 **	.017	.010	.083	-.065
Engagement target	.175 ***	.110 *	.181 ***	-.048	.017
Disengagement target	-.079	.040	.091 +	.036	-.004
Repatriate x transition	.033	-.006	-.079	.005	-.068
Jewish x transition	-.035	-.001	-.009	.007	-.050
Turkish x transition	.056	-.009	-.004	.072	-.070
Repatriate x Engagement	.039	.096 +	.009	.015	-.087
Jewish x Engagement	-.031	.004	-.041	-.003	-.034
Turkish x Engagement	.043	.084	.030	-.078	.047
Repatriate x Disengagement	.111 +	.023	.025	.008	.026
Jewish x Disengagement	.091	.066	.017	.049	.042
Turkish x Disengagement	.088	-.076	-.006	-.013	-.008
R^2	.13	.28	.27	.09	.11

Note: $^+$ p < .10; * p < .05; ** p < .01; *** p < .001

were also unaffected by the transition to living together in young adulthood. Furthermore, none of the interactions with the transition was significant, so that existing differentials between the groups of native Germans and immigrants did not differ before and after the transition.

The analysis concerning adolescents' dating competence (as an instance of Competence among the Five Cs) revealed that adolescents who had accomplished this transition scored higher, and no interaction effect was found. In contrast, self-efficacy and self-esteem (representing Confidence among the Five Cs for the adolescence group) were not related to the transition to romantic relations in adolescence, but the transition to cohabitation in adulthood predicted higher levels of self-efficacy. With regard to delinquent beliefs (Character), the transition to first romantic relationships showed no effect nor did any of the interactions. Basically, the same applied for the young adults.

Finally, civic engagement, representing Caring among the Five Cs for both the adolescent and young adult groups, appeared to be higher after the debut of romantic relationships in adolescence, but with no differences between the ethnic groups, as evidenced by no significant interaction being found. Higher cultural capital also played a role in civic engagement. Possibly, romantic involvement creates a new awareness and provides opportunities for voluntary activities typical of young people, although of course the reverse may also be plausible. Among the adults, however, the transition was not relevant, nor was any interaction, but social capital seemingly played a role as it predicted higher levels of civic engagement.

Results for the two partnership transitions in adolescence and adulthood can be summarized as follows: Although the transitions played a role in the expected direction in four out of twelve instances, this effect was never moderated by the groups, that is, immigrants compared to Germans. Neither were differences between immigrants and Germans ever explained away by any of the three forms of capital, which in any case had no great overall effect, or by the regulation strategies, of which engagement was most closely related to a substantial number of outcomes in both adolescence and adulthood. The variance explained in the various analyses (R-Square) ranged between about 10 percent and 40 percent.

The analyses reported thus far treated the transitions at face value, but disregarded possible differences between the ethnic groups in the quality of the transitions. A relevant qualitative aspect is the level of sexual involvement, which we assessed following Smith and Udry (1985) with a sequence ranging from holding hands to kissing, French kissing, petting, and finally to intercourse, for which cultural equivalence was established in previous research (Brook, Balka, Abernathy, and Hamburg, 1994). Here we found quite remarkable differences (Chemnitz-Haifa-Jena-Team, 2009). Among the native German group, although holding hands and kissing was ubiquitous at around 90 percent and higher, from French kissing onwards the percentage of native Germans reporting having experienced each stage fell gradually to 44 percent having had sexual intercourse. The share of adolescents having had a particular experience in the other groups, particularly the Turks, fell to around half or less than that of the native Germans.

For example, only 19 percent of Turks who had ever had a romantic partner indicated that they had experienced intercourse. These differences were significant and indicated that the real divide was between the Turks and the other three groups. Having a romantic relationship with a boyfriend/girlfriend for the Turks meant a much less "advanced" stage of sexual involvement. In sum, although the transition effects showed many similarities across groups, it seems that the transition involved different experiences for the various ethnic groups studied. It is probably not the absolute level of romantic and sexual involvement that is decisive for developmental progress, but its match with cultural practice for the age group studied.

Concerning the adult transition to living together, there were also remarkable but not unexpected differences between the ethnic groups in our sample (Chemnitz-Haifa-Jena-Team, 2009). The clearest difference concerned whether a respondent was married when living with a partner (of those couples living together, 87 percent of the Turks, but only 15 percent of the native Germans were married) or whether there was an intention to marry. Here about 50 percent of the native Germans did not yet know when they might marry (or ruled out marriage), whereas the German repatriates and the Russian-Jewish immigrants were much more pro-marriage. Unfortunately, breaking the analyses further down to distinguish living together as being married versus unmarried was not possible due to small cell sizes. In sum, the main difference between the ethnic groups concerning the transition to cohabitation with a partner was the fact that among native Germans the likelihood is high that it will not end in marriage, whereas for the Turks this kind of living arrangement is almost exclusively reserved for married couples. For the German repatriates and the Russian-Jewish sample, cohabitation appears much more like a waiting arrangement before the ultimate act of marriage.

Seen against the qualitative differences in the nominally equivalent transitions just discussed, the commonalities in the results are impressive. Although the sexual involvement among Turkish adolescents was much less advanced compared to the other groups, as the regression analyses revealed, the degree of traditional partnership preferences seemed generally lower after the transition as was observed in the other groups. Further, in spite of the fact that living together in adulthood (between ages 20 and 30 without having children) meant marriage among Turks and ambivalence concerning such a commitment among the native Germans, these differences were never reflected in a differential effect on the psychosocial outcomes depending on the ethnic group. Obviously the background behind the wish for living together differs between young adults, but the effects in terms of the Five Cs are alike.

Conclusion and Outlook

The main question of our study was whether age-typical transitions in adolescence and young adulthood to more mature intimate relationships are related to select psychosocial outcomes that are of proven relevance for the realization of an individual's potential for achievement and well-being (Lerner et al., 2005).

Furthermore, we wanted to know whether the effect of the transitions varies as a function of the particular social group studied, that is, young German natives and ethnic German repatriates, Russian-Jewish immigrants, and members of the Turkish minority. To be precise, the presumed cause of any differences observed is not the transitions as such, but the particular experiences they provide to "alter how people are treated, how they act, what they do, and thereby even what they think and feel." (Bronfenbrenner, 2005, p. 53). The transition to romantic involvement in adolescence is a major step towards a new intimacy between people, provides opportunities for the exploration of commitments, and also requires discipline in handling new freedoms (Miller and Benson, 1999). The transition to living together as a couple brings two lives into alignment and interdependence over a large range of duties and pleasures, possibly with the added task of developing a perspective for procreation (Hsueh, Morrison, and Doss, 2009). Our findings, according to our particular cross-sectional approach, showed that these transitions are indeed related to several of the outcomes studied and basically there was no instance of a negative effect of the transition experience among those who reported an experience of partnership or of living together.

Perhaps the most important result of the study was, however, that the transition effects were not conditioned by membership of the ethnic groups under comparison. Thus, if there was a positive difference for a particular outcome between those approaching and those having achieved the transition, then this applied equally well to all groups, as indicated by the absence of any statistical interaction between ethnic group and transition in the regression results. This is so despite the fact that experiences related to the transition, such as the stage of sexual experiences in adolescence or the willingness to marry in early adulthood, were quite different between the various ethnic groups. This implies that the respective experiences do not tend to diminish the existing differences in psychosocial outcomes. We should admit, however, that for the immigrants in contrast to the natives new demands resulting from the combination of development and acculturation may challenge the immigrant individuals, and the lack of a differential gain between natives and immigrants we observed may in part be due to such competing challenges.

Another noteworthy result is that the effects of the ethnic groups on the psychosocial outcomes cannot be substituted by any of the three resources examined, that is, by economic, social, and cultural capital. The levels of these capitals varied remarkably across the groups studied, with the Turkish immigrants being especially low in educational attainment and social network capital. Although of relevance for some psychosocial outcomes studied as such, their effect did not eliminate the differences in outcomes as a function of ethnic group membership.

Our study has limitations, starting with the particular cross-sectional design employed in assessing effects of transitions, which prohibits any causal interpretations of effects found. Nevertheless, the groups of individuals before a respective transition compared to those after the transition did not report very different scores across a number of demographic, resource-related, and acculturation-related variables we used as controls to secure internal validity. This comparability of the participants before and after the transition in many relevant demographic and psychological variables was a prerequisite for the interpretations of the group differences as related to transition experiences. Certainly a follow-up in a longitudinal fashion would be helpful, but the data on the adolescent and adulthood transitions were not adaptable to this scenario. Further, the sample was confined to two large cities chosen because they have the highest density of non-native groups in Germany (Schönwälder and Söhn, 2009). We also have to admit that, due to the nature of the survey, the array of psychosocial outcomes had to be rather narrow, and the assessment instruments very short. Finally, the actual experiences related to a particular transition were not assessed directly.

Beyond these caveats, the study has obvious strengths, such as the possibility of assessing whether ethnic differences in the psychosocial outcomes investigated can be explained away by differences in the three capitals assessed, i.e. economic, cultural, and social capital (Bourdieu, 1986). According to a review by Heath, Rothon and Kilpi (2008) on second generation immigrants in Western Europe, the gap in socioeconomic background in most cases is not wide enough to account for minority disadvantages in educational outcomes. Among the additional mechanisms discussed are language fluency, ethnic segregation and discrimination.

In a nutshell, the two transitions to intimate relationships addressed seem to be associated with psychosocial functioning, and this applies to natives and immigrants alike. However, pre-existing differences in the level of functioning between the ethnic groups were not smaller in the groups having accomplished the transition. Whether these differences (even after the transitions) are undue differences in psychosocial functioning to the disadvantage of immigrants, or even reveal a missed chance to overcome a gap in socialization, is a different issue. We would warn against any premature conclusion. Scientists and policy-makers alike may consider ways in which transition experiences can be changed such that they are more likely to provide the best opportunities for psychosocial development among native Germans and immigrant groups.

References

Batalova, J. A., and Cohen, P. N. (2002). Premarital cohabitation and housework: Couples in cross-national perspective. *Journal of Marriage and Family, 64*, 743-755.

Bollen, K. A. (1989). *Structural equations with latent variables*. Oxford: John Wiley and Sons.

Boos-Nünning, U., and Karakaşoğlu, Y. (2007). Sexuelle Normen und Erfahrungen mit sexueller Aufklärung von jungen Frauen mit Migrationshintergrund [Sexual norms and experiences with sex education of young women with migration background]. *BzGA FORUM, 3-2007*, 28-33.

Bourdieu, P. (1986). The forms of capital. In J. Richardson (Ed.), *Handbook of theory and research for the sociology of education* (pp. 241-258). New York: Greenwood.

Bronfenbrenner, U. (2005). A future perspective (1979). In U. Bronfenbrenner (Ed.), *Making human beings human: Bioecological perspectives on human development* (pp. 50-59). Thousand Oaks, CA: Sage Publications Ltd.

Brook, J. S., Balka, E. B., Abernathy, T., and Hamburg, B. A. (1994). Sequence of sexual behavior and its relationship to other problem behaviors in African American and Puerto Rican adolescents. *The Journal of Genetic Psychology, 155*, 107-114.

Brown, B. B. (1999). Measuring the peer environment of American adolescents. In S. L. Friedman and T. D. Wachs (Eds.), *Measuring environment across the lifespan: Emerging methods and concepts* (pp. 59-90). Washington, DC: American Psychological Association.

Chemnitz-Haifa-Jena-Team. (2009). *Working Report: Comparisons of informal transitions to romantic relations in adolescence and early adulthood between ethnic groups in Germany and Israel.* Jena: Center for Applied Developmental Science.

Chen, H., Cohen, P., Kasen, S., Johnson, J. G., Ehrensaft, M., and Gordon, K. (2006). Predicting conflict within romantic relationships during the transition to adulthood. *Personal Relationships, 13*, 411-427.

Connolly, J. A., and McIsaak, C. (2009). Romantic relationships in adolescence. In R. M. Lerner and L. Steinberg (Eds.), *Handbook of adolescent psychology. Vol. 2: Contextual influences on adolescent development* (pp. 104-151). Hoboken: Wiley.

Diehl, C., König, M., and Ruckdeschel, K. (2009). Religiosity and gender equality: Comparing natives and Muslim migrants in Germany. *Ethnic and Racial Studies, 32*, 278-301.

Diener, E., Gohm, C. L., Suh, E., and Oishi, S. (2000). Similarity of the relations between marital status and subjective well-being across cultures. *Journal of Cross-Cultural Psychology, 31*, 419-436.

Dietz, B. (2000). German and Jewish migration from the former Soviet Union to Germany: background, trends and implications. *Journal of Ethnic and Migration Studies, 26*, 635-652.

Duyan, V., and Duyan, G. (2005). Turkish social work students' attitudes toward sexuality. *Sex Roles, 52*, 697-706.

Finckenauer, O. J. (1995). *Russian youth: Law, deviance, and the pursuit of freedom.* New Brunswick, NJ: Transaction Press.

Ganzeboom, H. B. G., De Graaf, P. M., and Treiman, D. J. (1992). A standard international socio-conomic index of occupational status. *Social Science Research, 21*, 1-56.

Granovetter, M. S. (1973). The strength of weak ties. *The American Journal of Sociology, 78*, 1360-1380.

Grau, I., Mikula, G., and Engel, S. (2001). Skalen zum Investitionsmodell von Rusbult [Scales for assessing the model of investments by Rusbult]. *Zeitschrift für Sozialpsychologie, 32*, 29-44.

Heath, A. F., Rothon, C., and Kilpi, E. (2008). The second generation in Western Europe: Education, unemployment, and occupational attainment. *Annual Review of Sociology, 34*, 211-235.

Heckhausen, J., and Schulz, R. (1993). Optimisation by selection and compensation: Balancing primary and secondary control in life-span development. *International Journal of Behavioral Development, 16*, 287-303.

Hetsroni, A. (2000). Choosing a mate in television dating games: The influence of setting, culture, and gender. *Sex Roles, 42*, 83-106.

Hsueh, A. C., Morrison, K. R., and Doss, B. D. (2009). Qualitative reports of problems in cohabiting relationships: Comparisons to married and dating relationships. *Journal of Family Psychology, 23*, 236-246.

Hurrelmann, K., and Albert, M. (2006). *Jugend 2006. 15. Shell Jugendstudie: Eine pragmatische Generation unter Druck* [Youth 2006. 15th Shell Youth Study: A pragmatic generation under pressure]. Frankfurt: Fischer.

Jerusalem, M., and Schwarzer, R. (1992). Self-efficacy as a resource factor in stress appraisal processes. In R. Schwarzer (Ed.), *Self-efficacy: Thought control of action* (pp. 195-213). Washington, DC: Hemisphere.

Lerner, R. M., Lerner, J. V., Almerigi, J. B., Theokas, C., Phelps, E., Gestsdottir, S., and van Eye, A. (2005). Positive youth development, participation in community youth development programs, and community contributions of fifth-grade adolescents: Findings from the first wave of the 4-H study of positive youth development. *Journal of Early Adolescence, 25*, 17-71.

Levenson, R. W., and Gottman, J. M. (1978). Toward the assessment of social competence. *Journal of Consulting and Clinical Psychology, 46*, 453-462.

Miller, B. C., and Benson, B. (1999). Romantic and sexual relationship development during adolescence. In W. Furman, B. B. Brown and C. Feiring (Eds.), *The development of romantic relationships in adolescence* (pp. 99-121). Cambridge: Cambridge University Press.

Nauck, B. (2001). Social capital, intergenerational transmission and intercultural contact in immigrant families. *Journal of Comparative Family Studies, 32*, 465-488.

O'Farrell, P., Murray, J., and Hotz, S. B. (2000). Psychologic distress among spouses of patients undergoing cardiac rehabilitation. *Heart and Lung: The Journal of Acute and Critical Care, 29*, 97-104.

Remennick, L. (2005). Cross-cultural dating patterns on an Israeli campus: Why are Russian immigrant women more popular than men? *Journal of Social and Personal Relationships, 22*, 435-454.

Ryff, C. D., and Heidrich, S. M. (1997). Experience and well-being: Explorations on domains of life and how they matter. *International Journal of Behavioral Development, 20*, 193-206. doi: 10.1080/016502597385289.

Sakallı, N. (2001). Beliefs about wife beating among Turkish college students: The effects of patriarchy, sexism, and sex differences. *Sex Roles, 44*, 599-610.

Schmitt-Rodermund, E., and Silbereisen, R. K. (2009). Immigrant parents' age expectations for the development of their adolescent offspring: Transmission effects and changes after immigration. In U. Schönpflug (Ed.), *Cultural transmission. Psychological, developmental, social, and methodological aspects* (pp. 297-313). New York: Cambridge University Press.

Schönwälder, K., and Söhn, J. (2009). Immigrant settlement structures in Germany: General patterns and urban levels of concentration of major groups. *Urban Studies, 46*, 1439-1460. doi: 10.1177/0042098009104575.

Silbereisen, R. K., Titzmann, P. F., Michel, A., Sagi-Schwartz, A., and Lavee, Y. (2012). The role of developmental transitions in psychosocial competence: A comparison of native and immigrant young people in Germany. In A. S. Masten, K. Liebkind and D. J. Hernandez (Eds.), *Capitalizing on migration. The potential of immigrant youth* (pp. 324-358). New York: Cambridge University Press.

Smith, E. A., and Udry, J. R. (1985). Coital and noncoital sexual behaviors of White and Black adolescents. *American Journal of Public Health, 75*, 1200-1203.

Smock, P. J. (2000). Cohabitation in the United States: An appraisal of research themes, findings, and implications. *Annual Review of Sociology, 26*, 1-20.

Statistisches Bundesamt [Federal Statistical Office]. (2008). *Statistisches Jahrbuch 2008 für die Bundesrepublik Deutschland* [Statistical Yearbook 2008 for the federal republic of Germany]. Statistisches Bundesamt [Federal Statistical Office] Retrieved from http://www.destatis.de.

Stoessel, K., Titzmann, P. F., and Silbereisen, R. K. (2011). Children's psychosocial development following the transitions to kindergarten and school: A comparison between natives and immigrants in Germany. *International Journal of Developmental Science, 5*(1-2), 41-55.

van der Gaag, M., Snijders, T. A. B., and Flap, H. (2008). Position generator measures and their relationship to other social capital measures. In N. Lin and B. H. Erickson (Eds.), *Social capital. An international research program.* (pp. 27-48). New York: Oxford University Press.

Walsemann, K. M., Gee, G. C., and Geronimus, A. T. (2009). Ethnic differences in trajectories of depressive symptoms: Disadvantage in family background, high school experiences, and adult characteristics. *Journal of Health and Social Behavior, 50*(1), 82-98.

Woellert, F., Kröhnert, S., Sippel, L., and Klingholz, R. (2009). *Ungenutzte Potentiale. Zur Lage der Integration in Deutschland* [Idle potentials. On the integration of migrants in Germany]. Berlin: Berlin-Institut für Bevölkerung und Entwicklung.

Zimmer-Gembeck, M. J. (1999). Stability, change and individual differences in involvement with friends and romantic partners among adolescent females. *Journal of Youth and Adolescence, 28*, 419-438.

Chapter 12

Transitions to Romantic Involvement and Living Together: A Comparison of Psychosocial Outcomes between Natives and Immigrants in Israel

Peter F. Titzmann, Rainer K. Silbereisen, Andrea Michel, Yoav Lavee, Avi Sagi-Schwartz, and David Mehlhausen-Hassoen

Across the life-span, individuals face various biographical transitions that are more or less normative for adaptive development within a society (George, 1993). Pearlin (2009) noted that "probably no concept is more instrumentally central than the notion of transitions, which usually refers to the movement into and exit from various institutional roles" (p. 2). Transitions provide new social roles, expose individuals to new ecological settings (Bronfenbrenner, 2005), and carry the potential for new adaptation and longer-term development of psychosocial functions (e.g., Walsemann, Gee, and Geronimus, 2009). The two major research questions are the same as in the previous chapter (Silbereisen et al., this volume). First, how are the biographical transitions to romantic involvement in adolescence and living together with a romantic partner in emerging adulthood related to select psychosocial outcomes? Second, are the associations of transitions and psychosocial outcomes moderated by membership in a particular ethnic group? However, in contrast to the previous chapter, we focused on ethnic groups in Israel here.

Israel is, by definition, a country of immigration and the Law of Return allows every Jew in the world to come to this country as *oleh*, someone who returns to the Promised Land (Ben-Sira, 1997). In our research, we were interested in three ethnic groups in Israel: Russian Jewish immigrants, Israeli Arabs, and a native Israeli reference group. More than 1.1 million Russian Jews, the first group, migrated to Israel between the 1990s and 2008, creating the largest migrant population in Israel. Probably due to the large numbers in a rather short period of time, Russian Jewish immigrants established a Russian infrastructure in Israel with Russian media and Russian-based organizations (Al-Haj, 2004; Mesch, 2002). A second substantial share of Israeli citizens is of Arab origin, altogether about 1.5 million (Central Bureau of Statistics, 2009). Arabs have lived in this area for centuries and are in itself a diverse group consisting of Moslem Arabs, Christian Arabs, and Druze (Horenczyk and Ben-Shalom, 2006). Arabs are more traditional (Feldman, Masalha, and Nadam, 2001), more collectivist, more focused on the family, and follow more traditional gender roles (Lavee and Katz, 2003; Pines and Zaidman, 2003). Not surprisingly, they were described as a caste-like minority (Shavit, 1990).

The research in Israel offered the opportunity to investigate the role of transitions in a context that, compared to Germany, appears much more experienced in accommodating and absorbing immigrants, although this is not the only difference which exists between these two countries (e.g., Titzmann and Silbereisen, 2012; Titzmann, Silbereisen, Mesch, and Schmitt-Rodermund, 2011).[1] Due to the parallel study design in Germany and Israel, we do not repeat all the details here. For more information, especially with regard to general concepts and methods, see the previous chapter (Silbereisen et al., this volume).

Biographical Transitions as Opportunities for Psychosocial Development in Natives and Immigrants

The cultural diversity in Israeli society was one of the starting points for our comparative research, because timing, experiences within a relationship, and onset can vary significantly between cultures (e.g., Coates, 1999). Differences between ethnic groups in Israel concerning intimacy (Elbedour, Shulman, and Kedem, 1997), gender roles (Seginer, Karayanni, and Mar'i, 1990), and openness for sexual involvement (Hetsroni, 2000) can especially be expected to reflect differential effects of the transition to romantic involvement on psychosocial outcomes.

Experiences related to romantic involvement should have an effect on relevant psychosocial outcomes, although the specific experiences related to such a transition may differ between the Israeli groups. For example, sexual contacts are prohibited for Arab adolescents. Furthermore, substantial variation exists between ethnic groups in Israel with regard to how the transition of living together is handled (Baloush-Kleinman and Sharlin, 2004). Among native Israeli young adults, living together as a couple can refer to marriage, but also reflect the early steps of a more serious relationship. However, in some Arab groups, living together as couple without being married is almost impossible (Baloush-Kleinman

---

1   This project "Regulation of Developmental Transitions in Second Generation Immigrants in Germany and Israel" was funded by the German Federal Ministry of Education and Research (BMBF; reference number 01GWS068) as part of the research consortium on "Migration and Societal Integration" (Director: Rainer K. Silbereisen). All responsibility concerning the content of this publication is with the authors. We thank our collaborators from the Chemnitz-Haifa-Jena team: Susanne Clauß, Falk Gruner, Yoav Lavee, Mohini Lokhande, David Mehlhausen-Hassoen, Bernhard Nauck, Avi Sagi-Schwartz, Anja Steinbach, and Katharina Stößel. We want to express our gratitude to all study participants in Germany and Israel for their collaboration.

and Sharlin, 2004), but marriage can precede the transition of living together as a couple for some time, because of the Islamic delay between the signing of the wedding contract and the start of conjugal relations (Savaya and Cohen, 2003). Therefore, our general expectation guiding the research was that the specific circumstances of the Israeli groups, as just illustrated, may alter the potential effects of the investigated biographical transitions to first romantic involvement in adolescence and to living together as couples in emerging adulthood. As such, these transitions, for better or worse, may be differently related to psychosocial outcomes between ethnic groups.

Positive Development as a Framework for Studying Adaptation

In addressing the question of whether developmental transitions are related to developmental psychosocial outcomes, we used the framework of the Five Cs (Competence, Confidence, Connection, Character, Caring) which are approaches taken from positive developmental psychology (Lerner et al., 2005). *Competence* is defined as a positive view of one's actions in specific domain areas including social, academic, cognitive, and vocational skills. *Confidence* refers to a global internal sense of positive self-worth and self-efficacy, *Connection* refers to positive social bonds with people and institutions, *Character* refers to respect for societal and social rules and to internal standards for correct (and moral) behaviors, and *Caring* refers to a sense of sympathy and empathy for others. Obviously, these broad concepts had to be specified for each transition to help establish comparability.

Resources and Regulation Strategies

Certainly, the experiences indexed by the transitions are not the only source of differences in psychosocial outcomes and therefore, we included several other important outcome antecedents. First, ethnic groups may differ substantially in the family resources available to them. Considering such differences is especially necessary in comparing groups in Israel, as the ethnic groups differ substantially in terms of income (Menaham, 2000) or education (Okun and Friedlander, 2005). Beyond differences in such general prerequisites, it is known that reactions to stressors vary across cultures (Laungani, 1995) and also across ethnic groups in Israel (Ben-Ari and Lavee, 2004; Pines and Zaidman, 2003). Thus, we were interested in the way individuals manage transition-related challenges, i.e., whether they actively try to change a challenging situation (engagement) or avoid dealing with such issues (disengagement). By including ways of managing typical transition-related challenges helped ensure that we could see whether effects of transitions, or ethnic group differences, may be partly explained by differences in the way individuals deal with everyday transition-related challenges.

Design and Assessments of the Study in Israel

As mentioned previously, this study was the Israeli portion of a German-Israeli cooperative research on the role of transitions on psychosocial development among immigrants, minority groups, and natives. Although the two studies were conducted in parallel, a few differences in the approach between countries were unavoidable (see previous chapter for the German portion). Particularities of the data protection laws led to a different approach in gathering our samples, namely relying on registry data in Germany and random digit telephone screening in Israel. Thus, the Israeli data included participants from all geographical regions in Israel.

Sample

The study in Israel was also designed such that "age brackets" specific to the particular transitions were defined, with the purpose of acquiring approximately equal numbers of participants who would be representative of the situations before and after the transition. For romantic involvement, the age bracket was 15 to 17 years and for living together, 20 to 29 years. As in the German study, we decided to only interview young adults without children in order to avoid confounding cohabitation and parenthood. As indicated in Table 12.1, the total sample size including all groups and transitions was 879 participants. Participants were interviewed by a bilingual interviewer of a reputed field research organization in Israel. Concerning romantic involvement, adolescents and their mothers were respondents, whereas, for the transition to living together, all information was gathered from the young adults themselves. An extensive procedure of translation and back-translation ensured that the questionnaire used was able to assess the equivalent questions in the various language versions (Hebrew, Russian, and Arabic). All questions originated from an English master version, jointly developed by the German and the Israeli research groups.

Transitions

The information in Table 12.1 is divided by transition status. Adolescents who indicated that they ever had a girlfriend or boyfriend were rated as having made the transition to romantic involvement, and emerging adults who indicated that they lived together with their partner were deemed having made the transition to living together as a couple. Further information on whether the nominal equivalence of the transitions in adolescence and adulthood actually camouflages qualitative differences between Arabs, Russian Jewish immigrants, and native Israelis will be provided when discussing the results.

Ideally, our research questions would be analysed using longitudinal assessments of the same people before and after the transition. However, this was not possible. Although we had a second wave of assessment, far too few adolescents and young adults made the transition between the waves. Thus, the

Table 12.1 Sample sizes by ethnic group and transition

	Adolescence			Early adulthood	
	Before [a]	After [a]	Mothers	Before [b]	After [b]
Native Israelis	51 (52%)	47 (48%)	98 (100%)	71 (55%)	59 (45%)
Russian Jews	31 (36%)	56 (64%)	87 (100%)	69 (69%)	31 (31%)
Arabs	39 (40%)	59 (60%)	98 (100%)	64 (63%)	37 (37%)
Total	121 (43%)	162 (57%)	283 (100%)	204 (62%)	127 (38%)
		566		331	
			897		

Note: Percentages in brackets refer to the share of respondents in an ethnic group who have not yet made ("Before") vs. already made the transition ("After"); [a] before/ after first romantic involvement; [b] currently living together with partner no = before, yes = after. Only for the adolescent transitions both mother and adolescent participated.

comparability of the groups before and after the respective transition, as defined, was crucial for our cross-sectional approach, although of course, such an analysis still does not allow any causal inferences with regard to the effects of transitions on psychosocial outcomes. This is why we performed a number of ANOVAs to ensure that individuals before the transition, at least, did not differ significantly from individuals after the transition. The results revealed only very few significant differences in socio-demographic aspects, family resources and acculturation-related variables between individuals before and after the transition. In the main, they were related to age, with older participants being more likely to have made the transition.

Measures

The measures were basically the same as described in the previous chapter for the German portion of the study. For this reason, we do not provide all the details here (for more information, especially with regard to sample items, see Silbereisen et al., this volume). Nevertheless, in two instances, one item had to be deleted as it did not equivalently measure across the various Israeli groups (Bollen, 1989).

Family resources were assessed in all ethnic groups based on the conceptual work of Bourdieu (1986), who differentiated between social capital, economic capital, and cultural capital. *Social capital* was assessed using a list of occupations (from unskilled labourer to physician), which differed in prestige (International Socio-Economic Index of Occupational Status; Ganzeboom, De Graaf, and Treiman, 1992). The social capital score was calculated as a mean of the prestige of all occupations in which the respondents indicated whether they knew someone sufficiently well and could informally request advice from this person (van der Gaag, Snijders, and Flap, 2008). This score could range from 0 (not knowing any person of the professions presented) to 56 (knowing persons of all professions presented). *Economic capital* referred to the family's finances. Respondents rated the financial situation on a five point scale between 1 (It's nowhere near enough) and 5 (I can afford to buy myself almost everything). *Cultural capital* was indicated by the respondents' highest educational level, using the International Standard Classification of Education (ISCED) ranging from 0 (no formal education) to 6 (PhD and higher).

In order to assess *regulation strategies* (Heckhausen and Schulz, 1993), we developed a new instrument. Participants received two vignettes that characterized challenging everyday situations related to the specific transition studied (all vignettes and the response scale used are accessible under: http://www.migration.uni-jena.de/project1/The_Assessment_of_Regulation_Strategies.pdf). For example, the vignette concerning the transition to romantic involvement refers to a situation in which the adolescent wants more autonomy than the parents are ready to grant. Respondents report their degree of endorsement for statements indicating *engagement* (active attempts at resolving the mismatch, encouraging oneself to try harder, or seeking help from others) or *disengagement* (avoid self-blame when failing, stop thinking about the unresolved situation).

The selection of psychosocial outcomes was guided by the *Five Cs* of positive development (Lerner et al., 2005) and is similar to the measures described in the previous chapter (see for sample items). *Competence* in adolescence was assessed as the ability to deal with a potential romantic partner in a competent way using three items taken from Levenson and Gottman (1978). *Competence* and *Confidence* for the young adult group was addressed by general self-efficacy beliefs taken from Jerusalem and Schwarzer (1992). The remaining Cs were assessed alike in the transitions concerning adolescence and young adulthood. *Connection* was operationalized by partnership preferences on the dimension of traditional orientations (i.e., based on parental consent to the partner chosen and the match of religion or ethnicity) and economic considerations (i.e., social status, finances, and education were prominent). This measure was based on Hetsroni's (2000) research. *Character* was indexed via a scale on delinquent beliefs taken from Finckenauer (1995). *Caring*, the final C, was defined in our study as the level of civic engagement. The items of this measure referred to the Shell-Youth-Study (Hurrelmann and Albert, 2006) and presented seven items that referred to voluntary activities for the benefit of others in society.

We conducted confirmatory factor analyses on all instruments. The procedure followed recommendations by Bollen (1989). Thus, as a result of these preliminary analyses, the measures demonstrated equivalency across ethnic groups in Israel, age groups, and gender. All scales showed sufficient psychometric properties. As the life circumstances substantially vary, especially in the Israeli society, additional information was gathered concerning the nature of the transitions. Adolescents reported the level of sexual involvement (Smith and Udry, 1985), which was found to have the same sequence in different cultures (Brook, Balka, Abernathy, and Hamburg, 1994), African American vs Puerto Rican. Additional information on partnerships included the marital status of couples. Not surprisingly, living together as a couple basically indicated marriage among Arab couples, which was not necessarily the case among Russian Jews and native Israelis.

Differences between the Groups in Resources and Psychosocial Outcomes

Before we discuss the main research question concerning the role of transitions for psychosocial development, we want to compare native Israelis, Russian Jewish immigrants and Israeli Arabs concerning commonalities and differences in the share of individuals who made the transitions, the various predictors and outcome variables. Note, that except for the percentage of transitions achieved, the effects reported are controlled for differences in age and gender. The following will highlight the most remarkable results only. The data on transitions accomplished are shown in Table 12.1. The Russian-Jewish and the Israeli Arabs reported a higher share of achieved transitions as compared to romantic involvements. These comparisons have to be interpreted with caution, however, as the transition to romantic involvement refers to fundamentally different experiences among Arabs, as we will describe later in this chapter. In addition, the two minority groups reported somewhat lower instances than the native Israelis with regards to the transition of living together as a couple.

With limited space to present comparisons across ethnic groups on all variables, we confined ourselves to comparing resources available to these groups (three types of capital). Basically, the Israeli-Arab group was highest in social capital, that is, they knew more people and/or people with higher occupational prestige. Differences in economic capital were much less pronounced, but Israeli Arabs reported somewhat lower levels in this regard than the other groups. Concerning cultural capital, the Russian-Jewish immigrant group were distinct with the highest levels of education, whereas, the Arabs reported lower cultural capital and the native Israelis were between these groups.

With regard to our outcome measures, the Five Cs, major differences were found between the three ethnic groups as shown in Table 12.2. Concerning the adolescent samples, dating competence was highest among Russian Jewish adolescents and lowest among Arab adolescents. Self-efficacy was lower among Arab adolescents as compared to Russian Jewish and native Israeli adolescents. Arab adolescents also scored lowest in self-esteem and differed significantly from the native Israelis. Russian adolescents were in between these two groups concerning their level of self-esteem and did not differ from either of the other groups. Traditional partnership preferences (e.g., attributing importance to having a same-ethnic partner) was lowest among Russian-Jewish and highest among Arab adolescents with all groups differing significantly from one another. Economic partnership preferences were significantly higher among Arab adolescents. They were also lowest in delinquency and highest in civic

Table 12.2   Means (standard deviation) of psychosocial outcomes of ethnic groups and respondents for transition to romantic involvement and living together as couple

	Native Israelis	Russian Jewish Immigrants	Arabs	F values (df)
Romantic relations				
Dating competence	3.2 b	3.6 [a]	2.8 [c]	10.52
	(1.5)	(1.1)	(1.0)	(2,280)
Self-efficacy	4.6 [a]	4.7 [a]	4.1 [b]	9.54
	(0.9)	(0.9)	(0.8)	(2,287)
Self-esteem	5.1 [a]	4.9 [a, b]	4.7 [b]	5.25
	(0.8)	(0.8)	(0.9)	(2,287)
Traditional partner preferences	3.8 [b]	3.2 [c]	4.8 [a]	41.08
	(1.3)	(1.2)	(1.2)	(2,286)
Economic partner preferences	3.6 [b]	3.8 [b]	4.3 [a]	7.05
	(1.1)	(1.2)	(1.2)	(2,286)
Delinquent beliefs	1.6 [a]	1.5 [a]	1.1 [b]	4.51
	(1.4)	(1.4)	(1.2)	(2,287)
Civic engagement	3.0 [b]	3.1 [b]	4.4 [a]	6.56
	(2.6)	(2.5)	(3.0)	(2,287)
Living together as couple				
Self-efficacy	4.7 [a]	4.7 [a]	4.3 [b]	5.14
	(1.0)	(0.9)	(0.9)	(2,328)
Traditional partner preferences	3.7 [b]	3.5 [b]	4.9 [a]	50.64
	(1.2)	(1.1)	(0.9)	(2,329)
Economic partner preferences	3.9 [b]	4.1 [b]	4.4 [a]	6.75
	(1.1)	(1.0)	(1.0)	(2,328)
Delinquent beliefs	1.4	1.2	1.1	1.12
	(1.4)	(1.4)	(1.2)	(2,329)
Civic engagement	2.4 b	2.1 [b]	3.6 [a]	8.40
	(2.4)	(2.5)	(3.2)	(2,329)

Notes: Means with different superscripts within a row are significantly different at $p < .05$ with post hoc LSD-test (least significant difference) as part of an ANOVA. All results are controlled for age and gender.

engagement, with the native Israelis and Russian Jews basically representing the opposite. Finally, several significant differences in the levels of our outcome measures among the young adults were identified as well. As for the transition to romantic involvement, the Arab group was distinct. They were lower in self-efficacy, higher in valuing traditional and economic partnership preferences, and higher in civic engagement. Russian and native Israelis basically represented the opposite and did not differ from one another on these variables. No differences between young adults of the three ethnic groups were found in delinquent beliefs.

In summary, the most impressive differences between the three ethnic groups in Israel concerned the group of Israeli Arabs as compared to the two Jewish groups. They are better equipped with social capital and can rely on a strong network of weak ties that presumably is organized around one's own ethnicity (unfortunately we have no data on the ethnic composition). The fact that civic engagement was highest among Arabs probably reflects the higher level of collective action in less advantageous communities (Foster-Fishman, Cantillon, Pierce, and Van Egeren, 2007). Our data also highlights the more traditional nature of intimate relationships in the Arab group with more traditional and economic partner preferences and lower dating competences. All this does not rule out mutual affection, but romance and partnerships seem to be more guided by expectations held in the family.

The main aim of the study was to analyse whether the transitions studied are related to psychosocial outcomes, and if so, whether the effects also differ between ethnic groups. For that purpose, we conducted several regression analyses, separate for each outcome and transition, including demographics and ethnic group dummy-variables, the three types of capital, the transition status (before, after), regulation strategies of engagement and disengagement, and the interactions between ethnicity x transition and ethnicity x regulation strategies. The results are shown in Tables 12.3a (Transition to Romantic Involvement) and 12.3b (Transition to Living Together as a Couple).

Focusing on the role of the transition to romantic involvement in adolescence, we found, not surprisingly, higher dating competence among those who had already begun a romantic relationship. Moreover, having had made this transition corresponded to a lower valuing of traditional and economic partnership preferences. Furthermore, compared to those adolescents who had not yet had a girlfriend or boyfriend, delinquent beliefs were less pronounced, and civic engagement was higher. Thus, this transition seems to be related to a considerable number of outcomes in the young adolescent's life. Concerning the transition to living together in young adulthood, we again found an effect on traditional partnership preferences, but in the opposite direction as compared to the effect in adolescence. Those who had made the transition endorsed traditional preferences more, perhaps indicating a more realistic stance than the adolescents. No other main effects of the transition were found in the analyses.

In contrast to the results in the German samples, we found four interactions of ethnicity and transition in Israel. Three of them referred to particularities of the Israeli-Arab sample in adolescence and are depicted in Figure 12.1. First, among Israeli Arabs, dating competence was not higher among those who had accomplished the transition, whereas, this was true for the native Israeli and the Russian Jewish group. Consequently, whereas native Israelis and Russian Jewish adolescents had more competence in knowing how a potential partner feels or how to get a second date with a desired person after they have had a

Table 12.3a Regression results for the transition to romantic involvement (standardized coefficients)

	Dating competence	Self-esteem	Self-efficacy	Traditional partner preferences	Economic partner preferences	Delinquent beliefs	Civic engagement
Age of the child	.044	.068	.071	.072	.151 *	.051	.093
Sex (1 = male. 2=female)	-.110 *	-.044	-.059	.060	.046	-.068	.131 *
Arab (Dummy = 1)	-.097	-.027	-.173 +	.363 **	.276 **	-.083	.073
Russ_Jew (Dummy = 1)	.082	-.331 **	-.164	-.228 *	.069	.063	-.101
Social capital	.114 *	.042	.062	.020	.063	.029	-.043
Economic capital	-.072	.001	.132 *	-.024	-.035	.032	-.015
Cultural capital	.102	.263 **	.163 *	-.109	-.118	-.119	.062
Transition (0=no vs. 1=yes)	.253 **	.019	.097	-.144 **	-.135 *	-.106 +	.102 +
Engagement	.243 **	.098	.122 *	.073	.097	.069	-.001
Disengagement	.070	.077	.002	-.033	-.024	-.003	.034
Arab x transition	-.235 **	-.207 **	-.087	.017	-.027	.075	.211 **
Russian Jew x transition	-.029	.023	.056	.057	.087	.067	.089
Arab x active	-.070	.039	.023	.069	.153 +	.114	-.129
Russian Jew x active	-.102	-.074	-.078	-.100	.015	.042	-.118
Arab x passive	-.095	-.100	-.109	-.033	.000	-.274 **	.172 *
Russian Jew x passive	.061	.149 *	.074	.075	.084	-.001	.031
R2	.33	.20	.19	.33	.20	.14	.18

Note: $^+$ p < .10; * p < .05; ** p < .01; *** p < .001

Table 12.3b Regression results for the transition to living together as a couple (standardized coefficients)

	Self-efficacy	Traditional partner preferences	Economic partner preferences	Delinquent Beliefs	Civic engagement
Age of the child	-.079	-.099 +	.030	.047	.086
Sex (1 = male. 2=female)	-.143 *	.056	.131 *	-.031	-.057
Arab (Dummy = 1)	-.171 **	.432 **	.211 **	-.126 +	.151 *
Russ_Jew (Dummy = 1)	.036	-.048	.057	-.056	-.099
Social capital	.090	.058	.101 +	.109 +	.087
Economic capital	.093 +	.016	.071	.140 *	-.021
Cultural capital	.134 *	-.009	.075	-.164 **	.076
Transition (0=no vs. 1=yes)	.020	.130 *	-.090	-.073	-.066
Engagement	.216 **	.086 +	.209 **	.074	-.229 **
Disengagement	-.019	-.019	.010	.078	.022
Arab x transition	-.001	-.084	.030	-.095	-.078
Russian Jew x transition	.080	-.069	-.053	-.142 *	-.099
Arab x active	.022	.003	.077	-.063	-.112 +
Russian Jew x active	-.096	.021	.024	-.063	-.046
Arab x passive	-.043	-.130 *	-.147 *	-.012	-.035
Russian Jew x passive	.060	-.102 +	-.114 *	-.007	.002
R²	.14	.29	.15	.09	.15

Note: + p < .10; * p < .05; ** p < .01; *** p < .001

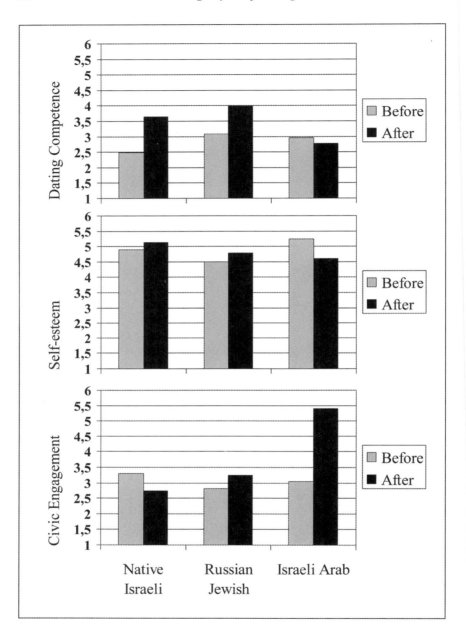

Figure 12.1   **Transition effects on dating competence, self-esteem, and
civic engagement in adolescence. Interactions are significant
on the p < .05 level and net all other variables entered into the
regression**

romantic partner, this competence was about equal among Arabs, independent of the fact whether or not they ever had a romantic relationship. However, self-esteem was lower and civic engagement was higher among Arab adolescents after the transition when compared with Arabs before the transition. These effects were not observed in the two Jewish groups. Overall, these results speak in favour of substantial differences between the three ethnic adolescent groups with regard to the effect of the transition to first romantic involvement on psychosocial outcomes. In early adulthood, only one significant interaction was found which revealed that only among Russian Jews' delinquent beliefs, for example tolerating items stolen from shops, were less often endorsed among those who reported to having moved in together as a couple.

Conclusion and Outlook

In our discussion, we will focus on the two main research questions of this chapter, namely, whether transitions were associated with psychosocial outcomes, and whether this association was moderated by ethnicity in the Israeli portion of our study. Altogether, we were able to identify four main transition effects across the 12 outcome variables studied. Especially, the transition to having a first romantic partner played an important role in adolescents' outcomes, being related to higher levels of dating competence (e.g., understanding a potential romantic partners feelings), lower levels of traditional partner preferences (e.g., wanting a same-ethnic partner), and lower levels of economic partner preferences (e.g., wanting a partner with high social status). It seems that adolescents' view about potential romantic partners and the skills for a dyadic relationship are very different afterwards as compared to prior the transition to a romantic relationship. For the transition of living together as a couple, we found one transition effect indicating more traditional partner preferences after moving in together. The different direction of this effect, as compared to the results in adolescence, may be explained by the nature of this transition. Living together most often involves more contact between family members of both partners and a similar ethnic background obviously helps in harmonizing family relations. Thus, our research shows that transitions seem to have the potential to enhance the psychosocial development of individuals in the Israeli context.

It is interesting to compare the effects found in the Israeli data set with those identified in Germany (previous chapter). Such a comparison reveals that the transition to romantic involvement seems to enhance similar psychosocial functions in Israel and Germany, because three main transition effects were found to be similar in direction and strength in the German and the Israeli sample. These similarities are the effects on dating competence and on partnership preferences. However, the transition to living together as a couple was related to different outcomes in Germany as compared to Israel. One can speculate whether the substantially higher living costs in Israel and the much more tense situation on the

Israeli housing market affects how the transition to living together as a couple has to be handled by young adults in Israel as compared to Germany.

Our second main question was whether these effects of transitions are moderated by the ethnic groups studied. Especially in adolescence, the Arabs were distinct in the comparisons of groups before and after the transitions. Whereas native Israelis and Russian Jewish adolescents seemed to profit from the transition in terms of dating competence, among Arabs, there were no differences between those before and after the transition in this regard. Furthermore, whereas it did not matter whether a native Israeli or Russian Jewish adolescent had accomplished the transition in terms of self-esteem or civic engagement, Arab adolescents, after the transition, reported lower levels of self-esteem and higher levels in civic engagement as compared to those before the transition.

In order to better understand this unexpected result, we examined some additional data. The major difference with the other ethnic groups was that, although about 60 percent of the Arab adolescents reported having had a girlfriend or boyfriend before the time of the survey, they were hardly engaged in any kind of sexual activity. Just four Arab adolescents reported experiences of kissing and none reported to have had intercourse. On the contrary, among Russian Jewish adolescents and native Israelis, 15 percent and 20 percent, respectively, reported to have had intercourse. About 80 percent of the Arab adolescents did not even hold hands with their partner. Thus, although adolescents of all groups reported to having made the transition to romantic involvement, the experiences related to this transition seemed to differ substantially, suggesting more traditional attitudes in sexuality among Arabs (Hetsroni, 2000; Lavee and Katz, 2003). In this light, it is plausible that experiencing a romantic affair is somewhat problematic for Arab adolescents, because romantic affairs are less accepted by their environment (Lavee and Katz, 2003). This would explain the lower scores in self-esteem among those classified as after the transition.

With regard to civic engagement, the effect observed among Arab adolescents may also be explained with a view on cultural differences. As dating is prohibited in many Arab contexts, adolescents in love have to meet outside their communities if they want to see each other (Lavee and Katz, 2003). Civic engagement may be one socially and culturally acceptable way to meet with a romantic partner in a setting outside school or home. Higher levels of civic engagement among Arab adolescents after the transition would be the result. An alternative explanation stressing the opposite direction of influences seems also possible. High levels of civic engagement could actually lead to more contact with same-aged peers and may create opportunities to fall in love. Romantic relations may thus be particularly likely among those adolescents highly engaged in civic affairs. It is questionable, however, why this alternative explanation for the link between romantic involvement and civic engagement should only apply to Arabs but not to native Israelis or Russian Jewish adolescents.

The only interaction between transition and ethnicity in the sample of young adults referred to delinquent beliefs. Russian Jews after the transition were lower in delinquent beliefs than the Russian Jewish young adults before transitioning, whereas in the other groups, no differences were found. One possible explanation based on delinquency research may provide some insight into this result. Russian Jews are the only group experiencing strain from the migration experience, known to result in higher levels of delinquency (Agnew and White, 1992). A steady relationship may counterbalance this acculturation effect (Sampson, Laub, and Wimer, 2006). However, we need to be cautious with this explanation, as the Russian Jewish young adults had been in Israel for quite some time when the study was conducted and it is questionable whether indeed acculturation effects are observed.

In addition to the insights related to the main questions on the role of transitions, many more results were found in this study. Especially pronounced in this regard were the higher levels of traditional and economic partner preferences among Arab participants in both age groups. This result highlights the ethnic boundaries in the Israeli society and the differences in traditional orientations, for instance in marriage arrangements (Lavee and Katz, 2003), and not a better or worse adaptation in a specific group. Furthermore, most of the differences seem to be based more in cultural than in social variations, as the various family resources did not eliminate ethnic differences in the psychosocial outcomes studied.

The study, as presented, also has several limitations. As in the German chapter, the results are cross-sectional and cannot be interpreted as causal effects. Another limitation refers to whether our results can be generalized beyond the particular groups studied in Israel. Especially among Arabs, the diversity in Israel is much higher than could be taken into consideration here. Our results refer mainly to Muslim Arabs, which are different to Druze or Christian Arabs (Horenczyk and Ben-Shalom, 2006), but even Muslim Arabs vary in the level of modernity, for example due to living in rural or urban environments (Lavee and Katz, 2003). Thus, the specific findings of our Arab sample may not necessarily apply to all Arab communities in Israel. A third limitation regards our assessments. In a survey-type study as this one covering a large number of constructs and variables, we needed to accept tolerable limits of the interview lengths. Therefore, the instruments had to be short and some worthwhile aspects, such as the actual transition experiences or challenges, were not assessed explicitly.

Despite these limitations, our study revealed clear and meaningful associations between the transition studied and various psychosocial outcomes, especially in adolescence. We could further demonstrate that transitions in adolescence are differentially related to outcomes depending on ethnic group membership, which is an interesting starting point for further research. Furthermore, effects of ethnic group membership on psychosocial outcomes were hardly explained by the various variables entered into our analyses. This seems to reflect a divide between the ethnic groups that goes beyond differences in the various family resources studied. Rather, the divide may lie in differences of cultural orientation (e.g., Feldman et al., 2001; Pines and Zaidman, 2003), in differences regarding the equality of opportunities in the Israeli society (Saad, 1991) or the ethnic context (Lavee and

Katz, 2003). All of our results are a rich source for further research on cultural differences in the development of individuals across various ethnic groups, for longitudinal analyses on the differential effects of transitions, and as a result, for understanding the interplay between individuals, ethnicity, and context.

References

Agnew, R., and White, H. R. (1992). An empirical test of general strain theory. *Criminology, 30*, 475-500.

Al-Haj, M. (2004). *Immigration and ethnic formation in a deeply divided society. The case of the 1990s immigrants from the former Soviet Union in Israel.* Leiden: Brill.

Baloush-Kleinman, V., and Sharlin, S. A. (2004). Social, economic, and attitudinal characteristics of cohabitation in Israel. *Journal of Family and Economic Issues, 25*, 255-269.

Ben-Ari, A., and Lavee, Y. (2004). Cultural orientation, ethnic affiliation, and negative daily occurrences: A multidimensional cross-cultural Analysis. *American Journal of Orthopsychiatry, 74*, 102-111.

Ben-Sira, Z. (1997). *Immigration, stress, and readjustment.* Westport, CT: Greenwood.

Bollen, K. A. (1989). *Structural equations with latent variables.* Oxford: John Wiley and Sons.

Bourdieu, P. (1986). The forms of capital. In J. Richardson (Ed.), *Handbook of theory and research for the sociology of education* (pp. 241-258). New York: Greenwood.

Bronfenbrenner, U. (2005). A future perspective (1979). In U. Bronfenbrenner (Ed.), *Making human beings human: Bioecological perspectives on human development* (pp. 50-59). Thousand Oaks, CA: Sage Publications Ltd.

Brook, J. S., Balka, E. B., Abernathy, T., and Hamburg, B. A. (1994). Sequence of sexual behavior and its relationship to other problem behaviors in African American and Puerto Rican adolescents. *Journal of Genetic Psychology, 155*, 107-114.

Central Bureau of Statistics. (2009). *Statistical abstract of Israel No. 60.* Jerusalem: Central Bureau of Statistics Retrieved from http://www.cbs.gov.il.

Coates, D. L. (1999). The cultured and culturing aspects of romantic experience in adolescence. In W. Furman, B. B. Brown and C. Feiring (Eds.), *The development of romantic relationships in adolescence* (pp. 330-363). New York, NY US: Cambridge University Press.

Elbedour, S., Shulman, S., and Kedem, P. (1997). Adolescent intimacy: A cross-cultural study. *Journal of Cross-Cultural Psychology, 28*(1), 5-22.

Feldman, R., Masalha, S., and Nadam, R. (2001). Cultural perspective on work and family: Dual-earner Israeli Jewish and Arab families at the transition to parenthood. *Journal of Family Psychology, 15*, 492-509.

Finckenauer, O. J. (1995). *Russian youth: Law, deviance, and the pursuit of freedom.* New Brunswick, NJ: Transaction Press.

Foster-Fishman, P., Cantillon, D., Pierce, S., and Van Egeren, L. (2007). Building an active citizenry: the role of neighborhood problems, readiness, and capacity for change. *American Journal of Community Psychology, 39,* 91-106.

Ganzeboom, H. B. G., De Graaf, P. M., and Treiman, D. J. (1992). A standard international socio-conomic index of occupational status. *Social Science Research, 21* 1-56.

George, L. K. (1993). Sociological perspectives on life transitions. *Annual Review of Sociology, 19,* 353-373.

Heckhausen, J., and Schulz, R. (1993). Optimisation by selection and compensation: Balancing primary and secondary control in life-span development. *International Journal of Behavior Development, 16,* 287-303.

Hetsroni, A. (2000). Choosing a mate in television dating games: The influence of setting, culture, and gender. *Sex Roles, 42,* 83-106.

Horenczyk, G., and Ben-Shalom, U. (2006). Acculturation in Israel. In D. L. Sam and J. W. Berry (Eds.), *The Cambridge handbook of acculturation psychology* (pp. 294-310). New York, NY: Cambridge University Press.

Hurrelmann, K., and Albert, M. (2006). *Jugend 2006. 15. Shell Jugendstudie: Eine pragmatische Generation unter Druck* [Youth 2006. 15th Shell Youth Study: A pragmatic generation under pressure]. Frankfurt: Fischer.

Jerusalem, M., and Schwarzer, R. (1992). Self-efficacy as a resource factor in stress appraisal processes. In R. Schwarzer (Ed.), *Self-efficacy: Thought control of action* (pp. 195-213). Washington, DC: Hemisphere.

Laungani, P. (1995). Stress in eastern and western cultures. *Stress and Emotion: Anxiety, Anger, and Curiosity, 15,* 265-280.

Lavee, Y., and Katz, R. (2003). The family in Israel: Between tradition and modernity. *Marriage and Family Review, 35,* 193-217.

Lerner, R. M., Lerner, J. V., Almerigi, J. B., Theokas, C., Phelps, E., Gestsdottir, S., van Eye, A. (2005). Positive youth development, participation in community youth development programs, and community contributions of fifth-grade adolescents: Findings from the first wave of the 4-H study of positive youth development. *Journal of Early Adolescence, 25,* 17-71.

Levenson, R. W., and Gottman, J. M. (1978). Toward the assessment of social competence. *Journal of Consulting and Clinical Psychology, 46,* 453-462.

Menaham, G. (2000). Jews, Arabs, Russians and foreigners in an Israeli city: Ethnic divisions and the restructuring economy of Tel Aviv, 1983-96. *International Journal of Urban and Regional Research, 24,* 634-652.

Mesch, G. S. (2002). Residential concentration and participation in local politics: The case of immigrants of the FSU in Israel. *Journal of International Migration and Integration, 3,* 157-177.

Okun, B. S., and Friedlander, D. (2005). Educational stratification among Arabs and Jews in Israel: Historical disadvantage, discrimination, and opportunity. *Population Studies, 59,* 163-180.

Pines, A. M., and Zaidman, N. (2003). Gender, culture, and social support: A male-female, Israeli Jewish-Arab comparison. *Sex Roles, 49*, 571-586.

Saad, I. A. (1991). Towards an understanding of minority education in Israel: The case of the Bedouin Arabs of the Negev. *Comparative Education, 27*, 235-242.

Sampson, R. J., Laub, J. H., and Wimer, C. (2006). Does marriage reduce crime? A counterfactual approach to within-individual causal effects. *Criminology: An Interdisciplinary Journal, 44*, 465-508.

Savaya, R., and Cohen, O. (2003). Divorce among Moslem Arabs living in Israel: Comparison for reasons before and after the actualization of the marriage. *Journal of Family Issues, 24*, 338-351.

Seginer, R., Karayanni, M., and Mar'i, M. M. (1990). Adolescents' attitudes toward women's roles: A comparison between Israeli Jews and Arabs. *Psychology of Women Quarterly, 14*, 119-133.

Shavit, Y. (1990). Segregation, tracking, and the educational attainment of minorities: Arabs and oriental Jews in Israel. *American Sociological Review, 55*, 115-126.

Smith, E. A., and Udry, J. R. (1985). Coital and noncoital sexual behaviors of White and Black adolescents. *American Journal of Public Health, 75*, 1200-1203.

Titzmann, P. F., and Silbereisen, R. K. (2012). Acculturation or development? The timing of autonomy among ethnic German immigrant adolescents and their native German age-mates. *Child Development, 83*(5), 1640-1654. doi: 10.1111/j.1467-8624.2012.01799.x.

Titzmann, P. F., Silbereisen, R. K., Mesch, G., and Schmitt-Rodermund, E. (2011). Migration-specific hassles among adolescent immigrants from the former Soviet Union in Germany and Israel. *Journal of Cross-Cultural Psychology, 42*(5), 777-794.

van der Gaag, M., Snijders, T. A. B., and Flap, H. (2008). Position generator measures and their relationship to other social capital measures. In N. Lin and B. H. Erickson (Eds.), *Social capital. An international research program* (pp. 27-48). New York: Oxford University Press.

Walsemann, K. M., Gee, G. C., and Geronimus, A. T. (2009). Ethnic differences in trajectories of depressive symptoms: Disadvantage in family background, high school experiences, and adult characteristics. *Journal of Health and Social Behavior, 50*, 82-98.

Chapter 13

First Romantic Relationships of Immigrant Adolescents in Israel and Germany: Does Acculturation Modify Ethnic Differences?[1]

Bernhard Nauck and Anja Steinbach

Introduction

The establishment of first romantic relationships is a central and almost universal developmental task of adolescence, in which close asymmetric intergenerational relationships are complemented by close symmetric relationships (usually) to the other sex. In general, the more universal and the more important a developmental task for a respective society is, the more likely that this developmental task will be normatively regulated and subject to social control. Moreover, if a developmental task remains stable in its importance and universality over time, it is also highly likely that its normative regulation will be deeply rooted in culture and backed by religious beliefs.

Romantic relationships have always been closely related to reproductive behaviour, both on the societal and individual level. On the societal level, it anchors the continuity of a socio-cultural group based on fertility and of the transmission of culture in general as well as religious beliefs specifically. On the individual level, it anchors the transmission of social status and the social integration of family and kinship systems. Because the relationship between romantic relationships and social reproduction is so close, it is patently obvious that institutional regulations on the societal level as well as investments in the social control of this

1   This chapter reports results from the project "Regulation of Developmental Transitions in Second Generation Immigrants in Germany and Israel" (Principal Investigators: Yoav Lavee, Bernhard Nauck, Avi Sagi-Schwartz, Rainer K. Silbereisen, Anja Steinbach), funded by the German Federal Ministry of Education and Research (BMBF). We thank our collaborators from the Universities of Chemnitz, Jena, and Haifa: Susanne Clauß, Falk Gruner, Mohini Lokhande, David Mehlhausen-Hassoen, Andrea Michel, Katharina Stößel and Peter Titzmann. The chapter builds upon previous analyses on the relationship between first romantic relationships and religion (Nauck and Steinbach, 2012). Necessarily, both works share some theoretical considerations.

developmental task on the part of parents are a fundamental part of the socialisation of offspring (Knafo et al., 2009). These normative regulations dictate how the younger cohorts' relationships are to be located within the life course, what forms of institutionalisation they require and how much sexual intensity is considered to be appropriate. Thus, first romantic relationships are an issue even in cases where these normative regulations are comparably restrictive and such relationships are not tolerated by the social environment (Nauck and Steinbach, 2012).

In principle, three different mechanisms influence engagement in first romantic relationships of migrant adolescents: changes in the opportunity structure, changes in social control and acculturation.

Firstly, migration may affect the composition of available partners. Migration flows typically start with an imbalance in the sex-ratio, i.e. the predominantly young, male pioneer migrants are confronted with a shortage of women in the partnership market of the same ethnic group in the receiving society. This situation produces a "marriage squeeze", which in turn may result in a delay of close relationships, an increased proportion of relationships with female members of the receiving society or an orientation towards the marriage market in their parents' homelands (Kane and Stephen, 1988; Kalmijn, 1993; Lievens, 1999; Klein, 2001; Gonzalez-Ferrer, 2006; Baykara-Krumme and Fuß, 2009; Kalter and Schroedter, 2010; Windzio, 2011).

Secondly, migration puts migrants in an ethnic minority situation, which may affect value orientations regarding the general value of close relationships, partnership choices and the timing of romantic engagements. The minority situation may result in increased intergenerational solidarity and increased efforts of the parental first migrant generation in intergenerational transmission of values and in social control and surveillance of their offspring in order to maintain the minority culture over generations. Accordingly, parents in migrant minorities have to organise more intergenerational transmission, will invest more time and energy in social control of their offspring and are more strict in the intergenerational maintenance of belief systems than parents in a similar situation in the country of origin or majority members in the receiving society. The latter can rely more on the effectiveness of social control in the broader environment, such as school or neighbourhood, than can members of minorities (Schönpflug, 2009; Nauck, 2001). Studies comparing intergenerational relationships in Turkish migrant families with those of natives in Germany as the receiving society and of natives in Turkey show that parents in the migrant families are more likely to adopt an authoritarian-controlling parenting style than German or native Turkish families. Moreover, co-orientation and similarities of perceptions and attitudes between generations are higher in migrant families than in families of those who remained in their country of origin (Nauck, 1995; 1997). In a study with a similar design that compared levels of religiosity of adolescents from Turkey as the society of origin, Turkish second-generation migrants and adolescents from Belgium as the receiving society revealed that Belgian adolescents showed lower and declining religiosity with age, whereas Turkish and Turkish Belgian adolescents were more religious regardless of age. However, religiosity was even more accentuated in Turkish Belgian adolescents as compared with Turkish adolescents in Turkey (Güngör, Bornstein and Phalet, 2012). Increased social control in minority situations may thus prevent "untimely" early romantic engagements and "wrong" partner choices, which under less controlled circumstances might have been more likely. This argument is already well-founded in classical assimilation theory, which proposes that changes in partnership and marital choices occur as a last stage, when other forms of assimilation have already reached a substantial level (Gordon, 1964).

Finally, the migrant adolescent is confronted by the values, beliefs and behaviours of the receiving society, which may induce acculturation processes in order to achieve status and social recognition (Nauck, 2008). Members of the receiving society, "successfully" performing the developmental task of establishing a close relationship to the other sex, may serve as role models. These role models may differ considerably from what may have been institutionalised in the respective societies of origin at the time the parents left these countries, as they were not influenced by social change that may have occurred there since. Thus, increased social contacts of the migrant adolescents to the receiving society (in kindergarten, at school, in vocational training) may result in higher levels of secularisation and acculturation as compared to the migrant parents.

One of the major social changes affecting not only affluent welfare societies is the weakened connection between the establishment of first romantic relationships and reproductive behaviour. Knowledge about effective contraceptive methods and about life-course scripts that separate romantic relationships from parenthood has now spread throughout the world (Thornton, 2005). Biographical trajectories have become less rigid because of changes in the standard life course such as earlier puberty, extended phases of education and intergenerational dependence and, consequently, the separation of partnership, parenthood, housing, education and occupation. Accordingly, former normative regulations primarily based on the *consequences* of social reproduction have lost much of their legitimacy. Moreover, they have lost much of their persuasive force and attraction for the adolescents now that establishing intimate relationships has become a right for everyone and the gap between puberty and reproduction has widened.

Leaving changes in the opportunity structure for migrant adolescents aside – a mechanism which will not be considered further in this analysis – two counteracting forces are at work. On the one hand, if increased social contacts of second-generation immigrants with members of the receiving society result in acculturation, then changes in first romantic relationships should occur over time, varying with length of stay and assimilation. On the other hand, if minority-based intergenerational transmission of values and increased social control of minority adolescents prevail, then first romantic relationships should be stable regardless of assimilation in other spheres.

Empirical research on the entry of migrant adolescents into early romantic relationships is scarce. Moreover, its evidence-based theoretical explanations are at a very early stage. Which of the two mechanisms noted above predominates, how they interact, and what variations distinguish different ethnic groups and social settings are questions that invite the inquiry described below. In contrary to the two previous chapters which focused on the impact of the biographical transition to romantic involvement to psychosocial outcomes and compared natives and immigrants in Germany (see Silbereisen et al., this volume) and Israel (see Titzmann et al., this volume) separately, the transition to first romantic relationships is investigated here depending on the degree of acculturation of different migrant (or ethnic minority) groups in two receiving countries simultaneously.

Method

The following analysis will investigate the impact of social change on the life-course transition to first romantic relationships in the case of three religious groups in two different social contexts with varying speed of experienced social change. The two contexts are Israel and Germany, the three religious groups are Christians, Jews and Moslems. The varying speed of social change is regulated by the migration experience. The following analysis explores empirically how these mechanisms are related to possible differences between the immigrant groups with regard to first romantic relationships. After a description of the study design and the data set, the variables used in this analysis are explained.

- A set of three constructs – which may be treated as representing causal order – captured the involvement of migrant adolescents in early romantic relationships, namely (a) *expectations* related to a partner and a partnership, which may differ between migrant groups and change with acculturation, (b) the extent of *involvement* in romantic relationships, which may be subject to social control, and (c) subjective *satisfaction* with the current state of romantic relationships.
- A set of two constructs captured the acculturation process and the social control of immigrant adolescents: (a) the retention of the language and culture of origin and the acculturation to the language and culture of the receiving society, and (b) the retention and acculturation of the mother and the extent of parental control.
- The correlation of acculturation and forms of involvement in early romantic relationships were checked for the effects of age and gender and for the effects of social characteristics related to the educational and religious climate of the family, the respective migrant minority group and the receiving country.

Data for the analysis were gathered in a research project on "Regulation of Developmental Transitions in Second Generation Immigrants in Germany and

Israel" (see also Silbereisen et al. and Titzmann et al. in this volume). Among the transitions studied, the involvement of adolescents in first romantic relationships was seen as a significant non-normative transition in the course of life. Data were collected between the autumn of 2007 and the summer of 2008 and comprised dyads of mothers and their children between 15 and 17 years of age from Germany and Israel. Sampling was based on regionally clustered register data in Germany and equivalent techniques in Israel. Five culturally different migrant groups were included, which were all comprised in the analyses: In Germany, German repatriates from Russia (n = 81), Turkish immigrants (n = 111) and Jews from Russia (n = 73); in Israel, Jews from Russia (n = 91) and Israeli Arabs (n = 110). The data were obtained by standardised, language-equivalent personal interviews using interviewers from the respective ethnic group. Respondents could choose to conduct the interview in the minority language (Turkish, Russian, Arabic) or in the majority language (German, Hebrew).

Measurement and Descriptive Results

Involvement in Romantic Relationships

In contrast to the operationalisation in Nauck and Steinbach (2012), latent class analysis was chosen for distinguishing the adolescents' partner preferences. The basic idea of this approach is that relationships can be characterised as a circumscribed set of types that are empirically manifested by combinations of observed variables (see for results regarding single items of natives and immigrants in Germany Silbereisen et al. and in Israel Titzmann et al., this volume). In this case, the theoretical motive was to establish a meaningful typology that reflects cultural differences of partner choices between groups. A technical motive was that most of the responses to the items about the characteristics a potential partner should have, which the respondents could rate between (1) "not important" and (6) "very important", were skewed. Therefore, all items were dichotomised. The solution finally comprised six indicators, discriminating best between four classes and showing reasonable statistical characteristics. This solution fitted the "elbow criterion" for L^2 and had the optimal value according to BIC. Table 13.1 shows the relationship between indicators and latent classes and the distribution of most likely class membership in the five migrant groups.

Analytically, the four classes distinguish between adolescents who are looking for social status and for maintenance of physical well-being through partnership (class 2), adolescents who are looking for a partner with social characteristics that most likely make them acceptable to their own social group (class 3) and thus increase social esteem within their own migrant minority, and adolescents who are looking for a partner who combines both requirements (status attainment and social esteem, class 4). Class 1 consists of adolescents who either show no partner preferences at all or whose preferences are related not to social but rather only to

Table 13.1   Latent class probabilities and average latent class distribution of important partner characteristics across migrant groups and gender

Important partner characteristics[*]	Status - Esteem -	Status + Esteem -	Status - Esteem +	Status + Esteem +
Educational background	.32	**.81**	.43	**.96**
Favourable social status	.06	**.57**	.21	**.95**
Good financial prospects	.03	**.52**	.24	**.97**
Approval of my parents	.12	.46	**.62**	**.92**
Similar religious background	.11	.38	**.81**	**.90**
Similar ethnic background	.06	.01	**.88**	**.94**
Total latent class distribution	37 %	26 %	20 %	17 %
German repatriates	43 %	42 %	9 %	6 %
German immigrant Jews	59 %	29 %	8 %	4 %
Turkish immigrants in Germany	27 %	27 %	23 %	23 %
Israeli repatriates	53 %	36 %	8 %	3 %
Israeli Arabs	21 %	9 %	38 %	32 %
Male adolescents	43 %	24 %	22 %	11 %
Female adolescents	33 %	31 %	16 %	20 %

Note: *Latent class probabilities greater than .5 are shown in bold.

individual characteristics such as age, physical appearance or psychological traits. Choices based on individual characteristics frequently occurred in combination with social characteristics and did not constitute a class of its own.

The lower part of Table 13.1 distinguishes significantly between two groups of migrant adolescents with regard to partner preferences (Eta = .46***). Christian and Jewish immigrants from Russia showed only low levels of preferences for social characteristics of potential partners and looked only for individual traits. Muslim adolescents with Turkish origin, and Israeli Arab minorities even more so, showed strong preferences for social characteristics, with the Turks being more status seeking and the Israeli Arabs looking more for esteem and conformity. Similar differences occurred for gender (Eta = .11**). Whereas female adolescents were more interested in status and securing physical well-being – in combination with social esteem from their own ethnic group – male adolescents either have no pronounced preferences or are more interested in individual characteristics and social similarity.

Migrant adolescents were asked whether they had ever had a romantic relationship and what kind of sexual activity was involved. Table 13.2 shows the respective proportions of the five migrant groups, controlled for the age and sex of the respondents, by means of multiple classification analysis (MCA). Additionally, it shows the results for an index of the sexual intensity of the romantic relationship (cumulative for the first six columns) in column 7.

As a general result, there was a similar decrease in the percentages for all five categories from the experience of a romantic relationship from holding hands to sexual intercourse. This result justified the construction of a cumulative index (column 7 in Table 13.2). However, level differences between these six groups were significant and to a large extent due to religious affiliation, creating a strong divide between the Christian and Jewish adolescents originating from Russia on the one hand, and the Muslim Turks in Germany and the Israeli Arabs on the other.

The third dimension of the romantic relationships of migrant adolescents is satisfaction with the current state of involvement (column 8 in Table 13.2). Although the level of sexual intensity in romantic relationships between German repatriate adolescents and the Israeli Arab adolescents differed most, their level of satisfaction with this situation did not. In fact, the involvement in romantic relationships of the Muslim youth showed a distinct pattern: 68 per cent of the Turkish adolescents in Germany and 63 per cent of the Israeli Arabs reported having or having had a romantic relationship, of which only a small fraction was ever accompanied by some intense form of bodily contact. This clearly suggests that "having a partner" had different meanings for the Turkish and Israeli Arab adolescents than for the three other immigrant groups. For them, partner choices had already been made with a view to future marriage (Table 13.1), and this led to a generally high level of partnership satisfaction despite low sexual involvement. Accordingly, the "partnership experience" as such (Beta = .08) and the "satisfaction with the partnership situation" (Beta = .23) showed the smallest differences between the groups.

Acculturation

Following Berry's typology (1997) of "acculturation strategies" (Nauck, 2008), the dimensions selected were operationalised two-dimensionally, comprising both the culture of origin and the culture of the receiving society. With a combination of both dichotomised dimensions, four different types result: "integration", "assimilation", "segregation" and "marginalisation". In order to replicate this typology for the analysis of acculturation effects on early romantic relationships of migrant adolescents, again methods of latent class analysis were used in operationalisation, both for theoretical and additional technical reasons, as the distribution was skewed for the majority of indicators. Again, the accepted models (Table 13.3 and 13.4) best met statistical and theoretical criteria. The dimensions chosen were language competence and identification.

With regard to language competence, the adolescents were asked to assess their competence in understanding, speaking, reading and writing the language of (their parents') origin (LO) and the language of the respective receiving society

Table 13.2   Adjusted proportions of migrant adolescents with partnership experience (MCA)[1]

	Partnership experience (percent)	Holding hands (percent)	Kissing (percent)	French kissing (percent)	Petting (percent)	Intercourse (percent)	Sexual intensity (mean)	Partnership satisfaction (mean)
German repatriates	74	71	71	61	38	27	3.41	4.35
German Jews	63	59	55	49	36	23	2.85	3.87
Turks in Germany	68	61	57	38	16	8	2.47	4.40
Israeli repatriates	65	67	63	55	47	9	3.07	3.63
Israeli Arabs	63	16	8	7	7	3	1.03	4.40
Beta[1]	.08*	.42***	.47***	.40***	.35***	.27***	.38***	.23***

Note:[1] Results adjusted for age and gender

Table 13.3   Language acculturation of immigrant adolescents

	Integration	Assimilation	Segregation	Marginalisation
Reading LR	.99	.99	.02	.38
Writing LR	.94	.99	.02	.10
Reading LO	.98	.02	.99	.13
Writing LO	.84	.01	.99	.08
Total latent class distribution	34 %	31 %	17 %	19 %
German repatriates	15 %	64 %	0 %	21 %
German Jews	30 %	38 %	0 %	32 %
Turks in Germany	57 %	15 %	9 %	19 %
Israeli repatriates	22 %	48 %	6 %	24 %
Israeli Arabs	38 %	0 %	56 %	6 %

(LR). Reading and writing were chosen as the most discriminating factors with regard to acculturation.

Table 13.3 shows that the indicators discriminated well between the four types of language acculturation. High competence in both languages was the most frequent type; competence in the parent's language of origin was least frequent. However, some extreme differences between migrant groups exist (Eta = .34***). Whereas 56 per cent of the Israeli Arabs could read and write only in Arabic and 38 per cent could read and write in both languages, the reverse is true for the situation of German or Israeli repatriates, who were less competent in Russian, but highly competent in German or Hebrew. The majority of Turkish adolescents in Germany were fluent in both languages, probably because a higher proportion stayed in the receiving society from birth, but with different outcomes than for the Israeli Arabs who shared the same situation.

With regard to identification, the adolescents were asked how important it is for them to participate in activities and have friends from their migrant minority group and from the majority society. These items were chosen because an inclusion strategy of members of either social group has implications for the extent of the partnership market as well as for partner choices and for the desired partner attributes that may be important for such choices.

The first part of Table 13.4 shows that the indicators also discriminate well between the four types of identification acculturation. "Integration" was the most frequent type, followed by "segregation", whereas "assimilation and "marginalisation" were the least likely outcomes of the acculturation process of migrant adolescents. Again, differences between migrant groups were significant (Eta = .28***). German repatriates were most likely to have a balanced orientation towards their minority group and the majority society, whereas Israeli repatriates

Table 13.4   Identification acculturation of immigrant adolescents

	Integration	Assimilation	Segregation	Marginalisation
Activities minority	.93	.34	.69	.10
Friends minority	.99	.01	.97	.01
Activities majority	.99	.94	.01	.01
Friends majority	.85	.51	.37	.04
Total latent class distribution	33 %	19 %	28 %	20 %
German repatriates	46 %	20 %	17 %	17 %
German Jews	27 %	27 %	19 %	26 %
Turks in Germany	33 %	9 %	40 %	18 %
Israeli repatriates	22 %	37 %	22 %	19 %
Israeli Arabs	36 %	3 %	36 %	25 %

were most likely to orient themselves towards the majority society alone. Turks in Germany and Israeli Arabs showed the highest likelihood of segregation, and Jews in Germany the highest likelihood of marginalisation.

Parental Control

Parental influence on their adolescent children can be direct or indirect. A direct influence consists of surveillance and control of behaviour. Indirect influence comes from being an accepted role model available for imitation by the adolescent; this is thus intergenerationally transmitted.

Parental control   Perceived parental control by the adolescents was measured with a shortened 4-item scale ($\alpha = .68$) from Kerr and Stattin (2000), including items such as "Do you feel that your parents demand to know everything?" or "Do you feel that your parents interfere too much in your free time activities?", ranging from (1) "No, never" to (6) "Yes, always".

Educational level   Mother's educational level was used as a proxy for individual resources and options and for competence in information seeking, and thus for her effectiveness in influencing her adolescent children. It was classified according to the international ISCED scheme (UNESCO, 2006). The differences in levels between the groups are extreme. Whereas 52 per cent of the Turkish mothers and 21 per cent of the Israeli Arab mothers had no or only elementary schooling, the share for the other groups was less than 5 per cent. Seventy per cent of the German Jewish mothers, 50 per cent of the Jewish repatriate mothers to Israel, 35 per cent of the German repatriates, 5 per cent of the Israeli Arab and only 1 per cent of the Turkish mothers had a tertiary education.

Table 13.5   Parental control and acculturation (MCA)

	Control (mean)	Education (mean)	Religiosity (mean)	Religiosity transmission
German repatriates	3.0	3.9	3.3	3.3
German Jews	3.2	4.6	2.7	3.6
Turks in Germany	3.2	1.4	4.4	3.2
Israeli repatriates	2.6	4.6	1.8	3.3
Israeli Arabs	3.2	2.4	4.6	4.1
Beta[1]	.22**	.80***	.65***	.26***

Note: [1]Results adjusted for age and gender

Mother's religiosity   Religiosity of the mother was used as an indication of strictness and an unambiguous set of values represented by her as a role model. It was measured with a single-item scale of self-perceived religiosity, ranging from (1) "not at all religious" to (6) "very religious". The group differences ranged from 4.6 for Arab mothers, 4.3 for Turkish mothers, 2.7 for the Jewish mothers in Germany and 1.8 for the Israeli repatriate mothers. High similarity between the extent of religiosity of mothers and adolescents was taken as an indication of effective intergenerational *religiosity transmission*.

Mother's identification acculturation   Adherence to the culture of origin and acculturation of the mothers was measured with the same items as for the identification of the adolescents. Similarly, a latent class model of their identification assimilation was established and compared to the results for the adolescents. Identical class membership was taken as an indication of effective intergenerational *identification transmission*; 37.1 per cent of mother-adolescent dyads showed identical class membership.

"Integration" and "marginalisation" were the most frequent types of identification acculturation of immigrant mothers. "Assimilation" and "segregation" were the least likely outcomes. Again, differences between migrant groups were significant (Eta = .14***), but much lower than for the adolescents. German repatriates are most likely to have a balanced orientation towards their minority group and the majority society, whereas Israeli repatriate mothers are most likely to orient themselves towards the majority society alone. Turkish mothers in Germany and Israeli Arab mothers showed the highest likelihood of segregation. Minority mothers in Israel showed the highest likelihood of marginalisation. When compared to their adolescent children (not shown), migrant mothers in Germany showed a higher level of identification acculturation than their children, which replicates and extends previous findings on repatriates (Steinbach and Nauck, 2000). However, in all five groups, they also showed a significantly higher level of identification retention with only moderate differences between these groups. The greatest differences existed between migrant groups with regard to educational level (Eta = .80***) and religiosity (.65***), clearly separating the more religious and less educated Turkish and Arab mothers from those originating from Russia.

Does Acculturation Matter?

Whether the acculturation strategy is related to partner preferences, involvement in romantic relationships and relationship satisfaction was tested with multivariate analyses. In each analysis, a base model (1) was established, which related the adolescent's immigrant group membership and his or her acculturation strategy to the respective dimension of romantic relationships. However, the unbalanced design of the study (no Christian immigrants in Israel) and available sample sizes made some data aggregations necessary. Because descriptive analyses showed rather small differences between the three migrant groups from Russia on the one hand and the Turkish and Israeli adolescents on the other, migrants were collapsed into a reference group of Christian/Jewish migrants from Russia and a group of *Muslim* migrant minorities. Together with the receiving society (Germany vs. Israel) this makes a 2 x 2 control for the immigrant groups, against which the effects of acculturation are set. Moreover, gender differences were systematically considered, as involvement in romantic relationships is differently gendered in the respective religious-ethnic migrant minorities. A second model (2) tests the extent to which a variation in the involvement in romantic relationships according to the acculturation process of the adolescents is induced or modified by parental control or intergenerational transmission.

Acculturation and Partner Preferences

With regard to preferences for partner characteristics, no differences between the two countries were found when controlling for migrant group membership and gender (Table 13.6). However, as already shown in the descriptive analyses (Table 13.1), differences between the respective immigrant groups were strong. Muslim immigrant minority members showed a strong preference for similarity in social characteristics of the partner and acceptance by their own family, together with status criteria with their economic overtones.

Acculturation mattered, even if group membership and gender were held constant:

- Adolescents who either place importance on social activities with their own group (segregation) or with members of their own minority and members of the receiving society (integration) were significantly more likely to optimise status and social esteem through partnership. They were less likely to look

Table 13.6   Acculturation and partner preferences (multiple, stepwise multinomial regression; Exp (B))

Reference: Status - and Esteem -	Status + and Esteem -		Esteem + and Status -		Status + and Esteem +	
	(1)[1]	(2)[1]	(1)[1]	(2)[1]	(1)[1]	(2)[1]
Female	1.98**	1.88*	1.21	1.18	3.02***	3.03***
Israel	.80	.98	1.77	1.82	1.19	1.35
Muslim minority	1.76	.55	8.23***	5.73***	10.84***	5.96**
Identification acculturation (reference: marginalisation)						
Integration	1.63	1.98*	2.70*	2.79*	9.81***	11.71***
Assimilation	1.55	1.64	1.14	1.18	5.92*	6.24*
Segregation	1.11	1.04	3.13**	3.12**	9.68***	10.61***
Language acculturation (reference: marginalisation)						
Integration	.43*	.49*	.77	.82	2.01	2.13
Assimilation	.44**	.42**	.84	.85	1.75	1.79
Segregation	.18***	.21**	.63	.69	3.96*	3.94
Parental control		.91		.97		1.26
Mother's education		.65***		.88		.80
Identification transmission		.77		1.05		1.15
Religiosity transmission		.80*		.99		1.01
Nagelkerke's R²	.37	.41				

Note:[1] controlled for the age of the respondent

for "individual" characteristics alone. Additional analyses (not shown) revealed no additional interaction effect with group membership, which indicates that acculturation strategies had an independent effect, additive to Muslim migrant minority membership.

- Language acculturation had a significantly different effect than identification acculturation, as it increased the likelihood of a primary preference for optimal individual characteristics, while status-criteria became less important compared to adolescents marginalized due to language.

Interestingly, the acculturation effects of the integration and the segregation mode operated in the same direction with regard to partner preferences, and even the assimilation mode showed the same tendency on a lower level of intensity. This finding suggests that the main divide with regard to partner preference was between marginalised and all other adolescents.

As compared to acculturation, the effects of parental influence and control were rather small, explaining only four per cent additional variance (model 2). The extent of parental control had no effect. The strongest effect was from the mother's education level. This indicates a rather indirect effect of the educational climate of the family, reducing the search for status and esteem through partnership in favour of individual characteristics. Inter-generational transmission effects were weak. Interaction effects, i.e., whether the effect of religiosity varies according to the respective religion, were insignificant.

Acculturation and Sexual Involvement

Contrary to the findings on preferences for partner characteristics, the receiving society plays an important role for sexual intensity in early partnership experiences of adolescents, as its level is significantly lower in Israel compared to Germany, even when parental influence, parental supervision and religious affiliation are held constant (Table 13.7). As the proportion of Jewish immigrants from Russia in Israel is much higher than any migrant minority in Germany, and as the Israeli Arab population is also a very large and visible minority in Israel, this result cannot be explained by shortages on the partnership market. Instead, it must be a result of a comparably "prohibitive" general social climate, due to more extensive social control in the neighbourhoods, irrespective of the direct parental control, which had a rather marginal "prohibitive" effect on the sexual activities of offspring.

As already revealed in Table 13.2, Muslim minorities (Turkish adolescents in Germany and Israeli Arabs) showed a much less intense sexual involvement in their early romantic relationships on average than members of other migrant groups. However, the direct effect becomes insignificant if preferences for social characteristics of the partner are controlled for. Especially those adolescents who seek partners with high social status and high acceptability in their own social group (most common among Muslims, especially females) deferred sexual relations most probably until wedlock. The framing of partnerships in the respective ethnic context and not the individual religiosity of the adolescent ($b = -.05$) or the religious transmission between mother and adolescent ($b = -.02$), clearly triggered this kind of behaviour (model 4).

The effect of acculturation on sexual intensity in early romantic relationships of migrant adolescents was relatively small. With regard to language acculturation, adolescents who were fluent in both languages or who were fluent in the language of origin (of their parents) showed less sexual intensity in their early relationships than marginalised adolescents, when the respective receiving country and the religious affiliation were controlled for (model 1 and 2). However, this effect became insignificant if partner preferences (model 3) were controlled for.

Thus, the study revealed no indication that an acculturation process of immigrant adolescents resulted in a more sexually "liberal" understanding of early romantic relationships. Instead, differences between immigrant groups, based on differences in the framing of early relationships and related scripts on how they are to be placed in the course of life, remained stable.

Table 13.7   Acculturation and sexual intensity of intimate relationship (multiple, stepwise regression)

	(1)[1]	(2)[1]	(3)[1]
Female	-.07	-.07	-.06
Israel	-.22***	-.22***	-.22***
Muslim minority	-.16**	-.16*	-.13
Identification acculturation (reference: marginalisation)			
Integration	.04	.04	.06
Assimilation	.05	.06	.07
Segregation	.03	.04	.06
Language acculturation (reference: marginalisation)			
Integration	-.12*	-.13*	-.12
Assimilation	.00	-.00	-.00
Segregation	-.14*	-.13*	-.12
Partner preference (reference: status - & esteem -)			
Status + & esteem -			-.04
Esteem + & status -			-.07
Status + & esteem +			-.12*
Parental control		-.05	-.05
Mother's education		-.01	-.02
Identification transmission		.04	.04
Religiosity transmission		.02	.02
R²	.17	.17	.18

Note:[1]Controlled for the age of the respondent

Acculturation and Relationship Satisfaction

As compared to partner preferences and the sexual intensity of early romantic relationships, the effect of migrant group membership and of the acculturation of the adolescents on relationship satisfaction was much smaller (Table 13.8). If only these two sets of factors were considered (model 1 in Table 13.8), then the group of Muslim minorities, who had the lowest level of sexual intensity in their relationships, was the most satisfied with their relationships. Adolescents who equally valued relationships with minority and majority partners were also highly satisfied. Adolescents marginalised in terms of identification acculturation, in contrast, were the most dissatisfied. Effects of parental control or influence were small and insignificant, but systematically negative (model 2).

If partner preferences and sexual intensity are also considered (model 3), satisfaction with the state of the partnership appeared to have two different sources. Adolescents were especially satisfied with sexually intense relationships

Table 13.8 Acculturation and relationship satisfaction (multiple, stepwise regression)

	$(1)^1$	$(2)^1$	$(3)^1$
Female	-.02	-.02	-.02
Israel	-.08	-.08	-.02
Muslim minority	.22***	.20*	.20*
Identification acculturation (reference: marginalisation)			
Integration	.22***	.22***	.18**
Assimilation	.12*	.11*	.08
Segregation	.16**	.15**	.11
Language acculturation (reference: marginalisation)			
Integration	-.07	-.06	-.05
Assimilation	.08	.08	.06
Segregation	-.00	.01	.01
Partner preference (reference: status - and esteem -)			
Status + and esteem -			-.02
Esteem + and status -			.02
Status + and esteem +			.16**
Sexual intensity			.27***
Parental control		-.08	-.07
Mother's education		-.04	-.03
Identification transmission		-.03	-.04
Religiosity transmission		-.04	-.05
R^2	.07	.08	.16

Note: [1]Controlled for the age of the respondent

(b = .27***). They were also satisfied if they strove for a partnership that provides both social status and esteem, and these are associated with low levels of premarital sex (Table 13.7).

Summary and Conclusion

The study's findings may be summarised as follows:

Adolescents from the five migrant and minority groups varied significantly on two different dimensions of acculturation. Identification acculturation reflects the importance of social relationships for adolescents of minority and majority populations. Language acculturation reflects competence in establishing relationships with one or the other group. German repatriates predominantly sought social relationships with both majority and minority members, based on their predominant competence in the German language. Jewish migrant adolescents in Germany were almost equally distributed over "integration", "assimilation" and "marginalisation" types and showed no tendency towards "segregation". Turkish adolescents in Germany were fluent in both Turkish and German but show the highest tendency to concentrate on relationships within their own ethnic group. To a greater extent than the German repatriates, Jewish migrant adolescents in Israel sought mainly to assimilate, judging by their competence in Hebrew. As did Turks in Germany, Israeli Arabs showed a strong segregation tendency, but in their case accompanied by language segregation.

The respective type of acculturation was related to marked differences in expectations towards romantic relationships. There was a clear divide between Muslim adolescents, who were primarily status oriented and expected increased social respect due to partner choice. On the other hand, Christian and Jewish migrant adolescents primarily sought appealing individual characteristics. These utility expectations of romantic relationships shaped involvement (for the relation of the transition to romantic involvement to selected psychosocial outcomes see Silbereisen et al. as well as Titzmann et al., this volume). Social status and esteem expectations were related to delayed or less intense sexual involvement. Personal attraction was related to earlier and more intense sexual involvement. Thus, the main effect of acculturation seemed to lie in its framing of expectations regarding early romantic relationships. For Christian and Jewish migrants these involved mainly an exploration of personal attraction. For Muslims, these involved the institutionalised initiation of the marital covenant. These frames were largely culturally bounded and showed little internal variation.

Cultural framing meant that the additional influence of parents was small. Neither intergenerational transmission of acculturation nor of religiosity exhibited significant direct influence on adolescents' partnership expectations or sexual behaviour. The only influence was indirect, with more personalised partnership expectations being more prevalent in better-educated families, irrespective of minority membership. Moreover, clear differences between the two receiving countries underscored that the broader social context played an important but as yet poorly understood role in the shaping of intimate relationships, with Israel being much more "prohibitive" with regard to early intense sexual involvement.

There were only minor differences among different migrant groups with regard to current partnership satisfaction, i.e. the adolescents seemed to follow their own distinct strategies of partnership selection with similar confidence and satisfaction. If all factors related to migrant status and acculturation were held constant, the only remaining variation between adolescents was the sexual intensity of their relationships.

The following conclusions can be drawn about the mechanisms through which migration affects early romantic relationships:

Firstly, there was no indication that specific *shortages on the partnership market* caused the behavioural outcomes observed. Otherwise, the similar levels of partnership satisfaction and the high coherence between partnership expectations and satisfaction among all migrant groups would be difficult to explain.

Secondly, there was only partial evidence in support of the proposition that contact with receiving societies has an immediate *acculturative effect* on the behaviour of migrant adolescents with regard to early romantic relationships. Obviously, migrant and minority adolescents behave differently in Israel and Germany, but these differences may be less due to acculturative shifts than to stable differences between groups. As the mode of acculturation has practicably no additional effect on behaviour in romantic relationships, it is very unlikely that country differences are a result of different pathways of acculturation.

And in conclusion, there is evidence that *cultural maintenance* of habits and frames regarding early romantic relationships was strong among immigrant minorities. Cultural maintenance was not so much a result of direct social control by the parents. It was more the result of their providing acceptable role models and scripts in which early romantic relationships are embedded. Accordingly, the expectations towards partnerships remained firm and distinct between migrant minority groups, and they determined the pathways of involvement in early romantic relationships, even if assimilation was high on other dimensions. Thus, choices in intimate relationships are clearly one of the realms in which assimilation happens last.

Clearly, these differences between the two groups of immigrants are consistent with deeply rooted cultural differences in the general modes of partner choice. While the migrant minorities from Russia shared the pattern of exogamous partner choice, Turks and Israeli Arabs shared the pattern of endogamous partner choice, preferably within their own kinship system and frequently in the form of cross-cousin marriages (Nauck and Klaus, 2008; Lewin, 2012). Whereas exogamous partner choices imply a longer search and exploration phase in adolescence and early adulthood, endogamous partner allocation reduces "choices" drastically and the matching of future spouses may occur quite early in the course of life. This may explain why marriages of Turkish migrants to (kinship member) candidates from the society of origin are more common than in other migrant minorities (Baykara-Krumme and Fuß, 2009; Huschek, de Valk, and Liefbroer, 2012). It may also explain why, despite a slightly increasing age of marriage in the Israeli Arab population (Lewin, 2012), the percentage of those early adolescents who claim to have partnership experience (without any sexual contact) is almost as high as for their Jewish counterparts in Germany and Israel.

An important limitation of the study was that relationship data was not event-based, which precluded the differentiation of level differences and timing differences. An event-history data set would have allowed for the inclusion of time-dependent covariates like time of migration, school profile, job history and marriage. Finally, migrant minority membership was inevitably confounded with socioeconomic status, placing the Muslim population in both countries in a distinctly disadvantaged position. Although untestable in this study, it may well be that the differences found between Muslim and Russian adolescents are related to an intergenerationally transmitted strategy of partner selection under conditions of scarce resources (for the two Muslim groups) and thus may also be found among populations with a different cultural backgrounds living in similar conditions.

References

Baykara-Krumme, H., and Fuß, D. (2009). Heiratsmigration nach Deutschland: Determinanten der transnationalen Partnerwahl türkeistämmiger Migranten. *Zeitschrift für Bevölkerungswissenschaft, 34*, 135-163.

Berry, J. W. (1997). Immigration, Acculturation, and Adaptation. *Applied Psychology: An International Review, 46*, 5-34.

Gonzalez-Ferrer, A. (2006). Who do Immigrants Marry? Partner Choice among Immigrants in Germany. *European Sociological Review, 22*, 171-185.

Gordon, M. M. (1964). *Assimilation in American Life.* New York: Oxford University Press.

Güngör, D., Bornstein, M. H., and Phalet, K. (2012). Cultural Patterns and Acculturation of Religiosity: A Study of Turkish, Turkish Belgian, and Belgian Adolescents. *International Journal of Behavioral Development, 36*, 367-373.

Huschek, D., De Valk, H., and Liefbroer, A. C. (2012). Partner Choice Patterns Among the Descendants of Turkish Immigrants in Europe. *European Journal of Population, 28*, 241-268.

Kalmijn, M. (1993). Spouse Selection among the Children of European Immigrants: A Study of Marriage Cohorts in the 1960 Census. *International Migration Review, 27*, 51-78.

Kalter, F., and Schroedter, J. H. (2010). Transnational marriage among former labour migrants in Germany. *Zeitschrift für Familienforschung, 22*, 11-36.

Kane, T. T., and Stephen, E. H. (1988). Patterns of intermarriage of guestworker populations in the Federal Republic of Germany: 1960-1985. *Zeitschrift für Bevölkerungswissenschaft, 14*, 187-204.

Kerr, M., and Stattin, H. (2000). What parents know, how they know it, and several forms of adolescent adjustment: further support for a reinterpretation of monitoring. *Developmental Psychology, 36*, 366-380.

Klein, T. (2001). Intermarriages between Germans and Foreigners in Germany. *Journal of Comparative Family Studies, 32*, 325-346.

Knafo, A., Assor, A., Schwartz, S. H., and David, L. (2009). Culture, Migration, and Family-Value Socialization: A Theoretical Model and Empircal Investigation with Russian-Immigrant Youth in Israel. In U. Schönpflug (Ed.), *Cultural Transmission* (pp. 269-296). Cambridge: Cambridge University Press.

Lewin, A. C. (2012). Marriage Patterns Among Palestinians in Israel. *European Journal of Population, 28*, 359-380.

Lievens, J. (1999). Family-Forming Migration from Turkey and Morocco to Belgium: The Demand for Marriage Partners from the Countries of Origin. *International Migration Review, 33*, 717-744.

Nauck, B. (1995). Educational climate and intergenerative transmission in Turkish families: A comparison of migrants in Germany and non-migrants. In P. Noack, M. Hofer and J. Youniss (Eds.), *Psychological Responses to Social Change* (pp. 67-85). Berlin/New York: de Gruyter.

Nauck, B. (1997). Migration and Intergenerational Relations: Turkish Families at Home and Abroad. In W. W. Isajiw (Ed.), *Multiculturalism in North America and Europe: Comparative Perspectives on Interethnic Relations and Social Incorporation* (pp. 435-465). Toronto: Canadian Scholars' Press.

Nauck, B. (2001). Intercultural Contact and Intergenerational Transmission in Immigrant Families. *Journal of Cross-Cultural Psychology, 32*, 159-173.

Nauck, B. (2008). Acculturation. In F. J. R. van de Vijver, D. A. van Hemert and Y. Poortinga (Eds.), *Multilevel Analysis of Individuals and Cultures* (pp. 379-409). New York: Lawrence Erlbaum Associates.

Nauck, B., and Klaus, D. (2008). Family Change in Turkey: Peasant Society, Islam, and the Revolution "From Above". In R. Jayakody, A. Thornton and W. Axinn (Eds.), *International Family Change* (pp. 281-312). New York: Lawrence Erlbaum Associates.

Nauck, B., and Steinbach, A. (2012). First Romantic Relationships of Adolescents from Different Religious Groups in Israel and Germany. In G. Trommsdorff and X. Chen (Eds.), *Values, Religion, and Culture in Adolescent Development* (pp. 290-311). Cambridge: Cambridge University Press.

Schönpflug, U. (2009). Theory and Research in Cultural Transmission: A Short History. In U. Schönpflug (Ed.), *Cultural Transmission* (pp. 9-30). Cambridge: Cambridge University Press.

Steinbach, A., and Nauck, B. (2000). Die Wirkung institutioneller Rahmenbedingungen für das individuelle Eingliederungsverhalten von russischen Immigranten in Deutschland und Israel. In R. Metze, K. Mühler and K. D. Opp (Eds.), *Normen und Institutionen: Entstehung und Wirkungen* (pp. 299-320). Leipzig: Leipziger Universitätsverlag.

UNESCO. (2006). *International Standard Classification of Education – ISCED 1997* (2nd ed.): UNESCO Institute for Statistics.

Windzio, M. (2011). Linked Life-Events. Leaving Parental Home in Turkish Immigrant and Native Families in Germany. In M. Wingens, M. Windzio, H. De Valk and C. Aybeck (Eds.), *A Life-Course Perspective on Migration and Integration* (pp. 187-209). Dordrecht, NL: Springer.

PART IV
Research on Diaspora Migration and its Implications for Research and Policy

Chapter 14

Diaspora Migration in Israel and Germany: Unique Contexts or Examples of a General Phenomenon?

Peter F. Titzmann and Katharina Stoessel

Diaspora immigrants differ in many ways from other immigrant groups. They not only share their religious, cultural, and ethnic background with the mainstream receiving society, but also receive privileged conditions and rights of immigration (Tsuda, this volume; Silbereisen, this volume). Their situation is also different from that of other migrants in that they have two cultures of origin: that of the homeland where their ancestors lived before the Diaspora and that of the sending culture represented by the country where Diaspora immigrants have lived for generations, typically absorbing its cultural imprint, before re-immigrating to their ancestral homeland. In addition, although Diaspora immigrants' receiving society and their ancestral homeland are identical at the first glance, the historic changes and modernizations that happened over decades or even centuries changed the ancestral homeland into a receiving society, which represents a different culture.

Whether these particularities of Diaspora immigrants relate to differences in psychological and socio-cultural adaptation is a matter of debate (Brenick and Silbereisen, 2012) that can only be answered by comparative research (Berry, Phinney, Sam, and Vedder, 2006; Fuligni, 2001). For this reason, the results of the research projects presented in this book are invaluable with regard to the theoretical and empirical understanding of differences in the adaptation of different types of immigrant groups.

The aim of this chapter is to move away from the close focus on immigration to Germany and Israel and to take a broader perspective on the acculturation of Diaspora immigrants by comparing empirical results concerning the psychological and socio-cultural adaptation of Diaspora immigrants with those yielded by research on other immigrant groups and in other parts of the world. A comprehensive overview covering different types of immigrant groups, different contexts, and various outcomes is, however, quite a complex task (Berry, Kim, Minde, and Mok, 1987). Researchers around the world use different instruments, different conceptual approaches, and mostly do not replicate results across various immigrant groups. Therefore, in order to compare research results across Diaspora and other types of immigrants, we used a theoretical framework by Colleen Ward (2001) as guideline for describing different approaches to the study of acculturation and adaptation. This framework allows similarities and differences in three crucial aspects of Diaspora immigrants' adaptation to be addressed. In the second section of the chapter we discuss some limitations of current research and suggest ways in which they can be addressed by comparative research focusing on various immigrant groups. We also discuss the necessity to place more emphasis on developmental aspects in immigration research, which is of particular interest for adolescents, because in this age-group normative developmental processes (psychological, social, and biological changes) co-occur with acculturation-related changes. For this reason, we focus primarily on the adolescent years throughout the chapter.

Diaspora Migration in Comparative Perspective: Three Approaches to Acculturation and Adaptation

In order to compare the adaptation of Diaspora immigrants with that of other immigrant groups we draw on the theoretical work of Ward (2001) and discuss three approaches to acculturation in detail. The first approach comprises stress and coping theories related to psychological affective outcomes. The second highlights socio-cultural learning theories related to socio-cultural behavioral outcomes, and the third covers identification theories and focuses on cognitive outcomes.

Stress-Research and Diaspora Migration

Stress and coping theories, the first approach described by Ward (2001), focuses on immigration-related challenges rooted in cultural transition from one country to another. Theories in this research tradition are usually used for studying affective outcomes of psychological adjustment (Berry et al., 1987), for which acculturative stress is seen as major risk factor. In these models, acculturative stress results from the "demands (that) stem from the experience of having to deal with two cultures in contact, and having to participate to various extents in both of them" (Berry, 1997, p. 18). Theoretically, acculturative stress is assumed to be detrimental as it represents challenges that individuals experience in addition to stress resulting from normative developmental tasks across the life span. Additional stressors can overburden individuals and may result in higher levels of depressive symptoms (Petersen, Sarigiani, and Kennedy, 1991) or antisocial behavior (Agnew and White, 1992), especially in adolescence.

Following this general idea of acculturative stress, research groups dealing with different receiving societies and different immigrant groups operationalized acculturative stress as hassles resulting from intercultural interactions. Approaches to measuring and quantifying such acculturation-related hassles vary widely and often require a series of qualitative field studies to make an initial assessment of the immigrant group's perceptions of their acculturation-related stressors (see for example Titzmann, Silbereisen, Mesch, and Schmitt-Rodermund, 2011).

Table 14.1   Acculturation-related hassles in studies on various immigrant groups

Authors	Number of dimensions	Types of acculturation-related hassles	Immigrant group
Titzmann, Silbereisen, Mesch, and Schmitt-Rodermund (2011)	3	Language hassles Discrimination hassles Family hassles (due to generational discrepancies in adaptation)	Diaspora Immigrants: Ethnic Germans in Germany and Russian Jews in Israel
Liebkind and Jasinskaja-Lahti (2000)	2	Language problems Discrimination	Diaspora Immigrants: Ethnic Fins in Finland
Hernandez and Charney (1998)	4	Language problems Perceived discrimination Perceived cultural incompatibilities Generational gaps	Hispanics in the US
Samaniego and Gonzales (1999)	3	Perceived discrimination Peer hassles (e.g., peer pressure) Family conflicts	Mexican American adolescents in the U.S.
Vinokurov, Trickett, and Birman (2002)	4	School (discrimination) Peer hassles (trying to make friends) Language hassles Family (due to generational discrepancies in adaptation)	Russian immigrants in the US
Safdar, Lay, and Struthers (2003) Lay and Nguyen (1998)	3	Family hassles (due to generational discrepancies in adaptation) Outgroup hassles (discrimination) Ingroup hassles (exclusion from ethno-cultural group)	European, black/ Caribbean and Vietnamese in Canada
Pan, Yue, and Chan (2010)	4	Language deficiency Academic work Cultural difference Social interaction	Chinese students in Hong Kong

Table 14.1 lists types of acculturation-related hassles found in various immigrant groups and societies. The commonalities are striking, particularly concerning discrimination hassles, hassles due to insufficient language proficiency, and family hassles related to parent-child differences in the pace of adaptation to the new culture, which are found repeatedly.

The finding that Diaspora immigrants share hassles due to intercultural contact in the receiving society with other types of immigrants shows that Diaspora immigrants experience a cultural distance to the receiving country, even when they share their ethnic or religious background with the mainstream culture of the receiving country. It also suggests that most of them were culturally well-adjusted to the mainstream culture of the sending country and that they had lost a meaningful cultural bond to their homeland (Remennick, 2006; Tsuda, 2009). In addition, empirical evidence suggests that acculturation-related hassles have similar effects on the psychosocial functioning of Diaspora immigrants and other immigrant groups: In studies among non-Diaspora immigrants, higher levels of acculturation-related hassles were related to lower levels of well-being, social participation, or more psychophysical symptoms (Pan, Yue, and Chan, 2010; Safdar, Lay, and Struthers, 2003; Vinokurov, Trickett, and Birman, 2002). Similar associations were found among Diaspora immigrants, with higher levels of acculturative hassles being related to higher levels of distress or delinquency (Michel, Titzmann, and Silbereisen, 2011; Titzmann, Silbereisen, and Mesch, 2013). Taken together, the everyday hassles related to being an immigrant, which are typically perceptions of discrimination, difficulties with the new language, and intergenerational conflicts within families, can be seen as a unifying experience that also applies to Diaspora immigrants and can be assumed to be one of the crucial experiences of acculturation-related stress.

A question that is still open for research is whether or not Diaspora immigrants differ in the level of acculturation-related hassles or in the pace of changes in these hassles over time. Due to differences in the answering formats or time frames of scales used, results stemming from different studies cannot be directly compared. One may argue on the one hand that Diaspora immigrants experience less acculturative stress, as they identify with the receiving country even prior to their migration (Lomsky-Feder and Rapoport, 2001) or as they seem to get into contact with natives rather easily (Titzmann, Silbereisen, and Mesch, 2012). On the other hand, however, the perceived affiliation to the receiving context may have the downside that immigrants' expectations are too positive so that frustrations and stress after immigration are higher than in other immigrant groups (Mirsky, 2001; Tsuda, 2009). However, in order to examine differences in levels and rates of change between Diaspora immigrants and other types of immigrants, further longitudinal comparative research is required.

Socio-cultural Adaptation and Diaspora Migration

The second approach to research on acculturation and adaptation described by Ward (2001) refers to socio-cultural learning theories. Socio-cultural adaptation is defined as the acquisition of culture-specific skills and knowledge, which facilitates interactions with members and institutions of the receiving country (Ward and Kennedy, 1999). According to this definition, friendships between natives and immigrants can be assumed to be a benchmark for socio-cultural integration into a new context (Khmelkov and Hallinan, 1999). However, despite the fact that level of friendships with natives is seen as benchmark of socio-cultural integration, research usually shows that individuals mainly form friendship bonds to members of their own group (Harris and Cavanagh, 2008). This phenomenon is called friendship homophily (McPherson, Smith-Lovin, and Cook, 2001). Diaspora immigrants have been found to show tendencies for friendship homophily, despite their cultural and ethnic commonalities with the receiving population, although the level is known to differ depending on the length of time since immigration. For example, newcomer Diaspora immigrant adolescents in Germany reported a friendship network consisting of about 100 percent Diaspora immigrants (Silbereisen and Titzmann, 2007), but this was found to decline during the seven years after immigration, and eventually to plateau so that after seven years, no overall change is observed. Diaspora immigrant adolescents have reported having about 60 percent to 70 percent Diaspora immigrants in their friendship network (Titzmann and Silbereisen, 2009). The same tendency of choosing Diaspora immigrants as friends was also observed with regard to best friends. In addition, about 85 percent of Diaspora immigrant adolescents reported having another Diaspora immigrant as their best friend (Titzmann, Silbereisen, and Schmitt-Rodermund, 2007). Similar or even higher levels of friendship homophily were found for other Diaspora immigrant groups, such as Russian Jewish immigrants in Israel (Titzmann et al., 2012; Titzmann et al., 2007).

Although these levels of friendship homophily may seem rather high, they basically reflect findings from other immigrant or minority groups. For example, Harris and Cavanagh (2008) report levels of homophily in friendship networks of 75 percent among Afro-American adolescents, of 40 percent for Asian adolescents and of 55 percent for Hispanic adolescents in the US. Similarly, the likelihood that the best friend is of similar origin is 85 percent for Afro-American adolescents, 62 percent for Hispanics, and 43 percent for Japanese students (Kao and Joyner, 2004). Among Turkish adolescents in Germany, a share of about 70 percent Turkish friends was found in friendship networks (Nauck and Kohlmann, 1998). These numbers highlight similarities in the socio-cultural adaptation of Diaspora immigrants and other immigrant groups.

The acquisition of socio-cultural knowledge, especially of knowledge in the new language, also seems to be strongly associated with the formation of friendships. This strong association can also explain the fact that the decrease in friendship homophily resembles a learning curve with an initial pronounced decrease and the reaching of a plateau later on. One mechanism behind this association is that language is a vehicle transporting many other characteristics, such as values or self-esteem (Remennick, 2003; Schnittker, 2002), which ease intercultural friendships through closing the cultural gap between groups. It is unlikely, however, that this process is unidirectional. In one direction, a higher use of the new language can explain levels and rates of change in friendship homophily among Diaspora immigrants in Germany and Israel (Titzmann et al., 2012), but intercultural friendships are also known to be effective in transmitting socio-cultural knowledge from natives to immigrants (Furnham and Alibhai, 1985).

In short, the socio-cultural adaptation of Diaspora immigrants seems to be highly similar to that of other immigrant or minority groups and marked by a focus on friendships with other Diaspora immigrants. Furthermore, interindividual differences in levels of friendship homophily seem to be strongly related to other indicators of socio-cultural adjustment, such as language knowledge. This is another indication that, despite sharing ethnic, cultural or religious roots with the population in the receiving country, Diaspora immigrants have to bridge a substantial gap to the cultural mainstream.

Cultural Identification and Diaspora Migration

The third group of theoretical and empirical approaches focuses on cognitive aspects of the acculturation process, such as identification with cultural groups and mutual intergroup perception (Ward, 2001). These approaches are mainly based on social identification theories that assume self-ascribed membership of social groups guides individuals' intergroup attitudes and behaviors (Tajfel and Turner, 1986; Turner, Hogg, Oakes, Reicher, and Wetherell, 1987). These approaches are especially interesting with regard to Diaspora migration, as the feeling of belonging to the receiving culture is often a driving force in the decision to return to the country of their ancestors (Schmitt-Rodermund, 1997).

Not surprisingly, therefore, the identification of Diaspora immigrants has been of considerable interest to research on their acculturation and adaptation. In general, it has been argued that immigrants identify with the sending and receiving culture at the same time (Phinney, Berry, Vedder, and Liebkind, 2006). While this also seems to apply to Diaspora immigrants, studies show that they tend to identify more with their sending culture than with their respective receiving culture (Phinney et al., 2006; Stoessel, Titzmann, and Silbereisen, 2012). Moreover, both these dimensions of cultural identification have been found repeatedly to be negatively correlated (Phinney et al., 2006; Stoessel et al., 2012). For example, most groups of adolescent Diaspora immigrants in Finland, Germany, and Israel showed substantial negative associations between their sending and receiving culture identification, suggesting that these adolescents have difficulties to identify simultaneously with both cultures. It seems, however, that these results are not a unique characteristic of Diaspora immigrants, as comparably high identification with the sending culture as well as negative associations between sending and receiving culture identification have also been found among other immigrant groups in various receiving societies (Phinney et al., 2006).

One aspect that also needs to be considered when discussing identification with cultural groups is the normative process of identity development. This involves developing a sense of cultural belonging, which is particularly relevant among immigrant and minority youth (Phinney, 1993; Quintana, 1998). This normative development, together with processes of socio-cultural adaptation (Berry, 2005; Ward, 2001), can be assumed to result in intraindividual changes in the cultural identification of adolescent immigrants. In line with these arguments, longitudinal studies among Diaspora immigrants showed an overall increased identification with the sending culture shortly after immigration compared to the pre-migration level (Mähönen and Jasinskaja-Lahti, 2012), and considerable interindividual variation in later changes in identification with sending and receiving culture (Stoessel et al., 2012). However, these changes were not directed in terms of an average group increase or decrease, but rather very individual without a normative trend. These results obtained among Diaspora immigrants are again similar to those revealed in studies among adolescents belonging to other immigrant groups (Eschbach and Gómez, 1998; Fuligni, Kiang, Witkow, and Baldelomar, 2008; Hitlin, Brown, and Elder, 2006).

As social identification theories (Tajfel and Turner, 1986; Turner et al., 1987) would argue, these highly individualized trajectories of immigrants' cultural identification have been shown to correspond to changes in intergroup perception. A higher and increasing identification of Diaspora immigrant adolescents with the respective receiving culture was related to immigrants' positive attitudes towards contacts with natives and to immigrants' perception of receiving culture members' positive attitudes and behaviors towards immigrants (Jasinskaja-Lahti, Liebkind, and Solheim, 2009; Mähönen and Jasinskaja-Lahti, 2012; Stoessel et al., 2012; Tartakovsky, 2009). This result corresponds to findings among members of other immigrant and minority groups (Badea, Jetten, Iyer, and Er-rafiy, 2011; Eschbach and Gómez, 1998; Hong et al., 2006; Rumbaut, 2005).

Taken together, results of existing research concerning cultural identification and cognitive outcomes of the acculturation process suggest great similarities between Diaspora immigrants and members of other immigrant groups: Both share the bi-dimensional structure of cultural identification and both show a rather strong identification with the sending culture in which they were enculturated. Thus, Diaspora immigrants do not necessarily identify more with the new cultural context, although they have ethnic and cultural roots in the respective receiving culture/homeland. Whether a higher identification with the sending culture relates to lower receiving culture identification or not, seems to be specific for the immigrant group and not so much related to the fact whether or not the specific immigrant group has a Diaspora background. Among Diaspora immigrants and other immigrant groups alike, a higher identification with the receiving culture relates to higher participation within the receiving culture in terms of positive intergroup attitudes towards natives as well as to a more positive perception of the acculturation context receiving society.

Comparative Perspective

Taking the results concerning acculturative stress, socio-cultural adaptation, and cultural identification together, the similarities in adaptation of Diaspora immigrants and other immigrant groups are striking. This may seem surprising given the rather favorable immigration conditions and the homecoming motive of Diaspora migrants. Nearly 80 percent of ethnic Germans reported, for example, that they moved to Germany "to live as a German among other Germans" (Schmitt-Rodermund, 1997). In addition, Diaspora immigrants receive citizenship as well as social benefits immediately after entry into the new country (Shuval, 1998; Slonim-Nevo, Mirsky, Nauck, and Horowitz, 2007).

In order to explain these similarities in acculturation and adaptation between Diaspora immigrants and other immigrant groups, it is useful to look more closely at the Diaspora immigrant groups that have so far been the subject of research. As the vast majority of studies have focused on Diaspora migration from the former Soviet Union, much of the literature cited in this chapter refers to this cultural background. This is the case for ethnic German immigrants in Germany (Dietz, 2000), for Russian Jewish immigrants in Israel (e.g., Mirsky, 2001; Remennick, 2006), for ethnic Ingrian-Fins in Finland (e.g., Mähönen and Jasinskaja-Lahti, 2012), or Pontic-Greeks in Greece (Motti-Stefanidi, Asendorpf, and Masten, 2012). All these groups have lived in the former Soviet Union for several generations and were to some extent forced to assimilate to the mainstream Russian culture. This assimilation was also reinforced through intermarriages with Russians (Al-Haj, 2004; Dietz, 2006). As a result, more than 80 percent of these Diaspora immigrants speak Russian as first language (Dietz, 2000; Jasinskaja-Lahti and Liebkind, 1998; Remennick, 2003). In addition, Diaspora immigrants' ideal of being German, Jewish, Finnish, or Greek is rarely represented by their actual knowledge of the respective receiving country or in their skills for dealing with members of these societies. It could well be, therefore, that hassles related to immigration, such as feelings of not belonging to the new context and a re-identification with the sending culture, are the result of this unexpected cultural gap to the native population.

The situation may be different when other Diaspora groups are considered, such as migrants of Italian or Spanish origin returning from North America, highly skilled Chinese returning to Taiwan, African migrants from Asia, other African countries and the Americas returning home, or the Armenians resettling from Europe (Ember, Ember, and Skoggard, 2005; Tsuda, 2009; White, 2007). These groups are fundamentally different and the existing research on Diaspora migrants from the Soviet Union may yield biased interpretations when being overgeneralized to these other Diaspora groups. Moreover, even Diaspora migrants with Russian background do not constitute a homogenous group, but often differ considerably with regard to the degree to which they had retained the culture of their ancestors and concerning their cultural distance to the respective receiving country.

Heterogeneity in adaptation to the receiving society is also evident when comparing the return of Diaspora migrants to their ancestral homeland and other groups involved in return migration. Here, although sometimes used interchangeably, it is important to distinguish between these two types of migration. Diaspora migration refers to "groups that migrated or were driven from their native land (the "homeland"), and subsequently found their way to other places (a "diaspora") where, over lengthy time periods, they maintained their own distinct communities and dreamed of one-day returning to their Ancient Home" (Weingrod and Levy, 2006, p. 691). Return migration however, refers to the remigration of individuals after shorter periods of time living and working in a different country. These return migrants were enculturated in the receiving country and are likely to have maintained first-hand contact with individuals in that culture. A well-studied case is the return migration to Hong Kong (Sussman, 2011): Before the Chinese authorities took over Hong Kong in 1997, many Hong Kongese left their homeland to settle in Western countries; most of them returned after 1997. Although in our chapter, we have confined ourselves to research on Diaspora immigrants, we can nevertheless assume that the cultural gap between migrants and individuals of the receiving country is significantly smaller among return immigrants than among Diaspora immigrants. This is likely to change the course of adaptation significantly and to hamper the applicability of findings from Diaspora immigrant groups to return immigrants.

These two examples, Diaspora migration with other than Russian background and return migration, demonstrate that more comparative research is necessary in order to understand adequately the large diversity of immigrant groups around the world. Such research could also contribute substantially to identifying similarities in adaptation, and thereby the possibility of generalizing results on the one hand, and group-specific aspects of adaptation and limits of generality on the other. This corroborates the importance of results presented in this book. However, further research would advance current knowledge even more by identifying the crucial dimensions on which immigrant groups differ from one another. One possible starting point for such comparative dimensions is a taxonomy by Berry and colleagues (1987) who differentiated between voluntariness and mobility of acculturating groups. Additionally, factors such as extent of cultural distance, group-specific tendencies for culture retention, characteristics of the receiving country, and, particularly for Diaspora or return immigrants, time spent outside the home country, may also be of importance. Research would profit substantially if studies would compare immigrant groups according to such theoretical criteria and taxonomies of immigrant groups, as it would also enable making predictions for under-studied rare immigrant groups based on criteria, such as voluntariness, naturalization, endowment with resources, and so on.

Conceptual Considerations: A Comparative Developmental Perspective

The second part of this chapter is dedicated to conceptual and methodological considerations for the future study of Diaspora migration. Although such approaches can help to expand our knowledge on the development of Diaspora migrants within the receiving society, it is important to note that they refer to immigrant groups in general and not exclusively to the study of Diaspora immigrants. Nevertheless, the specific situation of Diaspora immigrant groups has to be considered when such approaches are applied.

The first conceptual issue that deserves more attention in migration research is that individuals experience not only changes related to acculturation or adaptation to the new cultural setting, but also changes related to normative development across the life span. Such changes refer, for example, to biological processes of growth and decline, psychological transformations in cognitive functioning, and in the adoption of new social roles. These changes are reflected in developmental tasks for specific age-periods (Havighurst, 1972), in subjective estimations of when developmental transitions are expected to occur (e.g., Neugarten and Neugarten, 1996), and in the way contexts are structured to reinforce or hinder inappropriately early or late transitions (Nurmi, 1993).

These aspects of normative development are likely to interact with the challenges and tasks of acculturation and adaptation outlined earlier. The results of a longitudinal study among newcomer and experienced Diaspora immigrants and a native comparison group illuminate such competing processes (Michel et al., 2011): Normative increases in depressive symptoms during adolescence were found among natives and experienced immigrants, but not among newcomers. A plausible answer for this finding is that the adolescent-typical increase in depressive symptoms was counteracted by the acculturation-specific decrease in depressive symptoms in this group that is due to the improvement of coping skills for dealing with acculturation-specific stress. Ignoring normative development and its interplay with acculturation-related changes in immigration research can yield highly misleading results and may be erroneously interpreted as an indication for (un-)successful adaptation. Similarly, ethnic differences found empirically may in reality be based in different stages of the acculturation process due to group differences in length of residence or in different phases of normative development.

The need for differentiating normative development from acculturation leads to the question of how empirical research can disentangle these two processes (Fuligni, 2001; Michel et al., 2011; Titzmann and Silbereisen, 2012). A major step in accomplishing this task is the inclusion of one or more comparison groups as reference point. Comparisons of immigrants with same-aged native individuals in the sending country inform about the normative development in the sending culture, whereas same-aged natives in the receiving society tell about developmental norms there. In addition, comparisons with other immigrant groups that differ in the cultural distance to the receiving society, in the endowment with resources, or in their legal situation in the receiving country may help in a better understanding of the specificities of Diaspora migrant groups' adaptation compared to other immigrant groups. Choosing meaningful comparison groups for the study of Diaspora immigrants can, however, be an especially challenging task: A comparison group in the sending society could, for example, comprise individuals with similar Diaspora background still living in the Diaspora, or it can comprise a native group from the sending society.

Another requirement for research aimed at disentangling normative development from acculturation-related changes is to account for changes that occur within individuals over time. Although cross-sectional comparisons of groups differing in age and/or length of residence can reveal insights into general trends, the gains of longitudinal research can be expected to be significantly larger. Longitudinal studies map not only interindividual differences at a particular point in time, but also interindividual differences in intraindividual changes over time. Therefore, longitudinal studies enable the comparison of the average trajectory in an immigrant group with that of one or more reference groups. This permits researchers to estimate whether cultural differences in the outcomes studied remain stable, decrease, or increase over time. In addition, longitudinal studies allow factors that accelerate or decelerate the psychosocial adaptation within a particular immigrant group to be identified. For longitudinal assessments among Diaspora immigrants, it may be especially important for research to start already in the sending country, because their process of migration starts very early, involves multiple administrative steps, and is often marked by high expectations regarding their future in the homeland (Mähönen and Jasinskaja-Lahti, 2012; Mirsky, 2001).

A third facet refers to explorative research applying person-oriented methods (Bergman, Magnusson, and El-Khouri, 2003), as immigrant groups can be expected to be quite heterogeneous in their trajectories of adaptation. For example, Berry and colleagues (Berry et al., 2006) found four distinct patterns of adaptation to a new culture that correspond to immigrants' orientation towards the sending and receiving culture. Applying person-oriented approaches to longitudinal data may help in differentiating between immigrant adolescents who do not differ from natives in terms of their adaptation trajectories from those who deviate from normative patterns. Such methods seem especially promising with regard to the study of Diaspora migrants as the high expectations regarding the own acculturation and adaptation process found among Diaspora immigrants (Mähönen and Jasinskaja-Lahti, 2012; Mirsky, 2001) may result in frustration and in withdrawal into the ethnic communities among some individuals, whereas others may be more proactive in fostering their adaptation to the new context.

A fourth conceptual consideration concerns the outcomes studied. Thus far, we have focused on psychological adaptation of Diaspora immigrants, but the adaptation process to a new society is more complex. In particular, sociological life course outcomes, such as education, employment, or family formation, are interrelated with psychological functioning; educational attainment being especially important for immigrants' successful societal participation. However, migrants still have a lower likelihood of achieving higher education (Baumert and Schümer, 2002), and even where they are successful in graduating, they face more problems of finding appropriate positions. Blatant discrimination due to an unfamiliar and obviously foreign family name is not unknown (Kaas and Manger, 2010). Interestingly, Diaspora migrants in Germany seem to do somewhat better compared to other immigrant groups with regard to educational attainment (Woellert, Kröhnert, Sippel, and Klingholz, 2009). In order to understand the reasons for such outcome differentials, interdisciplinary research is necessary, as is the consideration of multiple outcomes (see Kristen et al., this volume). Related to this is the need for research on adaptation across multiple contexts, as the adaptation to the receiving culture may be positive in one context (e.g., in school), but may result in greater adaptation challenges in another context (e.g., the family). Such discrepancies can overburden the coping abilities of immigrants (Titzmann, 2012), but may be counteracted by strengthening a bicultural adaptation (Leyendecker et al., this volume).

Finally, future research aimed at disentangling normative from acculturation-related changes may profit from investigating potential interactions. Trajectories in adaptation may depend on the level of another variable and may thus not be applicable to the immigrant group as whole. For example, a study among immigrants in Greece (including Pontic Diaspora immigrants) found that immigrant adolescents were less popular in their class-rooms than native Greek adolescents (Motti-Stefanidi et al., 2012). This result, however, was only based on those immigrants who were the minority in their class, and even in this group, immigrant adolescents gained in popularity over time. Similarly, the association between risk or protective factors and outcome variables may differ depending on the level of other variables. In our own research, for example, associations between predictors and minor delinquency varied depending on Diaspora immigrants' length of residence. Among newcomer immigrant adolescents, some protective factors were not related to delinquency and some risk factors were much more strongly linked to delinquency than was to be expected, given the results of more experienced immigrants or native adolescents (Titzmann, Raabe, and Silbereisen, 2008). A likely explanation is that, due to the transition to a new country, social systems (e.g. social support network in the neighborhood) that would typically stabilize individuals' development are no longer available and need to be reestablished before they can deploy their buffering effect (Granic and Patterson, 2006). The support received immediately after entry into the new country may provide Diaspora immigrants with the resources needed to counteract risks more quickly, so that associations between predictors and outcomes may differ from those found in other immigrant groups.

All these considerations represent promising starting points for further research on the adaptation of Diaspora immigrants. Several suggested requirements were already applied in the projects presented in this book, such as comparative designs comprising several immigrant/minority groups, the study of multiple outcomes, and the interdisciplinary perspective that is needed for a better understanding of Diaspora migrants' adaptation. The continuing relevance of this research for today's societies is supported by the increasing levels of Diaspora migration around the world (Tsuda, 2009) and by the growing challenges faced by modern societies in dealing with diversity and immigration as a whole.

References

Agnew, R., and White, H. R. (1992). An empirical test of general strain theory. *Criminology, 30*(4), 475-500. doi: 10.1111/j.1745-9125.1992.tb01113.x.

Al-Haj, M. (2004). *Immigration and ethnic formation in a deeply divided society. The case of the 1990s immigrants from the former Soviet Union in Israel.* Leiden: Brill.

Badea, C., Jetten, J., Iyer, A., and Er-rafiy, A. (2011). Negotiating dual identities: The impact of group-based rejection on identification and acculturation. *European Journal of Social Psychology, 41*(5), 586-595. doi: 10.1002/ejsp.786.

Baumert, J., and Schümer, G. (2002). Familiäre Lebensverhältnisse, Bildungsbeteiligung und Kompetenzerwerb im nationalen Vergleich. [Family life, educational participation, and achieving competence in a national comparison]. In J. C. Baumert, C. Artelt, E. Klieme, M. Neubrand, M. Prenzel, U. Schiefele, W. Schneider, K.-J. Tillmann and M. Weiß (Eds.), *Pisa 2000 – Die Länder der Bundesrepublik Deutschland im Vergleich* (pp. 159-202). Opladen: Leske + Budrich.

Bergman, L. R., Magnusson, D., and El-Khouri, B. M. (2003). *Studying individual development in an interindividual context: A person-oriented approach.* Mahwah, NJ: Lawrence Erlbaum Associates.

Berry, J. W. (1997). Immigration, acculturation, and adaptation. *Applied Psychology: An International Review, 46*(1), 5-34.

Berry, J. W. (2005). Acculturation: Living successfully in two cultures. *International Journal of Intercultural Relations, 29*(6), 697-712.

Berry, J. W., Kim, U., Minde, T., and Mok, D. (1987). Comparative Studies of Acculturative Stress. *International Migration Review, 21*(3), 491-511. doi: 10.2307/2546607.

Berry, J. W., Phinney, J. S., Sam, D. L., and Vedder, P. (Eds.). (2006). *Immigrant youth in cultural transition: Acculturation, identity, and adaptation across national contexts.* Mahwah, NJ: Lawrence Erlbaum Associates.

Brenick, A., and Silbereisen, R. K. (2012). Leaving (for) home: Understanding return migration from the diaspora. *European Psychologist, 17*(2), 85-92. doi: 10.1027/1016-9040/a000119.

Dietz, B. (2000). German and Jewish migration from the former Soviet Union to Germany: Background, trends and implications. *Journal of Ethnic and Migration Studies, 26*(4), 635-652. doi: 10.1080/713680499.

Dietz, B. (2006). Aussiedler in Germany: From Smooth Adaptation to Tough Integration. In L. Lucassen, D. Feldman and J. Oltmer (Eds.), *Paths of Integration. Migrants in Western Europe (1880-2004)* (pp. 116-136). Amsterdam: Amsterdam University Press.

Ember, M., Ember, C. R., and Skoggard, I. A. (2005). *Encyclopedia of diasporas: Immigrant and refugee cultures around the world.* New York: Springer.

Eschbach, K., and Gómez, C. (1998). Choosing Hispanic identity: Ethnic identity switching among respondents to high school and beyond. *Social Science Quarterly, 79*(1), 74-90.

Fuligni, A. J. (2001). A comparative longitudinal approach to acculturation among children from immigrant families. *Harvard Educational Review, 71*, 566-578.

Fuligni, A. J., Kiang, L., Witkow, M. R., and Baldelomar, O. (2008). Stability and change in ethnic labeling among adolescents from Asian and Latin American immigrant families. *Child Development, 79*(4), 944-956.

Furnham, A., and Alibhai, N. (1985). The friendship networks of foreign students: A replication and extension of the functional model. *International Journal of Psychology, 20*(6), 709-722.

Granic, I., and Patterson, G. R. (2006). Toward a comprehensive model of antisocial development: A dynamic systems approach. *Psychological Review, 113*(1), 101-131.

Harris, K. M., and Cavanagh, S. E. (2008). Indicators of the peer environment in adolescence. In B. V. Brown (Ed.), *Key indicators of child and youth well-being: Completing the picture.* (pp. 259-278). Mahwah, NJ: Lawrence Erlbaum Associates.

Havighurst, R. J. (1972). *Developmental tasks and education.* New York: David McKay Company, Inc.

Hitlin, S., Brown, J. S., and Elder, G. H., Jr. (2006). Racial self-categorization in adolescence: Multiracial development and social pathways. *Child Development, 77*(5), 1298-1308.

Hong, Y.-Y., Liao, H.-Y., Chan, G., Wong, R. Y. M., Chiu, C.-Y., Ip, G. W.-M., and Hansen, I. G. (2006). Temporal causal links between outgroup attitudes and social categorization: The case of Hong Kong 1997 transition. *Group Processes and Intergroup Relations, 9*(2), 265-288.

Jasinskaja-Lahti, I., and Liebkind, K. (1998). Content and predictors of the ethnic identity of Russian-speaking immigrant adolescents in Finland. *Scandinavian Journal of Psychology, 39*(4), 209-219. doi: 10.1111/1467-9450.00081.

Jasinskaja-Lahti, I., Liebkind, K., and Solheim, E. (2009). To identify or not to identify? National disidentification as an alternative reaction to perceived ethnic discrimination. *Applied Psychology: An International Review, 58*(1), 105-128. doi: 10.1111/j.1464-0597.2008.00384.x.

Kaas, L., and Manger, C. (2010). *Ethnic discrimination in Germany's labour market: a field experiment.* Bonn: IZA.

Kao, G., and Joyner, K. (2004). Do race and ethnicity matter among friends? Activities among interracial, interethnic, and intra-ethnic adolescent friends. *The Sociological Quarterly, 45*(3), 557-573.

Khmelkov, V. T., and Hallinan, M. T. (1999). Organizational effects on race relations in schools. *Journal of Social Issues, 55*, 627-645.

Lomsky-Feder, E., and Rapoport, T. (2001). Homecoming, immigration, and the national ethos: Russian-Jewish homecomers reading Zionism. *Anthropological Quarterly, 74*(1), 1-14. doi: 10.2307/3318299.

Mähönen, T. A., and Jasinskaja-Lahti, I. (2012). Anticipated and perceived intergroup relations as predictors of immigrants' identification patterns: A follow-up study. *European Psychologist, 17*(2), 120-130. doi: 10.1027/1016-9040/a000114.

McPherson, M., Smith-Lovin, L., and Cook, J. M. (2001). Birds of a feather: Homophily in social networks. *Annual Review of Sociology, 27*(1), 415-444.

Michel, A., Titzmann, P. F., and Silbereisen, R. K. (2011). Psychological adaptation of adolescent immigrants from the former Soviet Union in Germany: Acculturation versus age-related time trends. *Journal of Cross-Cultural Psychology, 43*(1), 59-76. doi: 10.1177/0022022111416662.

Mirsky, J. (2001). A pre-immigration group intervention with adolescents: An evaluation study. *Journal of Social Work Research and Evaluation, 2*(2), 307-318.

Motti-Stefanidi, F., Asendorpf, J. B., and Masten, A. S. (2012). The adaptation and well-being of adolescent immigrants in Greek schools: A multilevel, longitudinal study of risks and resources. *Development and Psychopathology, 24*(02), 451-473. doi: doi:10.1017/S0954579412000090.

Nauck, B., and Kohlmann, A. (1998). Verwandtschaft als soziales Kapital: Netzwerkbeziehungen in türkischen Migrantenfamilien. [Kinship as social capital: Social networks in Turkish migrant families]. In M. Wagner and Y. Schütze (Eds.), *Verwandtschaft. Sozialwissenschaftliche Beiträge zu einem vernachlässigten Thema* (pp. 203-235). Stuttgart: Enke.

Neugarten, B. L., and Neugarten, D. A. (1996). The changing meanings of age. In B. L. Neugarten and D. A. Neugarten (Eds.), *The meanings of age: Selected papers of Bernice L. Neugarten* (pp. 72-78). Chicago, IL: University of Chicago Press.

Nurmi, J.-E. (1993). Adolescent development in an age-graded context: The role of personal beliefs, goals, and strategies in the tackling of developmental tasks and standards. *International Journal of Behavioral Development, 16*, 169-189. doi: 10.1177/016502549301600205.

Pan, J.-Y., Yue, X., and Chan, C. L. W. (2010). Development and validation of the Acculturative Hassles Scale for Chinese Students (AHSCS): An example of mainland Chinese University students in Hong Kong. *Psychologia: An International Journal of Psychological Sciences, 53*(3), 163-178. doi: 10.2117/psysoc.2010.163

Petersen, A. C., Sarigiani, P. A., and Kennedy, R. E. (1991). Adolescent depression: Why more girls? *Journal of Youth and Adolescence, 20*(2), 247-271. doi: 10.1007/BF01537611.

Phinney, J. S. (1993). A three-stage model of ethnic identity development in adolescence. In M. E. Bernal and G. P. Knight (Eds.), *Ethnic identity: Formation and transmission among Hispanics and other minorities* (pp. 61-79). Albany, NY: State University of New York Press.

Phinney, J. S., Berry, J. W., Vedder, P., and Liebkind, K. (2006). The acculturation experience: Attitudes, identities, and behaviors of immigrant youth. In J. W. Berry, J. S. Phinney, D. L. Sam and P. Vedder (Eds.), *Immigrant youth in cultural transition: Acculturation, identity, and adaptation across national contexts* (pp. 71-116). Mahwah, NJ: Lawrence Erlbaum Associates.

Quintana, S. M. (1998). Children's developmental understanding of ethnicity and race. *Applied and Preventive Psychology, 7*(1), 27-45.

Remennick, L. I. (2003). Language acquisition as the main vehicle of social integration: Russian immigrants of the 1990s in Israel. *International Journal of the Sociology of Language, 164*, 83-105. doi: 10.1515/ijsl.2003.057.

Remennick, L. I. (2006). *Russian Jews on Three Continents: Identity, Integration, and Conflict.* New Brunswick, NJ: Transaction Publishers.

Rumbaut, R. G. (2005). Sites of belonging: Acculturation, discrimination, and ethnic identity among children of immigrants. In T. S. Weisner (Ed.), *Discovering successful pathways in children's development: Mixed methods in the study of childhood and family life* (pp. 111-162). Chicago, IL: University of Chicago Press.

Safdar, S., Lay, C., and Struthers, W. (2003). The process of acculturation and basic goals: Testing a multidimensional individual difference acculturation model with Iranian immigrants in Canada. *Applied Psychology: An International Review, 52*(4), 555-579. doi: 10.1111/1464-0597.00151.

Schmitt-Rodermund, E. (1997). *Akkulturation und Entwicklung. Eine Studie unter jugendlichen Aussiedlern* [Acculturation and development. A study on adolescent ethnic German immigrants]. Weinheim: PVU.

Schnittker, J. (2002). Acculturation in context: The self-esteem of Chinese immigrants. *Social Psychology Quarterly, 65*(1), 56-76.

Shuval, J. T. (1998). Migration to Israel: The mythology of uniqueness. *International Migration, 36*(1), 3-26.

Silbereisen, R. K., and Titzmann, P. F. (2007). Peers among immigrants – Some comments on 'Have we missed something?'. In R. C. M. E. Engels, M. Kerr and H. Stattin (Eds.), *Friends, lovers and groups: Key relationships in adolescence* (pp. 155-166). New York, NY: John Wiley and Sons Ltd.

Slonim-Nevo, V., Mirsky, J., Nauck, B., and Horowitz, T. (2007). Social participation and psychological distress among immigrants from the former Soviet Union: A comparative study in Israel and Germany. *International Social Work, 50*(4), 473-488.

Stoessel, K., Titzmann, P. F., and Silbereisen, R. K. (2012). Young diaspora immigrants' attitude and behavior toward the host culture: The role of cultural identification. *European Psychologist, 17*(2), 143-157.

Sussman, N. M. (2011). *Return migration and identity: A global phenomenon, a Hong Kong case.* Hong Kong: Hong Kong University Press.

Tajfel, H., and Turner, J. C. (1986). The social identity theory of intergroup behavior. In S. Worchel and W. G. Austin (Eds.), *The psychology of intergroup relations* (pp. 7-24). Chicago: Nelson-Hall.

Tartakovsky, E. (2009). Cultural identities of adolescent immigrants: A three-year longitudinal study including the pre-migration period. *Journal of Youth and Adolescence, 38*(5), 654-671. doi: 10.1007/s10964-008-9370-z.

Titzmann, P. F. (2012). Growing up too soon? Parentification among immigrant and native adolescents in Germany. *Journal of Youth and Adolescence, 41*(7), 880-893. doi: 10.1007/s10964-011-9711-1.

Titzmann, P. F., Raabe, T., and Silbereisen, R. K. (2008). Risk and protective factors for delinquency among male adolescent immigrants at different stages of the acculturation process. *International Journal of Psychology, 43*(1), 19-31.

Titzmann, P. F., and Silbereisen, R. K. (2009). Friendship homophily among ethnic German immigrants: A longitudinal comparison between recent and more experienced immigrant adolescents. *Journal of Family Psychology, 23*(3), 301-310.

Titzmann, P. F., and Silbereisen, R. K. (2012). Acculturation or development? The timing of autonomy among ethnic German immigrant adolescents and their native German age-mates. *Child Development, 83*(5), 1640-1654. doi: 10.1111/j.1467-8624.2012.01799.x.

Titzmann, P. F., Silbereisen, R. K., and Mesch, G. (2014). Minor delinquency and immigration: a longitudinal study among male adolescents. *Developmental Psychology 50*(1), 271-282. doi: 10.1037/a0032666.

Titzmann, P. F., Silbereisen, R. K., Mesch, G., and Schmitt-Rodermund, E. (2011). Migration-specific hassles among adolescent immigrants from the former Soviet Union in Germany and Israel. *Journal of Cross-Cultural Psychology, 42*(5), 777-794.

Titzmann, P. F., Silbereisen, R. K., and Mesch, G. S. (2012). Change in friendship homophily: A German Israeli comparison of adolescent immigrants. *Journal of Cross-Cultural Psychology, 43*(3), 410-428. doi: 10.1177/0022022111399648.

Titzmann, P. F., Silbereisen, R. K., and Schmitt-Rodermund, E. (2007). Friendship homophily among diaspora migrant adolescents in Germany and Israel. *European Psychologist, 12*(3), 181-195.

Tsuda, T. (2009). Conclusion: diasporic homecomings and ambivalent encounters with the ethnic homeland. In T. Tsuda (Ed.), *Diasporic Homecomings: Ethnic Return Migration in Comparative Perspective* (pp. 325-350). Stanford, CA: Stanford University Press.

Turner, J. C., Hogg, M. A., Oakes, P. J., Reicher, S. D., and Wetherell, M. S. (1987). *Rediscovering the social group: A self-categorization theory.* Oxford: Basil Blackwell.

Vinokurov, A., Trickett, E. J., and Birman, D. (2002). Acculturative hassles and immigrant adolescents: A life-domain assessment for Soviet Jewish refugees. *The Journal of Social Psychology, 142*(4), 425-445. doi: 10.1080/00224540209603910.

Ward, C. (2001). The ABCs of acculturation. In D. Matsumoto (Ed.), *Handbook of culture and psychology* (pp. 411-445). New York: Oxford University Press.

Ward, C., and Kennedy, A. (1999). The measurement of sociocultural adaptation. *International Journal of Intercultural Relations, 23*(4), 659-677. doi: 10.1016/S0147-1767(99)00014-0.

Weingrod, A., and Levy, A. (2006). Social thought and commentary: Paradoxes of homecoming: The Jews and their Diasporas. *Anthropological Quarterly, 79*(4), 691-716.

White, C. M. (2007). Living in Zion: Rastafarian repatriates in Ghana, West Africa. *Journal of Black Studies, 37,* 677-709. doi: 10.1177/0021934705282379.

Woellert, F., Kröhnert, S., Sippel, L., and Klingholz, R. (2009). *Ungenutzte Potentiale. Zur Lage der Integration in Deutschland* [Idle potentials. On the integration of migrants in Germany]. Berlin: Berlin-Institut für Bevölkerung und Entwicklung.

Chapter 15

Learning a Host Country: A Plea to Strengthen Parents' Roles and to Encourage Children's Bilingual Development[1]

Birgit Leyendecker, Jessica Willard, Alexandru Agache, Julia Jäkel, Olivia Spiegler, and Katharina Kohl

Introduction

In many Western industrialized nations, immigrants represent the youngest and fastest growing segment of the population (Hernandez, 2012). The majority population of most of these nations is likely to have a low birthrate, and it is foreseeable that they will depend on young immigrant families to fill this demographic gap. Consequently, the economic and social success of many nations will depend to a large extent on these immigrant families and their offspring. Social policies which facilitate the successful adaptation and integration of immigrants are therefore a pressing and timely issue. Some countries have adopted different social policies towards returning diaspora migrants and towards work-migrants or refugees. As outlined in the chapter by Tsuda (this volume), the term "returning diaspora migrants" refers to the descendants of migrants who have lived outside of their homeland for generations. However, aside from some privileges, such as fast access to work permits and citizenships, these returning diaspora migrants are likely to face challenges similar to the obstacles of other immigrants. Culture and language change and develop over time. If cultures are separated over time with little or no exchange, they are likely to progress in different directions. It is possible that diaspora migrants have either preserved the culture of origin from the time of their ancestors' departure and that values and behaviors have basically petrified (Greenfield and Suzuki, 2000), that the diaspora culture has developed over the generations from the time of departure but in a different direction than in the country of origin, or that the diaspora migrants have adopted the culture and language of their host country at least to some extent.

Studies on sojourners show that while they are in the host country, they feel like foreigners. However, once they are back in their country of origin, they come

1   This work was supported by grant No. 292 "Social Integration of Migrant Children: Uncovering Family and School Factors Promoting Resilience" (SIMCUR) from NORFACE ERA-NET.

to realize that they have adapted to the host culture in behaviors, cognitions, beliefs, and values, and they may experience an unexpected second culture shock (Matsumoto et al., 2001). Diaspora migrants are likely to have quite similar experiences and to underestimate the intercultural adjustment upon the "return" to their ancestral country. In addition, many diaspora migrants adopt the language of the host country, and they may now feel more at ease with the language of the majority society of their country of birth (e.g., Russian) than with the language of the country their ancestors migrated from centuries ago (e.g., German). Diaspora communities can be found all over the world, for example, ethnic Kurds living in Turkey, Iran, Irak, Syria, or Armenia, as well as Turks living in Greece, Azerbaijan, Kazakhstan, or Bulgaria. After the end of World War II, two diaspora communities have been particularly mobile and likely to immigrate – people of Jewish and German descent. Between 1948 and 1990, 1.2 million people left the Soviet Union, mostly people of Jewish (52 percent) or German (36 percent) ancestry (Bade, 2000). After the dissolution of the USSR, Jewish people and people with German roots became the two largest diaspora communities to leave the Former Soviet Union. While the majority of the former group migrated to Israel, the latter group was most likely to migrate to Germany. In these countries, they received special treatment inasmuch as they received a passport and support that were not granted to other immigrants. This support was based on the concept that they were returning to their ancestral countries.

For these diaspora families, the ethnic heritage, e.g., being Jewish or German, is not necessarily identical to the language spoken at home which can be Russian, Ukrainian, Romanian, Polish, or Bulgarian rather than Hebrew or German. For other immigrant families, e.g., Turkish immigrant families, the ethnic heritage and the home language are usually the same. In sum, all immigrant families, whether they are diaspora migrants or not, have to cope with the challenges of adapting to a new and strange country, to reconsider their values, and most likely to learn a new language. In the case of diaspora migrants, there is the possibility that both the immigrants themselves as well as the receiving country will underestimate these acculturation costs.

History Repeating?

This has implications for the social policies geared at these immigrant families. Specifically, one should not assume that the diaspora migrants will embrace the culture and language and will identify immediately with the receiving country. Instead, chances are that at least to some extent they will realize that the country their ancestors have lived in for many generations has made its impact over time and that they have adopted some of these values and beliefs (see the chapter by Walters, Armon-Lotem, Altman, Topaj, and Gagarina in this book). In addition, they may experience prejudices from the population of the receiving country. For example, ethnic Germans returning to Germany, the so-called "Aussiedler", were perceived as Germans in Russia. Once they have moved to Germany, however, they are likely to be perceived as Russians. Just as their German heritage was often not appreciated in the Russian context, the Russian heritage they have acquired over the course of generations and possibly through intercultural marriages is now in danger of being unappreciated and devalued. In order to avoid a repetition of this history, social policies geared towards these immigrant families should be re-evaluated. From a psychological perspective, we believe that it is necessary that social policies go beyond teaching children and their families the language and culture of the receiving society. Instead, we believe that it is important not to ignore the cultural capital they have accumulated during their diaspora stay. Therefore, we make a plea to change social policies towards acknowledging and supporting the bilingual and bicultural competencies of children from immigrant families. Bilingual and bicultural competencies are assets that can enrich the lives of individuals as well as of the society to which they belong.

The framework of social policies towards immigrant families and children is usually based on teaching them the language and culture of the host society in order to facilitate the transition from one culture to another. A few countries, such as Norway, fund mother-tongue instruction for children from immigrant families for a transition period until they are sufficiently proficient in Norwegian to participate in the regular classroom. The ability to follow general instructions given in the majority language is an explicit goal for all students and an important prerequisite for academic success and social integration. The focus on the host language, however, should not result in a devaluation of the children's mother tongue. De Houwer (2009) points out that all over the world, pre-school teachers, pediatricians, nurses, and speech therapists tend to be ignorant of the potential benefits of growing up bilingual. Instead, they often emphasize only the potential problems and give parents the one-sided advice to give up the mother tongue and to speak only the majority language with their children. Parents who want to provide the best learning environment for their children are likely to listen to the advice given by healthcare or language professionals.

In Germany, the visit of the Turkish prime-minister Erdogan in 2011 fueled a debate among politicians about the importance of the German vs. Turkish language spoken in immigrant Turkish families. While Erdogan emphasized the importance of Turkish parents fostering their children's Turkish language competence, German politicians were less keen to endorse bilingualism. Politicians and policy makers are still less likely to perceive the heritage culture and language (or in this case the language and culture they have acquired during their diaspora stay) as a resource. Instead, they are more focused on the importance of the majority language, as this is considered essential for social integration. While this approach is understandable from the perspective of teachers and administrators, ignoring bilingual and bicultural competencies of citizens is also shortsighted in an increasingly globalized world. In this chapter, we will point out the importance of strengthening the role of first generation immigrant parents by encouraging them to teach their children the language and culture they have acquired in the diaspora while at the same time facilitating their children's access to the language and culture of their new home country.

Adaptation and Integration of Immigrant Families – the Perspective of the Host Countries

For host countries such as Germany, the integration of returning diaspora families as well as of immigrant families from other regions of the world presents a challenge and a serious concern. Thus, selecting acculturation strategies becomes a pressing issue. To what extent is the majority population of a country willing to change and to endorse cultural diversity in order to accommodate the new immigrants? Or do the host country and its majority population expect only the immigrants to change and to adapt? Changes of national institutions towards embracing diversity are more likely to happen on a very exclusive level (e.g., international bilingual schools, companies or universities competing to acquire the best researchers) rather than in local schools with a high percentage of immigrant children who may not speak the same language as their teachers.

A social policy geared towards integration requires that the receiving society is willing to change and has an inclusive and open orientation towards new immigrants. As Berry (2002) points out, this model would require the immigrants to retain basic values of their culture of origin but also to be willing to develop a positive attitude towards the culture of the host country, and respect if not adopt at least the basic values. For the receiving country, willingness to integrate requires substantial changes to institutions such as early childcare, schooling, housing, or health care in order to meet the needs of both the immigrants and the majority population. Policy indices summarized in the Multiculturalism Policy Index (http://www.queensu.ca/mcp/, accessed February 27, 2013) show that few countries, such as Canada, Norway, and Sweden are willing to move in this direction. Most countries expect only the immigrants to change, to adapt to the host society, and to adopt the values and language of the majority society. In the case of returning diaspora migrants, chances that a host society will start to question these policies are even slimmer because these groups are officially perceived as part of the majority population.

Language, National and Ethnic Identities

Cultural differences and similarities are visible on many levels, such as attitudes, parenting behaviors, dress codes, or preferences for music or food. From the perspective of the host nation, however, language appears to be of utmost importance. First, learning the majority language spoken in the schools is considered to be an important prerequisite for children's access to the school systems and therefore for their economic future. Second, a common language facilitates communication and unifies people. Third, languages are often an expression of a national and/or ethnic identity and a common heritage. This is evident in a non-migrant context, e.g., the intricate emotional connection between cultural and ethnic identity and a common language such as Basque or Catalan spoken in Spain. In other countries, the official language is closely associated with the ethnic and national identity. Prominent examples of the close association of ethnic or national identity and language in an immigration context are Israel's concern to teach Hebrew to all newcomers, or the concern of the francophone part of Canada to preserve the French language and to attract French speaking immigrants.

Adaptation and Integration of Children – the Perspective of Immigrant Families

Children mature in multiple psychological domains. Three domains are particularly important: their social integration, their psychosocial adaptation, and their cognitive abilities and educational achievement. The first domain, social integration, includes both cultural competence and a sense of belonging. From the attachment theory, we know about the importance of children feeling secure and firmly grounded in their families. Cultural competence and successful adjustment require knowledge and identification with one's own culture as well as knowledge and access to the host culture. For children from immigrant families, a first and important step to developing a sense of belonging is to become firmly rooted in the family as well as in the culture of origin (Stuart, Ward, and Adams, 2010). Suárez-Orozco and Suárez-Orozco (2001) point out the importance that parents meet this balance and that children respect their parents, family, and culture of origin while at the same time develop bicultural competencies so they are able to take full advantage of the opportunities of both worlds. This parenting task may prove to be quite a challenge, especially for parents with limited access to the host culture who may fear losing their children to the new and foreign culture.

The second psychological domain mentioned above is psychosocial adaptation. This refers to the development of social and behavioral competence and of subjective well-being. The development of social and behavioral competences allows children to have positive interactions with other children and adults and to develop and foster friendships. While the first domain, social integration and sense of belonging, is more narrowly focused on the family, the second domain is more closely focused on the world outside of the family, for example, the social competencies to develop friendships with peers or other adults the children are likely to meet outside of their home environment.

The third domain concerns external functioning and educational achievement, such as doing well in school or at work and developing motivation and broad interests. Developing this domain requires both individual and contextual resources. Individual resources include information seeking and problem solving, mastery motivation, self-regulation, and self-control. Contextual resources include effective relationships with parents or substitute parents, caring teachers or other adults, pro-social, mutually supportive friends, and ideally the support of an active community (Masten and O'Dougherty Wright, 2010).

In the past ten years, an increasingly growing body of research points to the importance of bilingual and bicultural competencies for children from immigrant families (De Houwer, 2007, 2009; Grosjean, 2010). Immigrant parents who provide access to the majority language and pass on the home language to their children are not only ensuring that they share a common language with their children. They are also endowing their children with a resource others spend considerable effort attaining: the ability to communicate effectively in two languages. Research comparing bilingual and monolingual children has accumulated evidence that bilingualism can benefit family, socio-emotional, cognitive, and academic functioning.

Benefits of Becoming Bilingual: Family Cohesion

Few will debate the value of mastering a society's majority language, as it lays the fundamental groundwork for academic and occupational success and social integration. In most countries, policies are directed towards improving the host language skills of children from immigrant families. In Germany, for example, there is an abundance of educational programs and research projects targeting their German language development in the pre-school years (Caspar and Leyendecker, 2011; Dubowny, Ebert, von Maurice, and Weinert, 2008). However, there may also be a number of benefits for children who not only become native speakers of the majority language but who also develop and maintain their home language. This is especially the case if a child has at least one first generation parent with limited command of the majority language. In such a family constellation, developing the home language becomes a necessity for the child. Otherwise, when a child has little knowledge of the home language and the parent cannot fully express him- or herself in the majority language, there is no real mean of communication between the parent and the child. Fillmore (2000) documents a case of a Chinese immigrant family in the USA. Several of the children either did not develop a working capability of Cantonese or lost the ability to use it. The parents, due to their work circumstances, made little progress with their English. Ultimately, the parents felt estranged and separated from their children, found it hard to maintain a relationship, and even lost contact with their son. Perhaps this is an exceptionally severe case, but Fillmore also points out that there may be more subtle consequences when parents and children do not share a native language. If a first generation parent adopts solely the majority language for communicating with the child, a language in which he or she may not feel fully comfortable, and may find expressing slight nuances of meaning laborious, how shall the child perceive his or her parent as a competent speaker and authority figure? Furthermore, a parent speaking to a child exclusively in a newly acquired majority language may not be able to provide the same stimulating language environment as in their home language. A study by Place and Hoff (2011) on Spanish speaking parents in the U.S. indicates that interacting with a non-native speaker is less stimulating and therefore less useful for very young language learners than interacting with a native speaker. Place and Hoff (2011, p. 1847) conclude:

> This is not to deny the importance of English language skills for children or the importance of English input for the development of those skills. It is to suggest that the search for ways to improve the English language skills of children of immigrant parents should look elsewhere, for example, by providing exposure to multiple sources who are native English speakers, rather than by asking parents not to speak the language they know and instead to speak a language they do not know well.

Several studies have taken a closer look at the effects of home language maintenance and loss on children from immigrant families (De Houwer, 2007; Chumak-Horbatsch and Garg, 2006). Other studies on this topic stem from the acculturation gap research that contends that if there is a discrepancy between children's and parents' language skills and use, this "lack of fit" leads to distress and conflict (e.g., Costigan and Dokis, 2006). This means that children's loss of the home language is a source of conflict especially if the parents speak it well and use it frequently. For instance, in one study, whether children of Chinese immigrants in the USA used Chinese or not mattered especially if their mothers spoke a lot of Chinese. For the children of these mothers, using Chinese was connected to less intense family conflicts, fewer depressive symptoms, and higher achievement motivation (Costigan and Dokis, 2006). A review by Park (2007) on Korean American youth supports the relationship between family cohesion and children's ability to speak the home language. Interestingly, it does not always seem to be the *interaction* between parents' and children's language behavior that is associated with a certain outcome. There is also some evidence that children's home language proficiency can be directly related to family and child well-being (Birman, 2006; Collins, Toppelberg, Suárez-Orozco, O'Connor, and Nieto-Castañon, 2011; Oh and Fuligni, 2010; Park, Tsai, Liu, and Lau, 2012), regardless of parents' language skills. However, this may also have to do with all the parents in the samples being relatively adept speakers of the home language as many of them were first generation parents.

Benefits of Bilingualism: Psycho-Social Adaptation

To gain insight into possible socio-emotional advantages of bilingualism, Han and colleagues analyzed data from the large-scale Early Childhood Longitudinal Study (ECLS-K), which follows children from kindergarten (N = 21,260) to fifth grade (N = 11,820) (Han and Bridglall, 2009; Han, 2010, 2012; Han and Huang, 2010). The ECLS-K study measured children's language status both by the language spoken at home with the mother and father and by their English proficiency at school entry. Han and her colleagues compared several subgroups of immigrant children with a monolingual white reference group. The four subgroups were "fluent bilinguals" with good command of both their home language and English, English dominant bilinguals, non-English dominant bilinguals, and non-English monolinguals, who had very little knowledge of English. Overall, by fifth grade, teachers rated fluent bilinguals and non-English dominant bilinguals as exhibiting fewer problem behaviors and higher social skills than the English monolingual reference group. Furthermore, from kindergarten to fifth grade, these two bilingual groups tended to have lower growth rates for problem behaviors and higher growth rates for social skills than the English monolingual children. Growth curves analyses for Latino children who spoke little English revealed that this subgroup exhibited the lowest self-control and social skills and the highest level of internalizing problem behavior at the end of elementary school (Han, 2010).

Similar group comparisons on data from the Children of Immigrants Longitudinal Study (CILS) revealed differences related to bilingualism on numerous other outcomes (Portes and Hao, 2002). This study was conducted in Florida and Southern California in the 1990s. For this study, Portes and Hao (2002) compared several subgroups of bilingual children to children of immigrants who spoke only English but not their heritage language. Fluent bilinguals experienced a better family climate, had higher self-esteem, and had higher educational aspirations than those children of immigrants who were not fluent in their heritage language.

Outside of the family, being bilingual might prove to be advantageous to children and adolescents and broaden their access to various social networks. Specifically, these language skills may allow them to expand their social network and to communicate and develop friendships both within and outside of their heritage language group (Golash-Boza, 2005). This finding is supported by a study from Ledesma and Oppedal (2013) with pre-adolescents from Turkish immigrant families in Norway. Children with a good command of both Turkish and Norwegian were most likely to have friends from both of these ethnic groups. In sum, the ability to communicate with people within and outside of an immigrant community can foster family cohesion, broaden children's networks, and increase the likelihood that they have fewer behavior problems and higher academic aspirations when compared to monolingual children.

Benefits of Bilingualism: Cognitive Control and Academic Achievement

Are there advantages for bilinguals regarding cognitive development and academic achievement? Peal and Lambert (1962) report studies from the 1920s that have already addressed these questions. In their own study, Peal and Lambert (1962) found that bilingual 10-year old French-English students in Canada performed significantly better on verbal and nonverbal intelligence tests than their monolingual French speaking classmates. They concluded that the bilingual children have a more diversified set of mental abilities. Today, more than fifty years later, we have a better understanding of the potential cognitive advantages of bilingual children.

The cognitive advantages of bilingual children are mostly detected on tasks that require children to ignore distracting or conflicting information, to act flexible, and to exert cognitive control (Barac and Bialystok, 2012; Bialystok, 2009). These tasks require executive functioning. Executive functions refer to neurocognitive processes that allow information processing and behavior to vary adaptively according to the changing demands of a situation or task. Executive functions (EF) comprise three main components: cognitive flexibility, inhibitory control, and working memory. They have been found to be an important predictor for later academic achievement (Diamond and Lee, 2011). In a literature review, Zelazo and Carlson (2012, p. 355) conclude that "...the evidence suggests long-term stability of early individual differences in EF that have meaningful consequences for people's lives". A recent meta-analysis provides further support for a bilingual advantage on various cognitive tasks (Adesope, Lavin, Thompson, and Ungerleider, 2010). The reason provided for this finding is that bilingual children's two languages are both activated at the same time, even when only one of them is required (Rivera-Mindt et al., 2008). Most bilingual children have one language that is slightly more dominant than the other. When they speak one language, the words in the other language are activated as well, yet they need to be suppressed. This requires a permanent necessity to inhibit the other language, especially when the subdominant language is spoken (Rivera-Mindt et al., 2008). Hence, for a bilingual child it takes constant attentional focusing on one language (Bialystok, 2009) and suppressing one of the other languages to avoid, for instance, speaking in a complete garble of the two languages.

Bilingual children show a higher performance on EF tasks already at the age of three to four years, and their performance matches those of four to five year old monolingual children (Carlson and Meltzoff, 2008; Feng, Bialystok, and Diamond, 2007; Zelazo, Müller, and Marcovitch, 2003). These benefits are sustained across the lifespan and have been found capable to slow down the process of age-related cognitive decline (Bialystok, Craik, and Freeman, 2007; Gold, Kim, Johnson, Kryscio, and Smith, 2013). While most studies have focused on bilingual middle-class children in Canada, a recent study suggests that these findings can be applied to children from low socioeconomic status (SES) immigrant families as well. Engel de Abreu and colleagues (2012), who compared children from low-income Portuguese immigrant families living in Luxembourg with children from low-income families in Portugal, found that bilingualism enhanced the executive functions of these children. The bilingual children in Luxembourg performed better on these tasks than their monolingual counterparts in Portugal.

Speaking and understanding the majority language is a prerequisite for the academic achievement of children from immigrant families. Those who fail to acquire sufficient knowledge of the majority language are likely to decrease their academic achievement over time (Han, 2010, 2012). In addition, however, there are also indicators that children who can communicate in both host and home languages have advantages for their academic achievement. The abovementioned ECLS-K study found these advantages for bilingual first and second generation immigrant children in scores for math and reading (Han, 2012). In Germany, analyses of the DESI (*Deutsch Englisch Schülerleistungen International*) study on English as a foreign language revealed that bilingual adolescents received higher scores than monolingual German children when controlling for background variables such as parents' socioeconomic status (Hesse and Göbels, 2009).

Summary, Conclusion and Implication for Social Policies

A central motivation for many immigrant parents is to provide a better life for their children (Rumbaut, 1997). They hope that their children will take full advantage of the opportunities made available to them and that they will be academically successful on the basis of their merit. After the immigration process, however, many parents fear that they are losing their children to the host country. In addition, they may be confronted by a majority society which argues that parents should facilitate their children's access to the culture and language of the new country, yet at the same time has little appreciation for their heritage language and culture. In the case of diaspora migrants, both the receiving society as well as the migrants themselves may underestimate the impact of the language and culture the migrants have lived in for generations. For a society that welcomes the returning diaspora immigrants, supporting bilingualism and thereby also biculturalism does present a challenge. Languages are not separate from culture, and we can assume that raising a bilingual child means to some extent also raising a bicultural child. This requires some tolerance from the receiving societies and the acceptance that despite their similar ethnic roots, diaspora migrants may differ in some aspects from the majority society.

Developmental psychology shows that it is important for children to become firmly rooted in their family. The development of autonomy and connection are not opposites but rather dependent on each other. Being firmly rooted in their families facilitates children's emerging maturity and autonomy and thus allows them to explore the environment and to expand their knowledge and competence. This is particularly important for immigrant children who need a safe space for building their sense of identity and belonging whilst integrating two cultures. Therefore, the task for immigrant parents is twofold inasmuch as they are faced with the challenge to uphold both a connection to the family and culture of origin as well as to facilitate their children's exploration of the majority culture.

Research with a focus on positive development of children from immigrant families points to the importance of bilingualism. Growing up bilingual can enrich a child's life. Learning the language spoken at home facilitates communication with parents and grandparents and helps children to become rooted in their families and culture of origin. Learning the societal language is important for their academic achievement and social integration. Becoming bilingual has an additional value inasmuch as these children have advantages for the socio-emotional and cognitive development during childhood and adolescence. They fare better on tasks of executive functions, their bilingual competencies broaden their choices of potential friends, and they are less likely to show problem behaviors. So far, the research presented here was centered around the question of what bilingualism can do for children and adolescents and how growing up in two language worlds can foster their development. However, once they are grown up, the perspective can be extended to the question, what children can do with their bilingual competencies. Here, it is safe to assume that being bilingual and bicultural may be advantageous when they choose their careers in an increasingly globalized world.

Learning two (or more) languages, however, does require commitment from the children's families as well as from the society in which they grow up. Becoming bilingual and maintaining bilingual competencies requires active support from the children's families as well as from the pre-schools and schools they attend. As Chumak-Horbatsch (2012, p. 85) points out, "young children require a language-rich environment and meaningful interaction to acquire a second language". If they do not have sufficient exposure and opportunities to practice a language in everyday activities they may lose this language again (Leyendecker and De Houwer, 2011).

Implications for Social Policies

The findings on the importance of fostering children's bilingual development call for suggestions to adapt social policies to encourage and to appreciate children's bilingual potential. In a best case scenario, the education sector, especially early childhood education, and families work together to facilitate children's bilingual development. Studies on bilingual development of children point to the pivotal role of parents to maintain the home language (De Houwer, 2007; Chumak-Horbatsch and Garg, 2006, Chumak-Horbatsch, 2008). Parents who immigrate with their children or whose children are born in the new country may have given little thought to the language they speak to their children. Speaking the mother tongue is natural and most likely to happen. However, experts from the medical and educational sector may be more concerned about children learning the majority language and less likely to emphasize the importance of maintaining children's home language. Monolingual schools, even when they have adopted positive and supportive attitudes towards children's home language, were found to play a negligible role in maintaining the home language (Chumak-Horbatsch and Garg, 2006).

Parents have to deal with many issues and questions during the immigration process. Upon their arrival, they need to be assured and informed about the importance of nurturing the linguistic (and cultural) advantages of their children. In addition, they need support and advice in order to consider strategies to ensure that they acquire and maintain both the home and the majority language. Children have the best chances to become bilingual if they have continuous and meaningful experiences in both language worlds and if parents work as a team to facilitate their children's bilingualism (Chumak-Horbatsch, 2008, 2012). According to Chumak-

Horbatsch (2012), children will have the chance to navigate in two language worlds if they have parents who *believe* that they are able to pass on their mother tongue to their children, who *commit* themselves to the task of maintaining the home language, who *adopt strategies* to provide their children with meaningful experiences involving the home language, and who *acknowledge* the importance of the majority language as well. As children grow older, the home language is likely to become the weaker language. Grosjean (2010) therefore recommends that parents look for additional language input from other family members or friends to provide children with a stronger base.

Conversely, early childhood educators and teachers at elementary schools face a similar task geared at facilitating children's access to the societal language. In classrooms with children from very diverse linguistic backgrounds, teaching the home language is not an option. Instead, it is important that teachers are informed that becoming bilingual is neither going to confuse children nor hinder their academic success. They need to be made aware that becoming bilingual can enrich the life of a child. Pre-school teachers as well as teachers of older grades can actively support children's bilingual competencies by acknowledging children's competencies in their home language, by adopting a positive and supportive attitude towards the home language, and by providing a stimulating environment for learning the societal language taught in the classroom. Following Chumak-Horbatsch's (2012) suggestions for linguistically appropriate practice in classrooms with children from diverse minority groups, teachers should believe that children can become bilingual, commit themselves to the task of teaching the societal language, provide a stimulating language environment, and acknowledge and appreciate children's bilingual competencies.

In summary, several different strands of research converge in showing that learning the home language as well as the language of the country of residence may have various benefits. The possible advantages reach beyond the individual child's cognition and well-being and into the realm of the family and school. These results do not negate other findings on the less fortunate correlates of bilingualism, such as smaller vocabularies in each individual language (Bialystok, 2009) or achievement gaps between certain groups of bilingual and monolingual children. Certainly, more research is required to tease apart the exact contexts which lead children who maintain their home language to flourish. Overall, however, these findings are substantial enough to be taken seriously. In this chapter, we make a plea to strengthen the role of first generation parents by encouraging them to teach their children their mother tongue and their heritage culture while at the same time facilitating their children's access to the language and culture of the host country. Likewise, we make a plea to early childhood educators to provide an enriched linguistic environment for these children, to teach them the majority language, and to appreciate their knowledge of the heritage language and culture. A good example for this policy is the website sponsored by the School of Early Childhood Education of Ryerson University in Toronto (My language – hold on to your home language: http://www.ryerson.ca/mylanguage/). This website pursues the goal of providing parents, teachers, and childcare workers with information for maintaining the minority languages spoken in the children's homes.

References

Adesope, O. O., Lavin, T., Thompson, T., and Ungerleider, C. (2010). A systematic review and meta-analysis of the cognitive correlates of bilingualism. *Review of Educational Research, 80*(2), 207-245.

Berry, J. W. (2002). Conceptual approaches to acculturation. In K. M. Chun, P. B. Organista, and G. Marin (Eds.), *Acculturation: Advances in Theory, Measurement and Applied Research* (pp. 17-37). Washington, DC: American Psychological Association.

Bade, K. (2000). *Europa in Bewegung. Migration vom späten 18. Jahrhundert bis zur Gegenwart.* München: C.H. Beck.

Barac, R. and Bialystok, E. (2012). Bilingual effects on cognitive and linguistic development: Role of language, cultural background, and education. *Child Development, 83* (2), 413-422.

Bialystok, E. (2009). Bilingualism: The good, the bad, and the indifferent. *Bilingualism: Language and Cognition, 12*(01), 3-11. Retrieved from http://dx.doi.org/10.1017/S1366728908003477.

Bialystok, E., Craik, F. I. M., and Freedman, M. (2007). Bilingualism as a protection against the onset of symptoms of dementia. *Neuropsychologia, 45,* 459-464.

Birman, D. (2006). Acculturation gap and family adjustment. *Journal of Cross-Cultural Psychology, 37*(5), 568-589. doi:10.1177/0022022106290479.

Carlson, S. M., and Meltzoff, A. N. (2008). Bilingual experience and executive functioning in young children. *Developmental Science, 11,* 282-298.

Caspar, U., and Leyendecker, B. (2011). Deutsch als Zweitsprache. Die Sprachentwicklung türkischstämmiger Vorschulkinder in Deutschland. *Zeitschrift für Entwicklungspsychologie und Pädagogische Psychologie, 43,* 118-132.

Chumak-Horbatsch, R., and Garg, S. (2006). Linguistic behaviors of Ukrainian-English bilingual children. *Psychology of Language and Communication, 10,* 3-26.

Chumak-Horbatsch, R. (2008). Early bilingualism: Children of immigrants in an English-language childcare center. *Psychology of Language and Communication, 12,* 3-28.

Chumak-Horbatsch, R. (2012). *Linguistically appropriate practice. A guide for working with young immigrant children.* Toronto: Toronto University Press.

Collins, B. A., Toppelberg, C. O., Suárez-Orozco, C., O'Connor, E., and Nieto-Castañon, A. (2011). Cross-sectional associations of Spanish and English competence and well-being in Latino children of immigrants in kindergarten:

International Journal of the Sociology of Language. *International Journal of the Sociology of Language, 2011*(208), 5-23.

Costigan, C. L., and Dokis, D. P. (2006). Relations between parent–child acculturation differences and adjustment within immigrant Chinese families. *Child Development, 77*(5), 1252-1267.

De Houwer, A. (2007). Parental language input patterns and children's bilingual use. *Applied Psycholinguistics, 28*, 411-424.

De Houwer, A. (2009). *Bilingual first language acquisition.* Bristol: Multilingual Matters.

Diamond, A., and Lee, K. (2011). Interventions shown to aid executive function development in children 4 to 12 years old. *Science, 333*, 959-964.

Dubowny, M., Ebert, S., von Maurice, J., and Weinert, S. (2008). Sprach-kognitive Kompetenzen beim Eintritt in den Kindergarten. Ein Vergleich von Kindern mit und ohne Migrationshintergrund. *Zeitschrift für Entwicklungspsychologie und Pädagogische Psychologie, 40,* 124-234.

Engel de Abreu, P. M. J., Cruz-Santos, A., Tourinho, C. J., Martin, R., and Bialystok, E. (2012). Bilingualism enriches the poor: Enhanced cognitive control in low-income minority children. *Psychological Science, 23*(11), 1364-1371.

Feng, X., Bialystok, E., and Diamond, A. (2007). Do bilingual children show an advantage in working memory? Paper presented at the Biennial Meeting of the Society for Research in Child Development, Boston, MA, March 2007.

Fillmore, L. W. (2000). Loss of family languages: Should educators be concerned? *Theory Into Practice, 39*(4), 203.

Golash-Boza, T. (2005). Assessing the advantages of bilingualism for the children of immigrants. *The International Migration Review, 39*, 721-753.

Gold, B. T., Kim, C., Johnson, N. F., Kryscio, R., and Smith, C. D. (2013). Lifelong bilingualism maintains neural efficiency for cognitive control in aging. *The Journal of Neuroscience, 33*(2), 387-396.

Greenfield, P., and Suzuki, L. K. (2000). Culture and human development: Implications for parenting, education, pediatrics, and mental health. In I. E. Sigel and K. A. Renningner (Eds.), *Child Psychology in Practice* (5th ed.) (pp. 1059-1109). New York: Wiley.

Grosjean, F. (2010). *Bilingual: Life and Reality.* Cambridge, MA: Harvard University Press.

Han, W.-J. (2010). Bilingualism and socioemotional well-being. *Children and Youth Services Review, 32*, 720-731.

Han, W.-J. (2012). Bilingualism and academic achievement. In C. Garcia Coll and A. K. Marks (Eds.), *The immigrant paradox in children and adolescents. Is becoming American a developmental risk?* (pp. 161-184). Washington, DC: American Psychological Association.

Han, W.-J. and Bridglall, B. L. (2009). Assessing school supports for ELL students using ECLS-L. *Early Childhood Research Quarterly, 24*, 445-462.

Han, W.-J., and Huang, C.-C. (2010). The forgotten treasure: Bilingualism and Asian children's emotional and behavioral health. *American Journal of Public Health, 100*(5), 831-838.

Hernandez, D. (2012). Resources, strengths, and challenges for children in immigrant families in eight affluent countries. In A. Masten, K. Liebkind, and D. J. Hernandez (Eds.), *Realizing the potential of immigrant youth* (pp. 17-40). New York: Cambridge University Press.

Hesse, H.-G., and Göbel, K. (2009). Mehrsprachigkeit als Kapital: Ergebnisse der DESI-Studie. In I. Gogolin and U. Neumann (Eds.), *Streitfall Zweisprachigkeit – The Bilingualism Controversy* (pp. 281-287). Wiesbaden: Verlag für Sozialwissenschaften.

Ledesma, H. M. and Oppedal, B. (2013). Role of linguistic and behavioral cultural competence in perceived social support in immigrant preadolescents. Paper presented at the Meeting of the Society for Research in Child Development, April 2013, Seattle, WA., USA.

Leyendecker, B. and De Houwer, A. (2011). Frühe bilinguale und bikulturelle Erfahrungen. In H. Keller (Ed.), *Handbuch der Kleinkindforschung* (4th ed.) (pp. 178-219). Bern: Huber.

Liu, L., Benner, Lau, A., and Kim, S. (2009). Mother-adolescent language proficiency and adolescent academic and emotional adjustment among Chinese American families. *Journal of Youth and Adolescence, 38*(4), 572-586.

Masten, A., and O'Dougherty Wright, M. (2010). Resilience over the lifespan. Developmental perspectives on resistance, recovery, and transformation. In J. W. Reich, A. J. Zautra, and J. Stuart Hall (Eds.), *Handbook of adult resilience* (pp. 213-237). New York: The Guilford Press.

Matsumoto, D., LeRoux, J., Ratzlaff, C., Tatani, H., Uchida, H., Kim, C., and Araki, S. (2001). Development and validation of a measure of intercultural adjustment potential in Japanese sojourners: The Intercultural Adjustment Potential Scale (ICAPS). *International Journal of Intercultural Relations, 25*, 1-18.

Multiculturalism Policy Index (http://www.queensu.ca/mcp/, accessed February 27, 2013).

My language – hold on to your home language: http://www.ryerson.ca/mylanguage/ accessed March 1, 2013.

Oh, J. S., and Fuligni, A. J. (2010). The role of heritage language development in the ethnic identity and family relationships of adolescents from immigrant backgrounds. *Social Development, 19*(1), 202-220.

Park, H., Tsai, K. M., Liu, L., and Lau, A. S. (2012). Transactional association between supportive family climate and young children's heritage language proficiency in immigrant families. *International Journal of Behavioral Development, 36*(3), 226-236.

Park, I. J. K. (2007). Enculturation of Korean American adolescents within familial and cultural contexts: The mediating role of ethnic identity. *Family Relations: Interdisciplinary Journal of Applied Family Studies, 56,* 403-412.

Peal E., and Lambert, W. E. (1962). The relation of bilingualism to intelligence. *Psychological Monographs, 76*(27), 1-23.

Place, S., and Hoff, E. (2011). Properties of dual language exposure that influence 2-year-olds' bilingual proficiency. *Child Development, 82*(6), 1834-1849.

Portes, A., and Hao, L. (2002). The price of uniformity: Language, family and personality adjustment in the immigrant second generation. *Ethnic and Racial Studies, 25*(6), 889-912.

Prevoo, M. J. L., Mesman, J., Van IJzendoorn, M., and Pieper, S. (2011). Bilingual toddlers reap the language they sow: Ethnic minority toddlers' childcare attendance increases maternal host language use. *Journal of Multilingual and Multicultural Development*, iFirst article, 1-16. doi: 10.1080/01434632.2011.609279.

Rivera Mindt, M., Arentoft, A., Germano, K. K., D'Aquila, E., Scheiner, D., Pizzirusso, M., Sandoval, T. C., and Gollan, T. H. (2008). Neuropsychological, cognitive, and theoretical considerations for evaluation of bilingual individuals. *Neuropsychological Review, 18*, 255-168.

Rumbaut, R. (1997). Ties that bind: Immigration and immigrant families in the United States. In A. Booth, A. C. Crouter, and N. Landale (Eds.), *Immigration and the family* (pp. 3-46). Mahwah, NJ: Erlbaum.

Suárez-Orozco, C., and Suárez-Orzoco, M. (2001). *Children of immigration.* Cambridge, MA: Harvard University Press.

Stuart, J., Ward, C., and Adam, Z. (2010). Current issues in the development and acculturation of Muslim youth in New Zealand. *ISSBD Bulletin, 58*, 9-13.

Zelazo, P. D., and Carlson, S. M. (2012). Hot and cool executive function in childhood and adolescence: Development and plasticity. *Child Development Perspectives, 6* (4), 354-360.

Zelazo, P. D., Müller, U., Frye, D., and Marcovitch, S. (2003). The development of executive function. *Monographs of the Society for Research in Child Development, 68*, 11-27.

Chapter 16

Diaspora Immigration from Countries of the Former Soviet Union to Israel: Some Social Policy Implications

Gustavo S. Mesch

This chapter explores the social policy implications of the results of research for the acculturation process of immigrants from the Former Soviet Union in Israel. Receiving societies face social policy dilemmas in various areas. A central issue is housing policy, as residential location can be a constraint or an opportunity in terms of access to education and labor market opportunities. Furthermore, one's place of residence shapes one's social, educational and identity options. The concentration of immigrants in residential areas is associated with fewer parental opportunities in the labor market and a high level of social segregation. However, residential dispersion is not an easy alternative, as housing costs may become a burden. A second dilemma is associated with schooling. Integration in regular classes creates hurdles for immigrant children with regard to learning a new curriculum in a new language. On the other hand, creating temporary special classes segregates them socially, exposing them to stereotyping and labeling. This chapter builds on the results of various studies to inform social policy concerning these dilemmas.

Social policy relates to guidelines for the changing, maintenance or creation of living conditions that are conducive to human welfare. Thus social policy is that part of public policy that has to do with social issues such as public access to social programs. Social policy aims to improve human welfare and to meet human needs for education, health, housing and social security (Gil, 1970). Social policy directed to the welfare of immigrants includes the principles and activities directed to provision of basic needs such as belonging, health, housing, education and employment.

This chapter builds on previous studies about the adjustment of immigrants from the Former Soviet Union to Israel. It explores the implications of these studies for social policies that support the acculturation process in general and in Israel in particular. Specifically, the chapter limits its discussion to the adaptation of children and young adults with regard to language, identity, school expectations and achievements.

From a sociological point of view, there are two major perspectives on the process of acculturation among young adults: the cultural view and the structural view (Portes and Rivas, 2011). These perspectives are important as they are behind the ultimate goals of social policy. The cultural view emphasizes the degree to which new immigrants assimilate into the cultural and linguistic mainstream. According to this view, largely developed in the context of American society, groups that come to a country in very large numbers tend to remain segregated residentially and therefore are not inclined to assimilate totally into their host society. These immigrants resist learning the language of the host country or using it as their first language, prefer the media and culture of their mother tongue are unlikely to involve themselves in the culture of their host country and may even be in conflict with the normative social behavior of the host country. According to this view, there are cultural forces within the immigrant community that prevent them from assimilating (Huntington, 2004). This situation is common the greater the cultural and religious difference between the host country and the immigrants. A large cultural gap will motivate immigrants to create social and cultural institutions that support resistance to learning the language and encourage consumption of immigrant media and culture.

A variation on this approach accepts that there is a process of acculturation that takes place, but it is more complicated than is generally assumed. According to this view, these immigrants do acculturate, but as they adapt to the society, they also change it. For policy makers this view implies the need to increase the exposure of these immigrants to the institutions of mainstream society, and the local culture and language. The cultural approach directs social policy to the support of the immigrant culture, both in terms of a separate media, separate school classes and encouragement in political participation based on immigrant organizations. The cultural perspective develops policies directed at the recognition of cultural differences and its reproduction.

The structural perspective emphasizes the role of the insertion of new immigrants into the social stratification structure of the society, particularly their ability to find jobs and be successful in school so they avoid the perils of unemployment, poverty and delinquency. Thus, in this view the key to acculturation is the ability to assimilate into the mainstream society and avoid becoming a separate ethnic group that is unable to achieve social mobility (Portes and Rivas, 2011). Those who support this approach argue that the community context into which new immigrants are received plays a central role because resources and opportunities are available at the local level. The structural perspective ultimate drives the development of social policies directed to a process of re-socialization of the immigrants in the new society, including learning and use of the local language both in cultural and educational activities and residential dispersion.

In Israel, the cultural perspective has been represented by the ethnicization hypothesis (Al-Haj, 2004). This hypothesis predicts that immigrants from the Former Soviet Union, who came to Israel in very large numbers, would want to remain a distinct cultural and social group. These immigrants would make such a choice not only because they constituted a large enough group to maintain their separateness, but also because they came with a high degree of human and cultural capital. They tended to look down on Israeli culture as less sophisticated than their own Soviet culture. The thesis predicted that the immigrants would adopt a selective approach to acculturation. While parents and children would eventually learn the local language and culture at least partially, they would also preserve their native language (Russian), values and customs, and develop a clearly Russian identity. Thus while they would develop a solid bond with the society, it would be sectorial in nature. They would consume locally produced Russian media create school activities oriented to increasing the academic achievement of children of immigrants from the FSU, access local and national resources through their own political organizations and support their own ethnic political parties. Furthermore, according to the ethnicization thesis, Israel has lost its ability to assimilate new immigrants. As a society, it has become too sectorial to be willing or able to fully incorporate newcomers. Like other Western countries, it is succumbing to the winds and pressures of multiculturalism and is drifting away from its goals of a unilingual and unicultural Jewish society.

On the other hand, the structural perspective has been represented by the assimilation thesis (Smooha, 2008). This view contends that the fate of the Russian immigrants of the 1990s will be both similar to and different from the fate of the immigrants who came to Israel in the 1950s. According to this thesis, the second generation will be Israelized and absorbed into the Ashkenazi ethnic group rather than become a separate ethnic group. They will not crystallize as a transnational community and will not be part of the Russian diaspora like the Russian minorities of the independent post-Soviet states. This prediction is based on several assumptions. First, the Russian immigrants and their leaders lack the collective goal of creating a separate community. Second, Russian immigrants will assimilate because of a lack of institutional arrangements for preserving a separate heritage. This perspective notes that these immigrants entered various strata of society, rather than being concentrated on the lower rungs of the social ladder. While many began at the bottom, they advanced quickly and although some remain at the bottom, their presence there does not seem to be due to ethnic stratification. In addition, while this perspective recognizes that Russian immigrants retained their language and culture, it emphasizes that this was made possible because the large size of the migration provided a critical mass that developed a vibrant written and electronic Russian media locally as well as television channel and theaters. The immigrant community adapted to the political culture of Israel. Conscious of its unique interests, it mobilized politically as a sectorial political party, as did other sectors of Israeli society. One party for immigrants that has been active since the 2006 elections (Yisrael Beitenu) won eleven seats, reflecting about half of the potential immigrant vote, and joined the ruling coalition. Yet, consistent with this argument in the 2013, following the creation of a joint list with the Likud party, for the first time since the beginning of the wave of migration in 1989, the immigrants from the Former Soviet Union will not be represented by a sectorial ethnic party. According to the structural view, Russian immigrants have entered the middle class because of their high aspirations, strong human capital and the opportunities available to them. Veteran Israelis are now ready to accept them, and they will merge into the Ashkenazi group to which they are increasingly drawn (Smooha, 2008).

After presenting the theoretical approaches, this chapter we will examine three central issues that have important implications for social policy with regard to immigration: homeownership and residential segregation, the acquisition of language and self-identity. We will conduct this examination in light of the theoretical perspectives delineated above and the implications of the results of studies that have been undertaken in Israel for social policy.

The Challenge of Housing

A basic need of immigrants is the attainment of housing and countries seeking to absorb large numbers of immigrants must develop housing policies. A country must decide whether to intervene in the process of home ownership and whether to encourage newcomers to settle in particular parts of the country. Residential location can be a constraint or an opportunity in terms of access to mainstream culture and language, as well as education and labor market opportunities. One's place of residence is known to shape the social, educational and identity options open to immigrants. The concentration of new immigrants together and low-income housing are both associated with reduced opportunities and a high level of social segregation. These conditions may shape the educational aspirations, achievements, and identity formation of young immigrants. Nevertheless, residential dispersion is not easy to achieve because housing costs may become a burden.

Israel's national social policy was instrumental in shaping the residential patterns of immigrants from the FSU. Using a direct immigration absorption policy (Smooha, 2008), the state provided new immigrants with an "absorption basket" of benefits, giving them the opportunity to make their own decisions in terms of residential location, language acquisition and job training. Unlike the policy applied to previous waves of immigrants, the state left decisions about where to live, what job to take and how to spend the money they received from the government to the immigrants themselves. The basket of benefits included subsidies for mortgages, Hebrew classes and tuition for higher education. Twenty-three years after the adoption of this policy for dealing with the massive immigration from the countries of Former Soviet Union, we can see two main outcomes of this policy with regard to housing: residential distribution and levels of homeownership.

The bulk of the evidence indicates that large numbers of these immigrants reside in medium-size cities such as Ashdod, Ashkelon and Nazareth in the north and south, away from the central part of the country. In addition, in a number of these localities, they became a substantial percentage of the city's population, which also led to changes in the local culture and patterns of behavior. This concentration has made it possible for the immigrants to create substantial social networks, and maintain their language and culture including Russian-language newspapers, television channels and theaters (Godner-Cohen, Eckstein, and Weiss, 2012). This finding reflects the soft argument of the cultural perspective, arguing that the reception of immigrants has the potential not only to affect their culture and language use, but that the effect is mutual, as the insertion of immigrants might produce changes in the cultural context of the local communities.

This process of settlement was gradual and a result of various changes in the national housing policy. At first, immigrants from the FSU settled in large cities such as Jerusalem, Haifa and Tel Aviv. Only later did they move to more peripheral areas. A study evaluating the housing settlement of diaspora immigrants found that the pull factor associated with this movement of large numbers of immigrants to medium-size cities was the improvement in their housing conditions (Cohen-Goldner, Eckstein, and Weiss, 2012). It was in these cities in peripheral parts of the country where new, relatively large and affordable housing was being built. It is interesting to note that in their choice of residence, immigrants traded job opportunities for less costly, better quality housing. For this reason, homeowners are more likely to live in small and medium-size cities where they can enjoy newer and larger homes, even if they have to endure a longer commute to work (Arbel, Ben Shahar, and Tobol, 2011; Mesch and Mano, 2006). Thus, the move to the periphery of the country was voluntary, and allowed the immigrants to improve the quality of their housing and their standard of living.

The second pull factor was that the movement to the periphery allowed the immigrants to increase their rate of homeownership. According to the official statistics, in 2008, 75.2 percent of the immigrants who arrived from the FSU in the early 1990s owned their own home compared with 81.7 percent of native Israelis (Arbel, Ben-Shahar, and Tobol, 2011). The high rate of home ownership and the short time it took for the immigrants to achieve this goal were made possible by a very generous package of housing benefits including mortgages at low interest rates provided to FSU immigrants. It is possible that the immigrants' expectations about and fulfillment of the goal of owning a home strengthened the ties of the FSU immigrants to Israel (Rehbun, 2009).

In terms of social policy, the challenge of housing a large number of immigrants can be achieved combining financial support for the achieving of housing together with a policy of housing building that is directed to the achievement of the social values (Benchetrit and Czamanski, 2009). The Israeli society has valued home ownership and a high percent of the population owns their homes. Housing building and financial support as a social policy should be directed to support immigrants to achieve the same socially valued housing as the local population. Otherwise a sense of relative deprivation among immigrants might develop.

Homeownership among diaspora immigrants is associated with several interesting factors. A study that investigated the likelihood of homeownership in Israel found that residence in an area in which half or more of the neighbors are natives was associated with a 13 percent increase in the likelihood of homeownership among immigrants. This finding suggests that homeownership among immigrants is more likely in integrated areas. In terms of social integration, homeownership is positively associated with being proficient in the Hebrew language and with expressing care about and concern for Israeli culture. Another dimension of social integration is participation in the local political context. The study found that immigrant homeowners are more likely than immigrants renting their homes to report participation in local elections (Arbel, Ben-Shahar, and Tobol, 2011). Thus, homeownership, promoted through a policy of subsidies and mortgages, is associated the acquisition of the local language, residence in neighborhoods with a mixed or a predominantly native population, integration into local networks and participation in the local political process.

An interesting feature of the integration of immigrants from the FSU is their living arrangements. Among earlier immigrants from the FSU who migrated to Israel and the US, those in Israel are less likely to live in an independent household than in the US. Furthermore, 28.8 percent of the elderly immigrants in Israel, but only 18 percent of the immigrants to the US, live in multigenerational households. The authors of this study conclude that multigenerational living arrangements in Israel are motivated in part by economic considerations, housing shortages, the paucity of public subsidies geared to older immigrants and the need for support (Burr, Lowenstein, Tavares, Coyle, Mutchler, Katz, and Khatusky, 2012). Younger parents are accepting of multigenerational households with older parents because the latter provide childcare and income sharing. While adult children are somewhat less satisfied with this type of living arrangement and prefer more independence (Lowenstein, 2002), as the duration of residence in the country increases, the predicted probability of living in a multigenerational household decreases (Burr et al., 2012). Social policy directed at the incorporation of immigrant groups have to take account of their demographic composition and direct part of the housing policy to the solution of housing problems of elderly and lone immigrants providing the building not only of housing for couples and families but for the elderly as well.

The Challenge of Social Identity

How do residential concentration and the frequency of multigenerational households affect the identity of diaspora immigrants? This is a key issue, because implicit in the idea of immigration to Israel is the notion of returning home and the mutual expectations on the part of the receiving society and the immigrants that the latter will become an integral part of the "homeland" and adopt the national identity. On a very basic level, social identity refers to the perception of membership in a defined social group along with the emotional significance of that perception (Tajfel, 1978). A recent study investigated the relative strength of the Israeli component of the immigrants' self-identity compared to the Jewish and Russian components. Of particular interest is that the study investigated changes over time. The data were collected in 2005 among immigrants who arrived in Israel between

1990 and 2005. We can compare its findings with those of a previous study by the same author conducted in the late 1990s (Leshem, 2008). Among immigrants 18 years of age and older, Jewish identity is the most common primary identity, a fact noted by 39.2 percent of respondents. A smaller number, 34.4 percent, mentioned their Israeli identity as their primary identity, while only 26.2 percent highlighted their Russian identity as primary. An important observation is that the respondents' primary social identity differs according to age. For the group aged 18-44 years old, the most frequent social identity mentioned was Israeli. Among younger people (18-24 years old) a majority (57.7 percent) indicated that their most salient identity was Israeli. This percentage declined to 40.4 percent among the 30-44 year olds. Nevertheless, the second social identity mentioned by all age groups was Russian, ranging from 24.6 percent among the younger group to 33.3 percent of the 30-44 year olds.

As is well known, the Israeli government does not consider a percentage of the immigrants as Jewish. Thus, it is not surprising that a higher percentage of non-Jewish immigrants than Jewish immigrants noted their primary identity as Israeli. Among the non-Jewish immigrants, 45.7 percent defined themselves as Russian, 41.5 percent as Israelis and 12.8 percent as Jewish. Among the Jewish immigrants, 30.7 defined themselves as Israeli, 52.9 percent as Jewish and 16.4 percent as Russian. Thus, while non-Jewish immigrants tended to be polarized in their self-identity almost equally between Israeli and Russian, for the Jewish immigrants, the most salient identity was Jewish. Immigrants felt overwhelmingly that the Israeli component of their identity had become more intense since they first arrived in the country. Concomitantly, the Jewish component of their identity had also grown stronger, but less so than the Israeli component. When comparing this study with previous findings, the author concludes that the identity that is shared by all immigrants, Jewish and non-Jewish, and that grows stronger with the length of time in the country is their Israeli identity (Leshem, 2008). At the same time, it is clear that there are different pathways to integration and that a sizeable group of the immigrant population, both Jewish and non-Jewish, still consider their Russian identity as the most salient even after living in the country for 15 years.

The constellation of different identities, expressed by both the older generation and the young generation, might create confusion among a sizeable portion of the population. The constellation of possible identities (Israeli, Jewish and Russian) is certainly a characteristic peculiar to Israeli society. However, from a policy point of view, it is an important consideration. Due to the lack of separation between religion and the state in Israel, the immigrant group from the FSU became heterogeneous in its religious composition. While the religious institutions use one definition of "who is a Jew," the State has used a broader and more inclusive definition, creating a sub-group of immigrants whose current status as citizens is still unclear. About 350,000 individuals in Israel are defined as "lacking national status." This sizeable percentage does not define themselves as Jewish and are not defined by the country as Jewish. Religious affiliation has an effect on social integration. Indeed, in some cases there is a direct association between this factor and the inability to integrate into the country, evident particularly in the stressful social consequences for individuals attempting to define their identity. Thus, the receiving society need to develop a clear social policy of integration of the definition of citizenship that will allow to all the legal immigrants to be full citizens. This might require urgent legislation, as the current gap is creating a sizable marginal group that feels discriminated and finds difficult to develop a shared identity with the rest of the population.

The Challenge of Education

The encounter between young immigrants and native youngsters and teachers in school has implications for social policy as well. In this encounter, the major issues involve the daily growing pains of becoming part of a new culture and perceptions about discrimination (Mesch et al., 2008; Titzman et al., 2011). One additional implication for social policy has to do with the school environment or climate and the extent to which teachers and principals are prepared for the encounter between immigrants, teachers and native-born children. Various studies of young immigrants in school have found that they often see the school climate as less open to them or prepared to deal with them. As a result, minor events or situations can create negative feelings such as annoyance, irritation, worry or frustration, underscoring the notion that the youngster's goals and plans may be more difficult or impossible to achieve (Suarez-Orosco, Rhodes, and Milburn, 2009).

One study focused on the frequency of three acculturation-related causes of distress: language, discrimination, and family. Insufficient command of the local language and a concomitant lack of communication with those in charge at school exacerbate the integration of new immigrants. Without a facility in the local language, it is difficult to deal with events that one sees as unfair or to respond to negative treatment, such as being verbally harassed or neglected by one's peers because of one's ethnic background. Problems with discrimination are related to out-group behavior and create barriers to the adaptation of immigrants. In addition, parents who object to the cultural adaptation of their children seeking to become part of the in-group can make their children's lives more difficult. One study found that immigrants in both Germany and Israel suffer from these issues, but they decline more rapidly in Germany as the length of the immigrants' stay in the country increases (Titzmann, Silbereisen, Mesch, and Schmitt-Rodermund, 2011). The existence of such issues calls for specific cultural sensitive training for teachers aimed at improving the school climate. Furthermore, given that many of these problems arise as the result of interactions between students, teachers trained in cultural sensitivity need to develop educational programs targeted at native-born students to ensure a safe and accepting environment in school.

Perceived discrimination is defined as a person's belief that he or she is being treated unfairly because of his or her origin. Such negative feelings are a source of stress. They also reflect the nature of the interaction between immigrants and the receiving society. Perceived discrimination is an indicator of the lack of congruence between the orientations of immigrants and the receiving society and the expectations each has of the other (Jasinskaja-Lahti, 2006). Some studies have found perceived discrimination particularly detrimental to adolescents, negatively affecting their perceived efficacy, their attitudes to school and their educational achievements (Liebkind et al., 2004). A longitudinal study that assessed the relationship between perceived discrimination and well-being in a sample of immigrant adolescents from the FSU (12 to 18 years old) found that variables that directly account for the acculturation process, namely, language use and length of residence in the country had no statistically significant effect on immigrants' well-being. However, at the same time, controlling for initial levels, perceived discrimination in public places and in school had a direct effect on psychological well-being, increasing self-reported depressive moods and decreasing perceived self-efficacy. Variables measuring social support were statistically significant as well, underscoring the important role of a supportive environment on improving well-being. Interestingly, this study found that contrary to expectations, perceived discrimination was not a factor directly related to the preference for socializing with fellow immigrants or with a Russian identity. Furthermore, increased use of the local language reduced the preference for social involvement with other immigrants. Thus, the results indicate that being treated differently at school by teachers and schoolmates is a daily experience that might have long lasting effects on social integration and school achievement. These findings expand our knowledge about the detrimental effect of unfair treatment at school and seem to indicate that perceived discrimination in school can have negative effects on school achievement (Mesch, Turgeman, and Fishman, 2008).

Immigration is a difficult process that involves the shift from one culture to another, from one normative environment to another. While the cultural distance between immigrants from the FSU and Israel is considered minimal, the discontinuity of the social environment and negative reactions at school are problematic. In their study of violence among young immigrants, Koren and Eisikovitz (2011) conducted in-depth interviews with young adolescents (aged 14-20) and found that violent youngsters differed from non-violent youth in a number of dimensions: their religious perceptions of themselves, their reason for immigrating and their identification with and acceptance of differences in cultural norms. The groups that were non-violent in the FSU and become violent in Israel were more likely to define themselves as Russians (non-Jewish) and felt confused about the norms of social behavior in the host country. The group that was violent in the FSU and continued to be violent in Israel reported feeling uprooted, frustrated, discriminated against and not part of either culture. Both groups reported that the decision to immigrate was a pragmatic search for a better lifestyle rather than an ideological, Zionist desire to return to the homeland of the Jewish people. The violent group felt they had little control over their lives, as reflected in their lack of input in the decision to immigrate to Israel and their perception of not having a clear identity and being strangers in the country (Koren and Eisikovits, 2011). From a policy viewpoint, we learn the importance of providing opportunities for participation and decision making to young immigrants in the absorbing country and creating opportunity structures for involvement that enhance their sense of self-identity, self-efficacy and confidence in their ability to influence the conditions of their own lives.

As we have seen before, adjustment to school plays a central role in the well-being and adjustment of young immigrants. For school age students, who are rarely involved in their parents' decision-making process concerning immigration, this is an especially complex process. It involves disconnecting with the society and school one knew and readjusting to a completely different social context. In addition to the social, psychological and linguistic adjustments, immigrant children are required to adapt to a new educational environment and meet new academic expectations. This process implies the need to learn a new language they are not familiar with and to use this language to learn a new school culture, teaching methods, instructional material and testing practices, all in a short period of time. Needless to say, parents are often unable to provide support for their children's educational endeavors because they are unfamiliar with both the language and the educational system. Thus, school, as the major acculturating institution of society, plays a central role in the process of adapting to the new society, shaping the content of the learning as well as the youngsters' motivations and aspirations to learn. The centrality of language is critical, both because it serves as the medium of instruction and because it introduces students to academic subjects other than those to which they were exposed in their countries of origin.

The integration of new immigrants poses a number of social policy dilemmas for the educational system. One key issue deals with the question of whether to integrate new immigrants immediately in regular classes or create separate classes for them. Integration in regular classes may present major hurdles with regard to mastering a completely new language and new curriculum. On the other hand, creating temporary special classes for diaspora immigrants can lead to their social segregation, exacerbating their efforts at integration.

In Israel, school principals have autonomy in terms of making decisions about whether to separate or integrate new immigrants. However, the policy is to support the incorporation of children of diaspora immigrants as much as possible in the Israeli curriculum and to do so as quickly as possible. In some schools, the policy is to limit institutional help to the provision of short-term classes in Hebrew to immigrant students (Eisikovits, 2000). The implicit goal is to return the students as quickly as possible to the regular classes, mixing them with native-born students both academically and socially. The implicit message here is a school policy that advocates rapid integration with an emphasis on the learning of the language. Other schools have adopted an alternative approach that does not limit the period of participation of immigrant students in second language classes in Hebrew. Furthermore, this approach is part of a general policy that supports gradual integration. Taking a more holistic view, it recognizes that in order to facilitate the transition to the new country, the school must pay attention not only to academic achievements and language acquisition, but also provide social support and guidance to parents as well as social guidance and academic support to the students. In some cases, new immigrants are allowed to take some of their matriculation exams in their own language (Eisikovits and Beck, 1990).

Thus, this approach deals with the issue of integration vs. segregation by enrolling immigrant students in regular classes and creating special classes that focus mainly on teaching Hebrew as a second language rather than creating special classes for other courses in the curriculum. Temporary and limited separation to meet the needs and demands of immigrant youngsters in regular schools is the main policy.

Teachers who meet students from the FSU are often struck by the sense that these new immigrant students have a higher level of cultural capital than native-born students (Cohen, Haberfeld, and Kogan, 2010). Studies have shown that cultural capital affects the academic success of students through two different mechanisms. One is through labeling. Teachers who are affected by the label attached to students from the FSU and believe they have a higher level of cultural capital might be inclined to give them better grades. The second mechanism is a scholastic one. Students with a higher level of cultural capital may be more likely to do homework and get better grades in school. However, Leopold and Shavit's (2011) recent study found that the level of an immigrant student's cultural capital did not affect the grades that teachers gave. According to the authors, teachers were not influenced by the labels attached to their students (Leopold and Shavit, 2011).

A large study that examined achievement in various mathematical and language skills concluded that the differences in student achievement are a function of their length of residency in Israel. The study indicates that immigrants require a substantial number of years to reach achievement levels similar to those of students who were born in the country. In particularly, for achievement in academic Hebrew for young immigrants from the FSU, years of residence proved to be a positive factor. The study concluded that it takes between two and seven years of residence and schooling to attain the levels of academic achievement similar to those of native-born students. For mathematical skills, the largest and most salient difference between immigrants and native-born Israeli students is in solving verbal mathematical problems (Levin and Shohamy, 2008).

Armon-Lotem et al.'s (2013) study that investigated the role of external factors such parental education and internal factors such as age, age when starting to learn a new language and length of family exposure to the target language in young children's linguistic performance produced similar results. The internal factors were associated with linguistic performance. The study found that Russian Jewish children immigrating to Israel fared better in the target language than diaspora immigrants to Germany who were more likely to maintain their native language. In addition, preferences for the mother tongue were associated with parental characteristics such as education and occupational status (Armon-Lottem et al., 2013).

Summary and Discussion

The integration of diaspora immigrants requires the development and implementation of a detailed social policy that often differs from country to country. The chapter focused on universal challenges to immigrants' integration, and illustrated them with specific examples from the Israeli context. As contexts of immigrants' integration, Israel and Germany share similarities in migration policies and challenges in immigrants' integration. Similar to Israel, Between 1992 and 2007, a large number of ethnic Germans from the former USSR emigrated to Germany. The Aussiedler and their descendants are struggling with their social identity as often native Germans consider them Russian. In everyday life they face a similar level of hassles as immigrants from the FSU in Israel (Titzman, et al. 2011). Recent studies show that in Germany, as in Israel there is substantial ethnic residential segregation between immigrants and native Germans. The extent of this segregation has been relatively stable over the last three decades and is particularly pronounced for low-educated workers. Ethnic residential segregation is reflected in occupational ethnic segregation in the workplace as well Glitz, 2012). Thus, despite the focus of the chapter mainly on the social policy in Israel, challenges are similar in both countries.

The goal of social adjustment to a new country is linked to the attainment of affordable and appropriate housing. In the process, there are various risks to monitor. One is the risk of residential and social segregation that may result in social marginalization instead of adjustment. The second is the risk that the native-born population may see residential concentration as a threat, increasing negative feelings, attitudes and behaviors toward the immigrants. Given that immigrants have difficulty finding jobs because of a lack of language skills and difficulty in transferring their skills and credentials, supporting a policy of homeownership can be a strategic signal that the host society is ready, willing and able to accept them and provide opportunities to ease their adjustment to their new lives. The development of a housing policy that promotes homeownership also reduces residential segregation, signals social acceptance and opens a venue to integration into the mainstream of the society. This is not an easy goal to achieve, but is one that Israel appears to have achieved over time. Such a policy was developed in Israel combining two components. The first, a national policy of subsidized loans to encourage private construction and provision of subsidized housing loans to immigrants. The second component requires job training programs and labor market placement that increases the social identification of the immigrants with the country and their desire to buy houses.

When dealing with immigrants, attention should be paid to policy inconsistencies that create heterogeneity in the immigrant population. The inconsistency in the definition of who is a Jew resulted in the consolidation of two groups among the diaspora immigrants to Israel. The vast majority was recognized as Jewish by the religious authorities, and the state provided them with immediate citizenship and equality of rights. For this group, the development of a Jewish and Israeli identity seemed not to be a difficult process. However, a sizeable minority was recognized as members of the Jewish people and eligible for citizenship by the government, but not by the religious authorities. This group found it difficult to identify as Jews or even as Israelis. Over time, the members of this group were more likely to remain socially unadjusted and engage in aggressive and violent behavior. This problematic inconsistency in definition, particularly in a country in which there is no separation between church and state, has the potential to create more feelings of alienation and even social adaptation problems in the second generation. Because the lack of separation of the religion and the state, and the role of religious parties in the governmental coalition, social policy had been directed at the implementation of a policy facilitating religious conversion. The government has provided funds and created state bodies with the aim to facilitate the process. Yet, for the ones that conversion is not an option, the path is unclear. More efforts at the social policy level are needed to overcome the potential for alienation and marginalization.

The school experience of immigrant children in Israel also requires the attention of policy-makers. Language learning for children is critical. At the same time, it is a complicated and difficult task that requires considerable time in order to bring them up to the level required for the mastery of verbal mathematical abilities as well as writing and reading comprehension. There is a need to develop an appropriate curriculum for new immigrants, provide intensive teacher training in dealing with the academic needs of new immigrants and create enrichment classes targeted at specific sub-groups of the immigrant population. It is apparent from the studies presented that teachers do not receive meaningful training about the needs of immigrant students or instructional strategies for accommodating these needs. School principals and teachers need to be provided with training programs based on principles of multi-culturalism. The literature shows that investing in these endeavors is worthwhile, because the difficulties of immigrant children in mastering the language and the school material that is learned in the local language persist for long periods of time.

References

Albrecht, G. (2012). Ethnic Segregation in Germany, CReAM Discussion Paper Series 1222, Centre for Research and Analysis of Migration (CReAM), Department of Economics, University College London.

Al-Haj, M. (2004). *Immigration and Ethnic Formation in a Deeply Divided Society*. Leiden: Brill.

Arbel, Y., Ben-Shahar, D., and Tobol, Y. (2011). The correlation among immigrant homewonershop: Objective and subjective characteristics and civic participation. *Urban Studies*, 1-21,

Armon-Lotem, S., Gagarina, N., and Waters, J. (2013). Social Identity in Russian-Hebrew and Russian-German Preschool. In R. K Silbereisen, Y. Shavit, and P. Titzmann (Eds.), *The Challenge of Diaspora Migration in Today's Societies*.

Benchetrit, G., and Czamanski D. (2009). Immigration and Home Ownership: Government subsidies and wealth distribution effects in Israel. *Housing, Theory and Society, 26*(3), 210-230.

Burr, J. A., Lowenstein, A., Tavares, J. L., Coyle, C., Mutchler, J. E., Katz, R., and Khatutsky, G. (2012). The living arrangements of older immigrants from the FSU: A comparison of Israel and the U.S. *Journal of Aging Studies, 26*, 401-409.

Cohen, Y., Haberfeld, Y., and Kogan, I. (2010). Who went where? Jewish migration from the former Soviet Union to Israel, USA and Germany, 1990-2000. *Israel Affairs, 17*(1), 7-20.

Cohen-Goldner, S., Eckstein, Z., and Weiss, Y. (2012). *Immigration and Labor Market Mobility in Israel, 1990-2009.* Boston: MIT Press.

Eisikovits, R. (2000). Gender differences in Cross-Cultural Adaptation Styles of Immigrant Youths from the FSU in Israel. *Youth and Society, 31*, 310-331.

Eisikovits, R., and Beck, R. H. (1990). Models Governing the Education of New Immigrant Children in Israel. *Comparative Education Review, 34*, 177-195.

Gil, D. (1970). A systematic approach to social policy analysis. *Social Service Review*, 411-426.

Goldner-Cohen, S., Eckstein, Z., and Weiss, Y. (2010). *The immigrations from the former Soviet Union to Israel; Evidence and Interpretation.* Discussion Paper No. 14-12, The Pinhas Sapir Center for Development, Tel Aviv University, Israel.

Huntington, S. (2004). *Who we are: the challenges to America's national identity.* New York: Simon and Schuster.

Jasinskaja-Lahti, I. (2006). Perceived Discrimination, Social Support Networks, and Psychological Well-Being among Three Immigrant Groups. *Journal of Cross-Cultural Psychology, 37*(3), 293-311.

Koren, C., and Eisikovits, Z. (2011). Continuity and Discontinuity of Violent and Non-Violent Behavior. *Sociological Focus, 44*, 314-339.

Leopold, L., and Shavit, Y. (2011). Cultural Capital Does Not Travel Well: Immigrants, Natives and Achievement in Israeli Schools. *European Sociological Review*, doi: 10.1093/esr/jcr086

Leshem, E. (2008). Being an Israeli: Immigrants from the Former Soviet Union in Israel, Fifteen Years Later. *Journal of Israeli History: Politics, Society, Culture, 2*(1), 29-49.

Liebkind, K. (2004). Cultural Identity, Perceived Discrimination, and Parental Support as Determinants of Immigrant's School Adjustments. *Journal of Adolescent Research, 6*, 635- 656.

Lowenstein, A. (2002). Solidarity and Conflicts in co-residence of three-generational migrant families from the FSU. *Journal of Ageing Studies, 16*, 221-242.

Mesch, G., and Mano R. (2006). Housing Attainment of Immigrants from the FSU in Israel: A Cost-Benefit Approach. *Housing Studies*, 21, 423-441.

Mesch, G. S., Turgeman, H., and Fishman, G. (2008). Perceived Discrimination and the Well-being of Immigrant Adolescents. *Journal of Youth and Adolescence, 37*(5), 592-604.

Suarez-Orosco, C., Rhodes, J., and Milburn, M. (2009). Unravelling the Immigrant Paradox Academic Engagement and Disengagement Among Recently Arrived Immigrant Youth. *Youth and Society, 41*, 151-185.

Portes, A., and Rivas, A. (2011). The Adaptation of Migrant Children. *The Future of Children, 21,* 219-246.

Rehbun, U. (2009). Housing adjustment among Immigrants in Israel: An application of complementary metric and non-metric measures. *Social Indicators Research, 92,* 565-590.

Smooha, S. (2008). The mass immigrations to Israel: A comparison of the failure of the Mizrahi immigrants of the 1950s with the success of the Russian immigrants in the 1990s. *The Journal of Israeli History, 27,* 1-27.

Tajfel, H. (1978). Social categorization, social identity and social comparison. In H. Tajfel (Ed.), *Differentiations between social groups: studies in the social psychology of intergroup relations.* London: Academic Press.

Titzmann, P., Silbereisen, R. K.., Mesch, G. S., and Schmitt-Rodermund, E. (2011). Migration-specific hassles among adolescent immigrants from the former Soviet Union in Germany and Israel. *Journal of Cross-Cultural Psychology. 42*, 777-794.

Index

Bold page numbers indicate figures. *Italic* numbers indicate tables.